WORKING DOGS

A portion of the proceeds from this book was donated to Roswell Park Volunteer Services in Buffalo, New York, and ÂNIMAS in Portugal. These two organizations carry out inspiring work with therapy dogs in hospitals, and the funds will support their efforts.

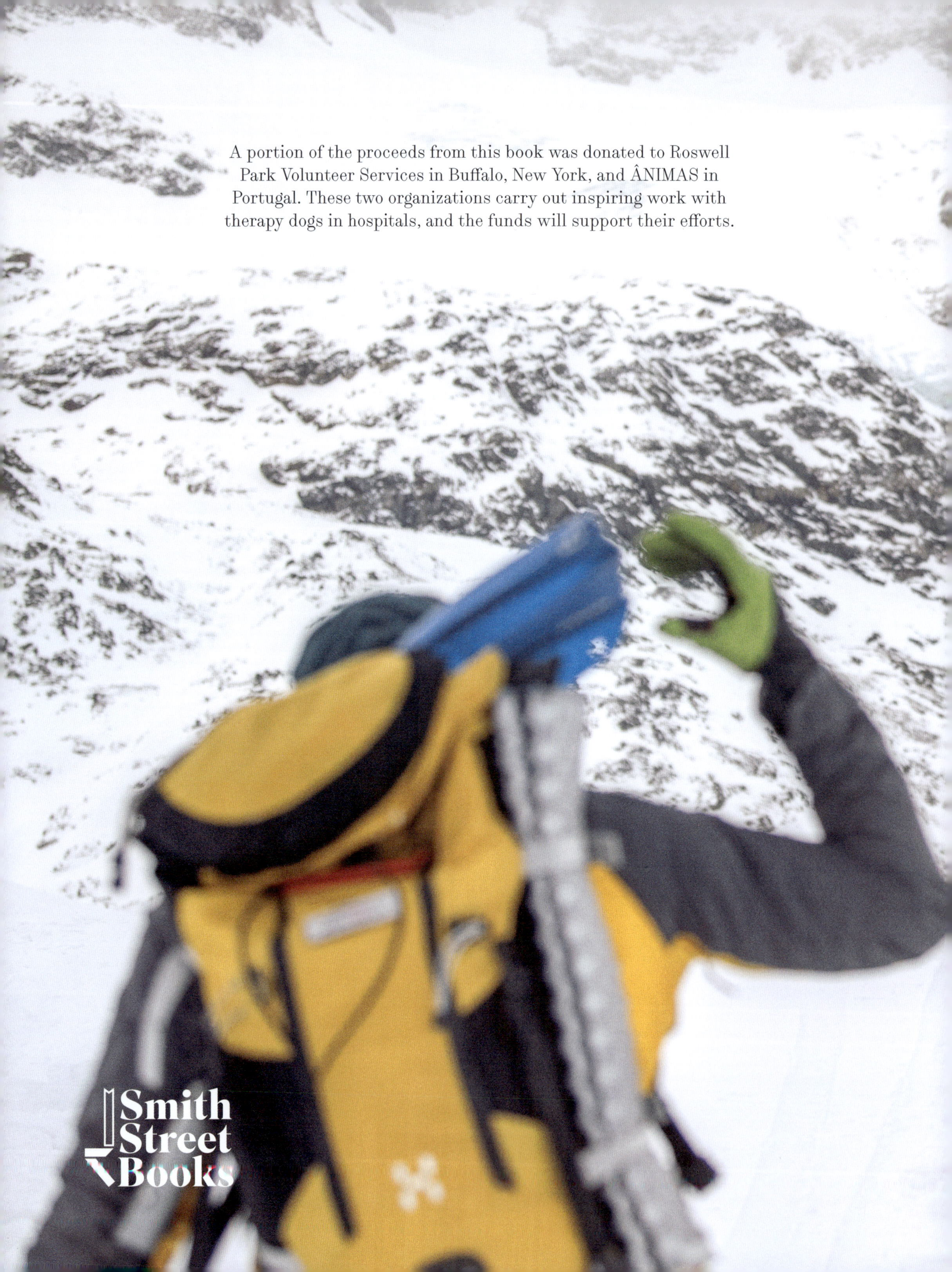

Smith Street Books

WORKING DOGS

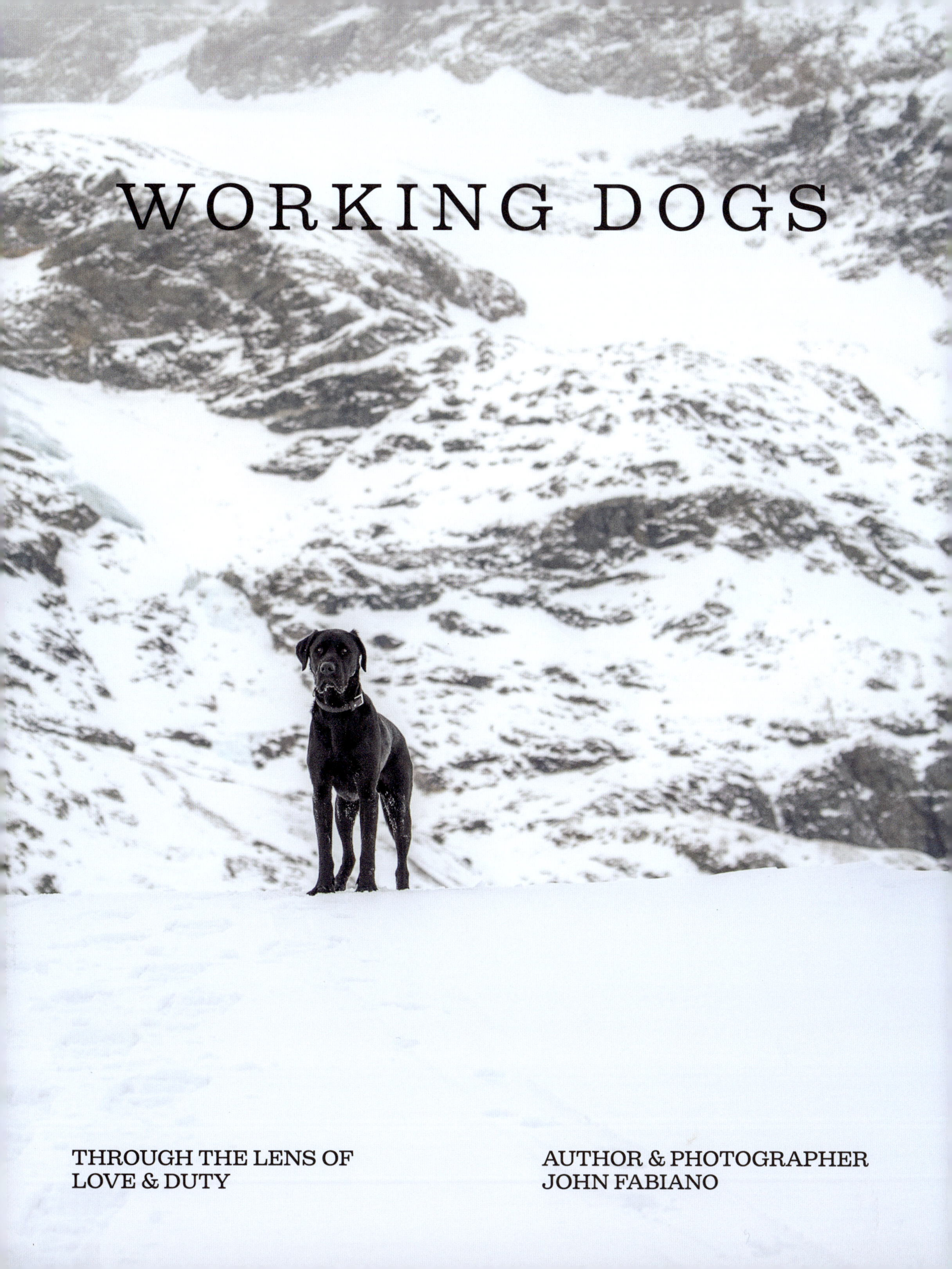

THROUGH THE LENS OF
LOVE & DUTY

AUTHOR & PHOTOGRAPHER
JOHN FABIANO

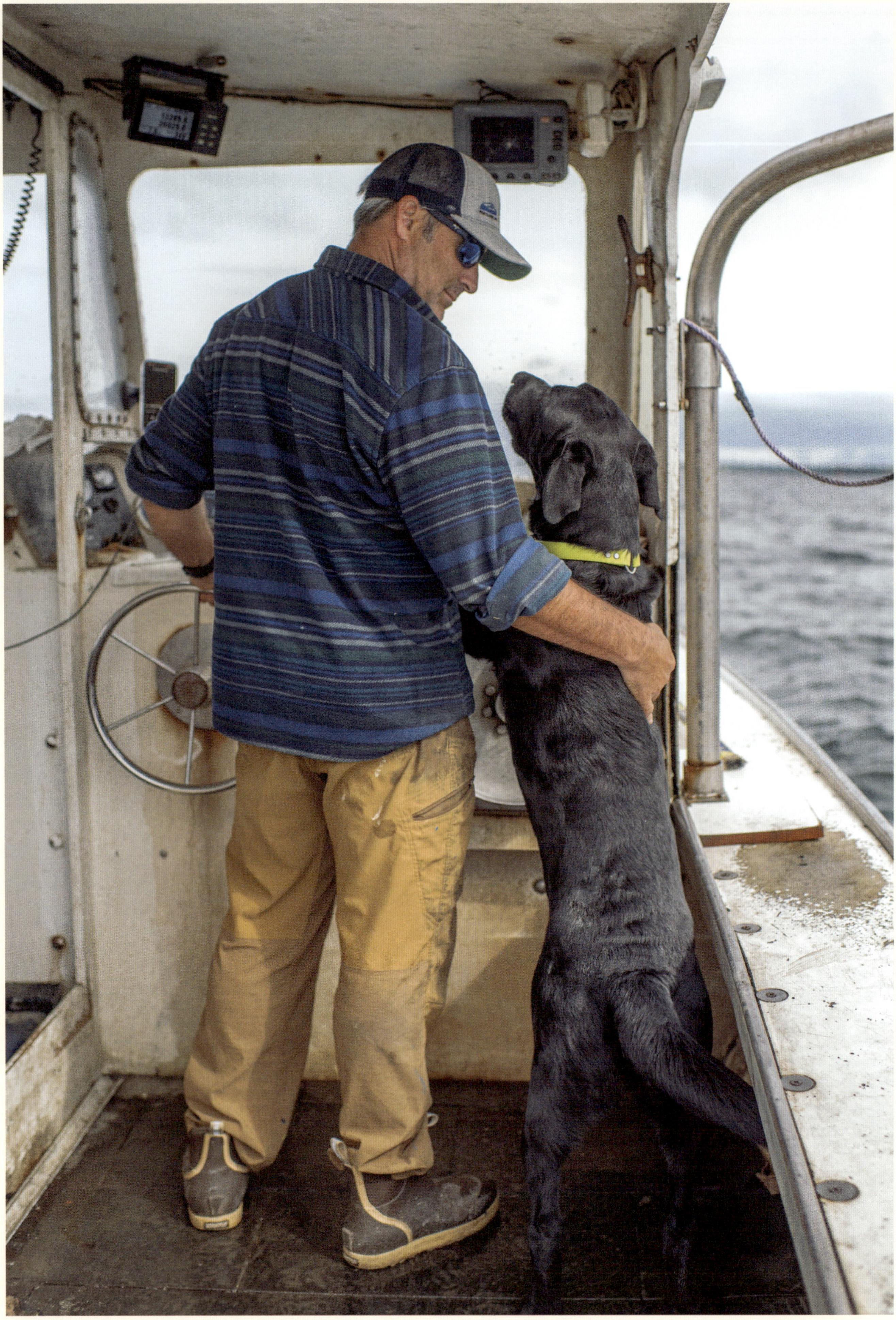

INTRODUCTION

It was always meant to be dogs.

Dogs: The creatures I have loved, idolized, and obsessed over my entire life. I was lucky to grow up with them – my version of generational wealth. My first true love was Lola, the little black mutt who quickly became my favorite family member. Our identities blurred, and if you graded my school papers or received a birthday card from me during my childhood, it was always inscribed "John and Lola."

When the pandemic hit in 2020, and shutdowns left me with a lot more free time, I bought my first camera. At that point, I had no photography experience aside from a high school course and snapping shots on my phone, but I needed a hobby.

It didn't take long to recognize that my favorite subject to photograph, by far, was dogs. I loved being outdoors with just them and a camera.

Some ideas fully consume the brain, living there rent-free day and night. For me, it was the dream of traveling the world to photograph dogs. I couldn't kick it. I dreamed of going far, going remote, and going places that no tourist seeks out, all to explore the relationships between dogs and humans in different cultures. In 2023, I finally boarded a plane to Germany with my camera, on my way to my first planned destination of many.

In my travels, from India to Australia and beyond, I have been impressed by all the dogs I photograph, whether they are pampered as pets, running wild in parks, flaunting at dog shows, or even thriving on the streets. Dogs, simply by existing, are magic. But as I've met more and more through photography, I've found those with jobs to be truly special. Working dogs were only a portion of my original travel plans, with trips to photograph sled dogs in Greenland and herding dogs in Australia on my initial itinerary. But as I've traveled, I've met so many working dogs that are doing exactly what they were born to do. Many of them would have made great family pets, spending their days at home, sleeping on the couch, but these dogs were fortunate to end up with owners who let their abilities shine out in the world.

As you'll see in the pages that follow, some jobs require significant, intensive training while others ask the dogs to just, well, be dogs. Working dogs showcase the unique capabilities of their species – their camaraderie, unrelenting work ethic, and eagerness to please. When asked, dogs will protect, bring peace, guide us through the world, and even help us survive. The wide range of jobs that dogs hold around the globe demonstrates their remarkable abilities and adaptability. From putting smiles on faces, to saving lives, their positive impact is felt in numerous ways.

Embarking on my photography journey was one of the greatest joys of my life, and I hope this book brings you even a fraction of the happiness I felt while creating it.

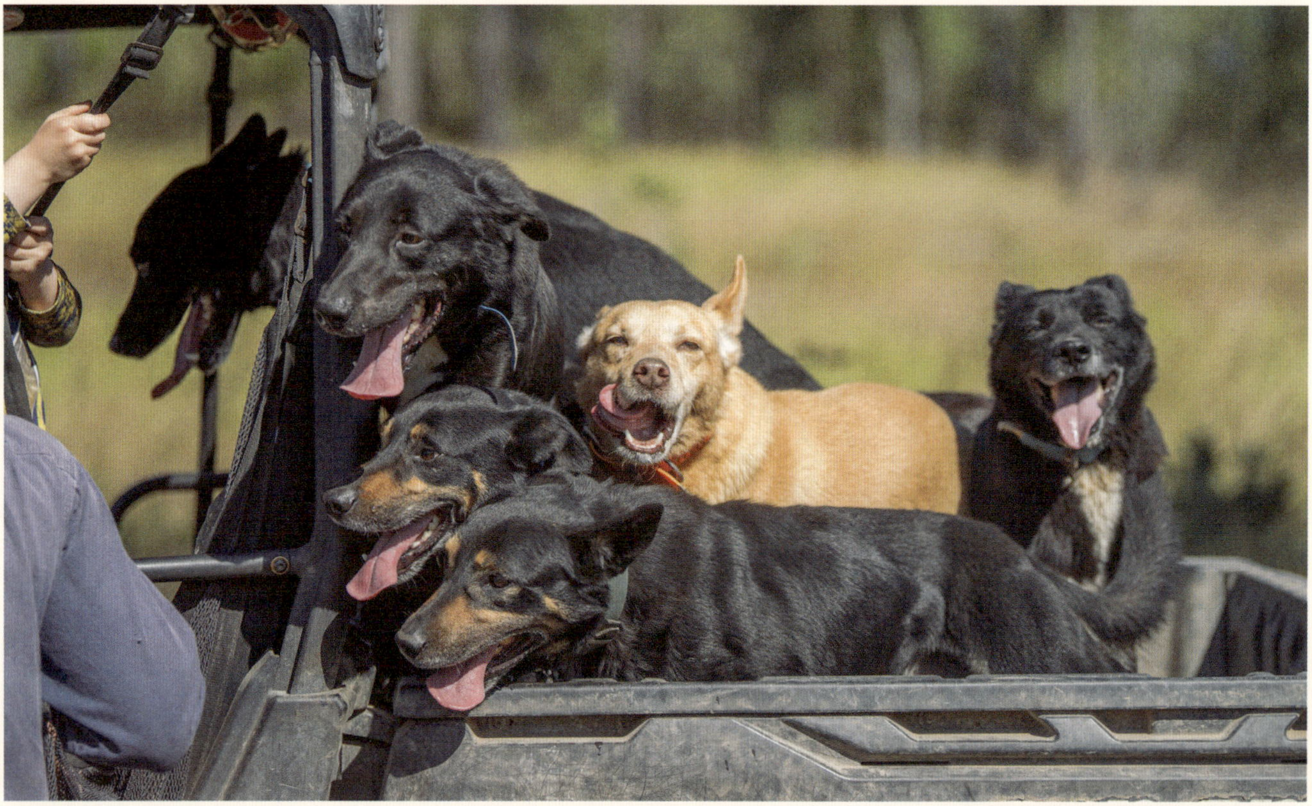

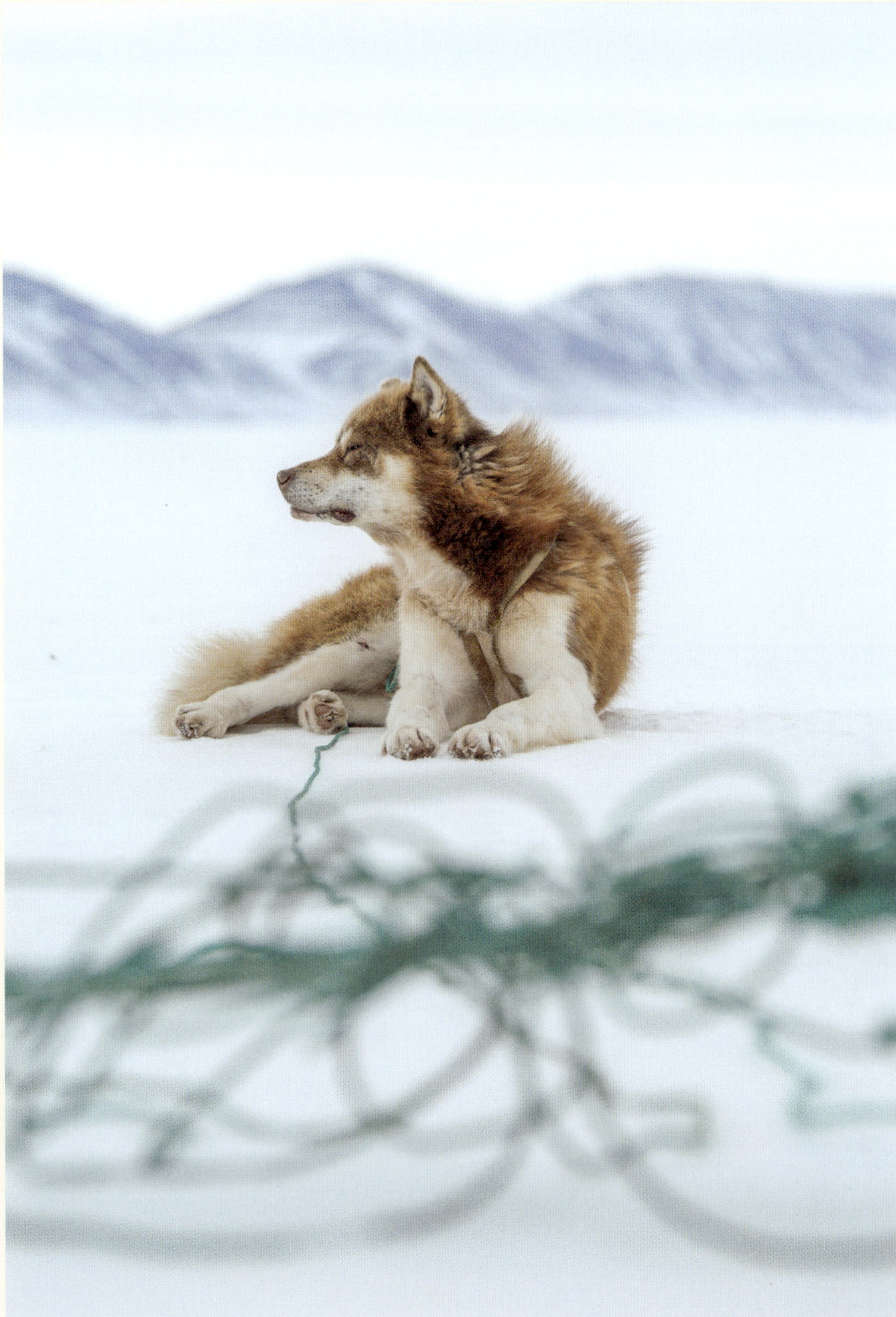

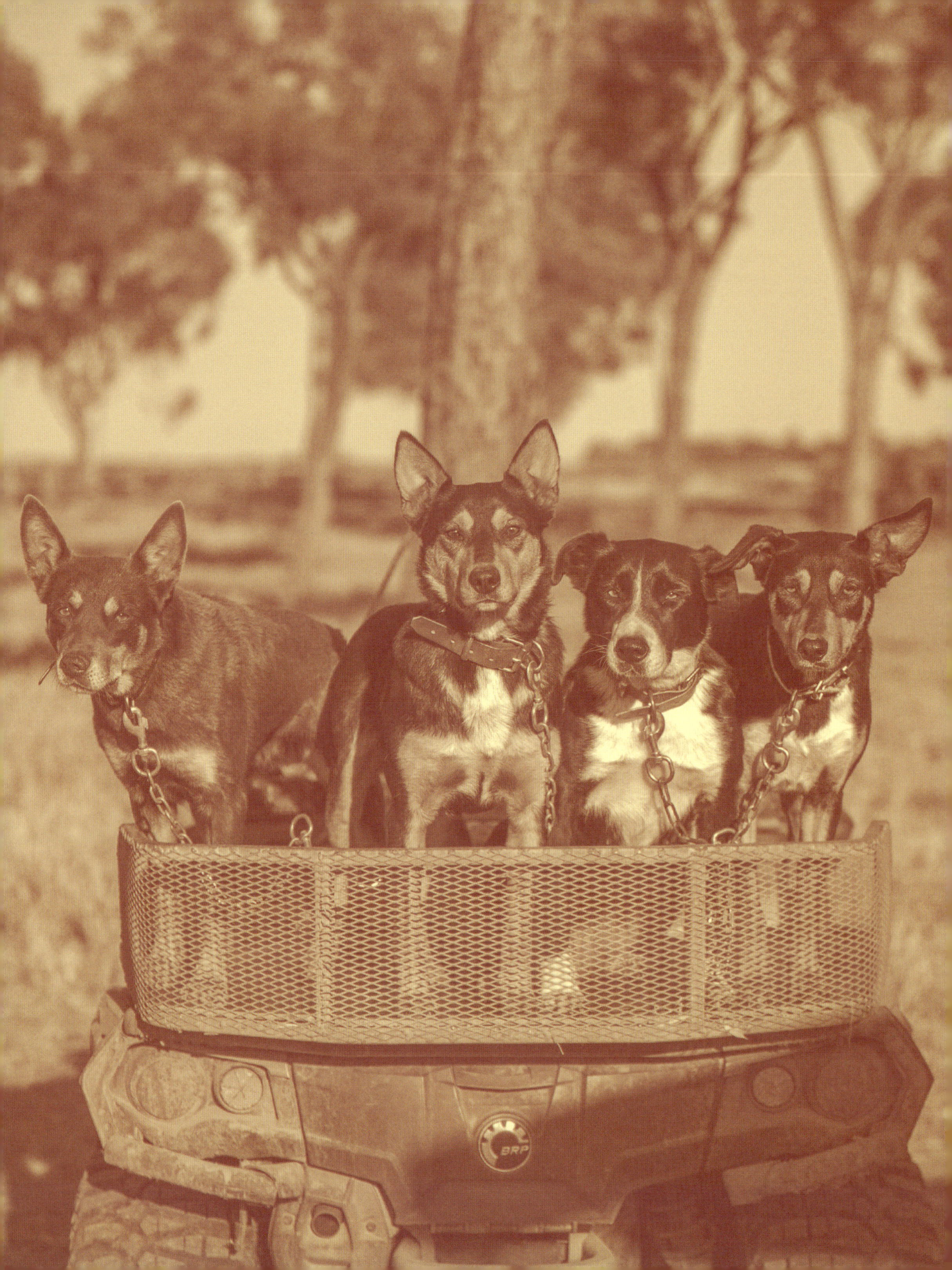

LOCATION	BREEDS	TASKS	SKILLS
New South Wales and Queensland, Australia	Kelpie, Border Collie, Stumpy Tail Cattle Dog, Australian Cattle Dog	Mustering, Holding Position, Working Independently	Organization, Endurance, Obedience

HERDING DOGS

AUSTRALIA'S ECONOMY has relied heavily on livestock industries, and the stockmen who manage those animals rely on (stock)man's best friend. Herding dogs have played a massive role in developing the country, and you'll find many of these whip-smart, active breeds, such as the Kelpie and the Border Collie, throughout its farms and cities.

Both breeds are excellent workers that tirelessly serve to round up livestock, nipping at the heels of sheep and cattle to usher them across large plots of land. They have their own styles of work – Kelpies are independent and don't require much guidance, while Border Collies will follow instructions to a tee. Many farms utilize both breeds for their complementary working styles.

I spent over a month in Australia photographing these dogs in action.

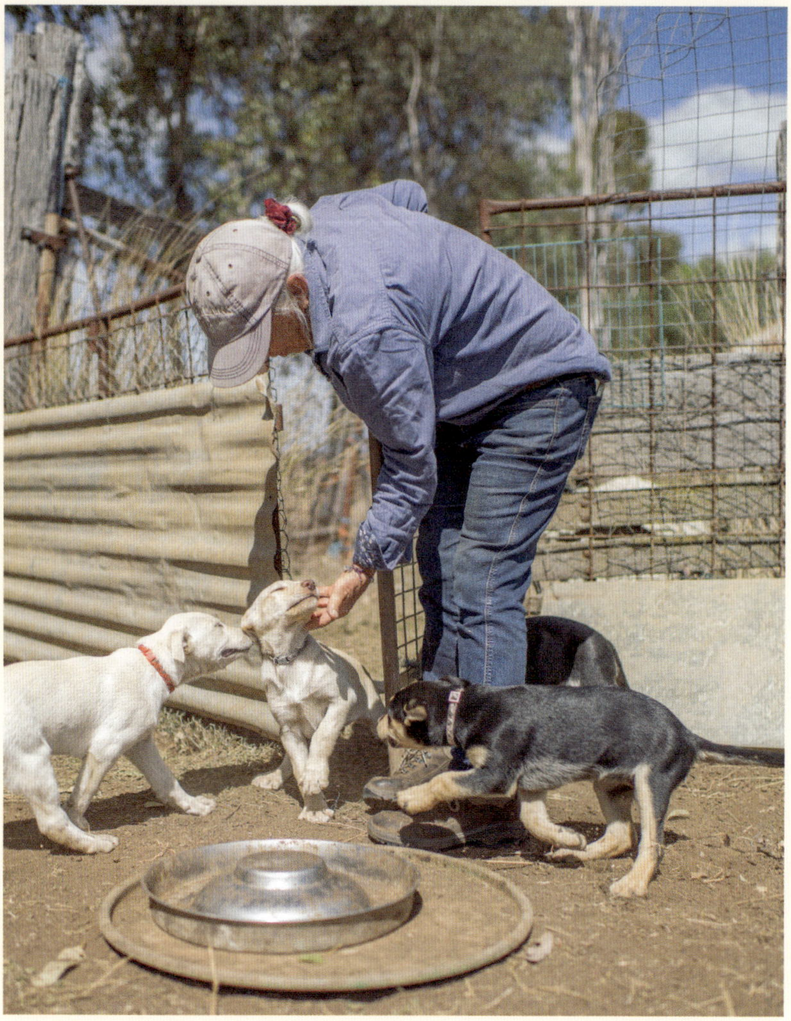

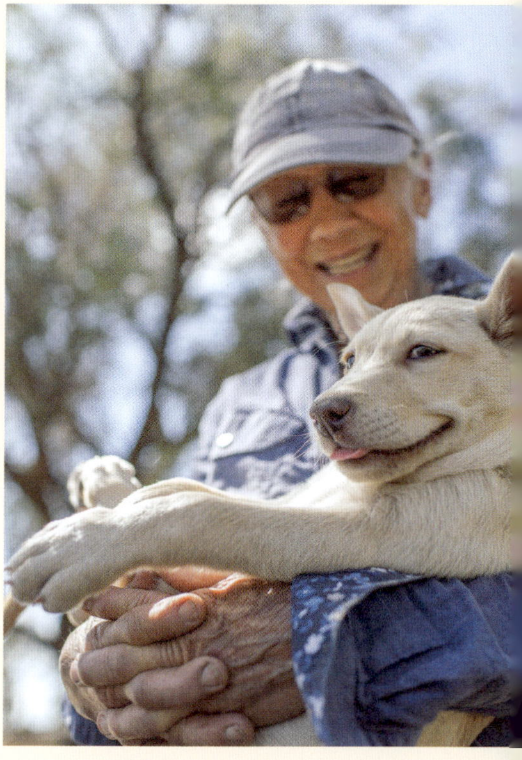

ABOVE I quickly found out that the star of the herding world in Australia is the Kelpie. Jan McIntyre is a breeder and owner of Karmala Kelpies, who specializes in the breed. Her dogs can be found all over the world.

RIGHT As a breeder, Jan is selective about where she sends her dogs: They need to be with owners who know how to handle breeds with a strong herding drive. Jan vets prospective owners, making sure that her dogs will be in good hands in their new homes.

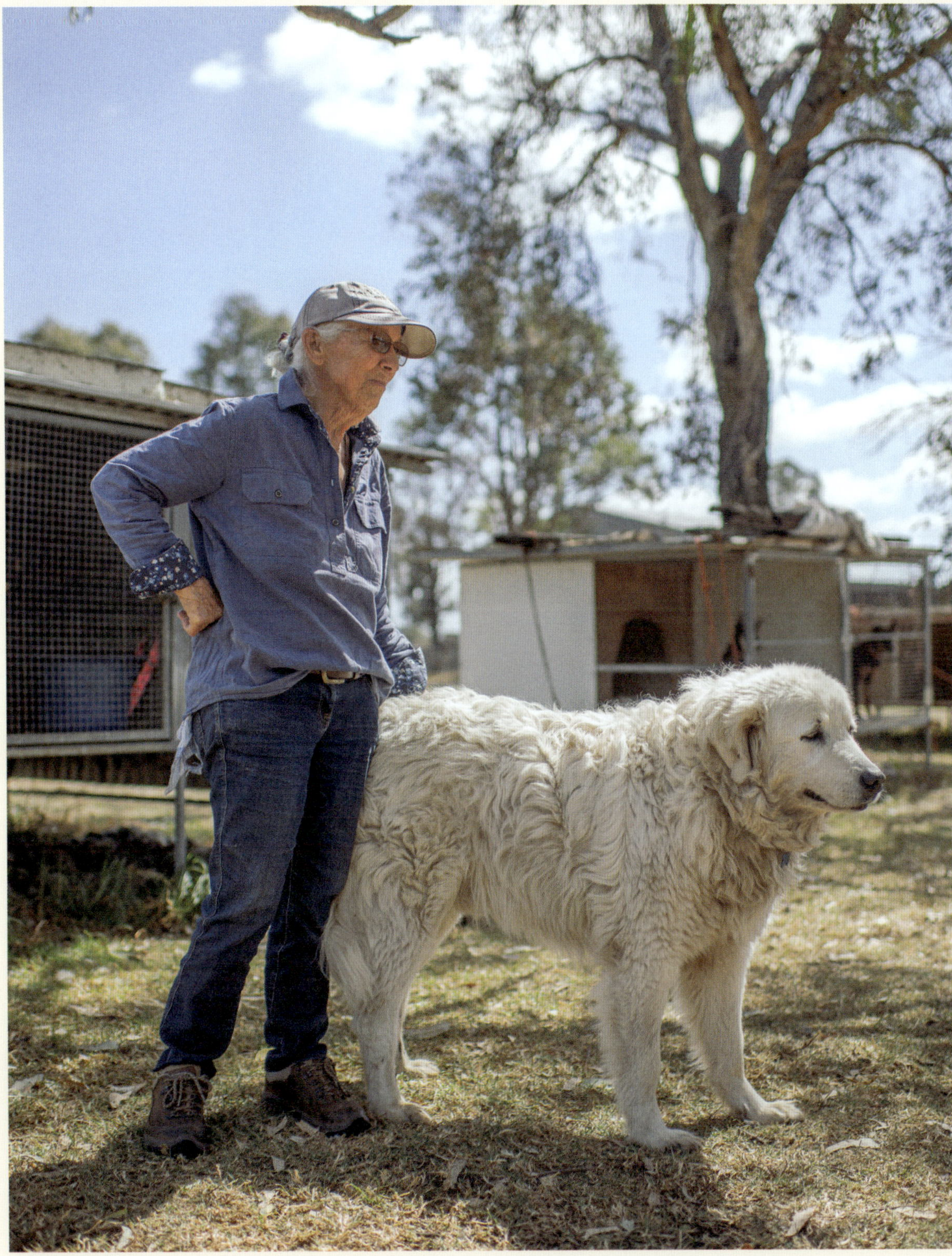

ABOVE While most of the dogs at Karmala are Kelpies, there was also Howie the Maremma, a type of livestock guardian dog with origins in Italy. Howie was a big, gentle dog who would be sure to flip a switch into protection mode if any Australian critters tried to mess with the puppies.

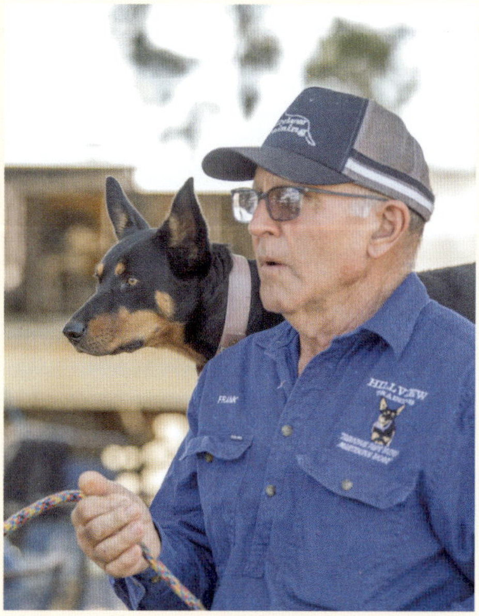

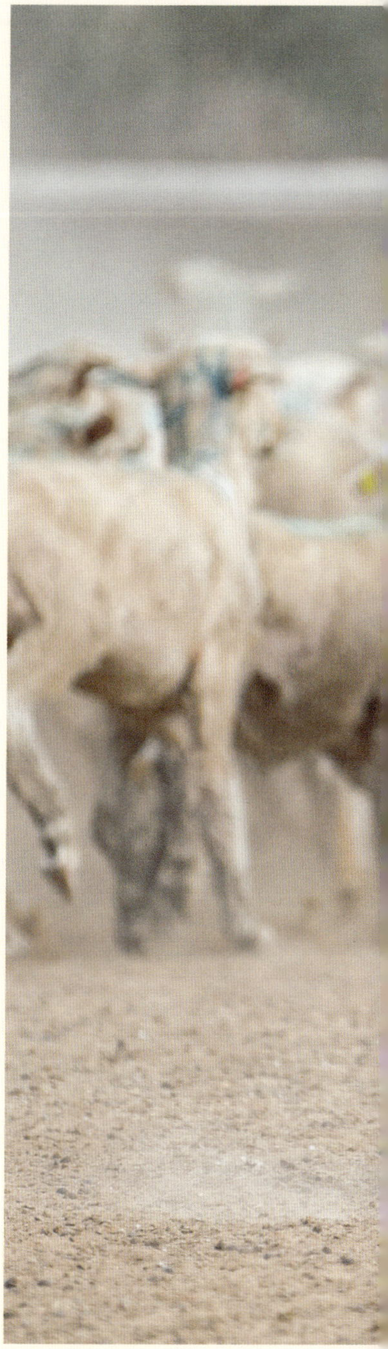

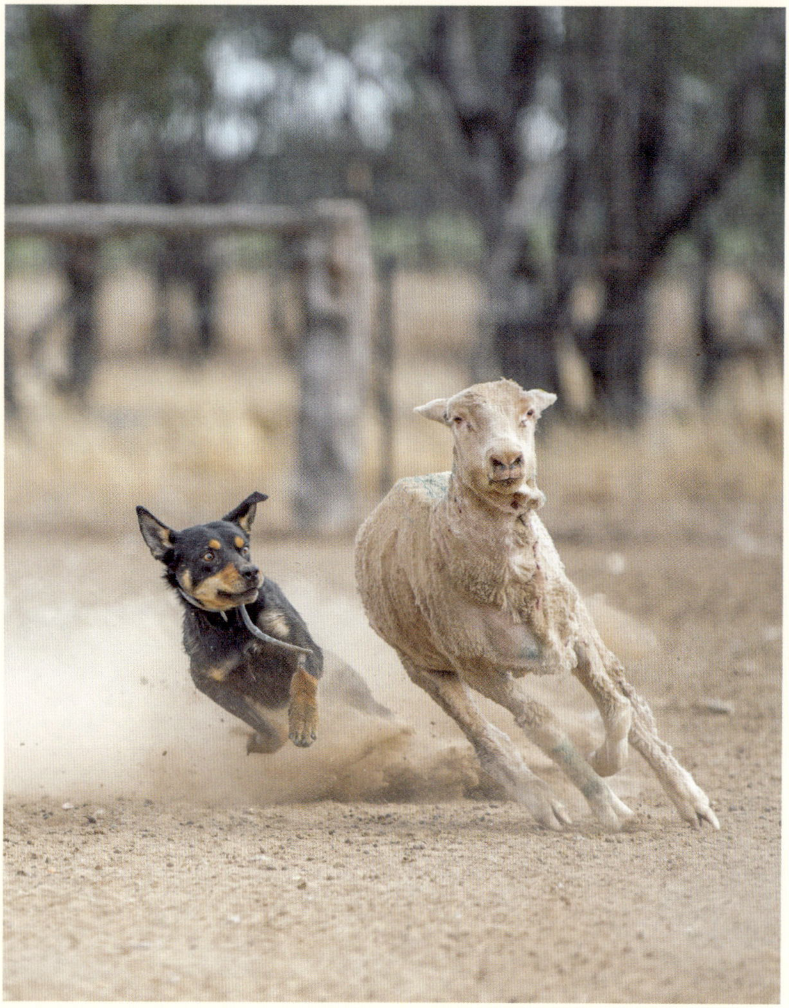

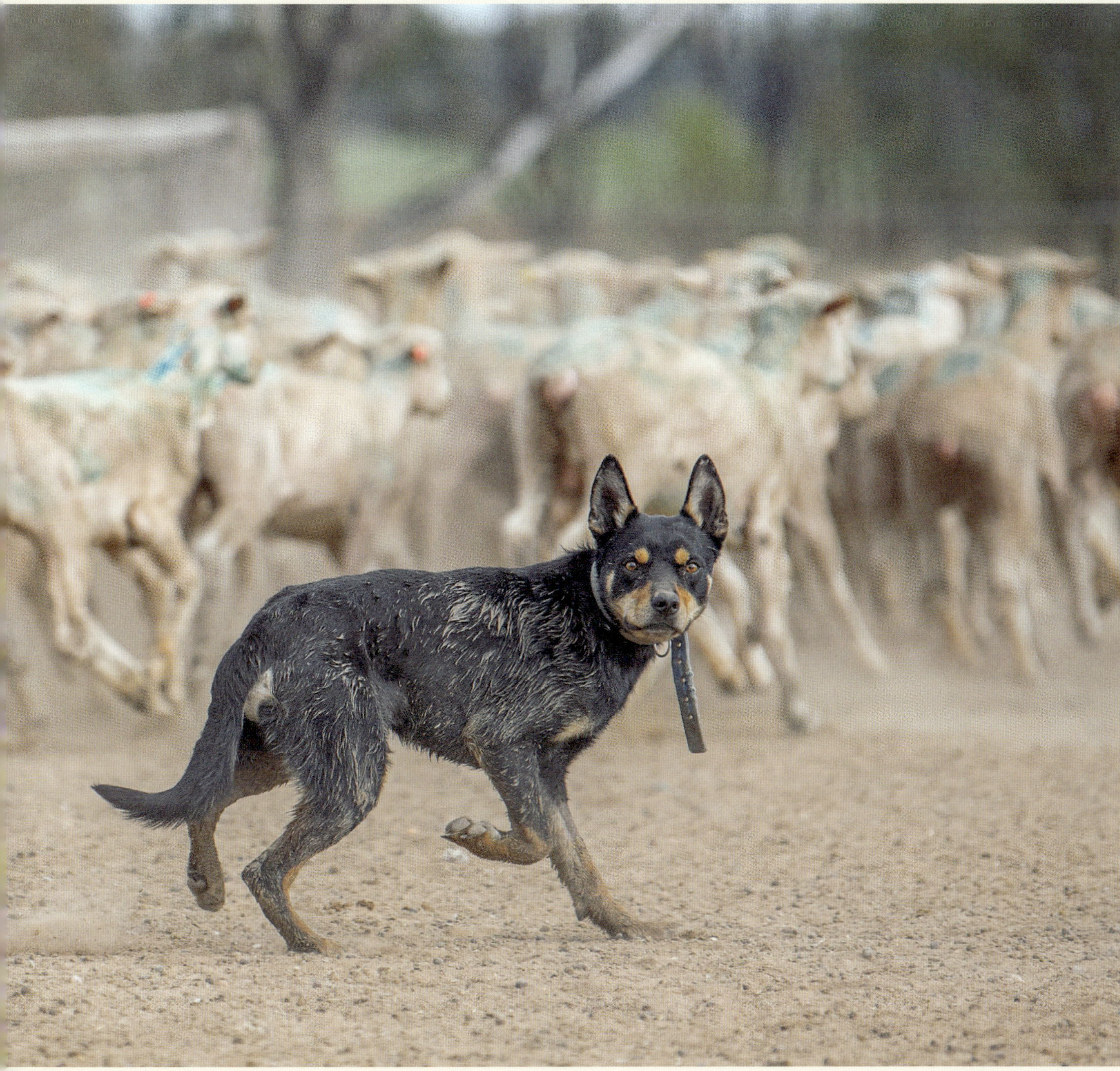

TOP LEFT Kelpies can reach a certain skill level through instinct and other dogs showing them the ropes, but to really excel, they need training. When it comes to trainers, Frank Finger knows a thing or two. He and his dog, Annie, won the dog training reality show *Muster Dogs.* He trains other pups at his school, Hillview Training, in Clermont, Queensland.

BOTTOM LEFT & ABOVE The Kelpie stare is intense. The dogs were hard at work, herding sheep at a wool farm in Collarenebri, New South Wales. The sheep had just been sheared, dewormed, and sprayed with an aqua-colored anti-lice treatment.

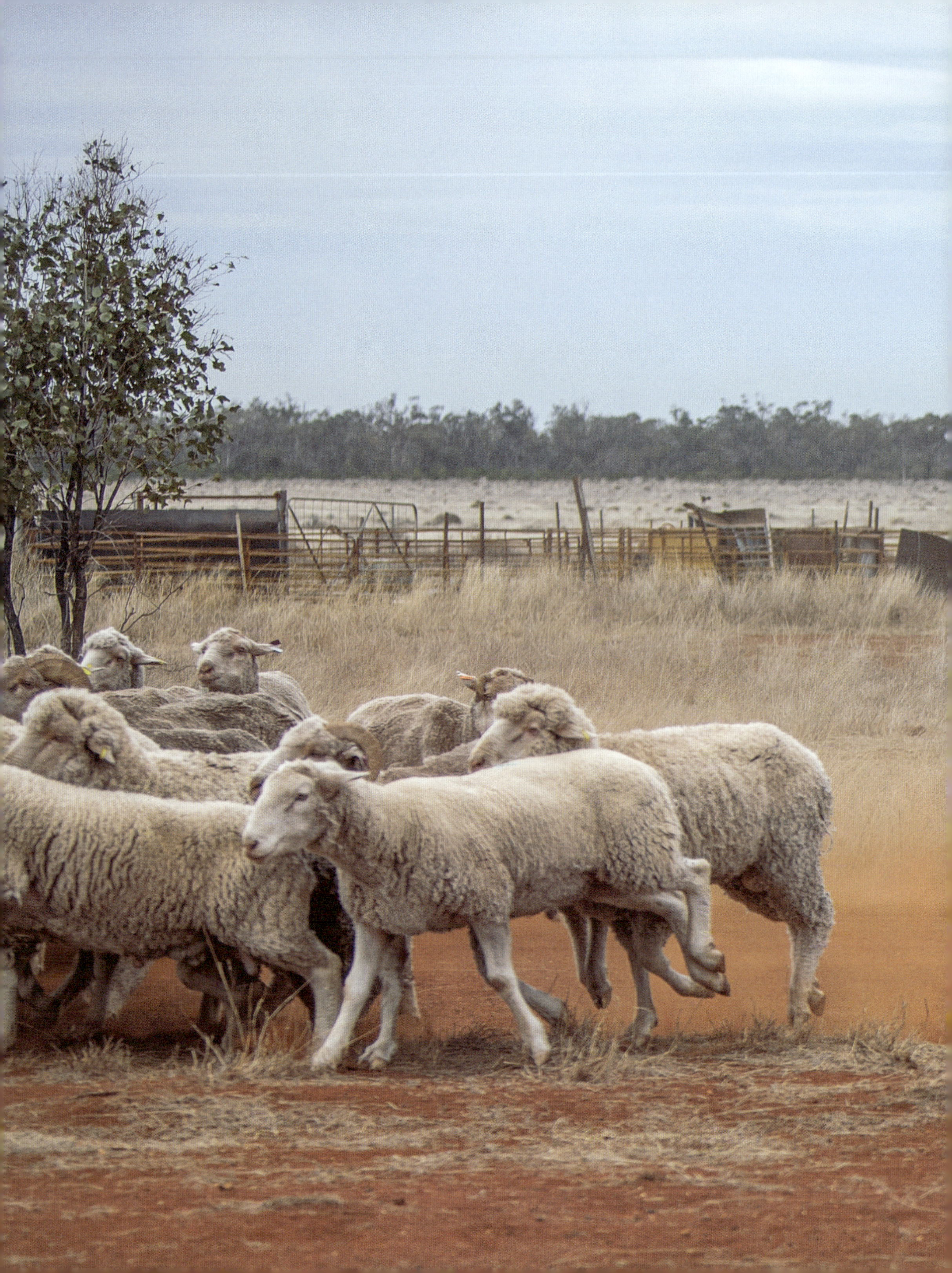

THIS PAGE The farmers moved sheep across this vast 9,000-acre plot mostly through the work of the dogs. They would hop on and off 4×4s until they heard the command, which was described as "send them and bend them." As soon as they received a command, or an animal stepped out of line, the dogs sprung into action, running side to side to bend in the flock and keep it tight.

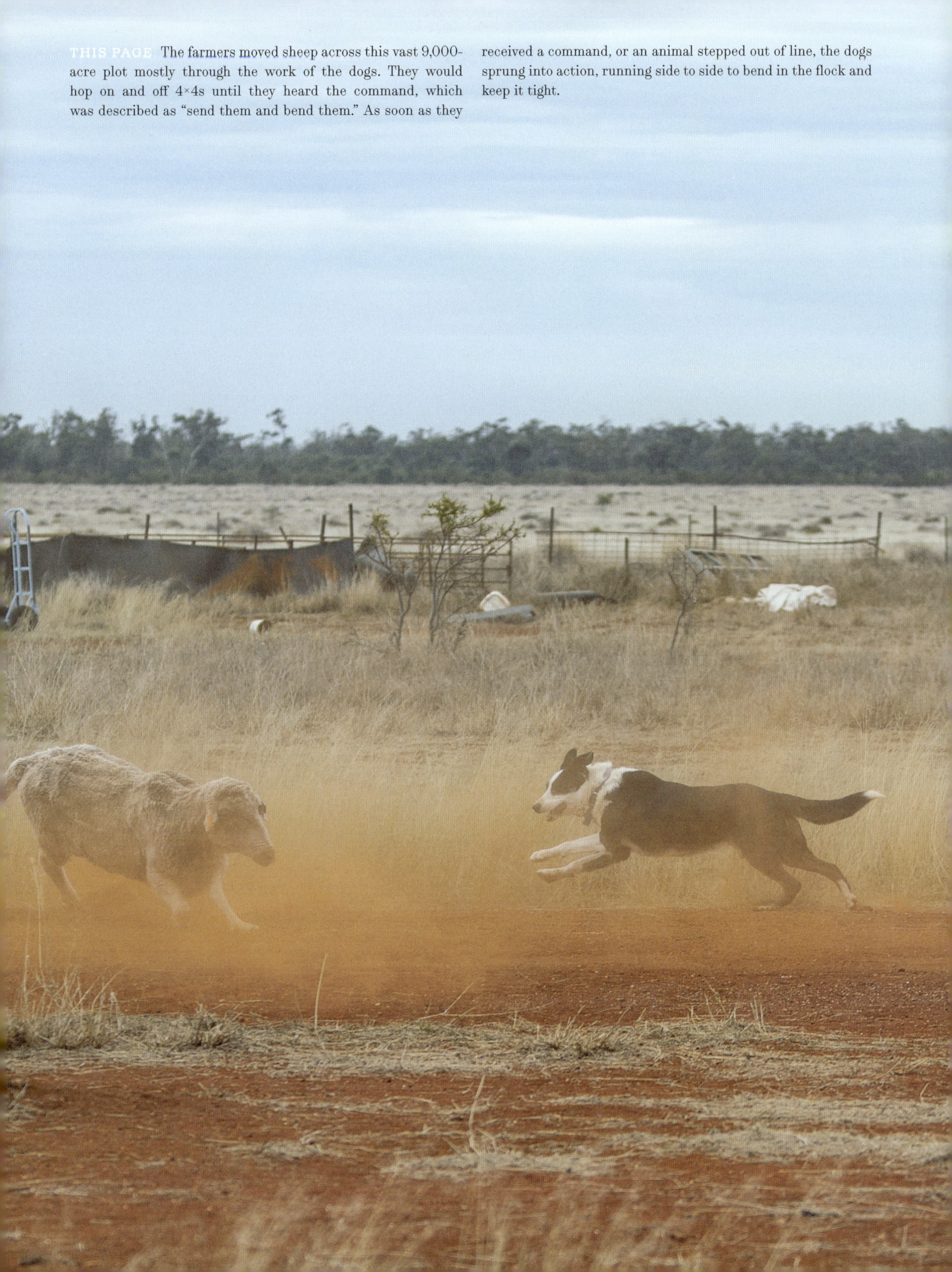

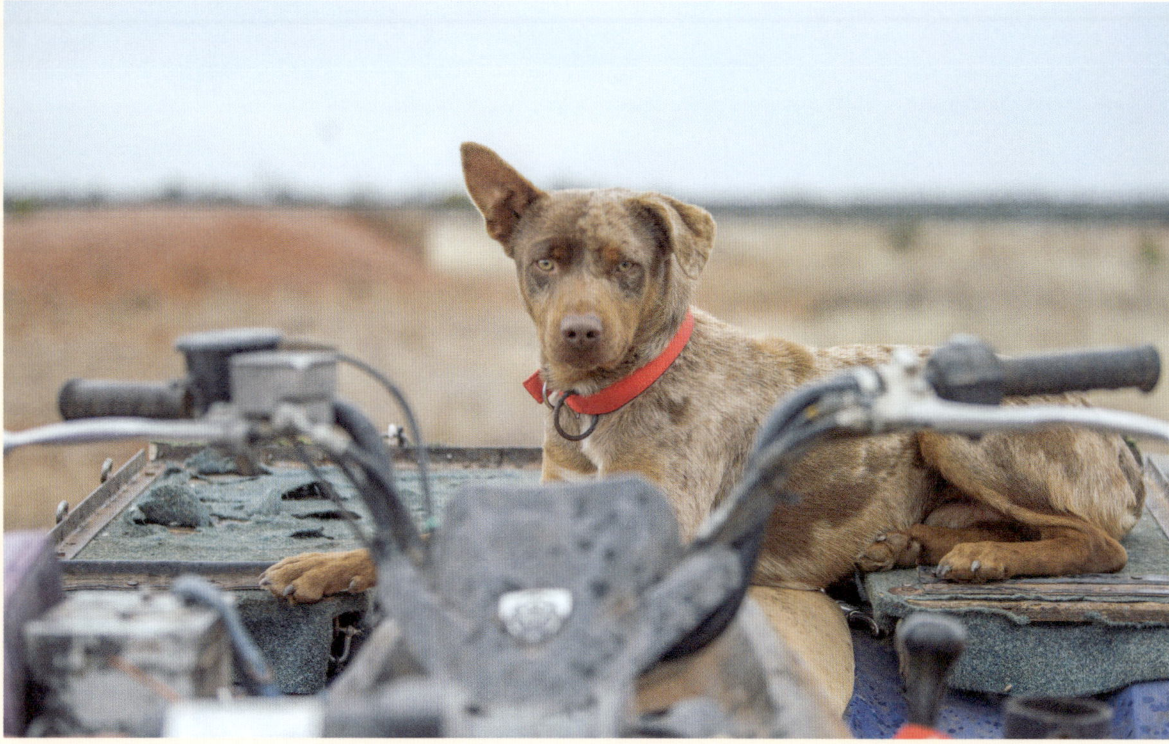

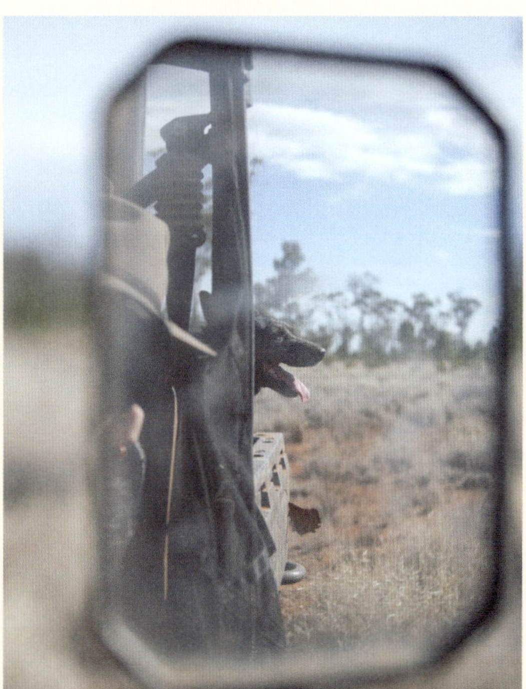

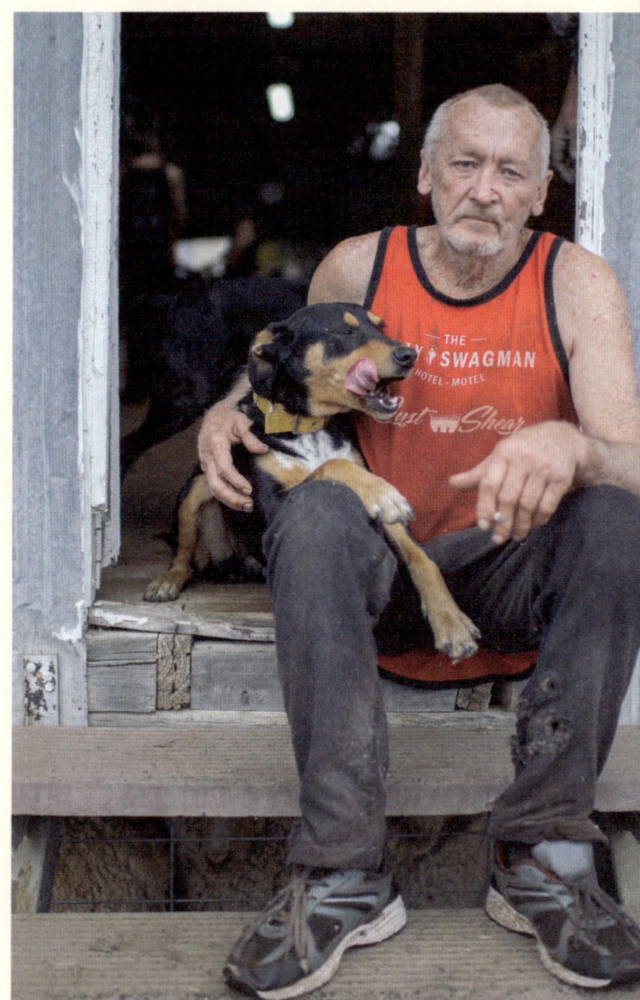
THE
SWAGMAN
HOTEL - MOTEL

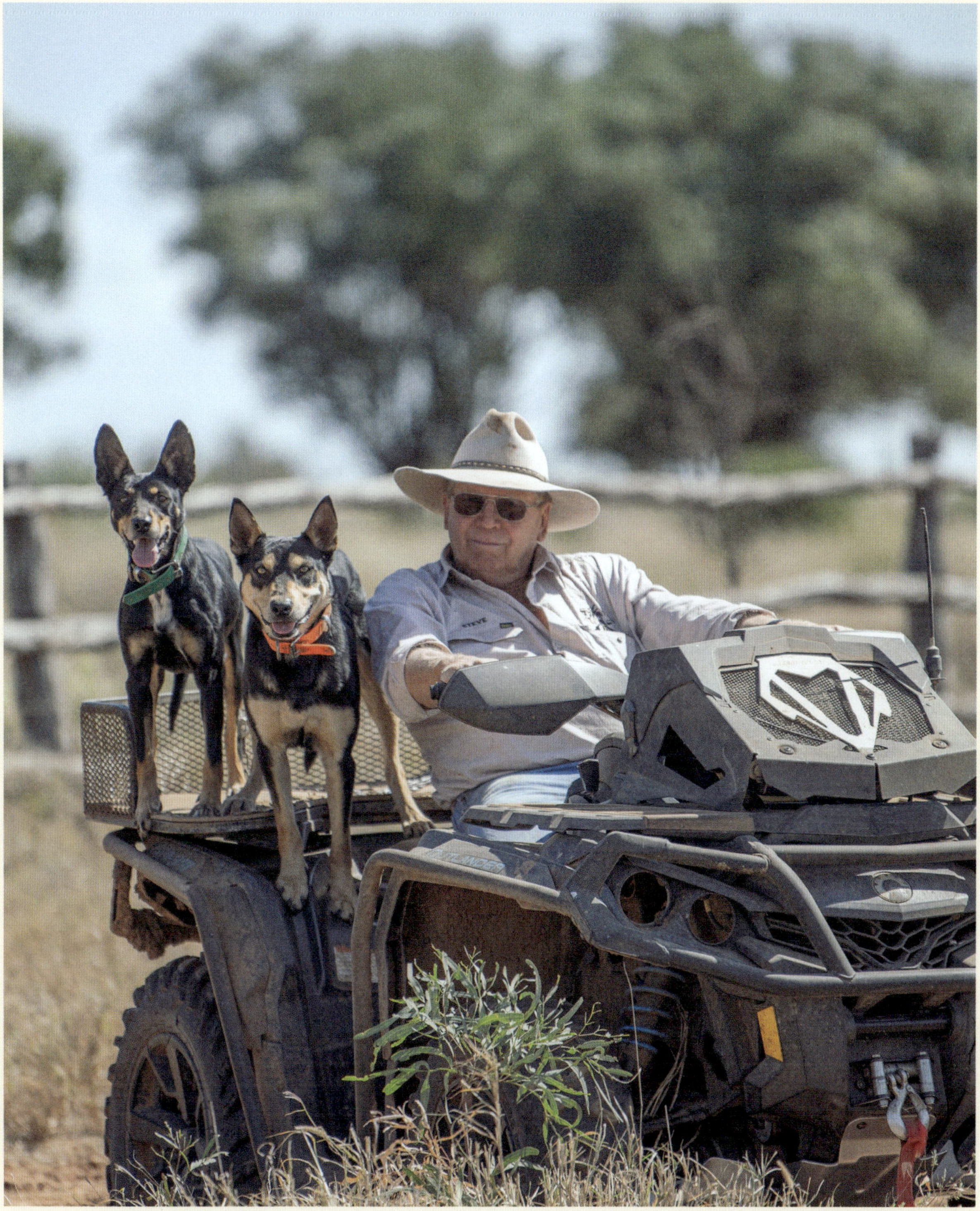

19

TOP & BOTTOM LEFT The dogs always found their way back to the ATVs for a ride with their owners across the expansive land, but they were ready to work at a moment's notice.

BOTTOM RIGHT A snapshot of coworkers. Shearers and dogs both play important roles in the wool industry.

ABOVE & NEXT PAGE A visit to Talki Station in Queensland gave me a glimpse of dogs working with cattle. Owners Mary and Steve Lund both manage their own packs of dogs and work in tandem to move cattle across their property.

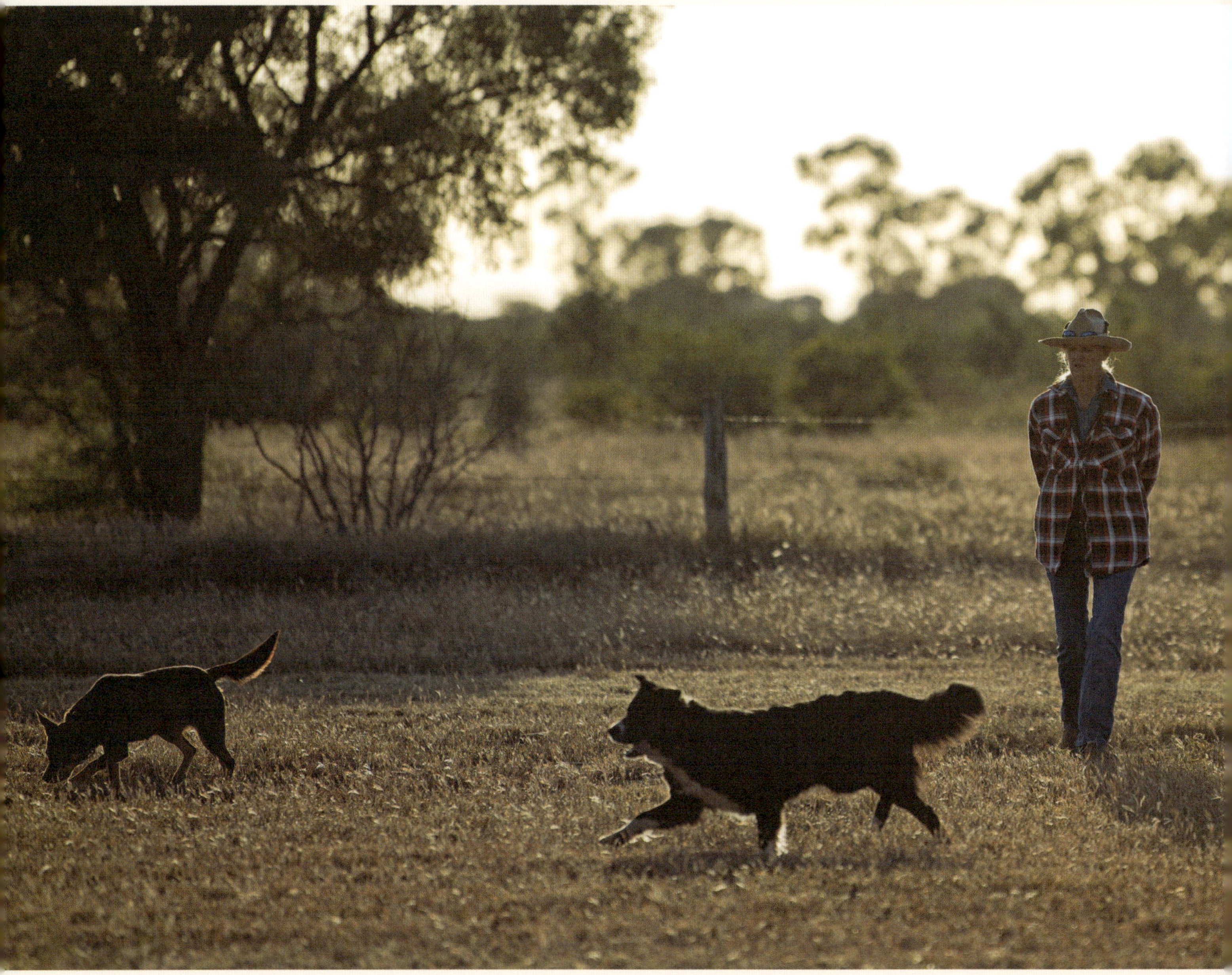

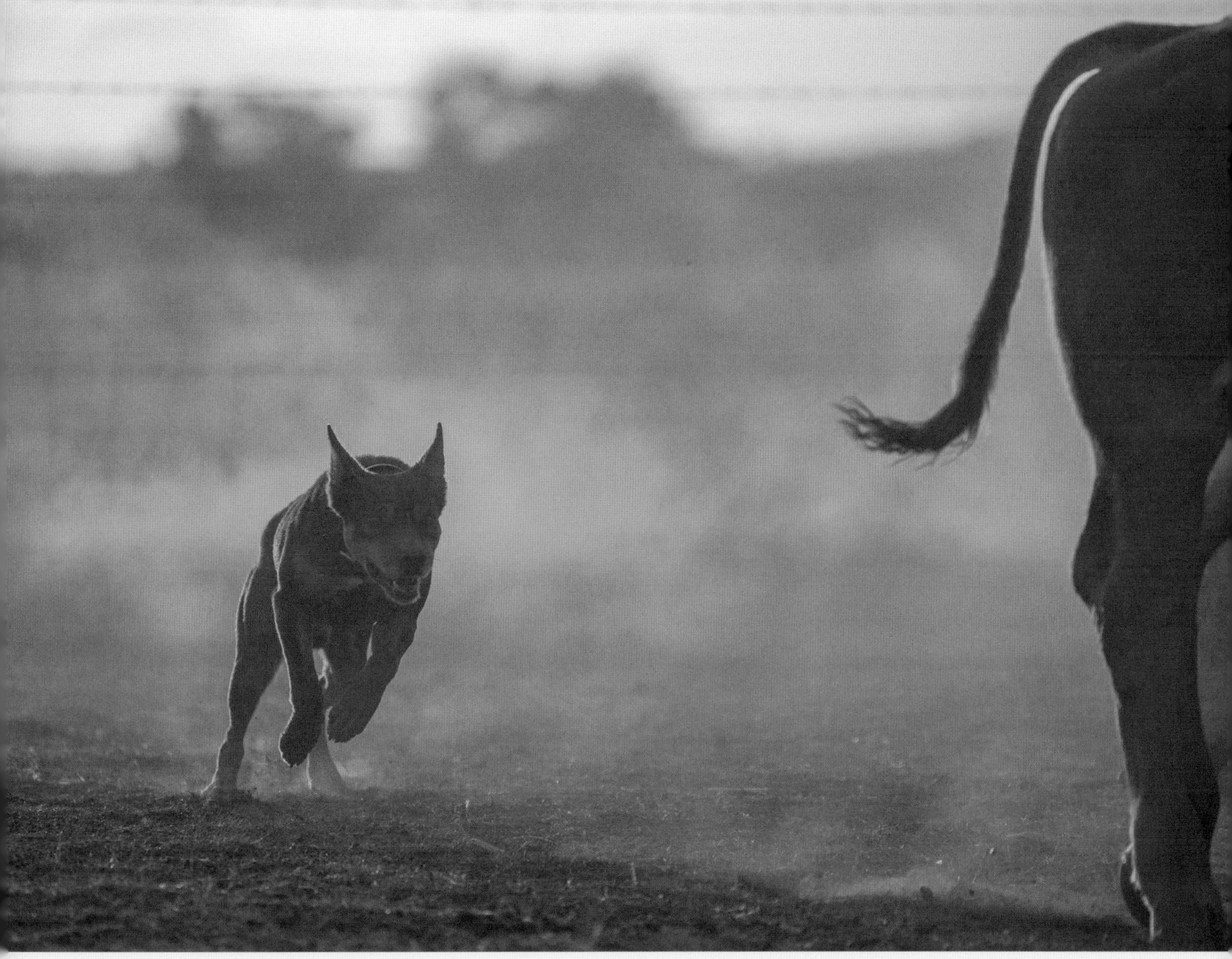

ABOVE It was an early start to a day spent moving hundreds of young cattle, also known as weaners.

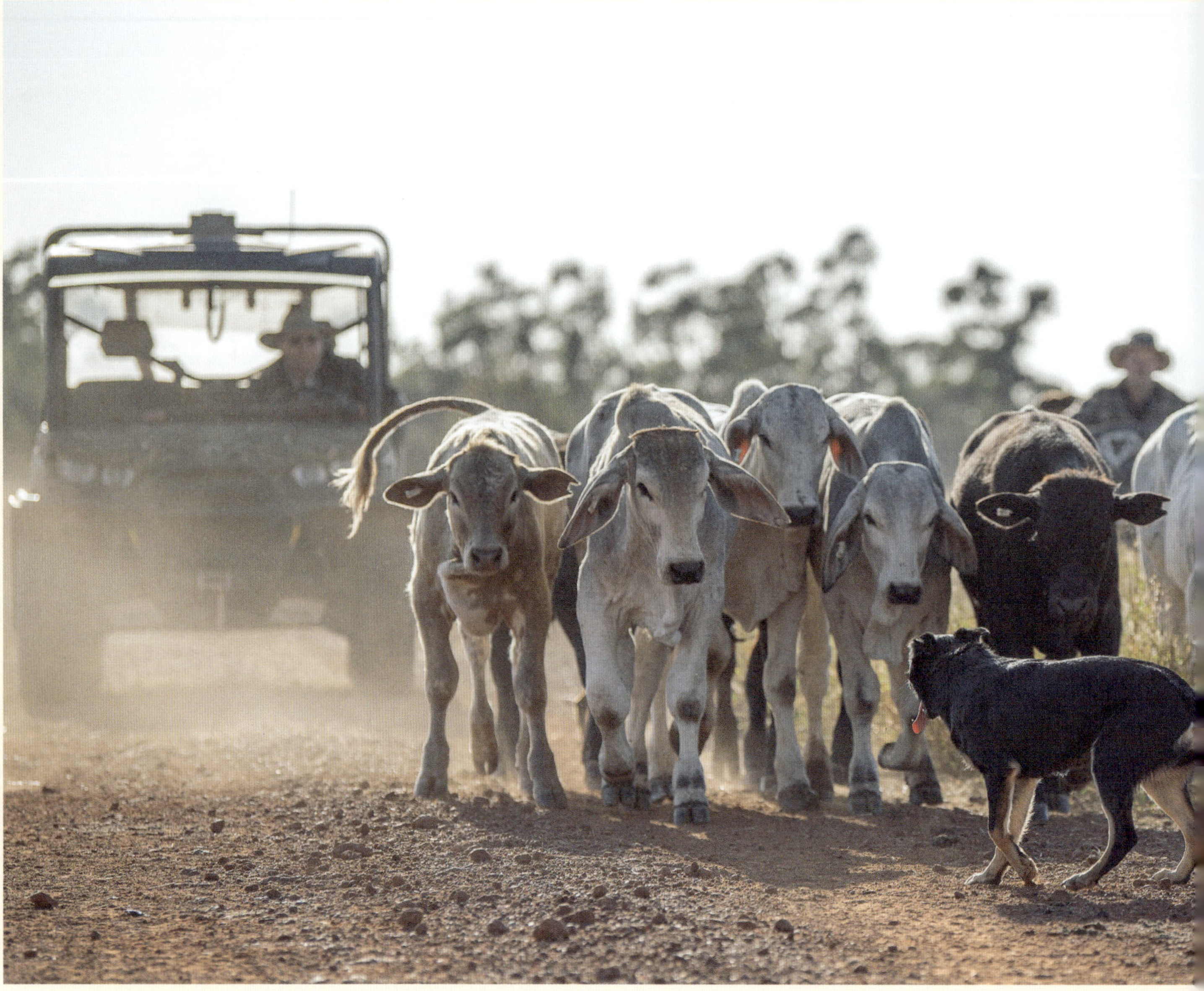

ABOVE Weaners are young cattle that have recently been separated from their mothers, so they no longer drink milk. They are often moved to new paddocks to start eating independently. Who moves them? Well, Mary and Steve are the brains behind the operation, but the dogs do the heavy lifting. Mary and her dogs lead the way and make sure none of the calves try to run ahead. Meanwhile, Steve and his dogs follow from behind to keep the stragglers moving along.

RIGHT TOP & BOTTOM As much as herding dogs want to always be on the move, they need to take commands to stop, stay, and lay: the same basic commands that every domesticated dog should know. While still, the dogs' eyes remain fixated on the livestock.

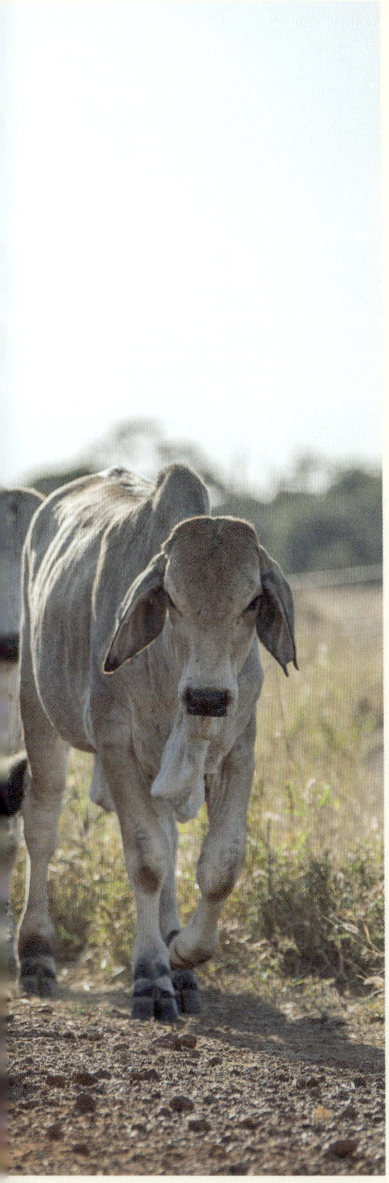

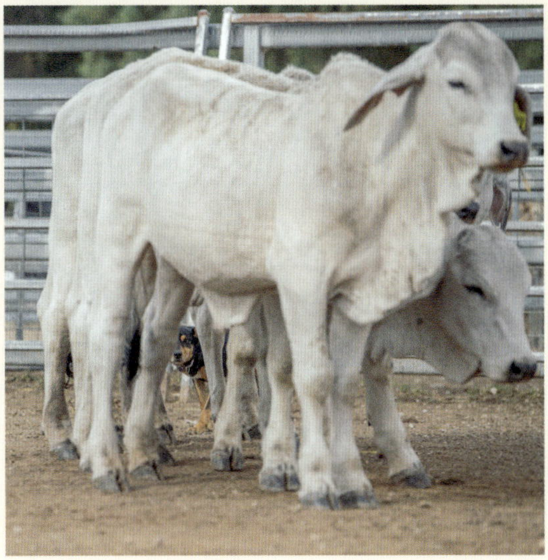

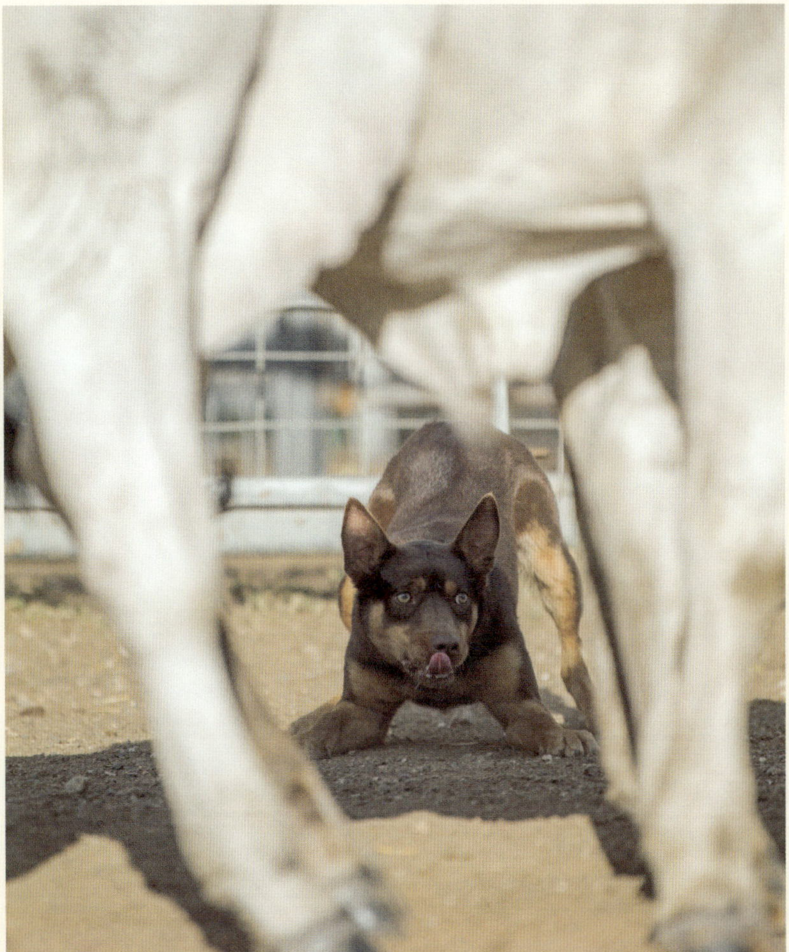

RIGHT After visiting with Steve and Mary, I witnessed more of their family's talents at their daughter Kim's property. She owns a cattle farm and Nitro Kelpies, where she breeds dogs. With a deep connection to her Kelpies, she is an excellent handler. Kim finds that her dogs are good at different things, which guides her on how to utilize them in varying situations.

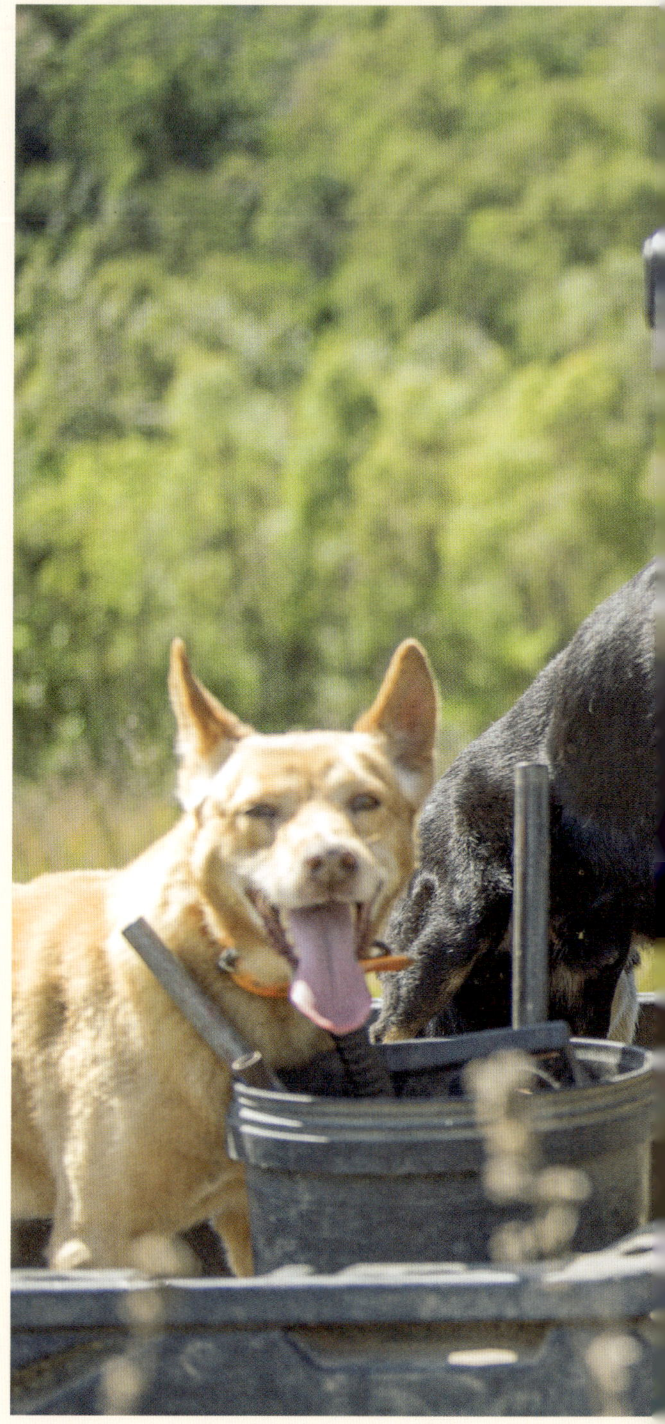

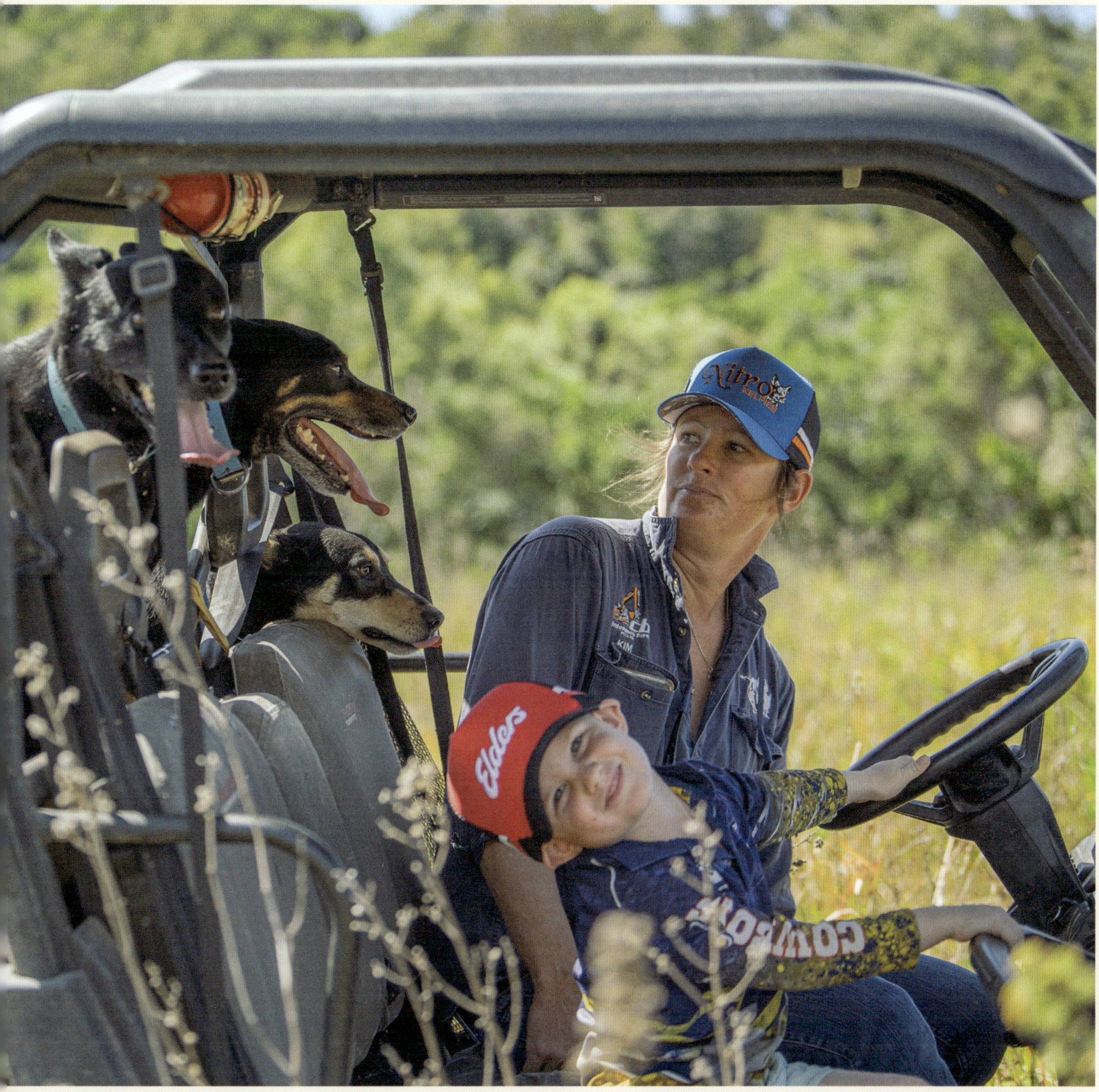

The dogs have an innate ability to work together, and Kelpies are renowned as independent thinkers. It doesn't take much human handling or direction to get them to work – they are born for this.

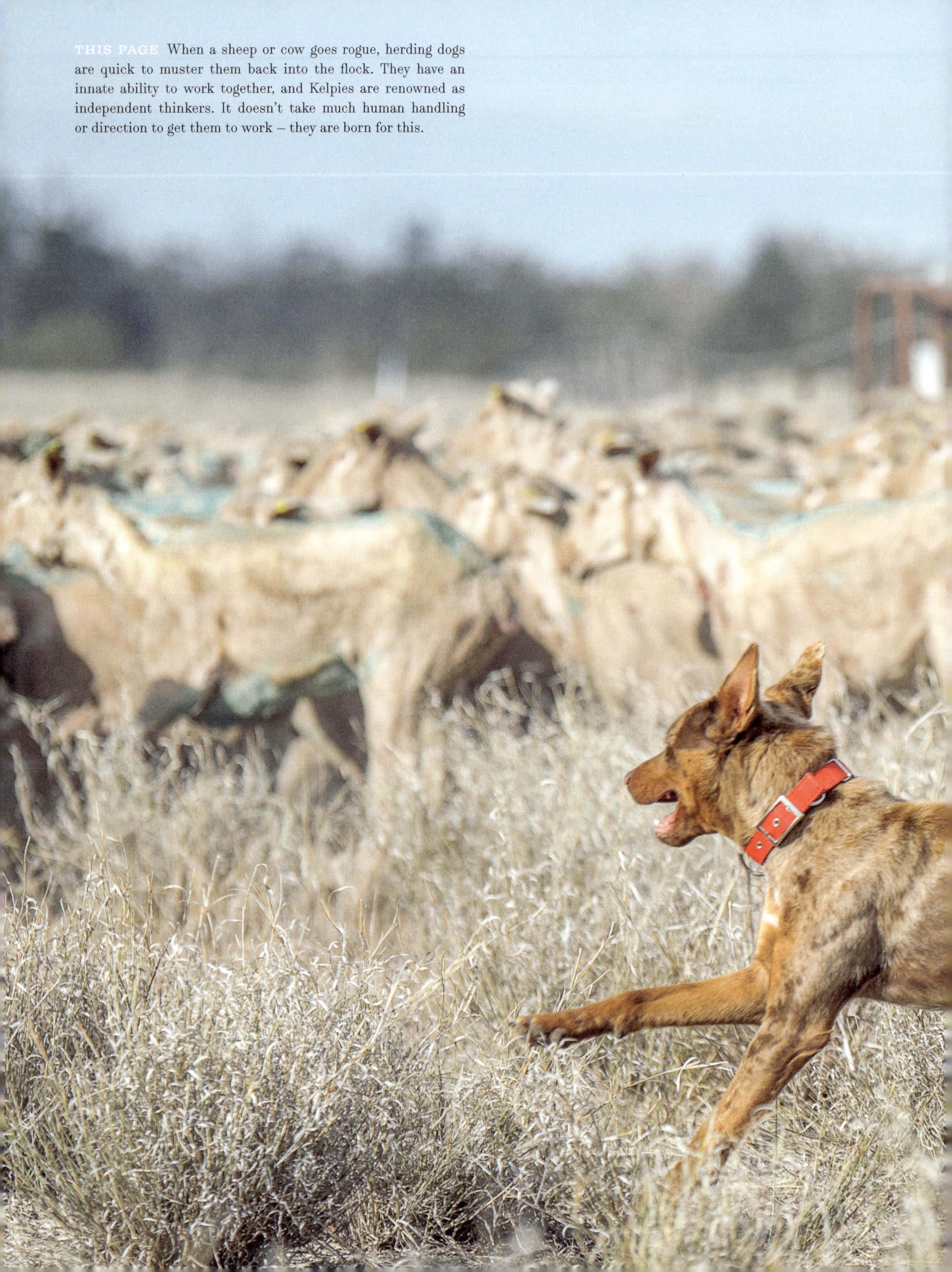

THIS PAGE When a sheep or cow goes rogue, herding dogs are quick to muster them back into the flock. They have an innate ability to work together, and Kelpies are renowned as independent thinkers. It doesn't take much human handling or direction to get them to work – they are born for this.

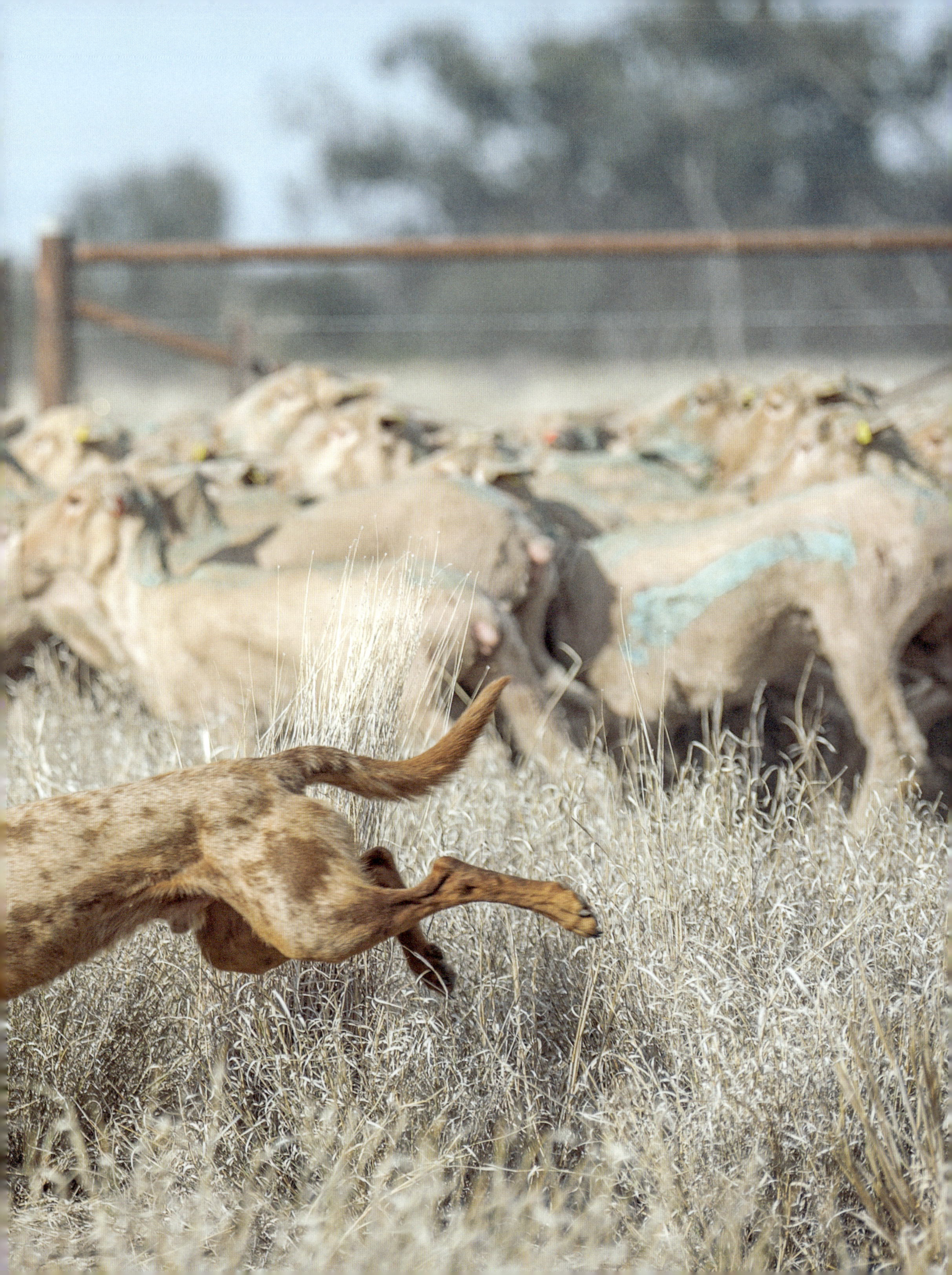

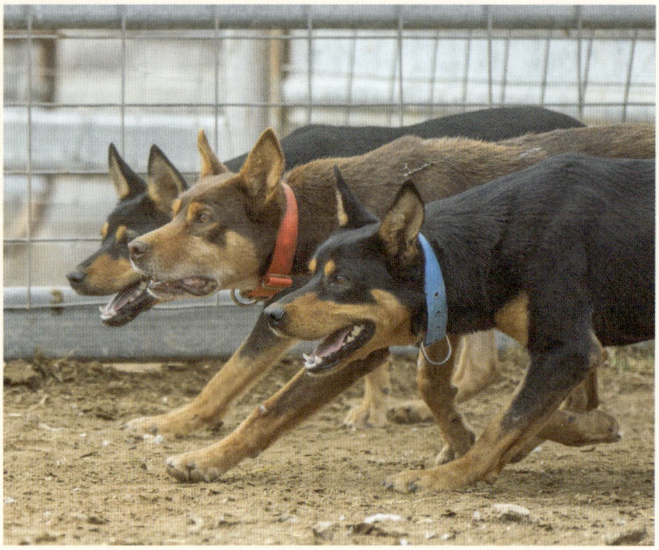

28

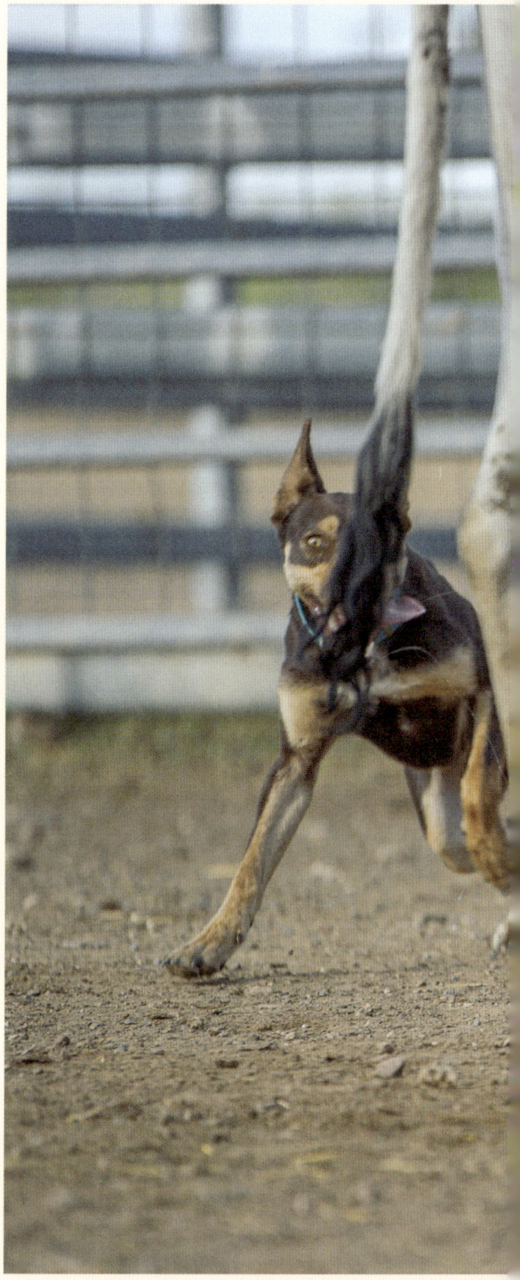

LEFT & BELOW Kelpies have a way of stalking livestock. They are stealthy, crouching low and lurking behind the animals they are mustering. As soon as they receive a command, or an animal steps out of line, the dogs spring into action. Some will instinctively bite at the ankles of animals: This is something handlers may try to train out of them. A kick from a cow will also make a dog think twice about getting that close again.

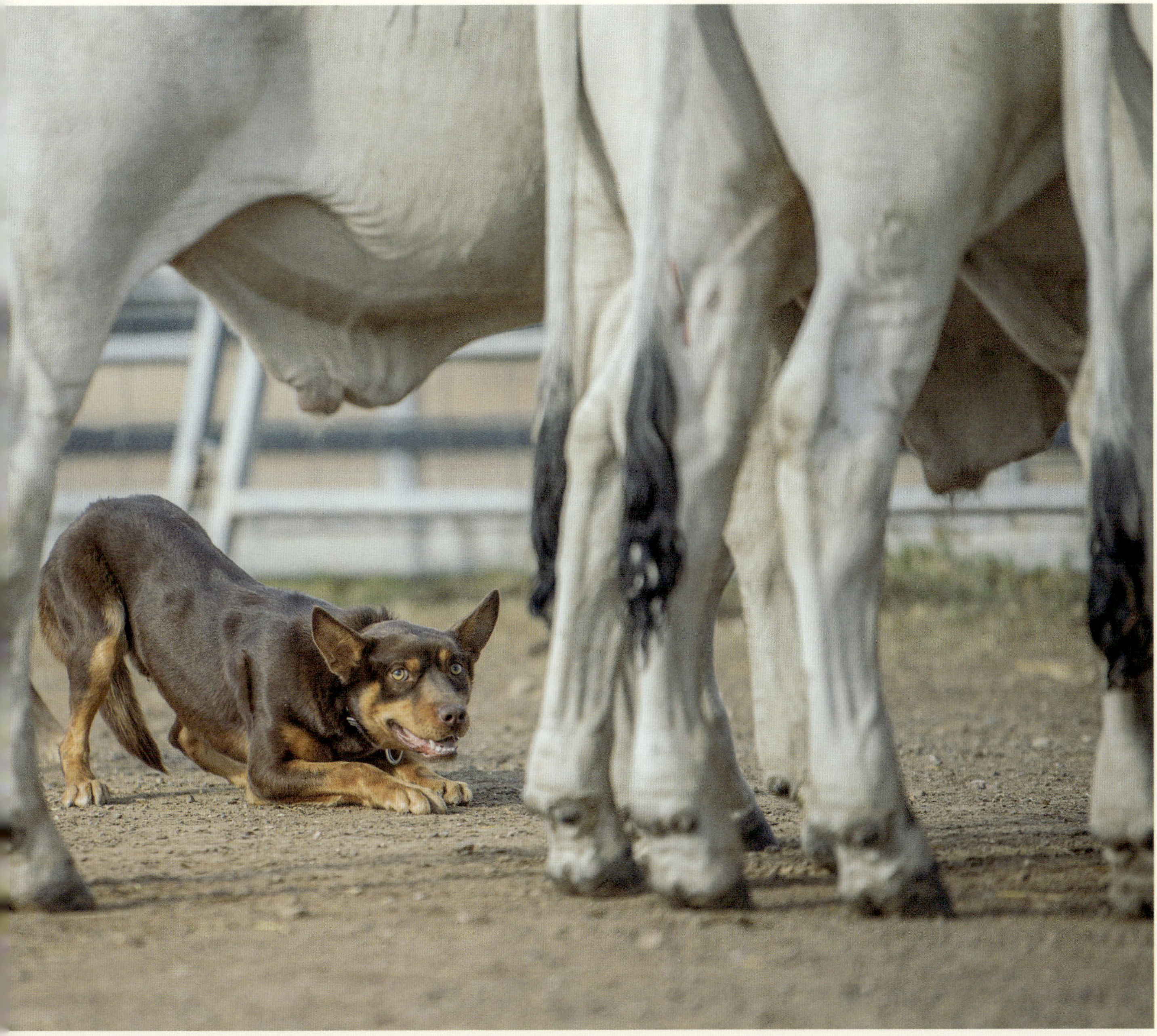

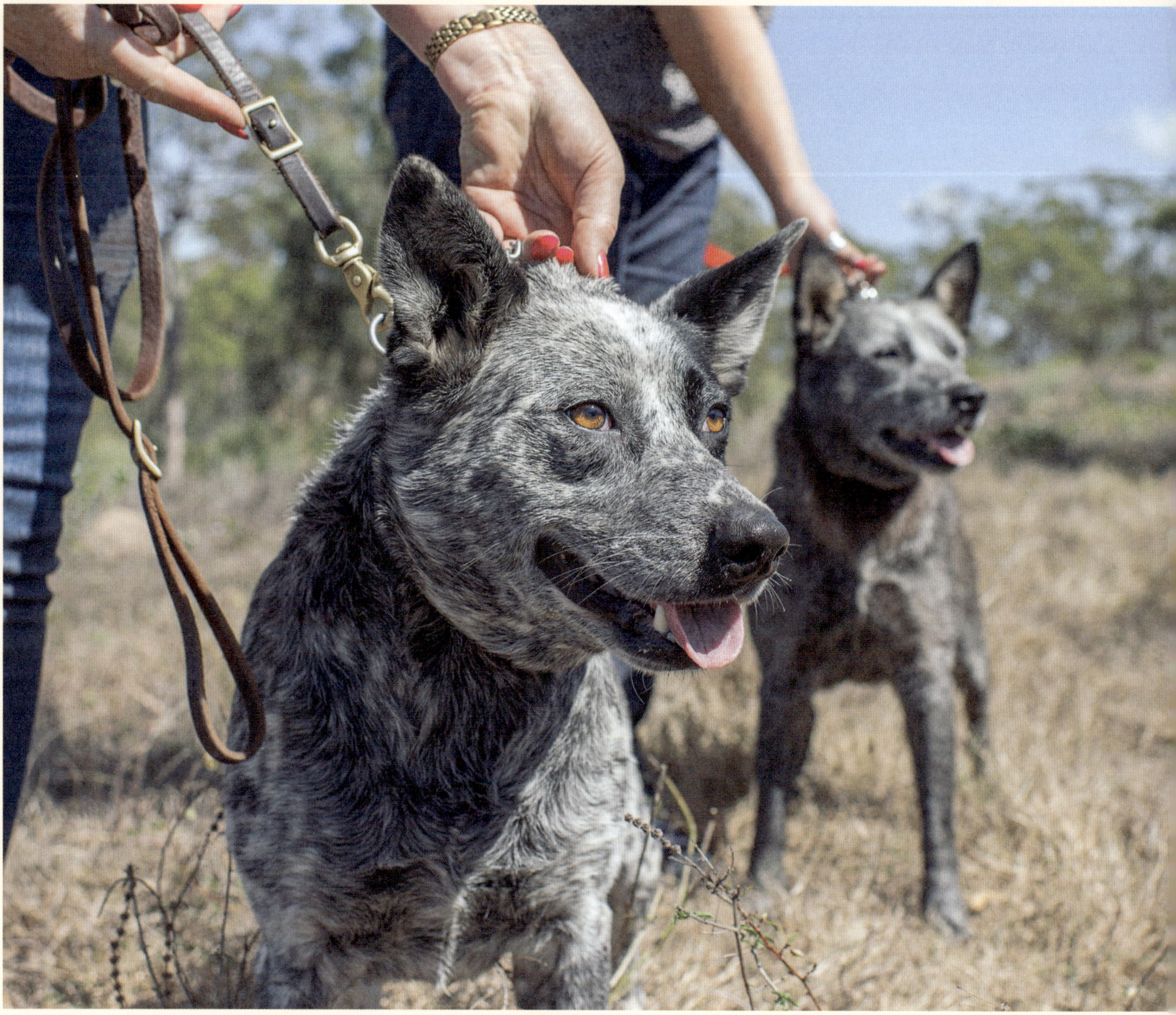

RIGHT The Australian Cattle Dog was widely used for over a century as a herding dog in Australia, but today it has fallen out of favor as a worker. However, this breed is still widely found across Australia – and the world – though not as the choice herding dog it once was. This dog was bred by Team Kombinalong, who adheres to the original breed standard from 1903: "That of a small, thickset Dingo."

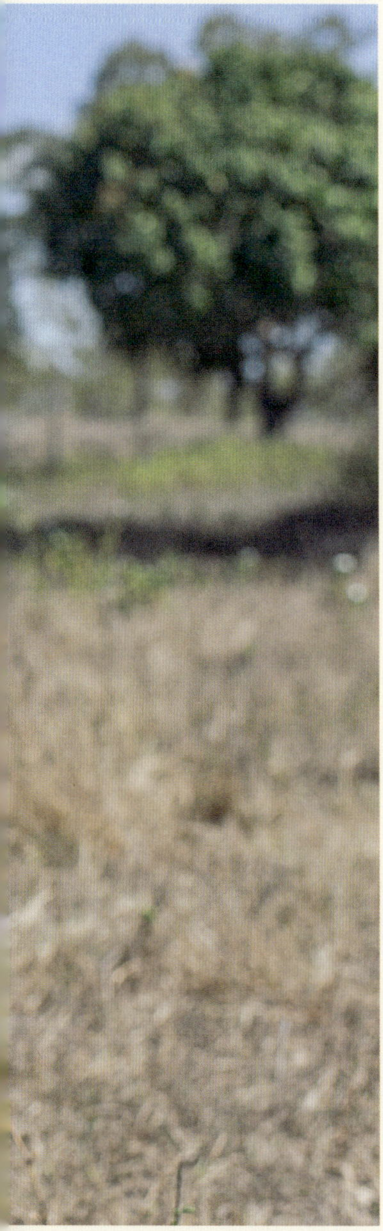

LEFT The Stumpy Tail Cattle Dog holds a place in Australian history, but once the work and the needs of stockmen changed, the breed faced extinction. Breeders have worked diligently, however, to preserve this cattle dog. Talelesshill Kennels owner Brendan Dalglish breeds gorgeous, award-winning dogs, and has rehomed his Stumpys all over the world.

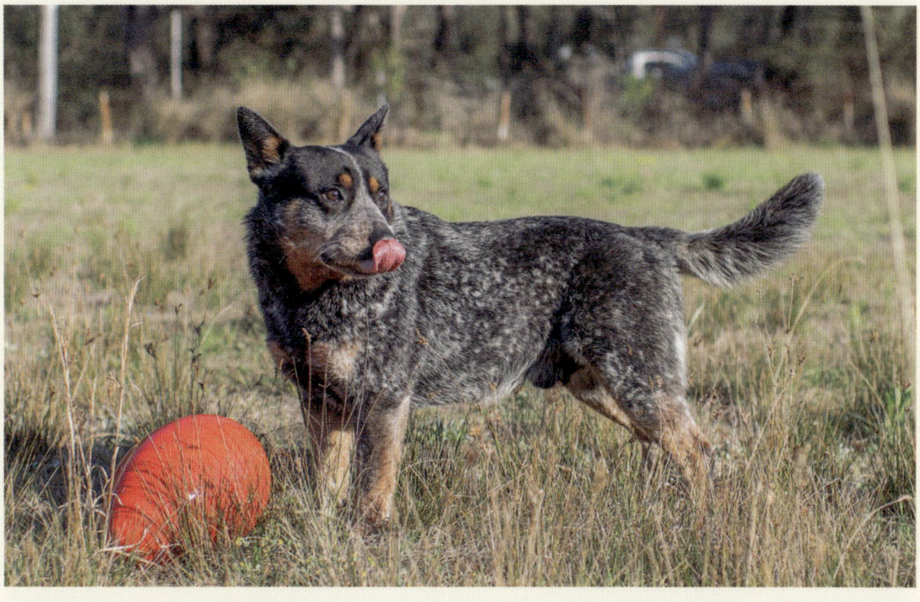

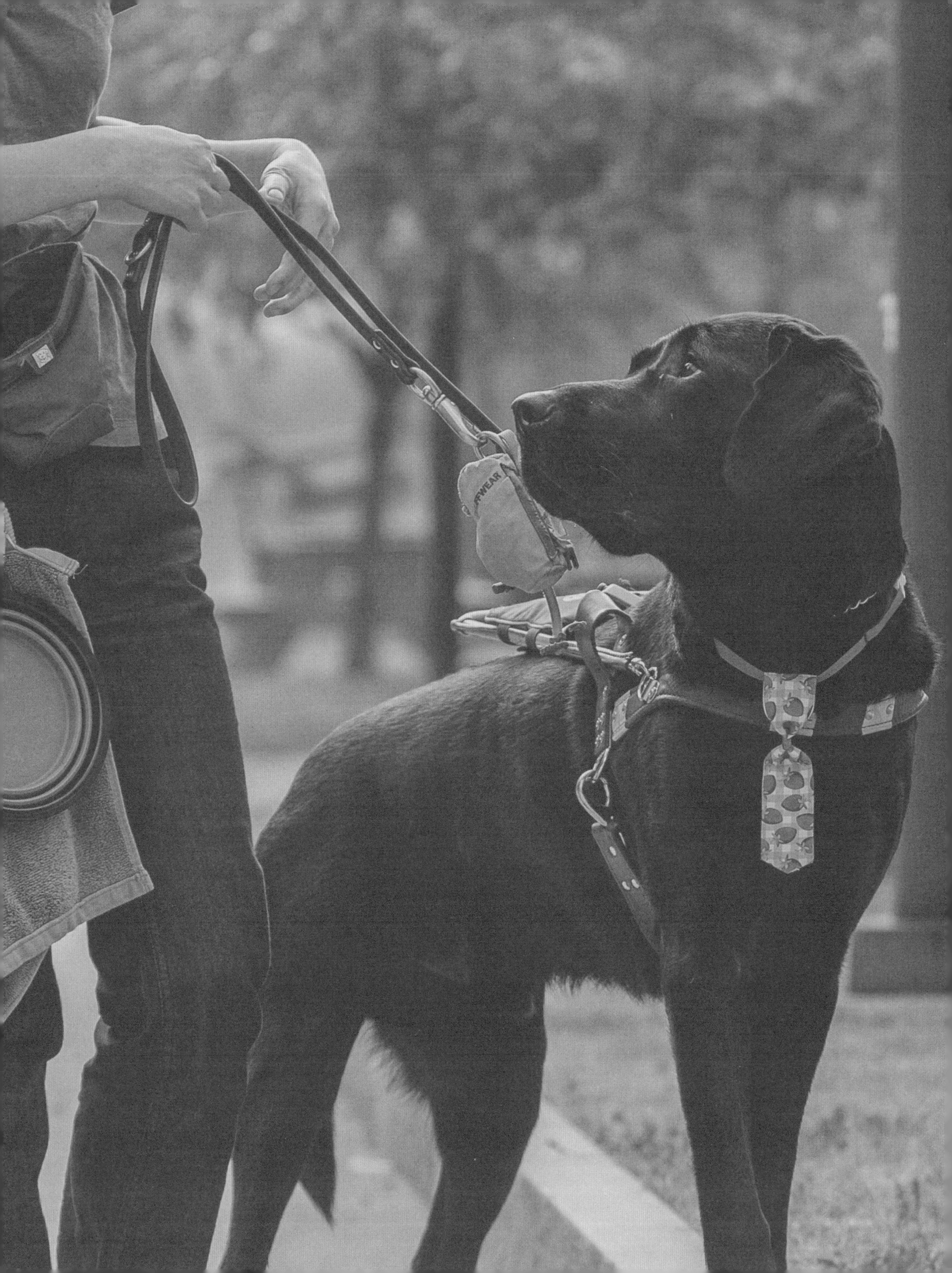

LOCATION	BREED	TASKS	SKILLS
Buffalo, USA	Labrador	Navigating, Avoiding Obstacles, Managing Crowds	Confidence, Adaptability, Sociability

GUIDE DOGS

OF ALL THE HUMAN–DOG RELATIONSHIPS I've photographed, the most special one I've witnessed is between guide dogs and their handlers. The capabilities of these dogs are remarkable, offering people with vision loss a greater sense of independence.

Guiding Eyes for the Blind breeds and trains guide dogs. The dogs are trained for years before they begin working with their handlers: a journey that starts well before a guide dog is born. The organization purposefully breeds dogs for the health and temperament needed for guide work. The most common breed they train is the Labrador, as these dogs have the traits required to excel. Guiding Eyes looks for dogs with strong, confident temperaments who have the enthusiasm for work and the ability to adapt to new environments.

I am incredibly grateful that I had the opportunity to meet two guide dog handlers, as I was able to learn about the immeasurable positive impact that their dogs have had on their lives.

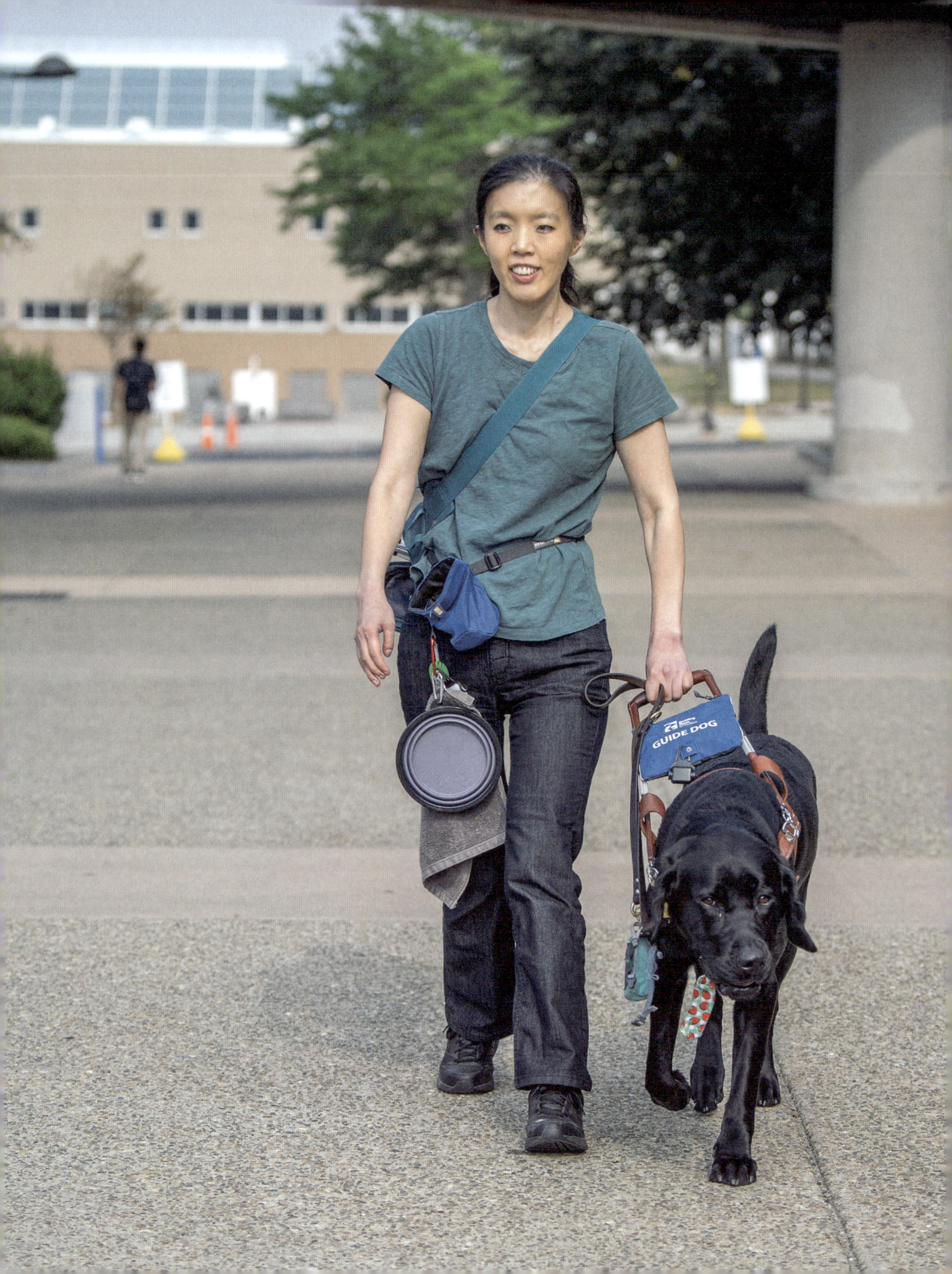
GUIDE DOG

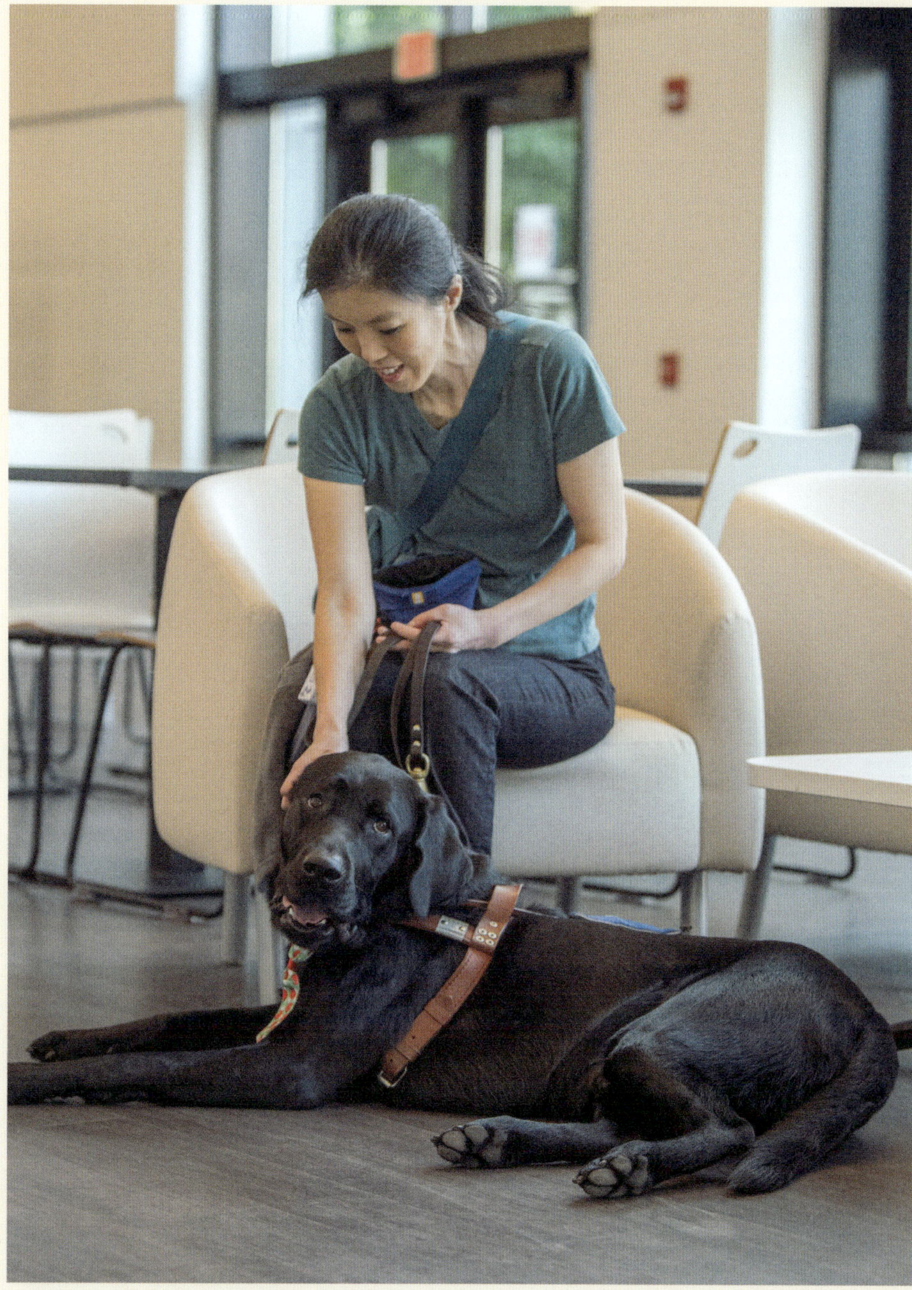

LEFT Guiding Eyes for the Blind has provided life-changing connections for over 70 years. In that time, they have graduated over 10,000 guide dog teams. They believe in the powerful, meaningful change that dogs bring to the lives of people facing the daily challenges presented by blindness and vision loss.

ABOVE I met Yoojin, along with her guide dog, Dennison, at the university where she is a graduate student. Dennison is not only her first guide dog, but her first dog in general, and he has completely transformed her life. When I met Yoojin, she'd been working with Dennison for less than a year, but the pair had already accomplished so much.

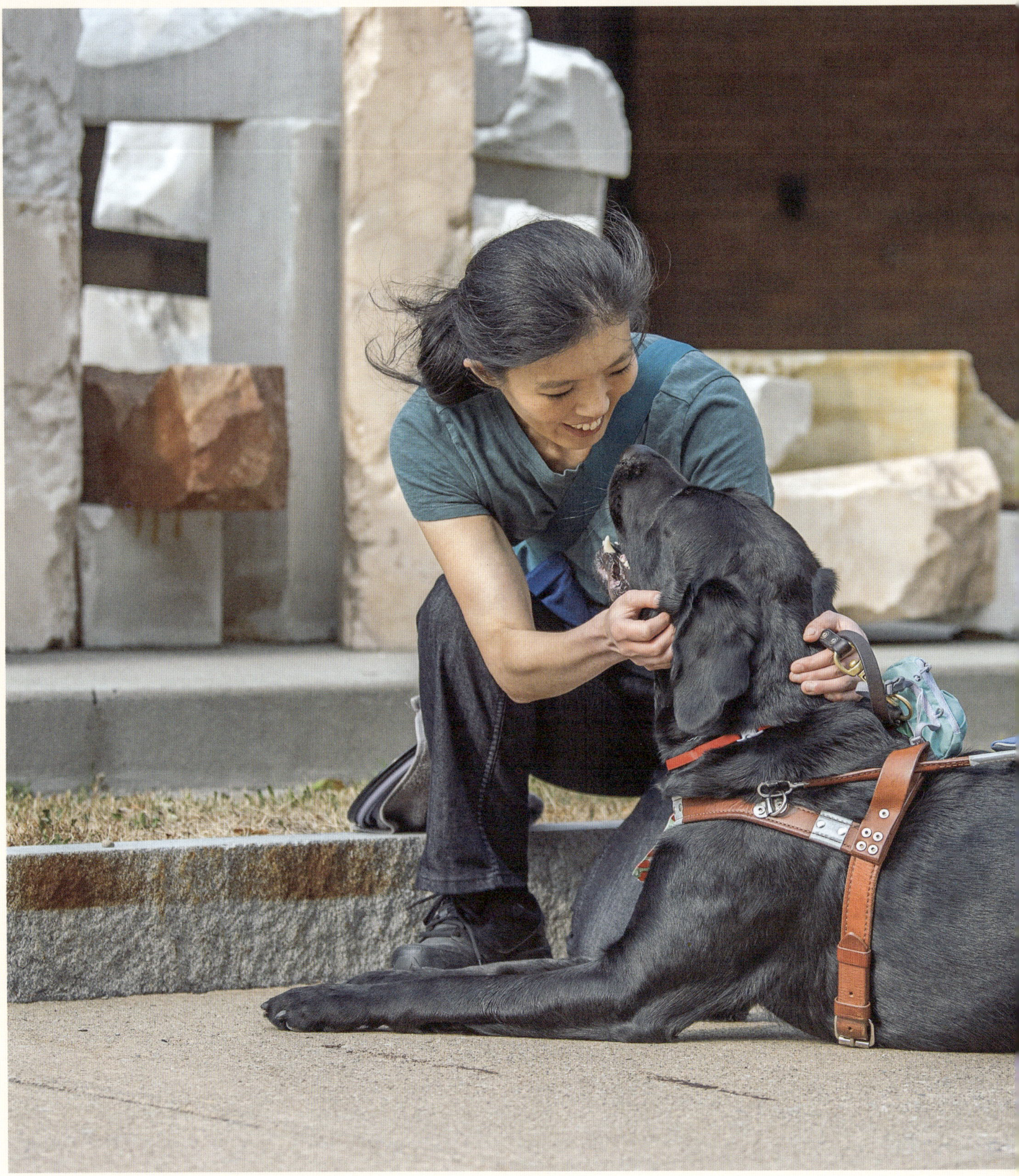

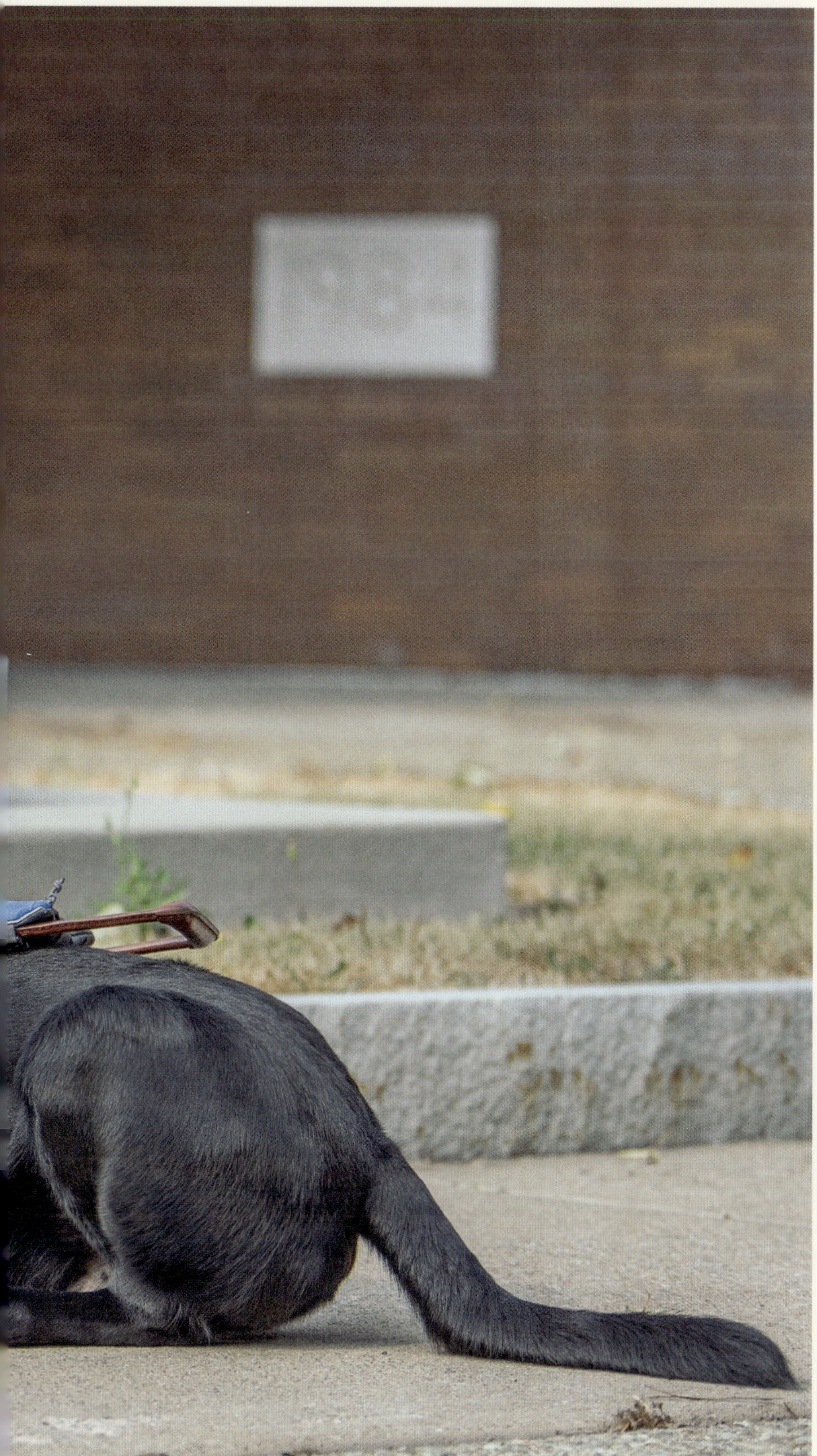

LEFT Yoojin had doubts before meeting Dennison. She wondered if they would click and worried that he might not like her. Looking back now, she finds those concerns silly, as would anyone else who encounters these two together. Their bond is so deep and special.

Yoojin struggles to put into words the profound impact that Dennison has had on her life, perhaps because no words can do it justice.

BELOW Once Yoojin got Dennison, she explored more of her hometown than she ever had before. Going out became exciting, and he even inspired her to take a trip to the Grand Canyon to hike the Bright Angel Trail. She struggles to put into words the profound impact that Dennison has had on her life, perhaps because no words can do it justice.

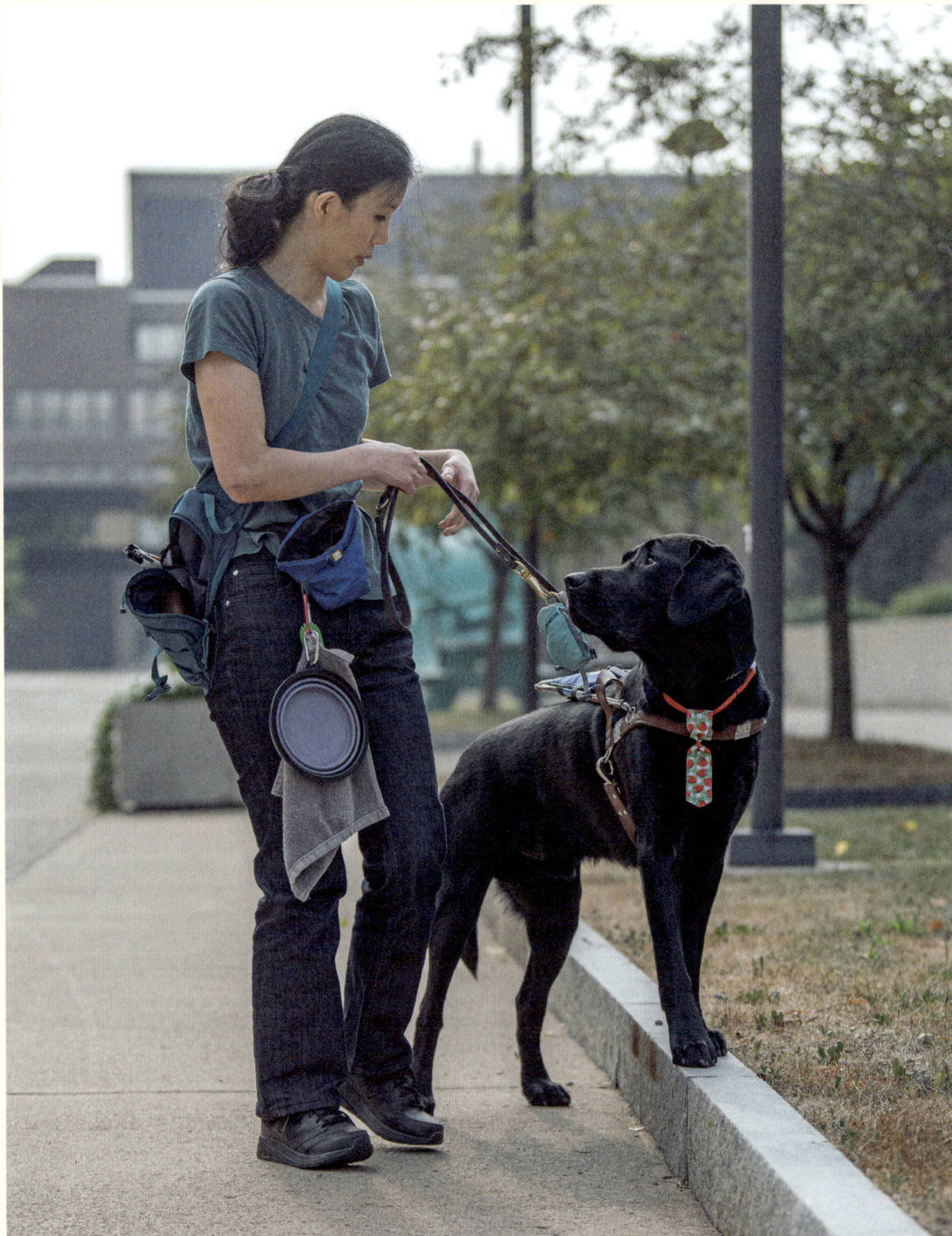

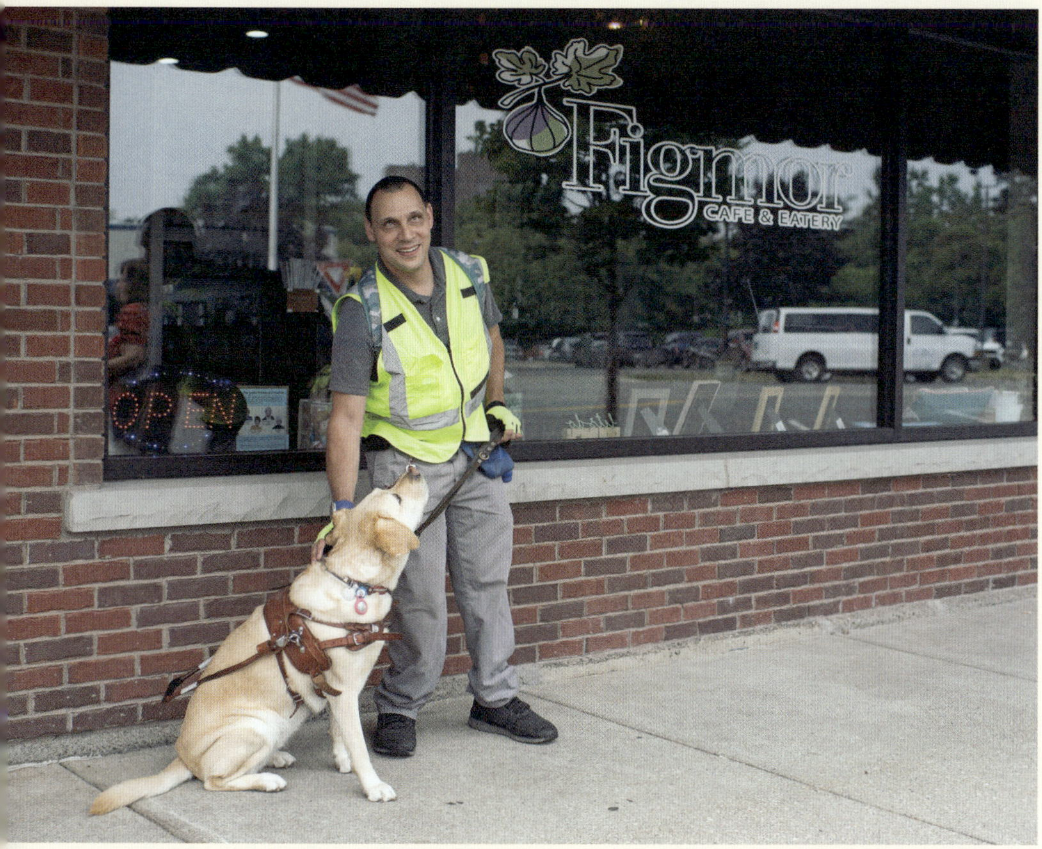

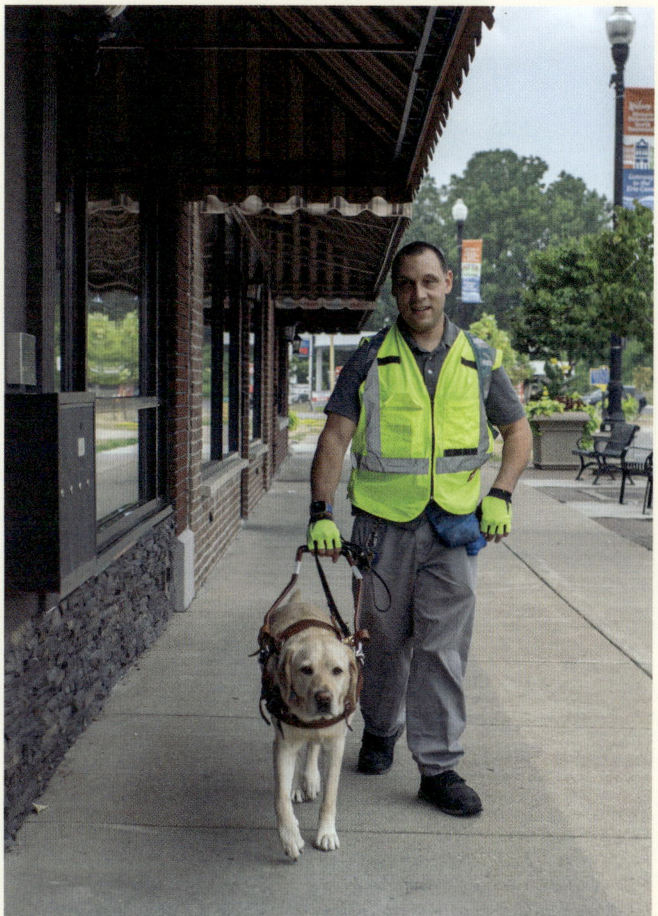

ABOVE Anthony and I met at Figmor Cafe, which has special significance for him as it was the first destination that he walked to alone with Lindsey, his guide dog. The staff loves it when the pair stops by for a meal.

RIGHT Anthony also struggled to articulate the feeling of freedom he has experienced since he was paired with Lindsey. He settled on telling me it's the best feeling in the world. He has used both a cane and a guide dog and remarked that a cane is an obstacle finder, while a dog is an obstacle avoider.

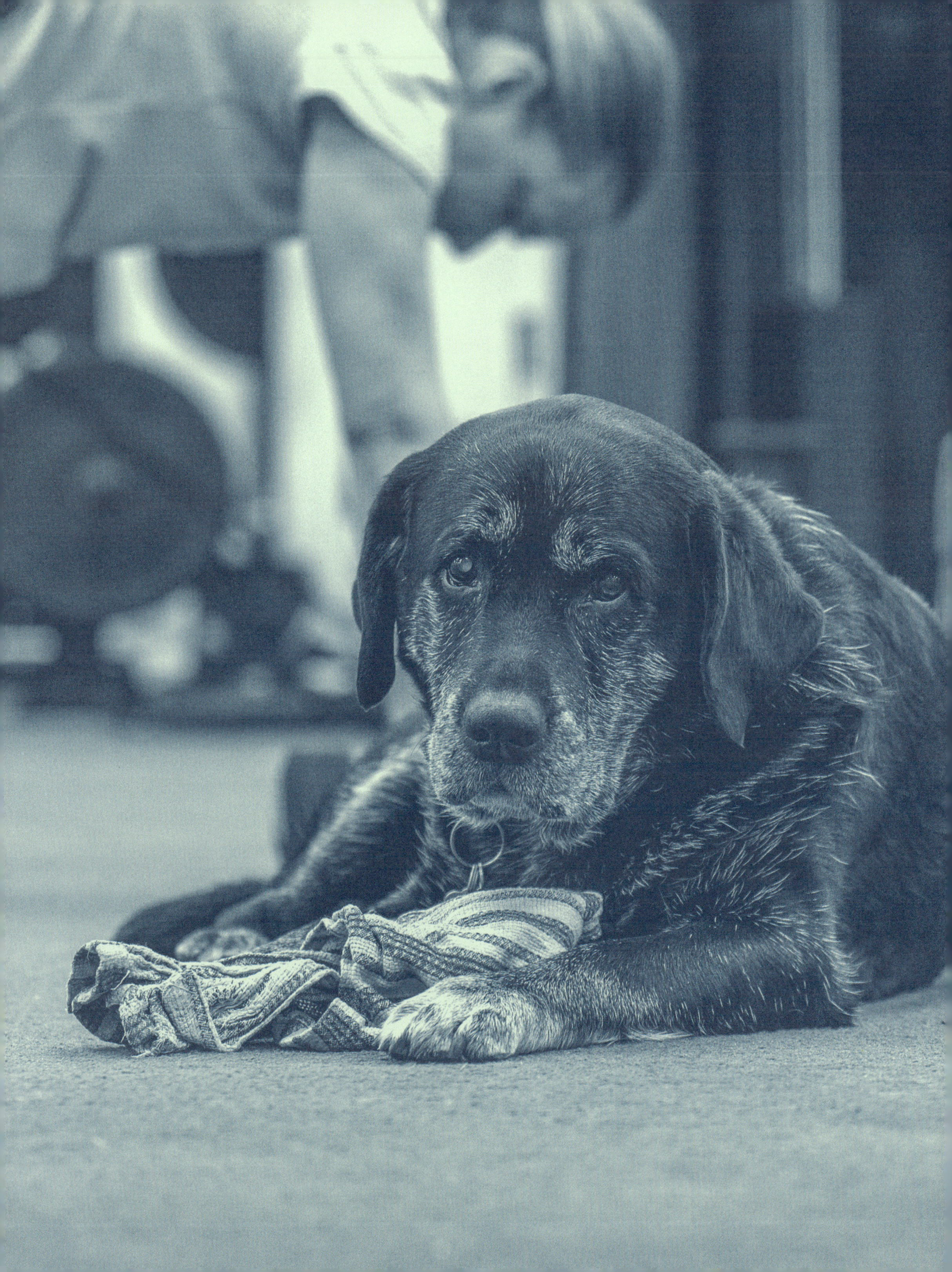

LOCATION	BREED	TASKS	SKILLS
Buffalo, USA	Labrador	Emotional Support, Companionship, Comic Relief	Stress Reduction, Motivation, Morale Boosting

PHYSICAL THERAPY DOGS

EARLY MORNING WORKOUTS are tough, especially in the winter. The bed is cozy, it's dark and cold outside, and it would be a lot easier to hit the snooze button and go back to sleep.

But the gym becomes a lot more appealing when you know there's a dog waiting there to greet you. Amanda Bevilacqua owns Prescribed Motion – a physical therapy and fitness studio – and her dog Roma loves to attend classes. Even if she's not physically helping gym-goers lift weights, it's well-known that dogs have a calming effect on humans, lowering stress hormones and reducing blood pressure. In Roma's case, she does this for them while they pump iron.

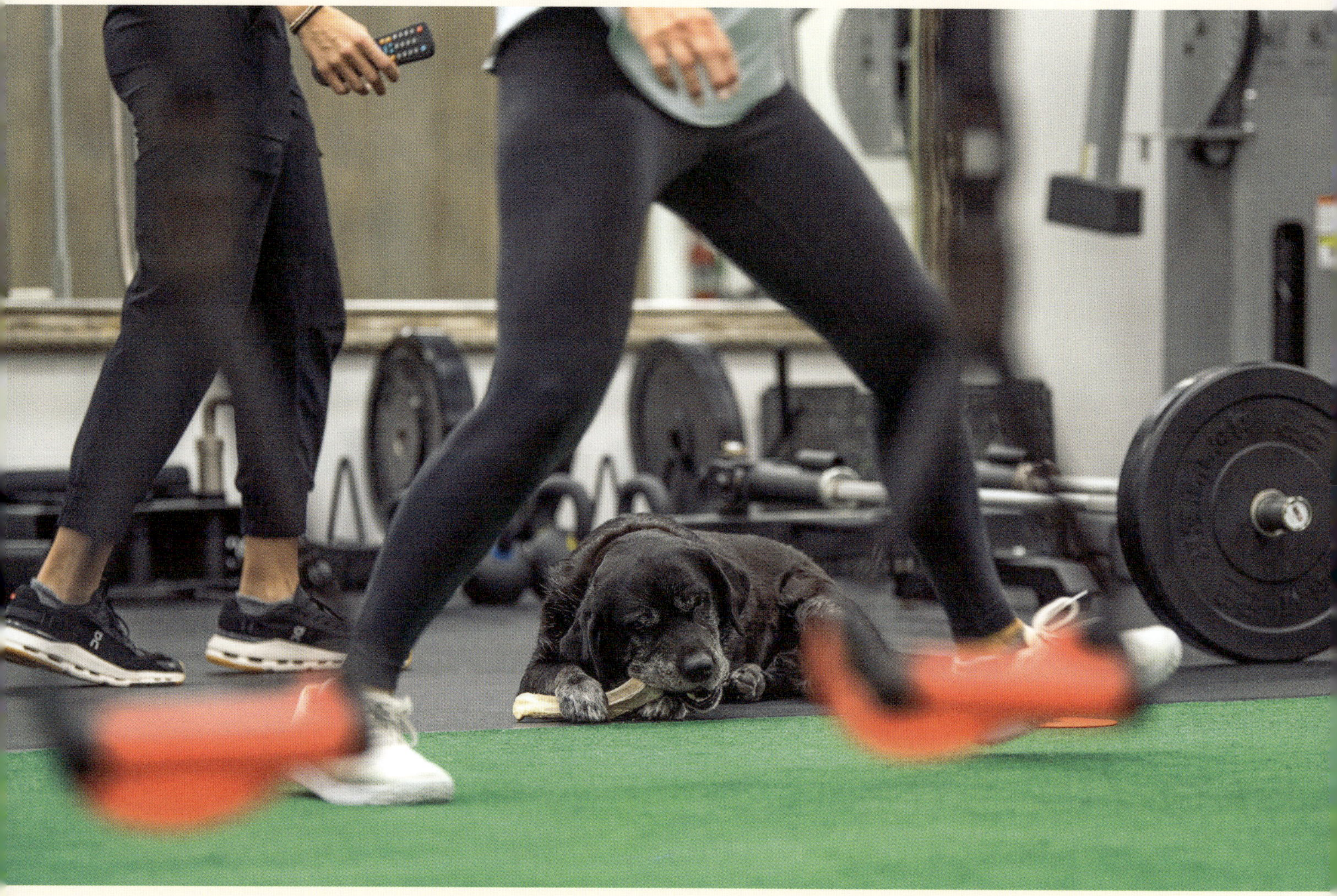

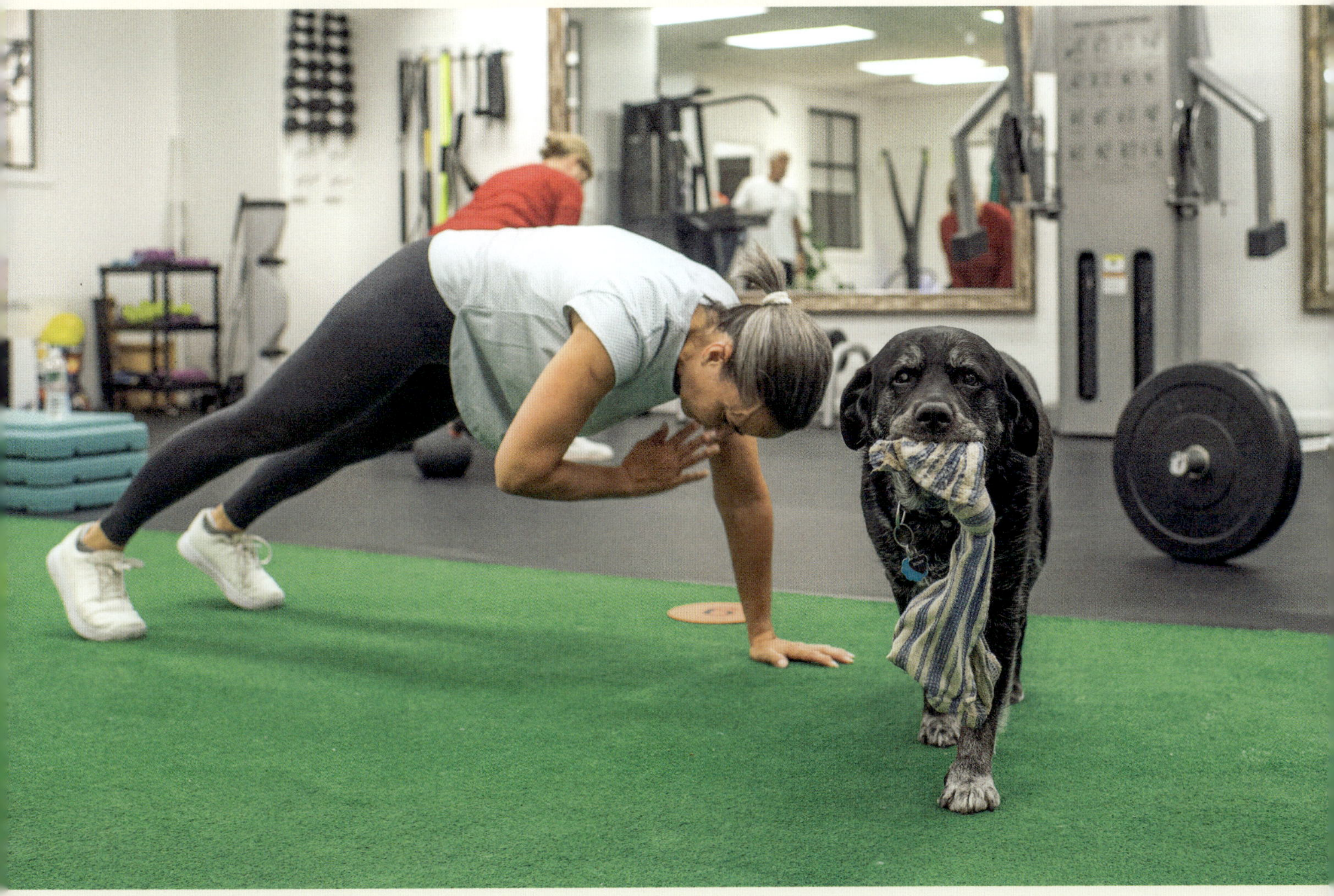

LEFT Roma likes to greet everyone when they arrive at the studio, but then it's right to work for her. She doesn't show up and relax. This is an exercise studio, not a spa.

ABOVE Roma has a big basket of toys and she likes to alternate through her equipment. Whenever she chooses something new, it is customary for her to parade it around the studio and show everyone.

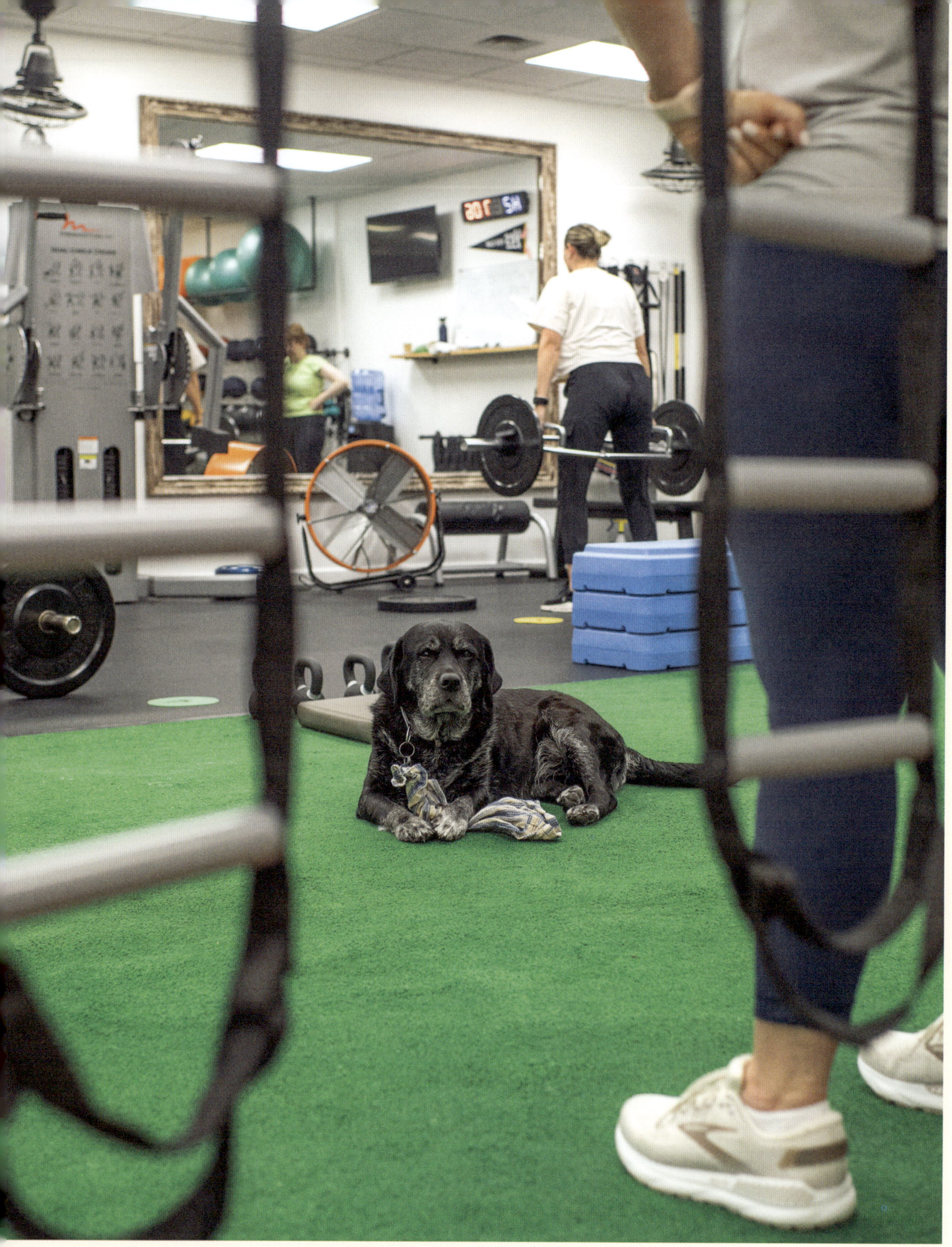

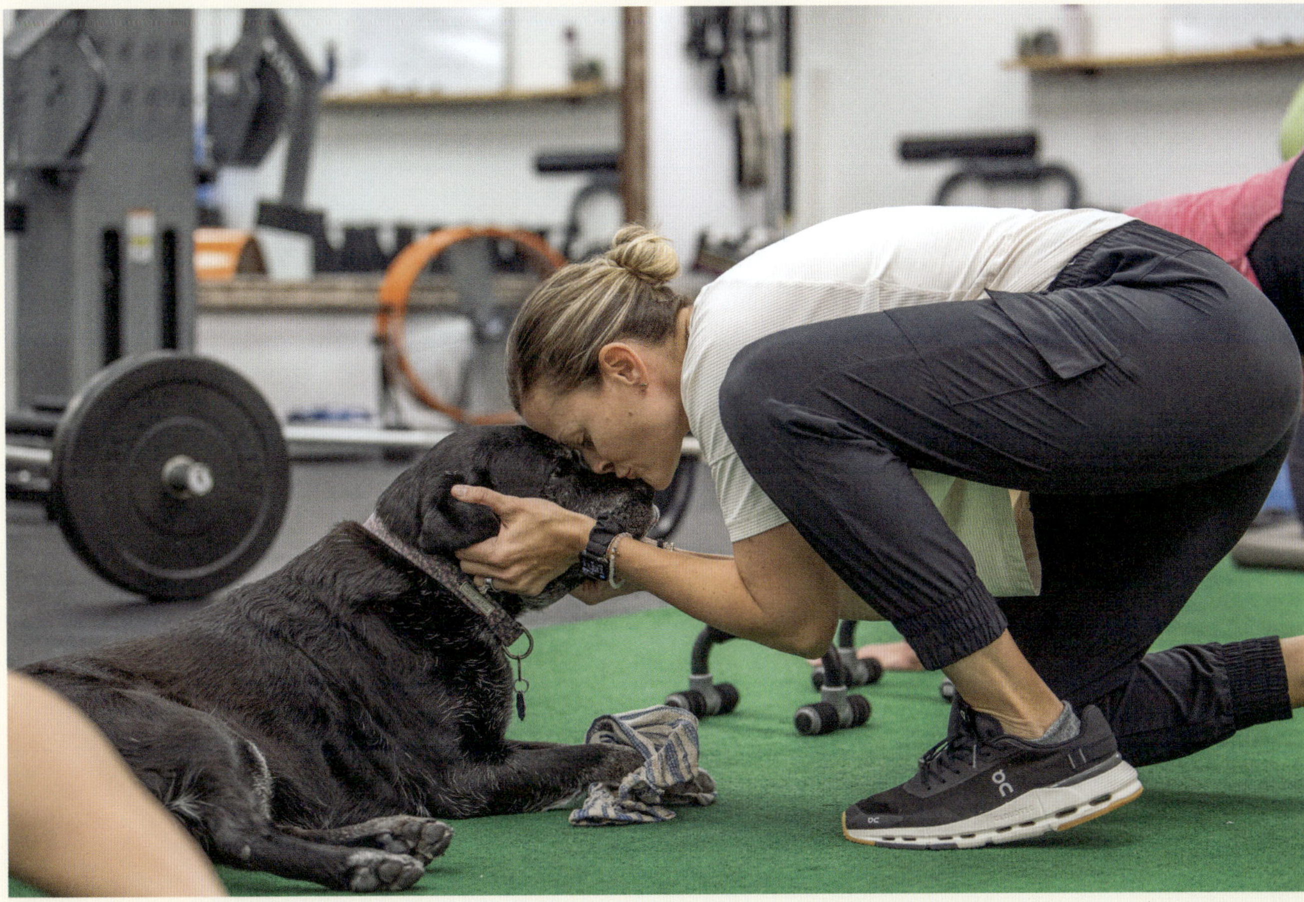

LEFT & NEXT PAGE The real benefit of having a dog around is the distraction. As the workout goes on, when the breath is short and muscles are aching, it's nice to lock eyes with a friendly dog whose mere presence provides gentle encouragement.

ABOVE Amanda is incredible at her job. She brings the energy during early morning workouts and leads her classes with kindness. She and her sweet dog Roma are a perfect match.

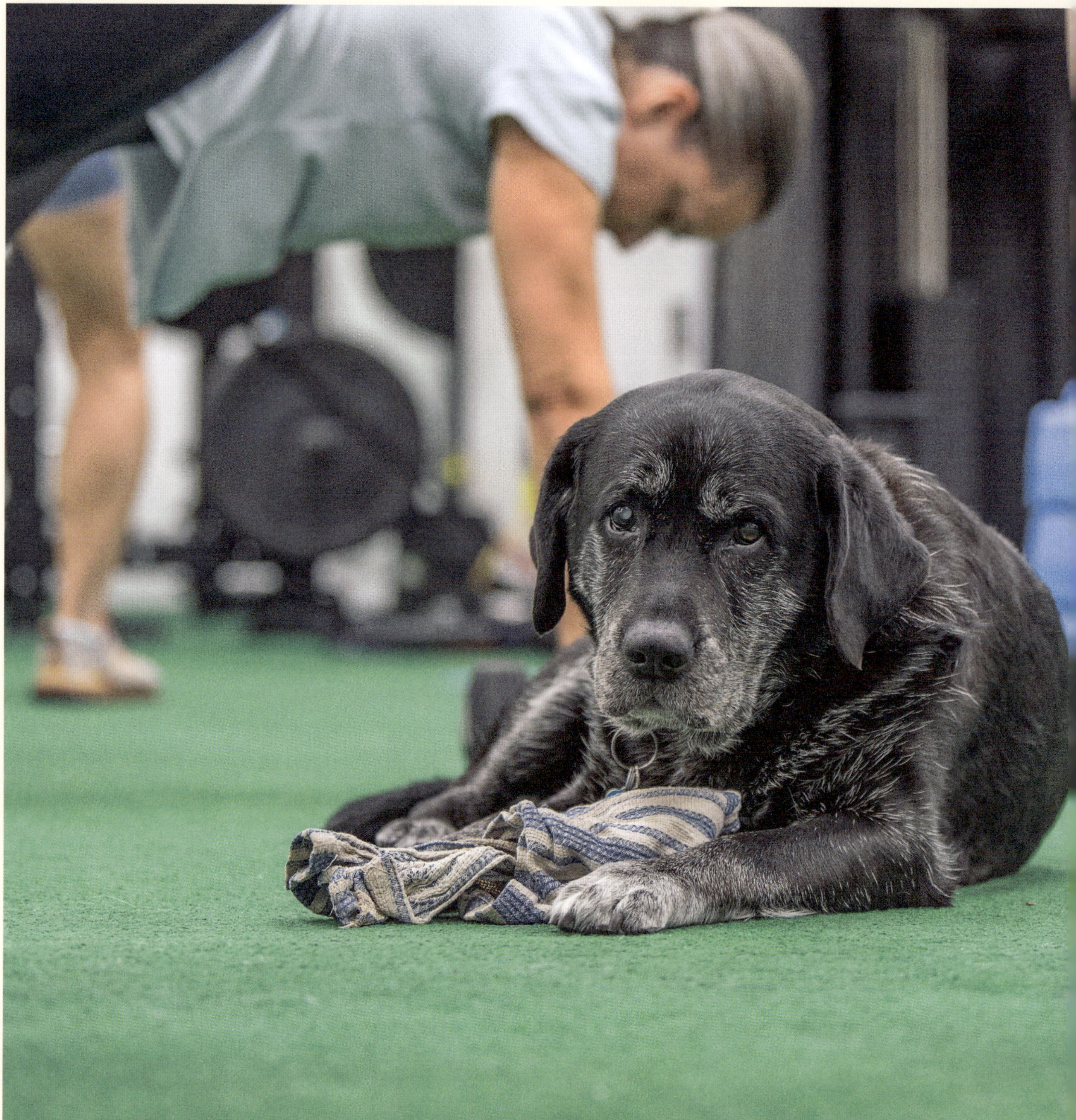

The real benefit of having a dog around is the distraction. As the workout goes on, when the breath is short and muscles are aching, it's nice to lock eyes with a friendly dog whose mere presence provides gentle encouragement.

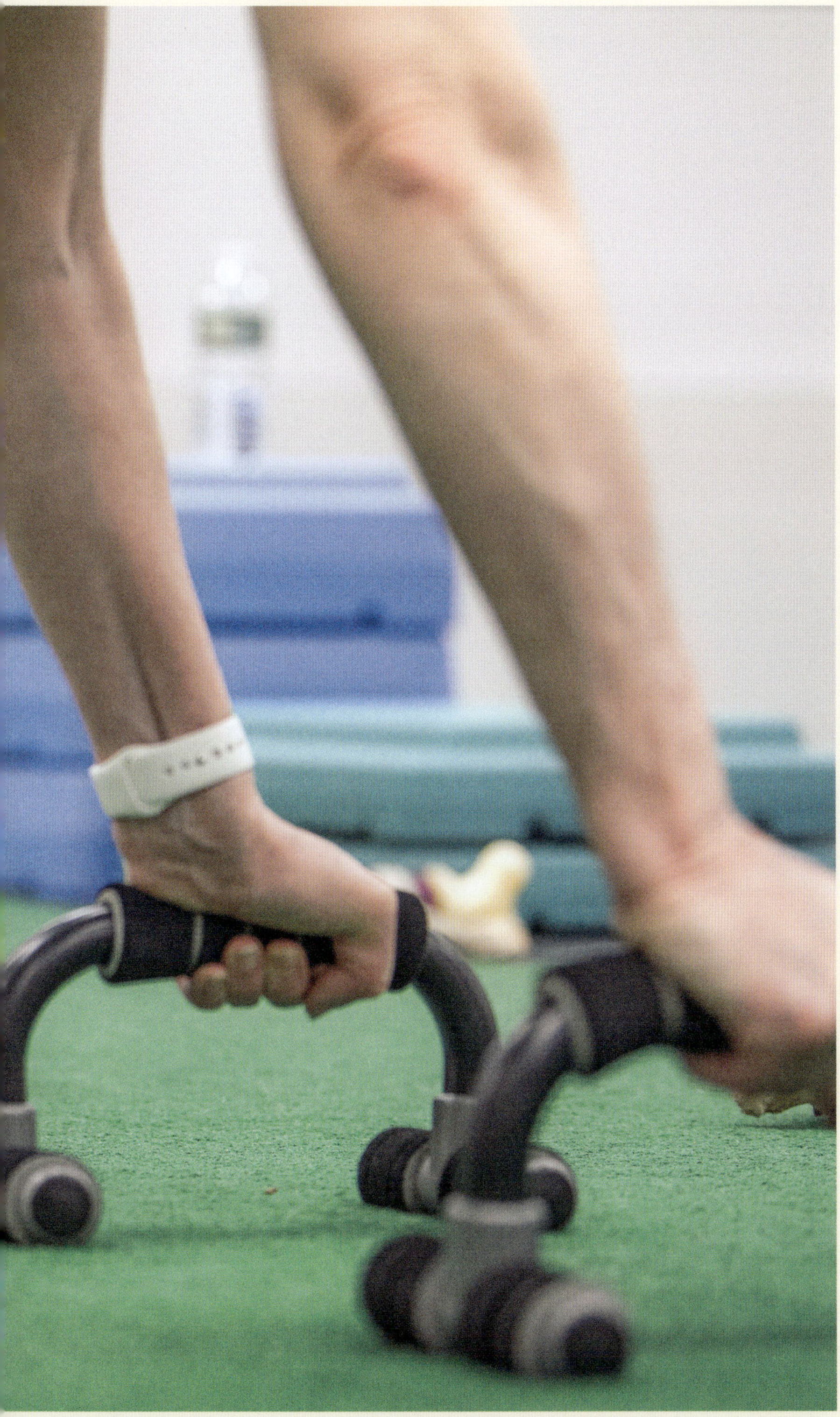

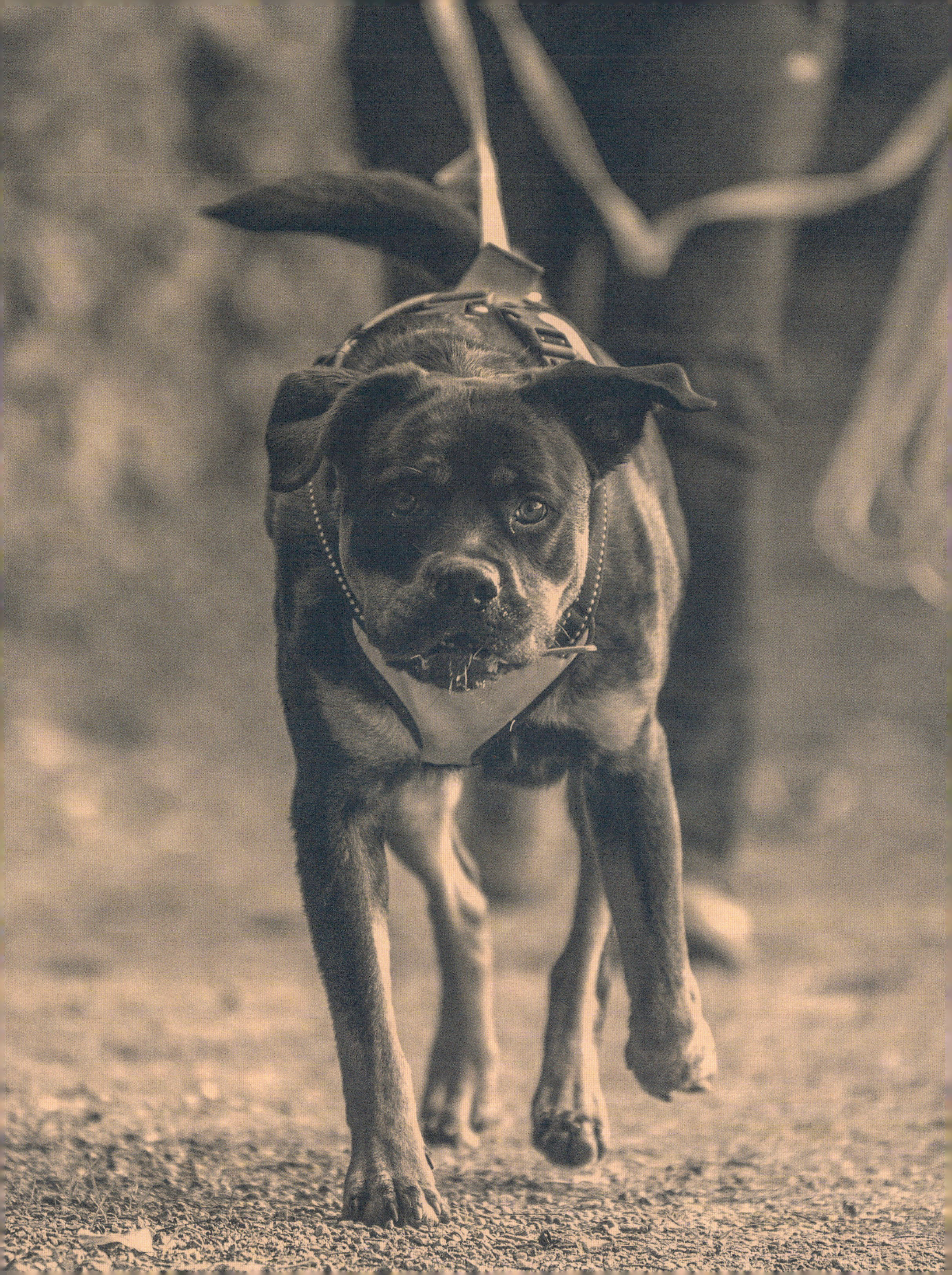

LOCATION	BREED	TASKS	SKILLS
County Cork, Ireland	Rottweiler	Searching, Detecting Scents, Alerting Handler	Sense of Smell, Evaluation, Navigation

SEARCH & RESCUE DOGS

A DOG'S MOST POWERFUL tool is its nose. While many primarily use that tool to sniff around for fallen food, some are trained to use their noses to save lives. While photographing dogs in Ireland, I had the opportunity to see what goes into training a dog for mantrailing: a search-and-rescue technique in which a dog takes the particular scent of a human and follows its trail. Sometimes dogs can pick up the scent of a person days after they were in an area.

Two Rottweilers, Doris and Daphne, were part of the training session while I was there. At the time, they were the only two Rottweilers in Ireland training as Search and Rescue Dogs. Rottweilers have a long history of working and these two proved that, when given the opportunity, the breed can excel at a job typically reserved for other dog breeds.

Rottweilers have a long history of working and these two proved that, when given the opportunity, the breed can excel at a job typically reserved for other dog breeds.

RIGHT Considered one of the oldest herding dogs, Rottweilers date back to Roman times in what is now Germany. From the Middles Ages onward, they were known as "the Butcher's Dog," as butchers would employ them to pull meat carts to the market. The dogs' owners were known to tie their moneybags to the dogs' necks – a sound security system.

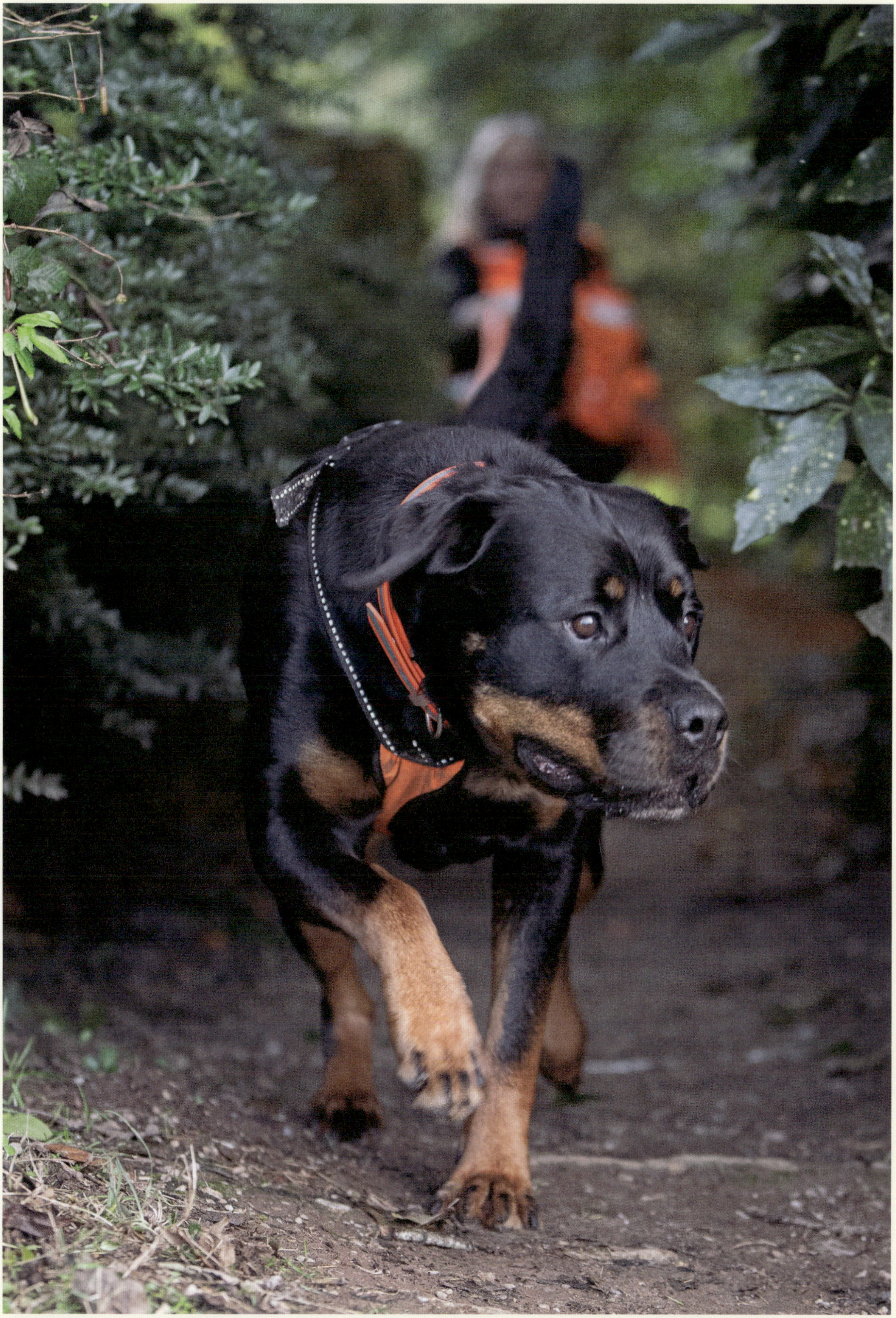

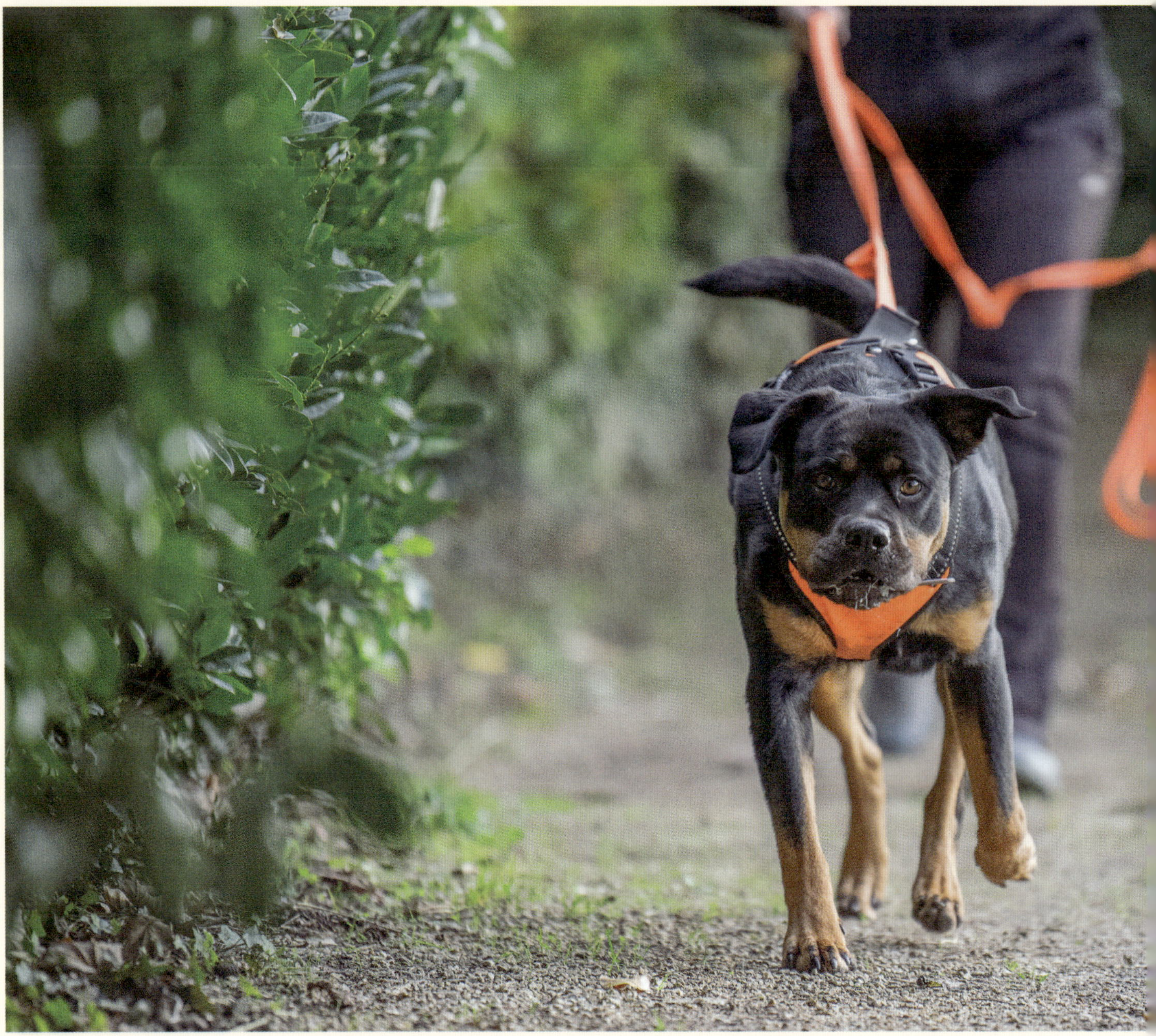

ABOVE During their mantrailing training, a trainer would hide and Doris and Daphne would take turns following the scent they were given. While I photographed the dogs, they would sniff me and then quickly keep moving as they recognized I was not the person they were searching for. When they find their target, the dogs are taught to sit down and wait for their owner to meet them.

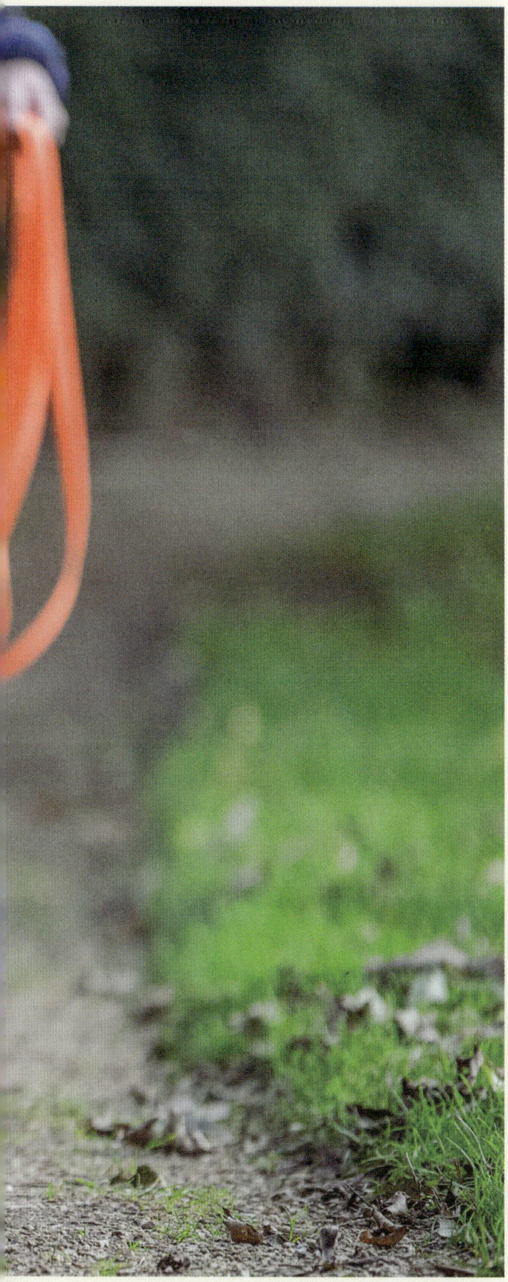

BELOW Every training session ends on a high note. Doris did an excellent job finding the hidden person, so she was rewarded with her beloved ball.

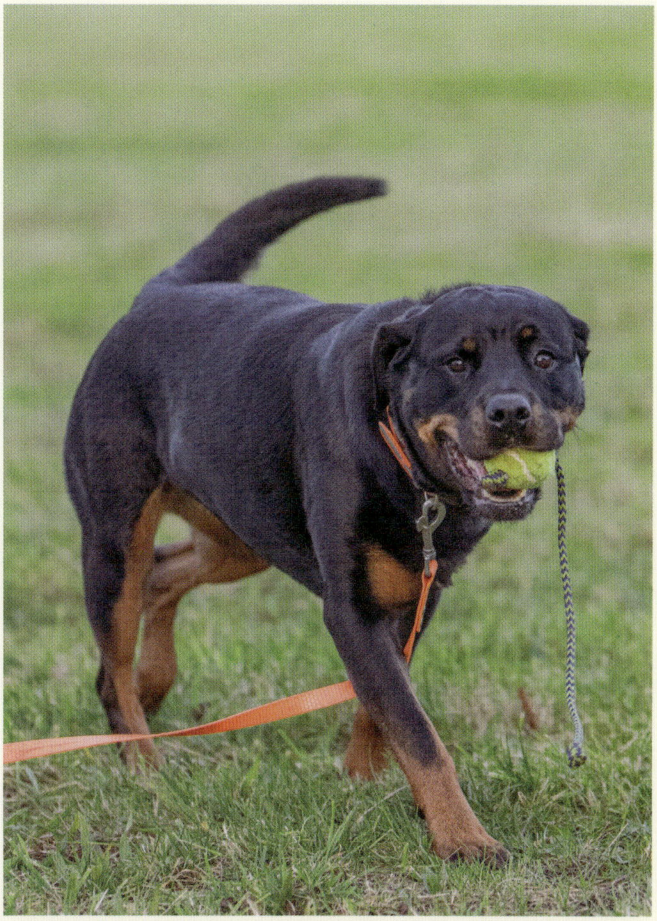

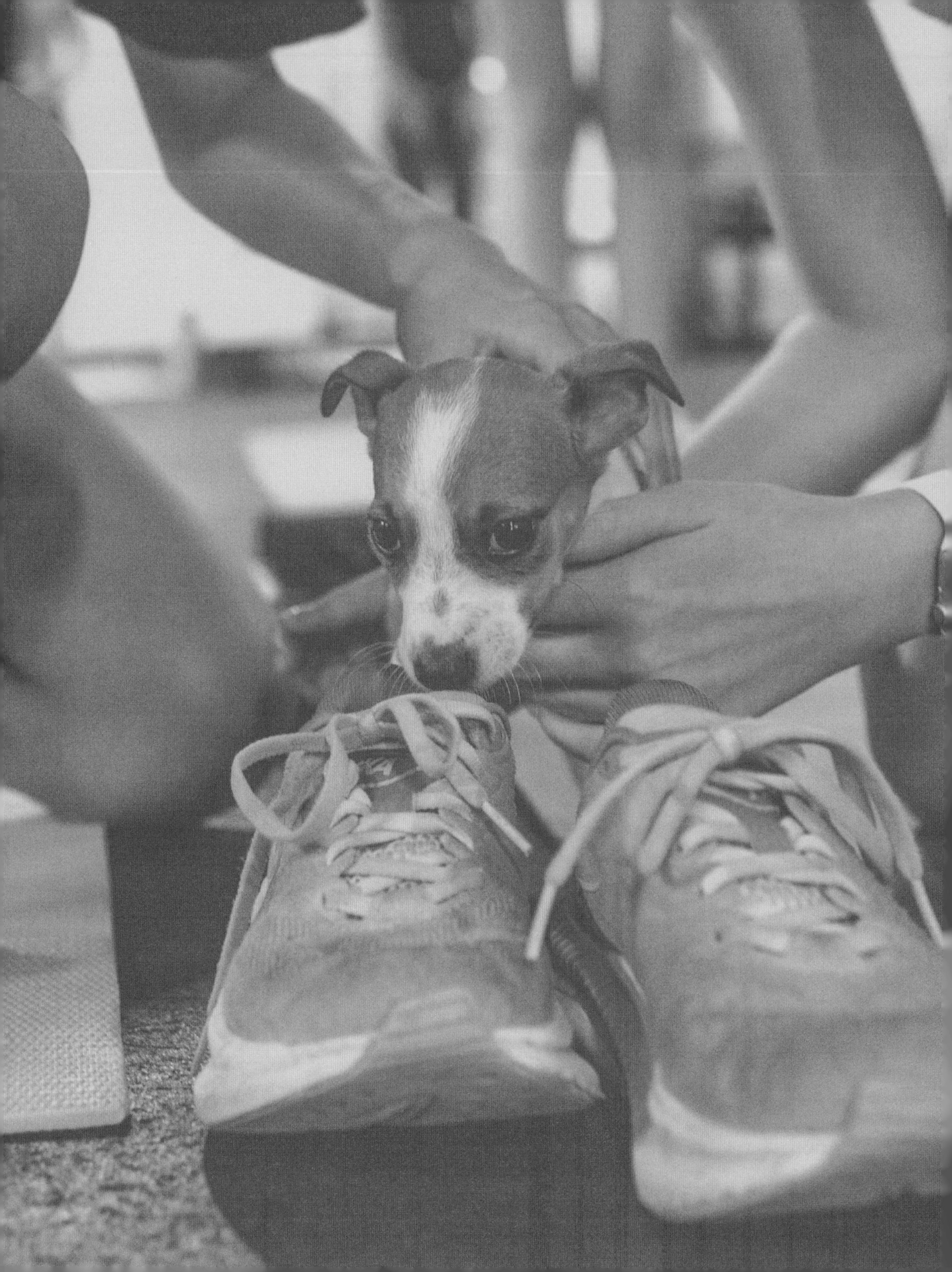

LOCATION	BREED	TASKS	SKILLS
Buffalo, USA	Shar Pei Mix	Socializing, Climbing on People, Being Held	Cuteness, Zoomies, Puppy Breath

YOGA PUPPIES

PUPPY YOGA HAS DEVELOPED a bad reputation, and in a lot of cases it's for good reason. Breeders will put profits over pups and are willing to loan out litters for multiple yoga classes in a single day. Overstimulation and exhaustion as a puppy can have long-term effects on a dog's behavior.

But when puppy yoga is done right, it can be a source of good. That was my experience photographing a yoga session hosted by 716 Paws, a rescue organization located in Buffalo, New York. They brought a recently rescued litter of puppies to assist with the class and raise money for their rescue efforts. They also use classes to help place the rescues in new homes.

The puppies did their best to help with pose techniques, but they didn't know much past upward and downward facing dog.

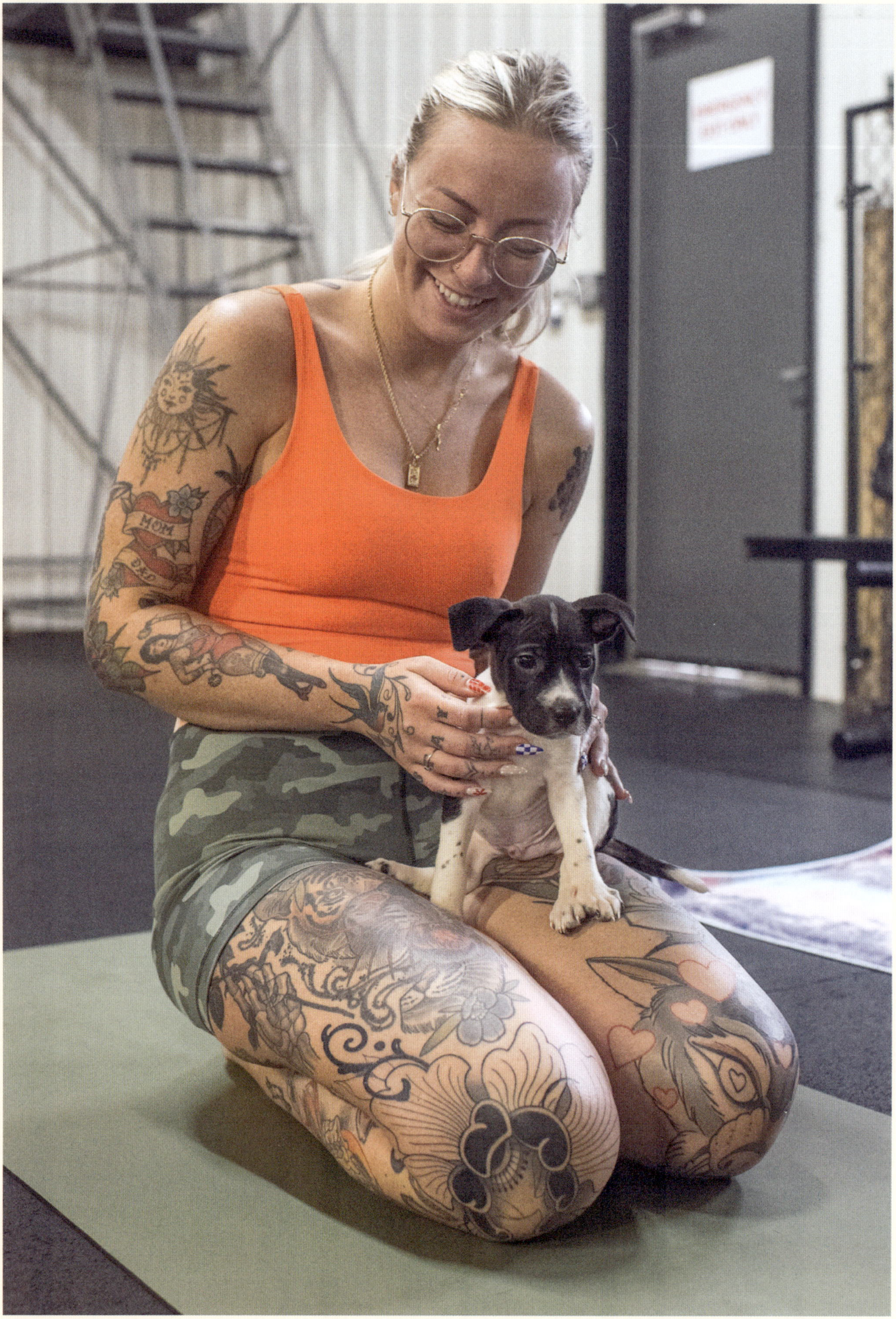
MOM
DAD

LEFT The class was hosted at Barkology, a combination indoor dog park and bar. It was led by a certified yoga instructor who did an excellent job creating a calm, controlled atmosphere. 716 Paws also had a half a dozen volunteers on hand looking after the puppies ... and cleaning up any messes they left behind.

BELOW Yoga was a part of the morning event, but the real draw was the puppies. The room was filled with dog lovers who wanted to spend time with the rescues.

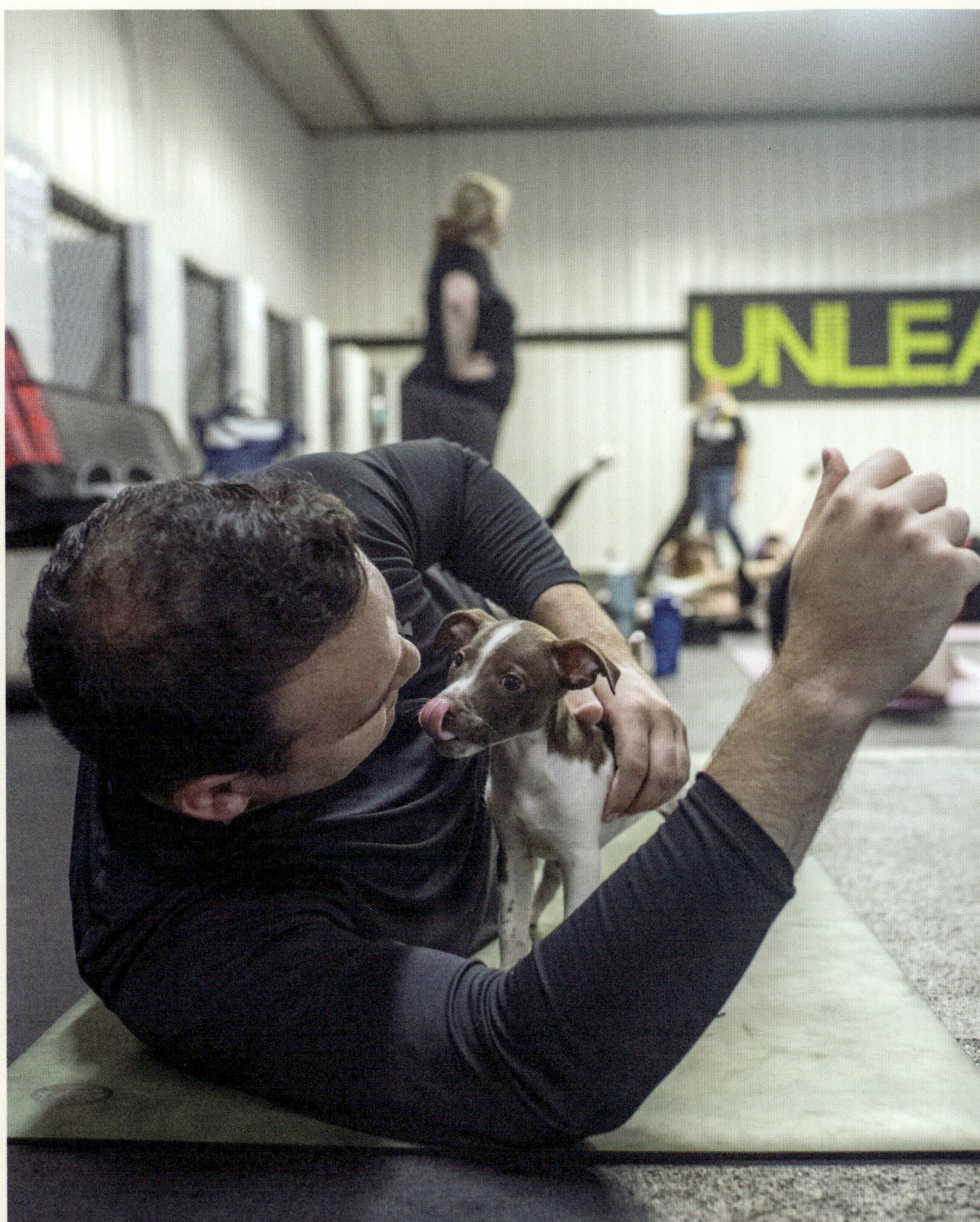

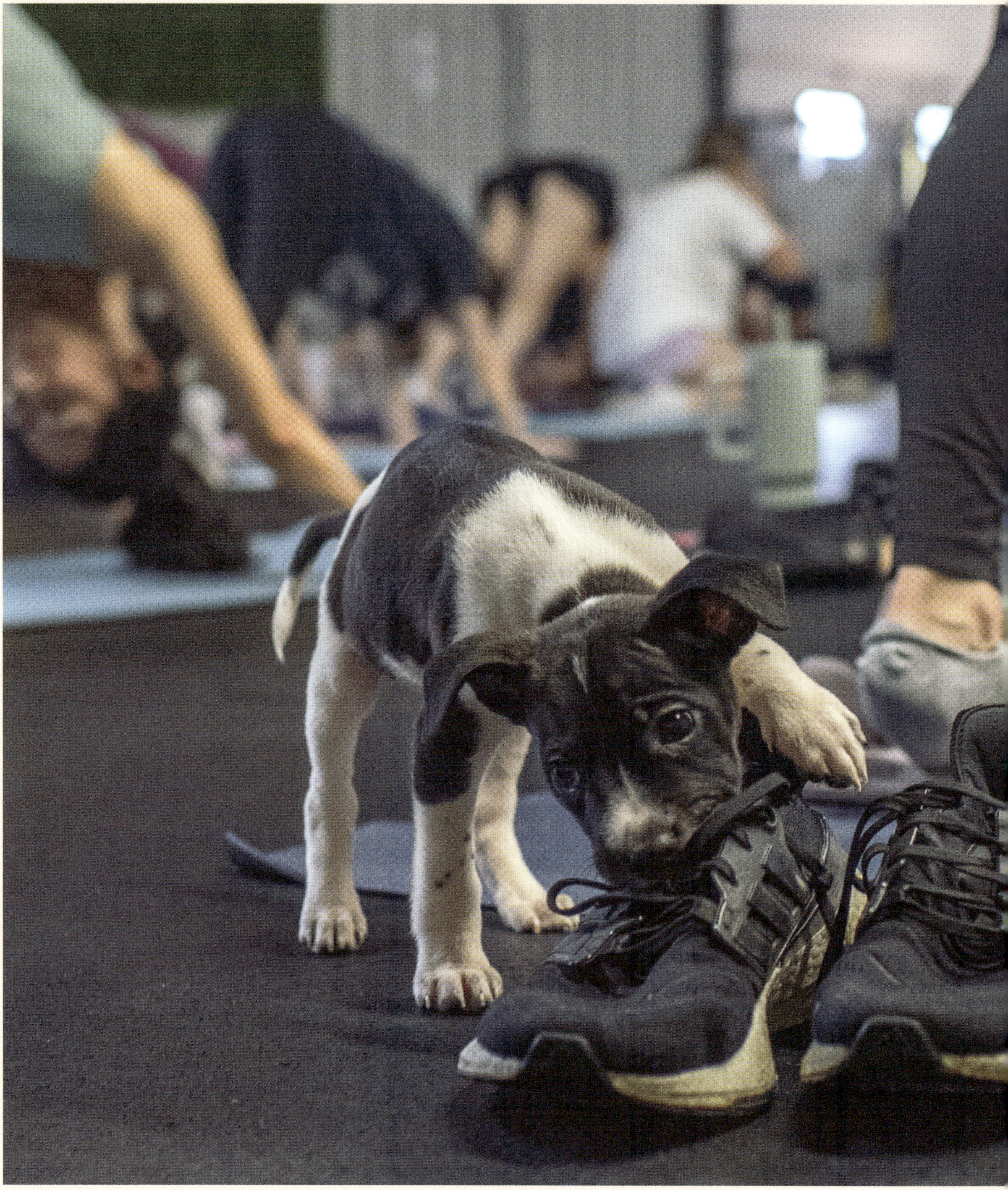

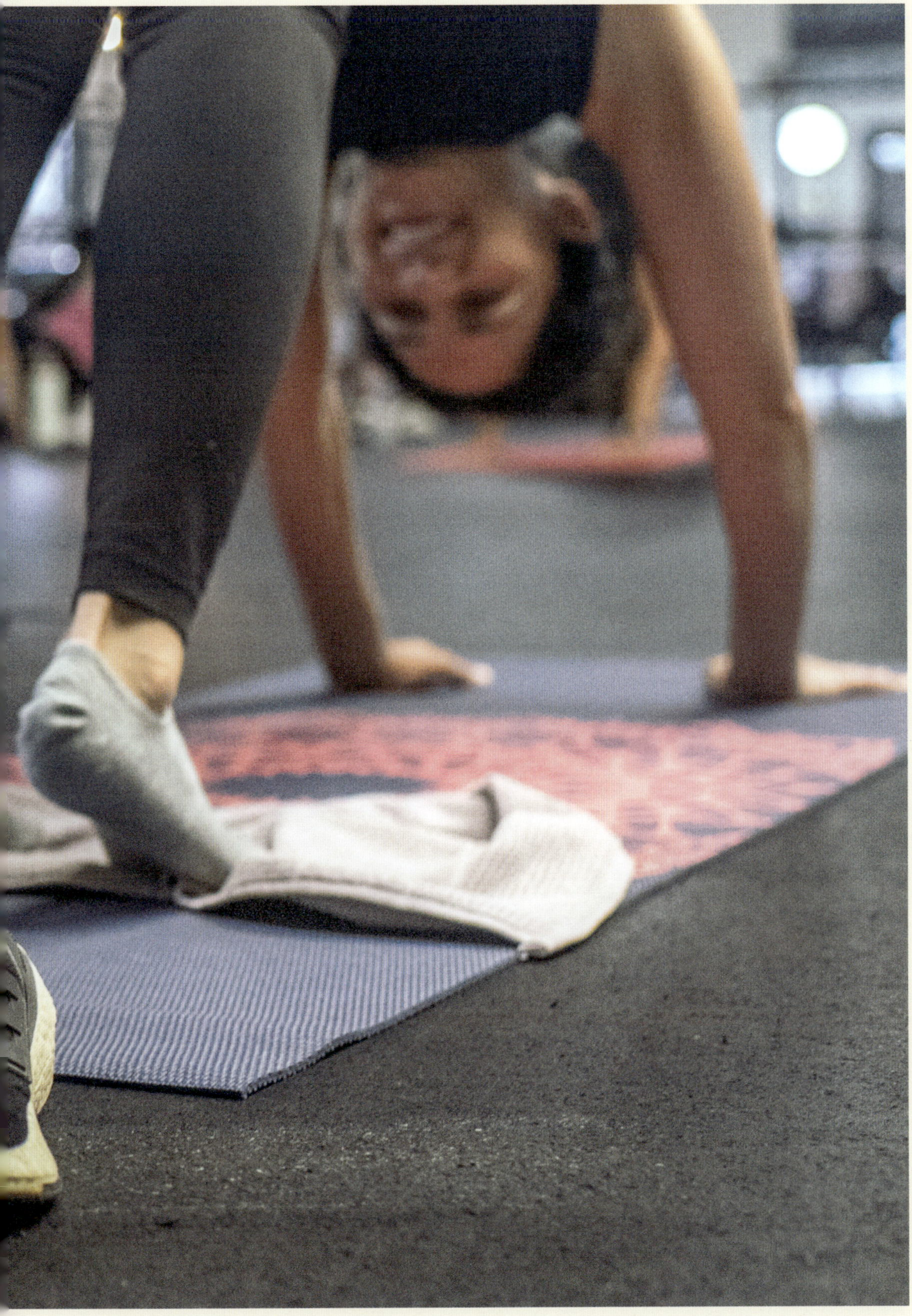

ABOVE Many of the participants' shoes were seen as toys, and the puppies enjoyed the sweet taste of shoelaces.

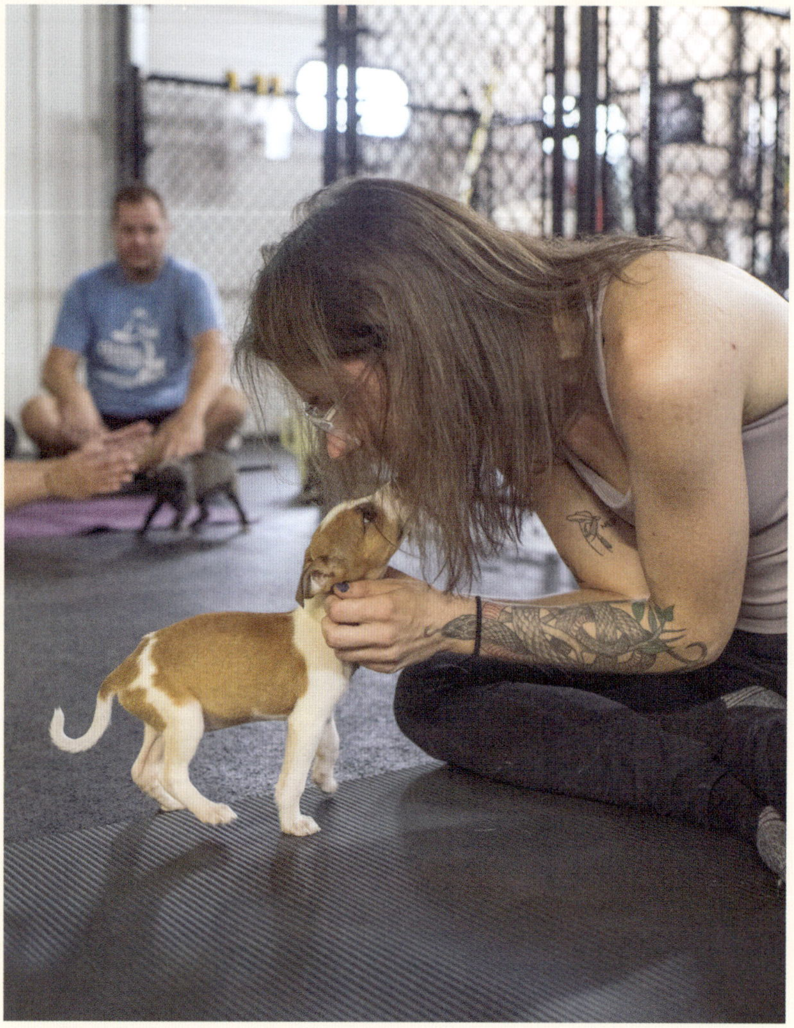

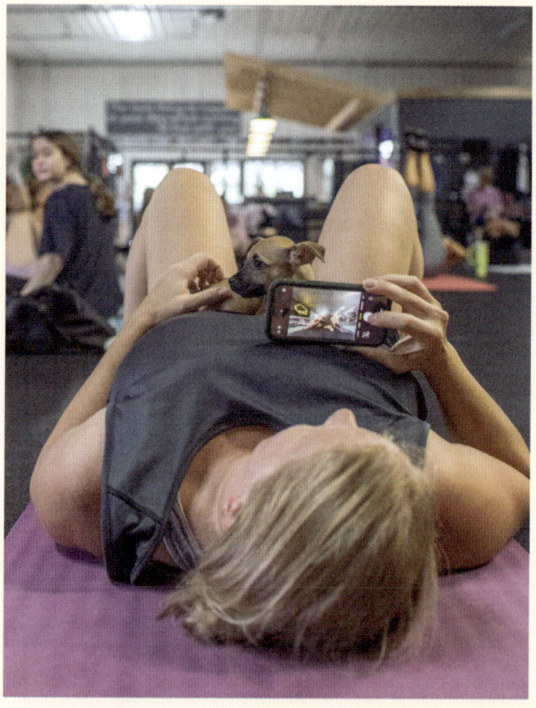

ABOVE & OPPOSITE For a litter that experienced a rough beginning in life, the wonderful volunteers at 716 Paws stepped up to show them love. This appreciation extended through the guests at the yoga class. Dog rescue organizations are always in need of resources, and with the money raised from these types of events, they are able to fund the rescue of future litters in need.

RIGHT I wasn't the only one taking photos. Most of the class participants kept their phones handy to snap shots of the dogs.

For a litter that experienced a rough beginning in life, the wonderful volunteers at 716 Paws stepped up to show them love. This appreciation extended through the guests at the yoga class.

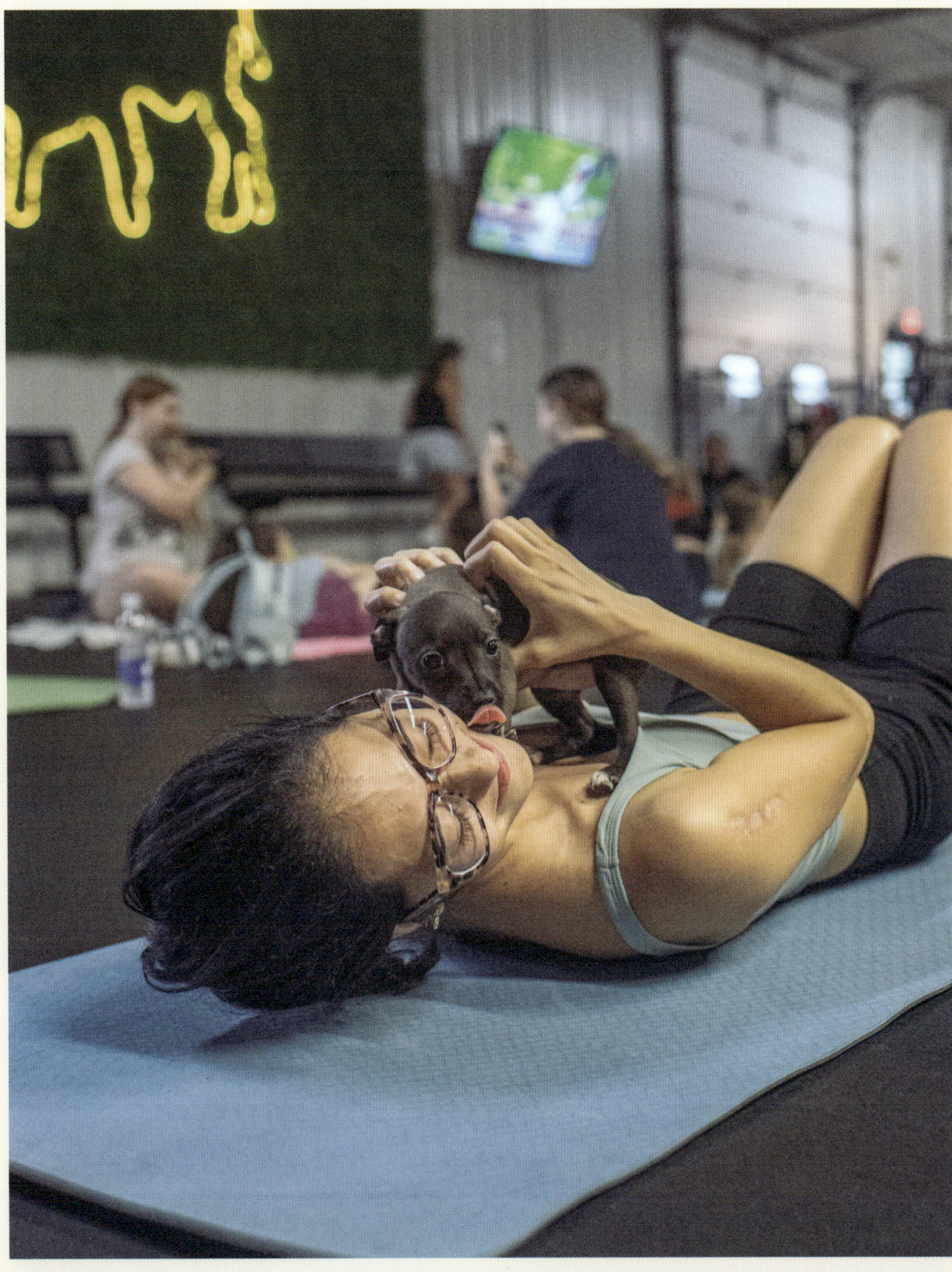

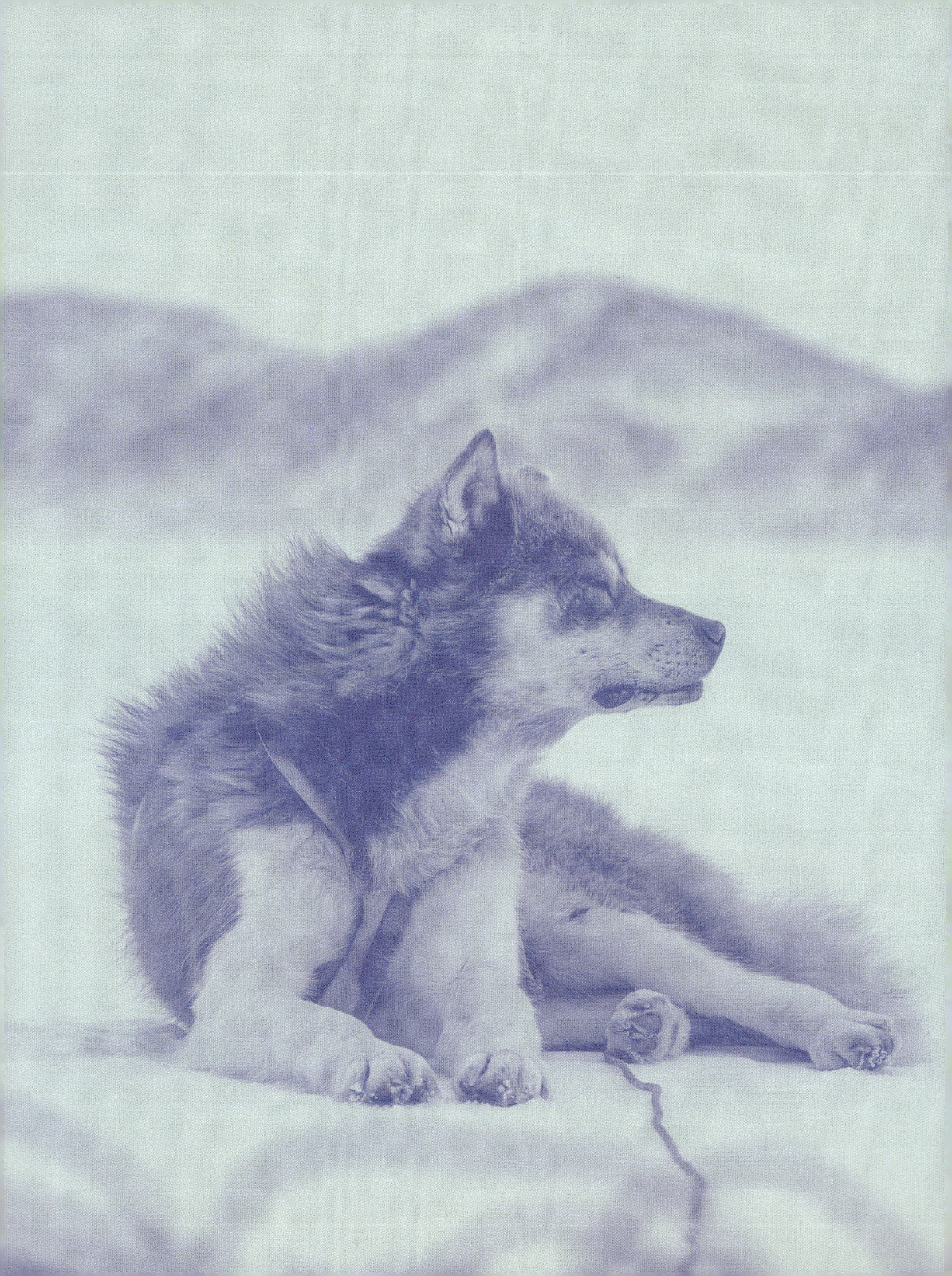

LOCATION	BREED	TASKS	SKILLS
Ilulissat, Siorapaluk, and Qaanaaq, Greenland	Greenland Dog	Pulling Sleds, Guarding, Providing Companionship	Strength, Endurance, Navigation

SLED DOGS

SLED DOGS IN GREENLAND are an inspiration. They do not have the easiest lives. Greenland Dogs are not pampered and they battle harsh conditions year-round, living in extraordinarily remote locations. Yet their work ethic is unmatched, and their companionship has been crucial to Inughuit culture for thousands of years in Northern Greenland, where the dogs pull sleds for hunters and those traveling between villages. I traveled as far north as possible in the country to visit Inughuit communities where these dogs are integral for survival.

Greenland Dogs are so important to Inughuit culture, and so specialized, that it is illegal to import any other dog breed north of the Arctic Circle. This law was implemented to preserve the purity of the breed. Greenland Dogs have thick double coats, padded fur-covered paws, and unique metabolisms that allow them to not just survive, but thrive, in such a frigid environment. Thanks to the massive role they play within Greenland Inughuit communities, they are deeply appreciated.

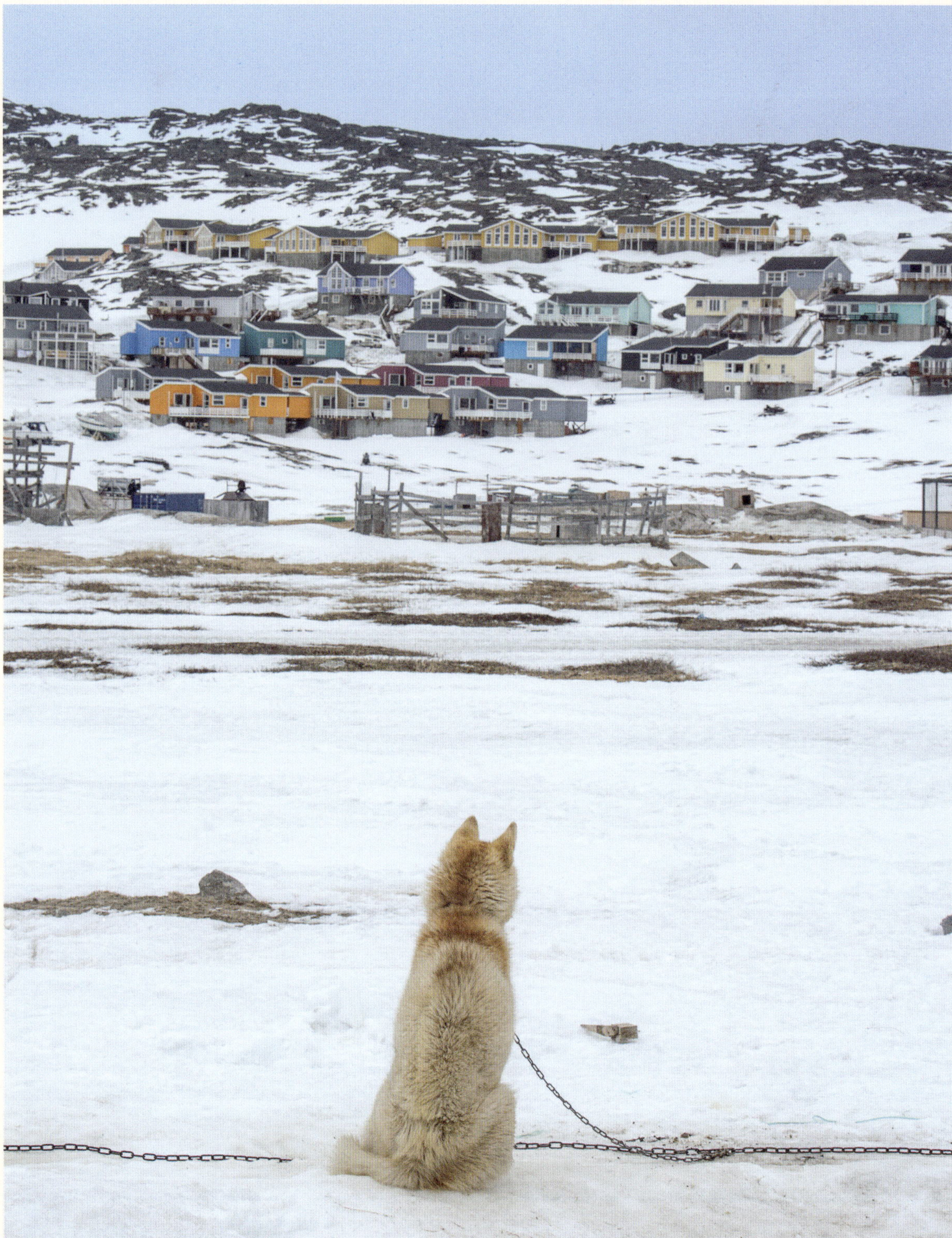

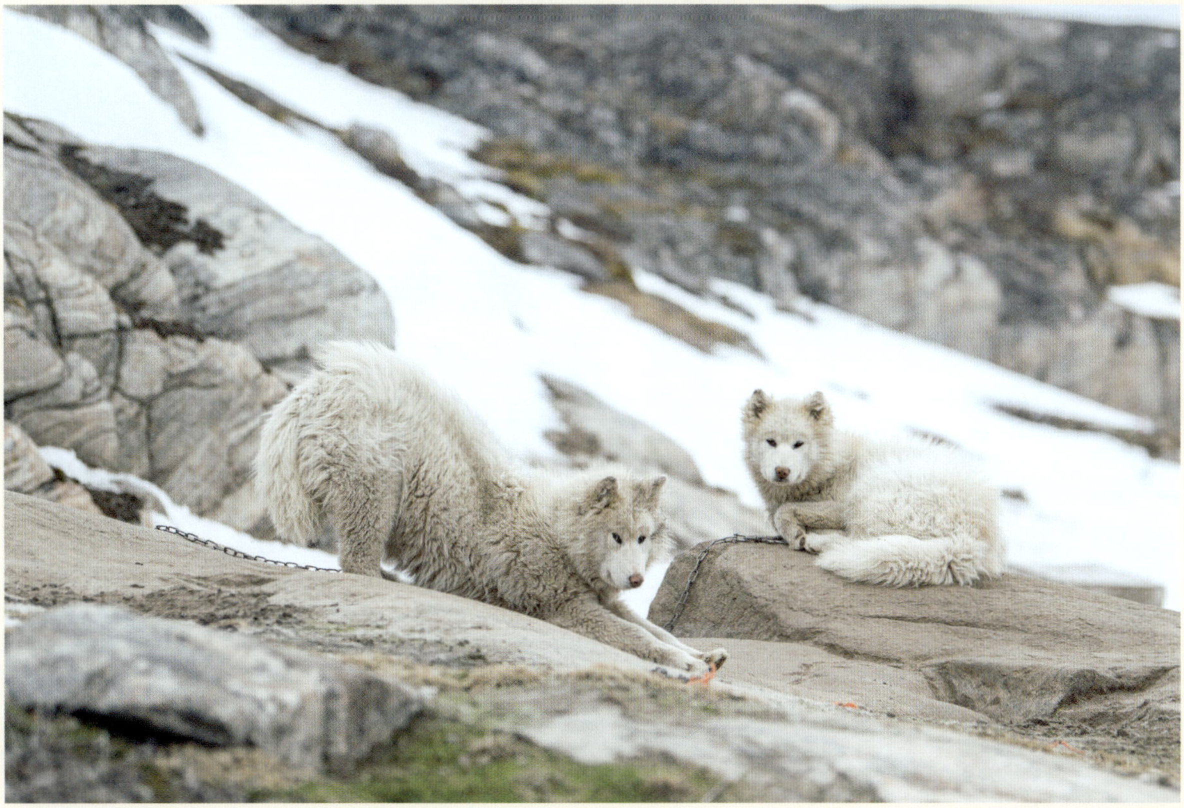

LEFT & ABOVE It didn't take long to see dogs upon my arrival, even in the larger city of Ilulissat. They are all around the city, living outside on properties. These dogs are used for tourist sled rides. I liked them, because I like all dogs, but these weren't the dogs I came to see.

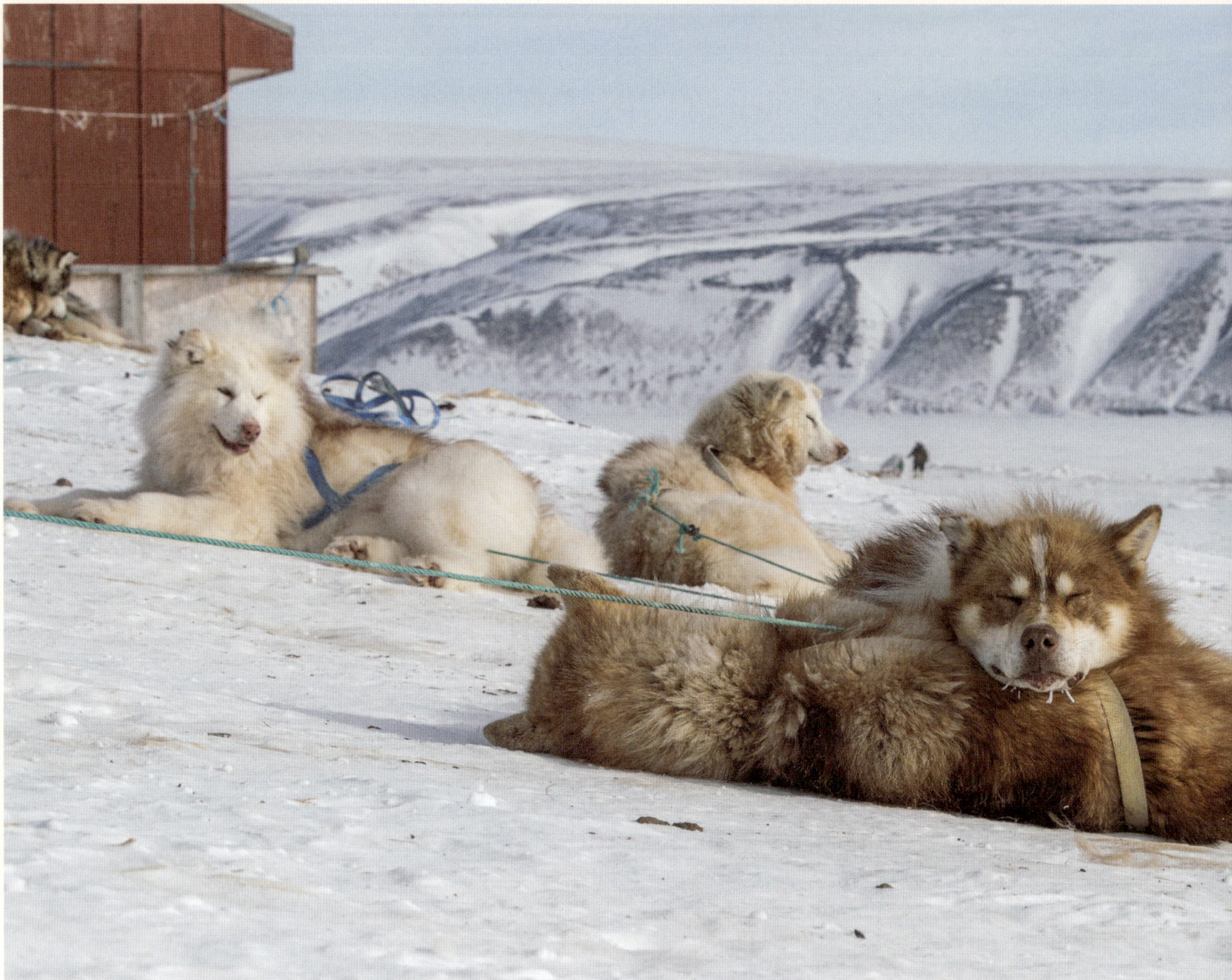

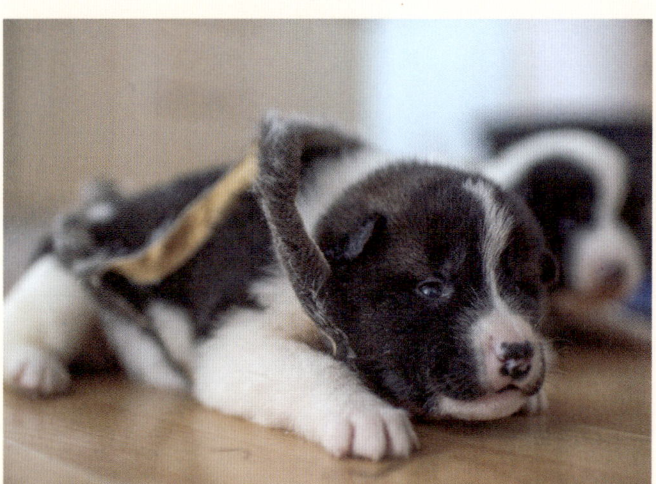

LEFT Sometimes puppies get the luxury of making a quick visit inside the home for a little warmth. These puppies were only weeks old, but they already looked the part of sled dogs with their little harnesses.

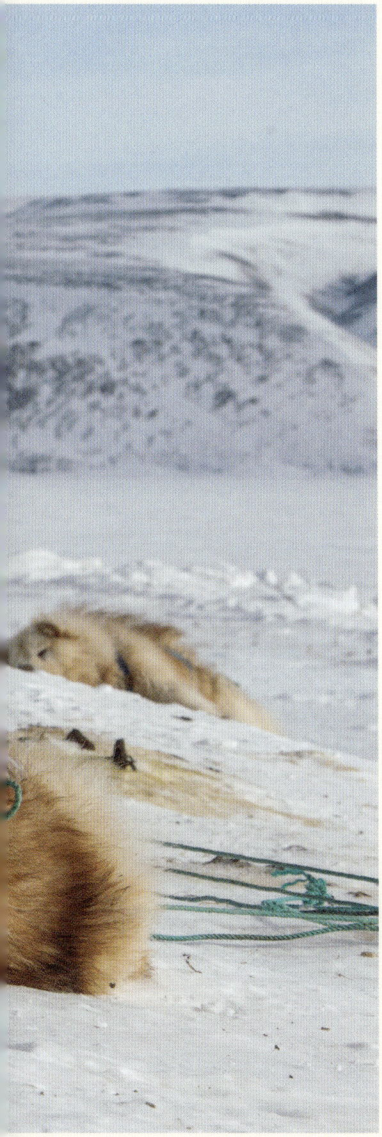

LEFT Siorapaluk is the northernmost Greenland Inughuit town in the country. Approximately 40 people live there and dogs outnumber the humans. The only way to travel to Siorapaluk is via helicopter or dog sled.

BELOW With bodies built to withstand temperatures that drop well below freezing, Greenland Dogs live outside year-round. Their barks and howls are the soundtrack for Northern Greenland communities. For working dogs, they are incredibly friendly and were happy to meet the new guy in town.

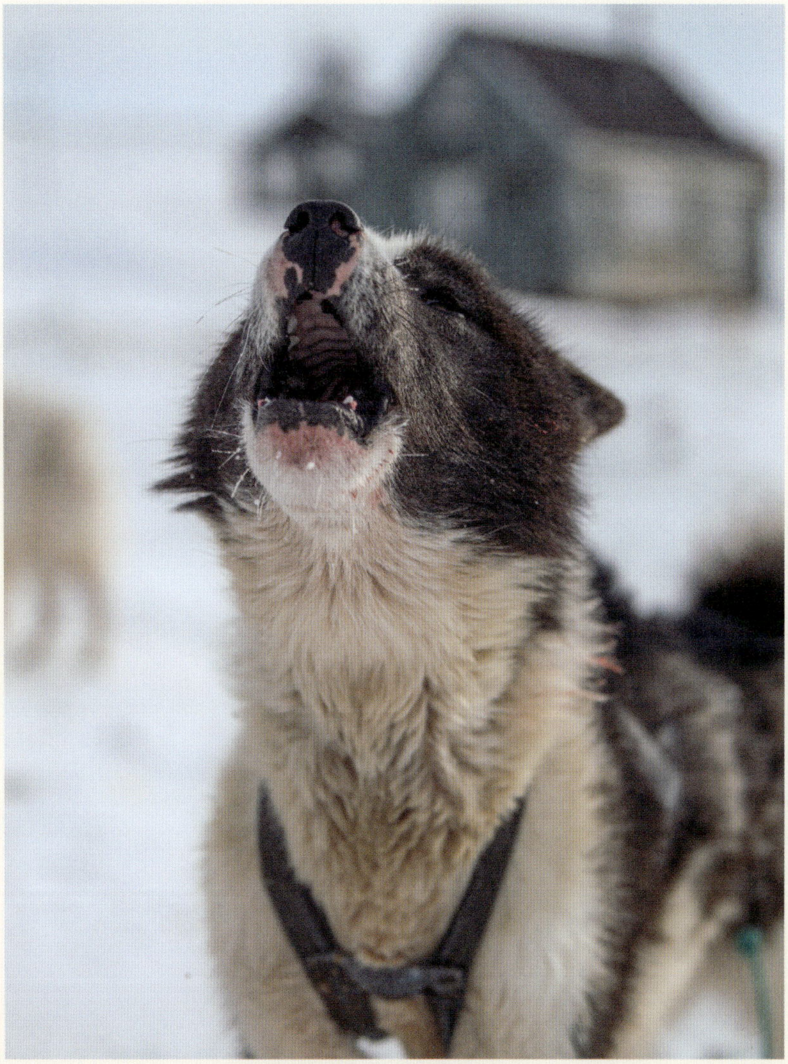

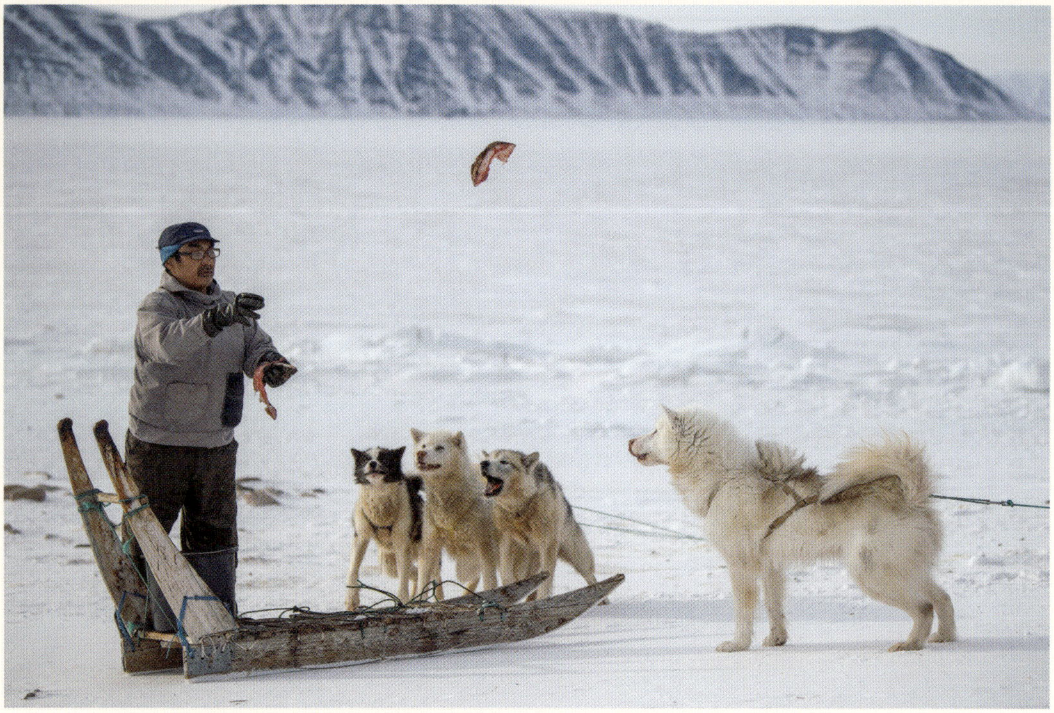

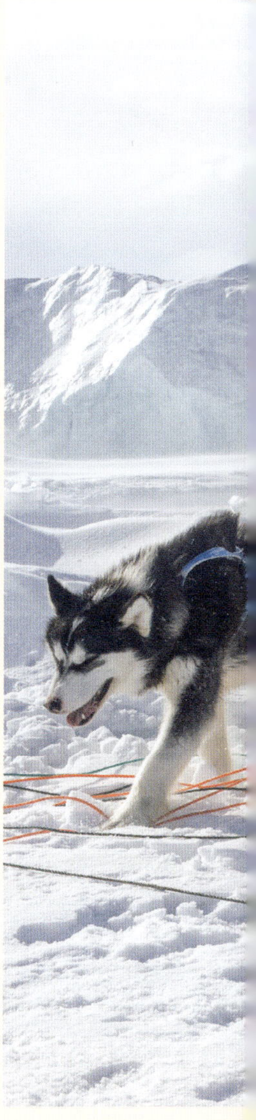

ABOVE Feeding time is a big event for the sled dogs. They aren't always fed every day, in part because of the scarcity of resources, so there is a lot of excitement when they hear the dinner bell. Their diet typically consists of seal, walrus, and narwhal – much different than the kibble most dogs around the world eat.

BELOW There is so much excitement when the dogs are getting strapped up to run. They all jump up and down with "Pick me!" enthusiasm. Once harnessed, they anxiously wait for the rest of their pack to join the team so they can sprint out onto the ice.

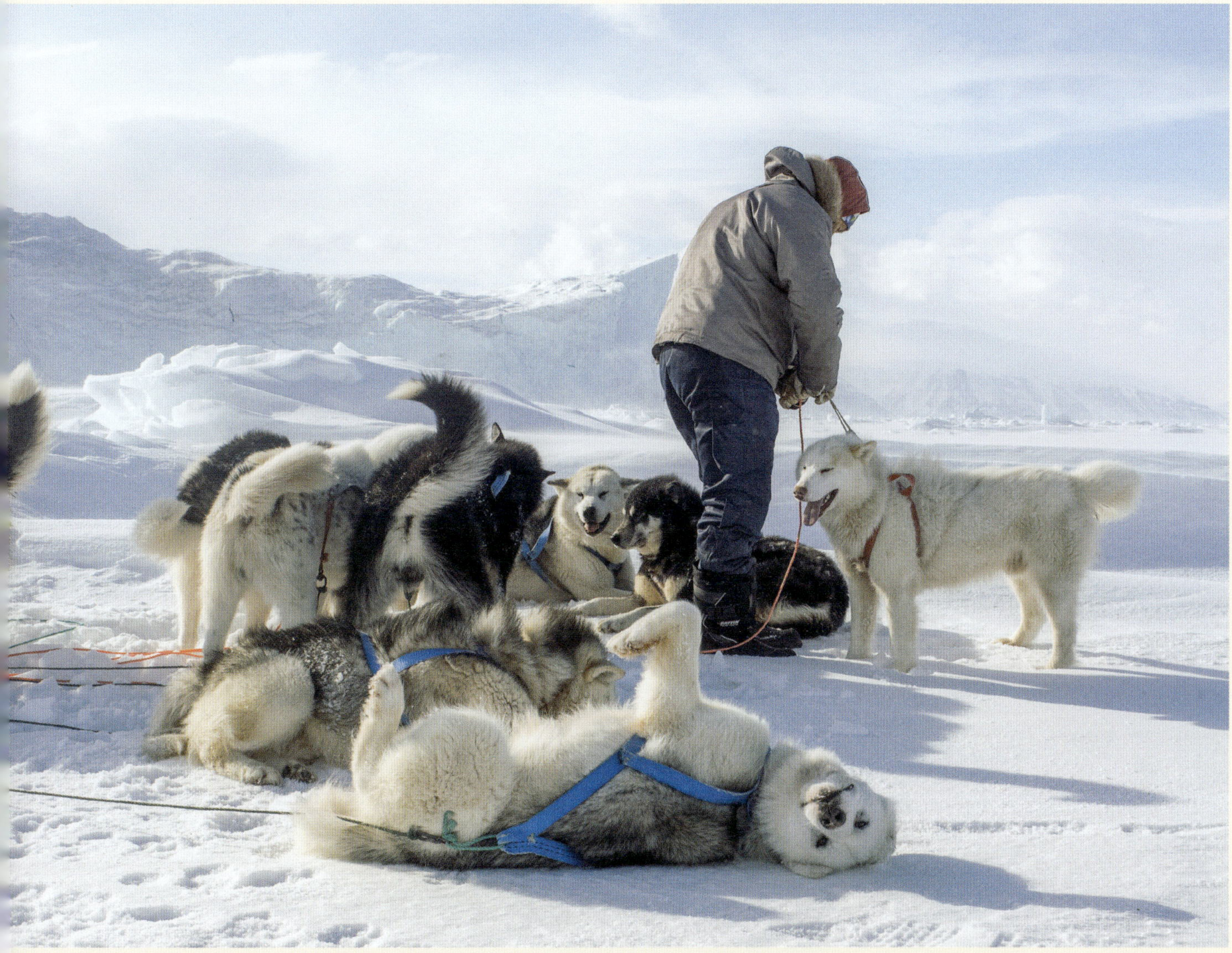

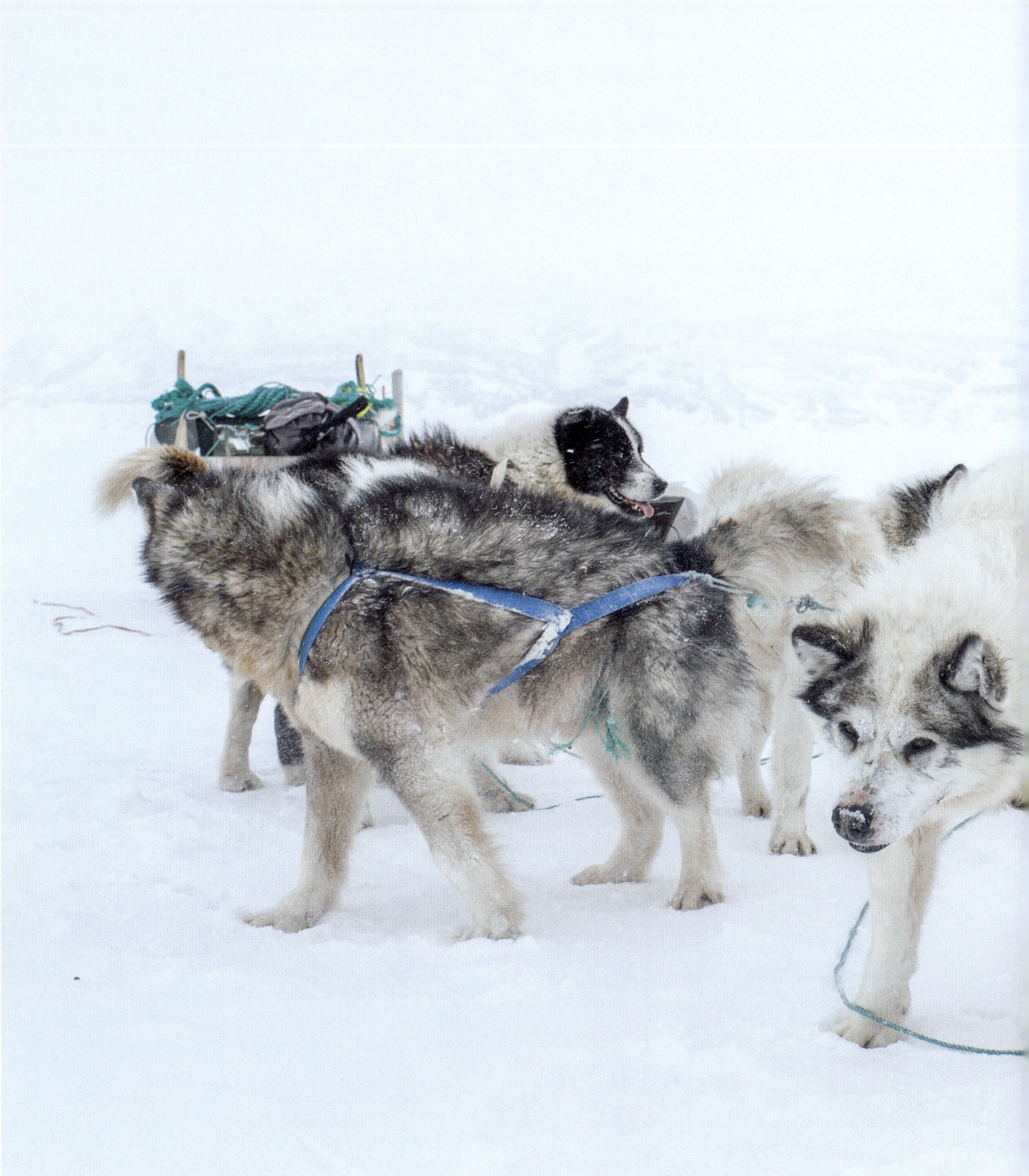

ABOVE We took a sled ride from Siorapaluk to Qaanaaq in whiteout conditions. I could barely see the wagging tails of the 13 dogs pulling our sled. We didn't have cell service, GPS, or any way to call for help if something were to go wrong, such as a crack in the ice or a run-in with a polar bear. My life was in the hands of Ilannguaq, a man in his late twenties who spoke little English and couldn't provide me with any updates.

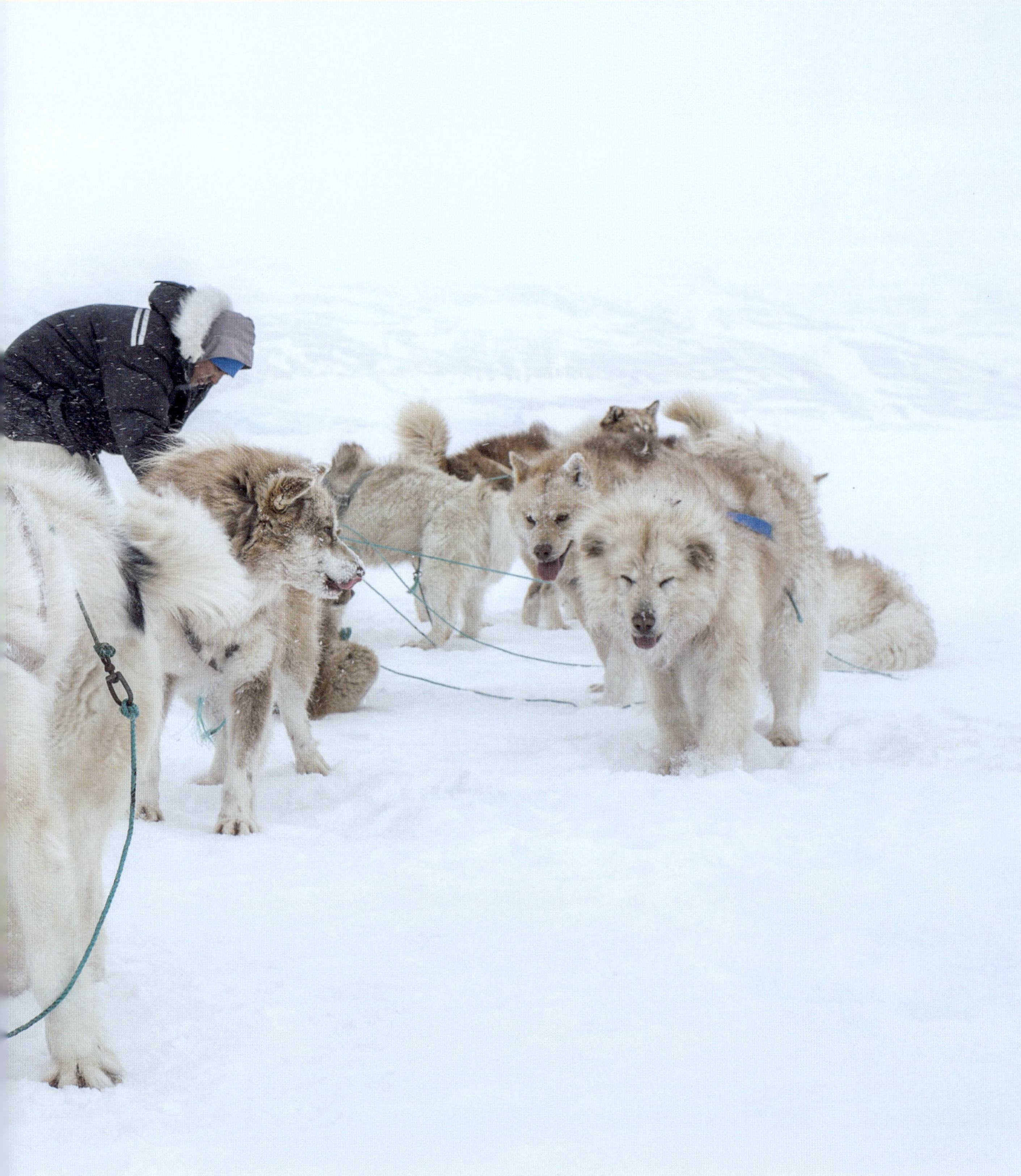

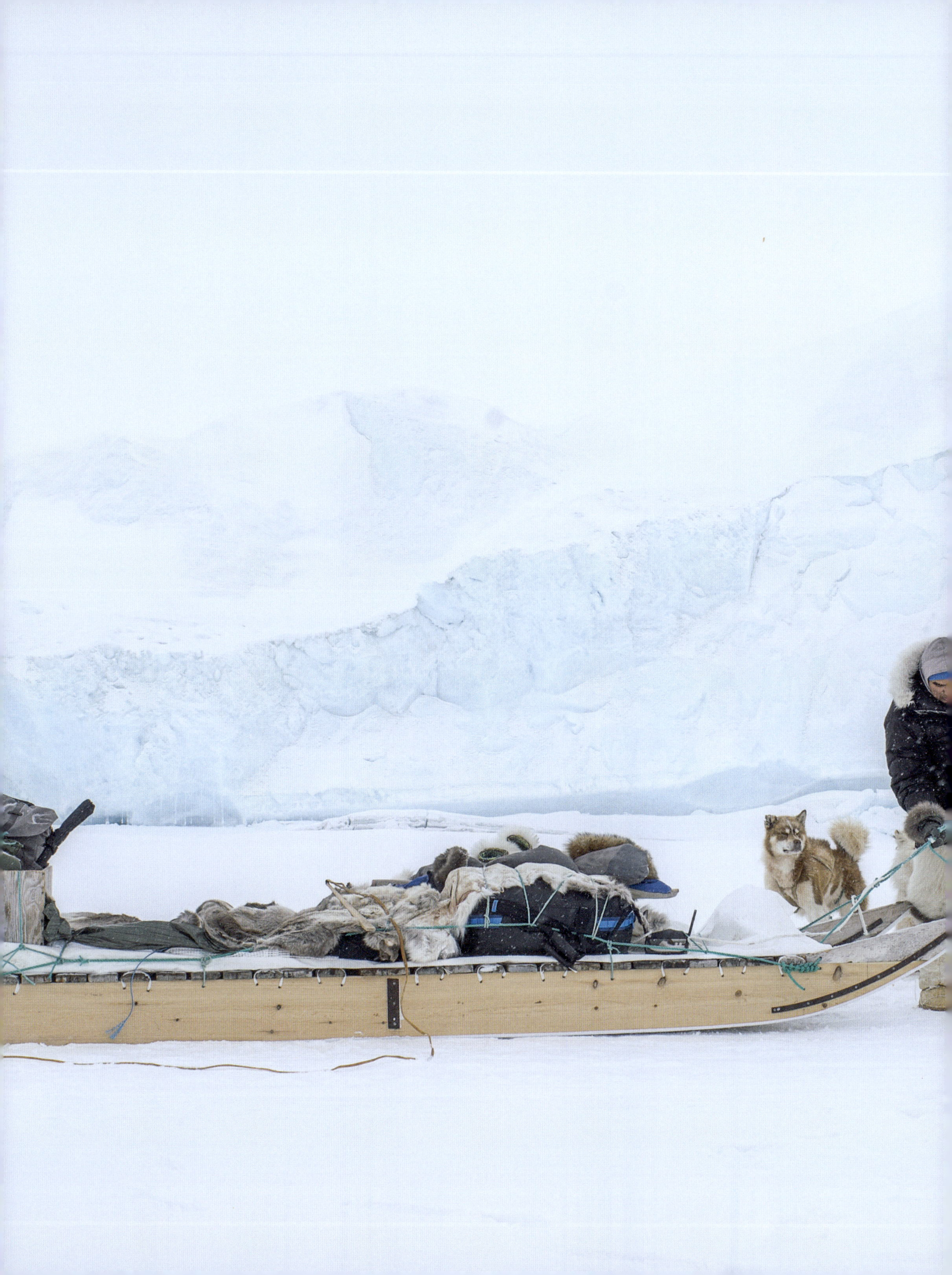

THIS PAGE At points where the ice was thin, we would have to move slowly so that we didn't break through. And every so often, we had to stop when we had a Greenlandic "flat tire," so Ilannguaq could untangle the ropes. The dogs watched on patiently until they could get back to their favorite thing in the world – running.

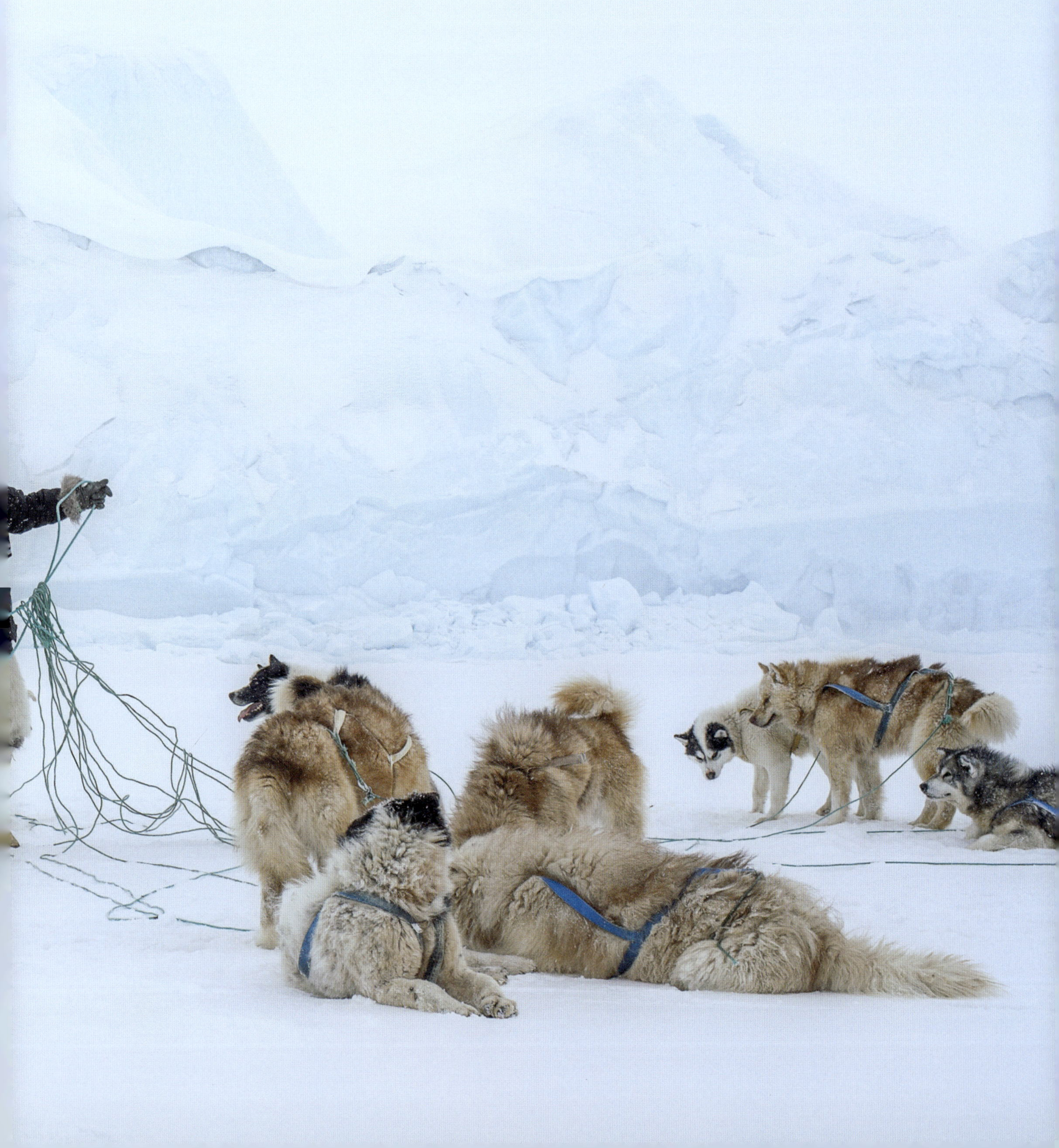

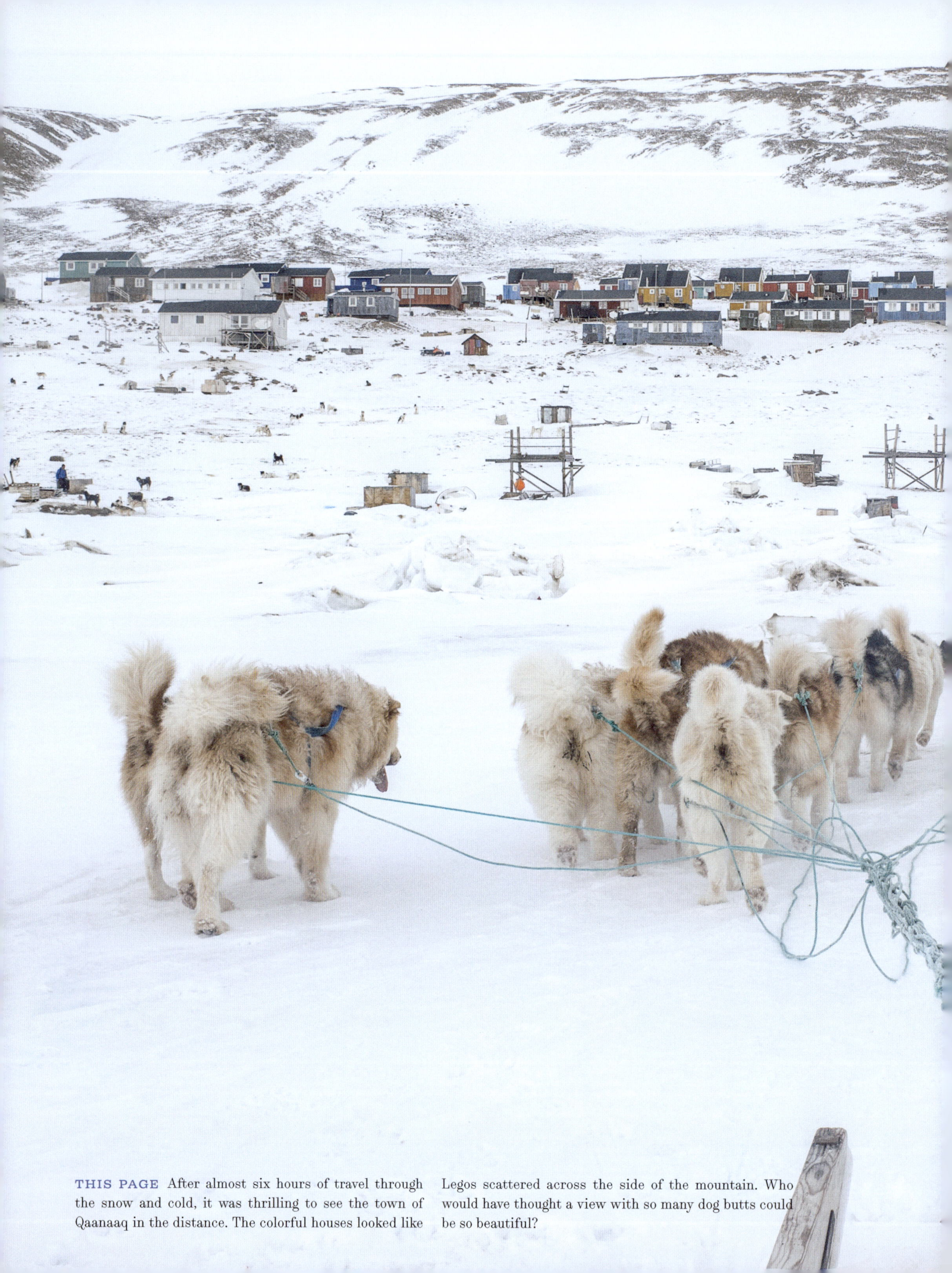

THIS PAGE After almost six hours of travel through the snow and cold, it was thrilling to see the town of Qaanaaq in the distance. The colorful houses looked like Legos scattered across the side of the mountain. Who would have thought a view with so many dog butts could be so beautiful?

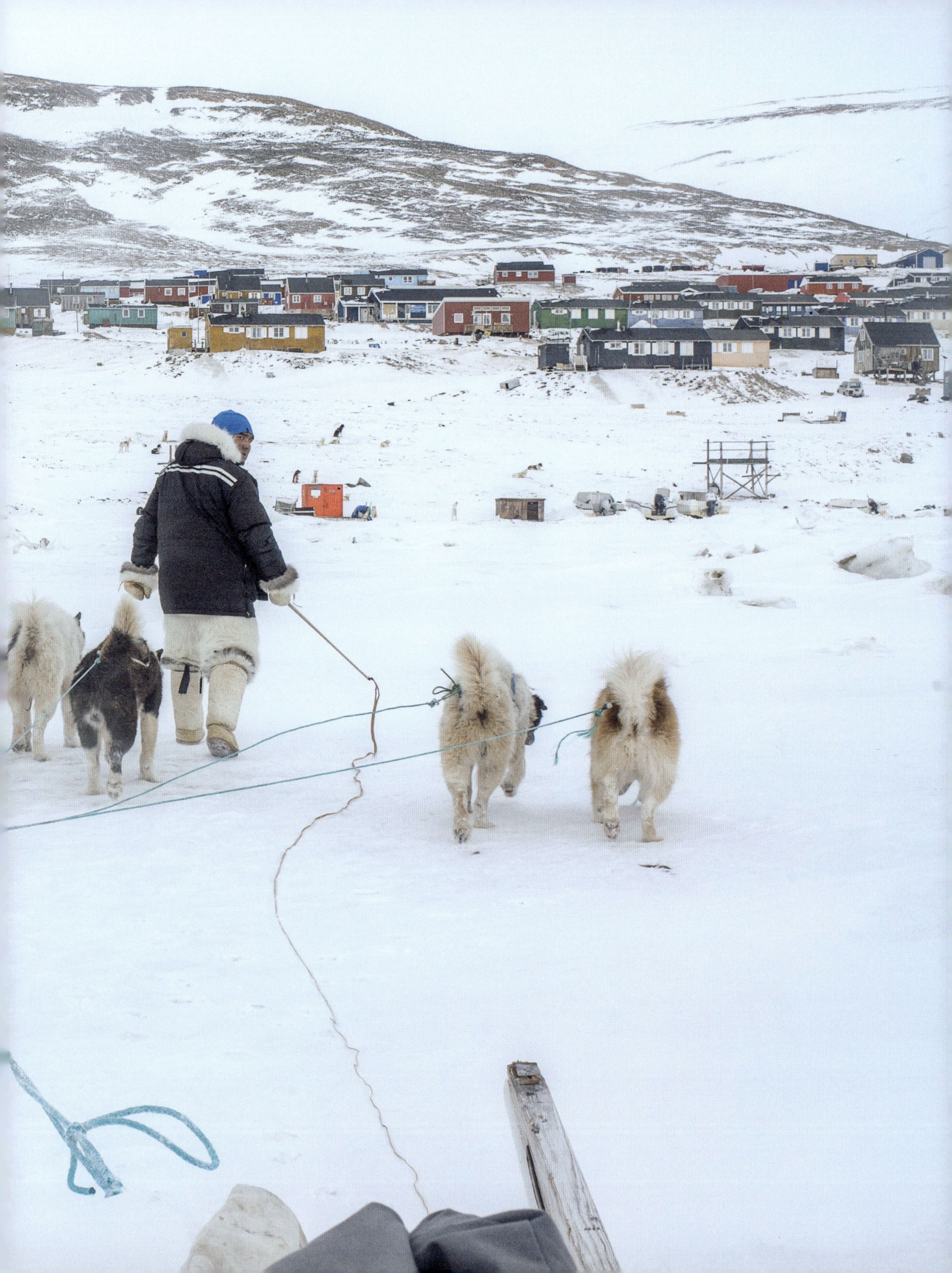

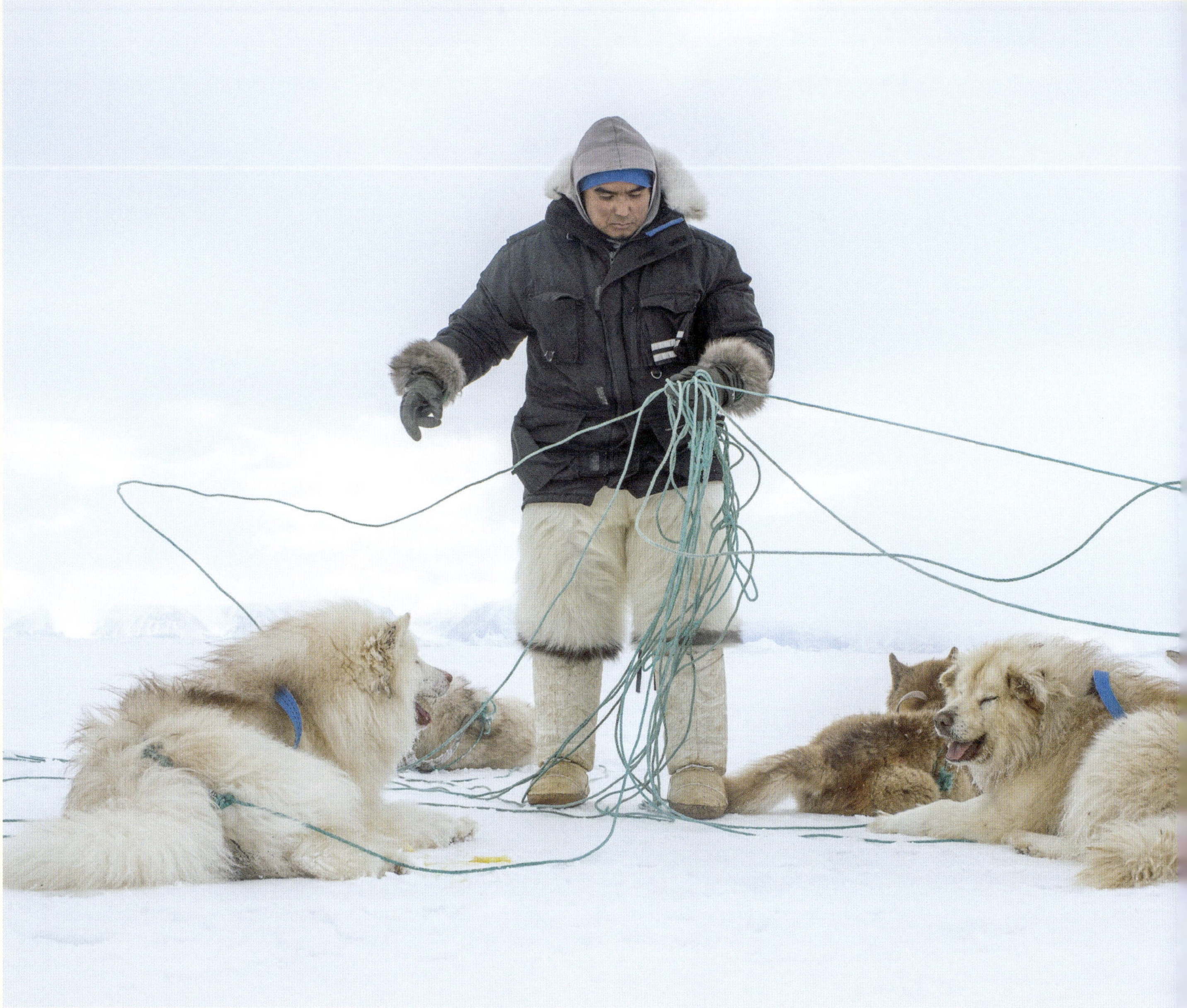

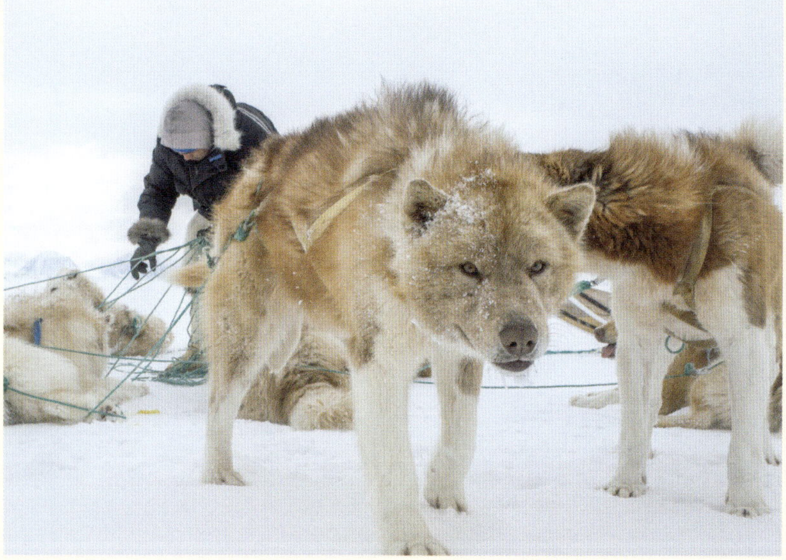

ABOVE & LEFT After arriving in Qaanaaq, the dogs were fed and the team was secured out on the ice. One by one, they curled up and fell asleep to rest up after the long journey.

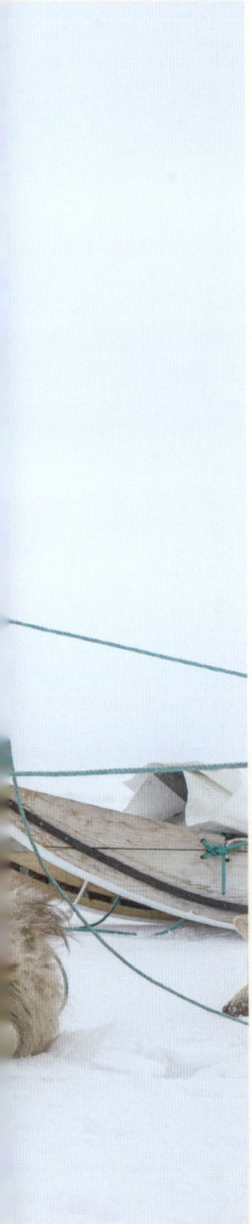

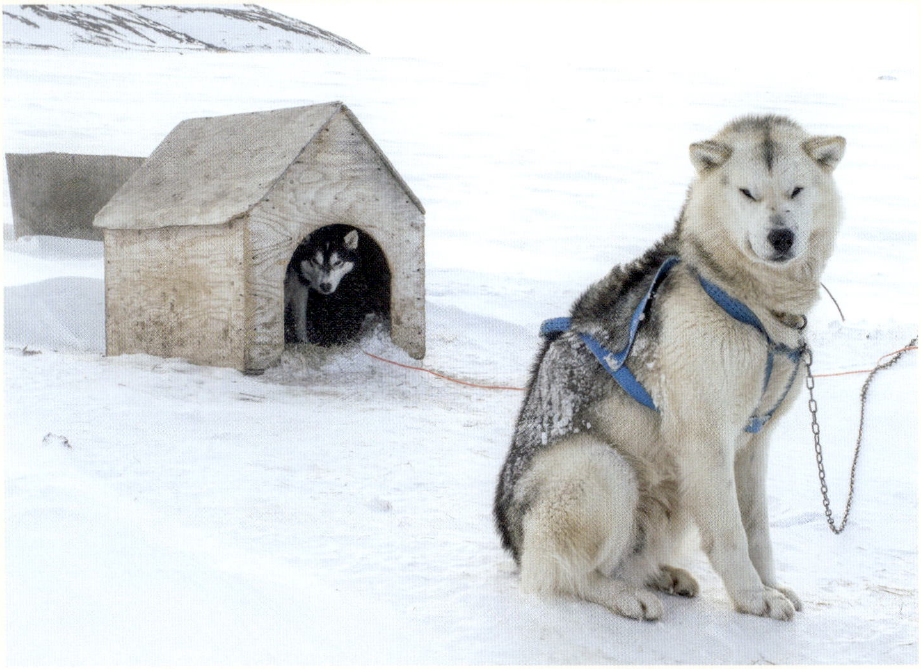

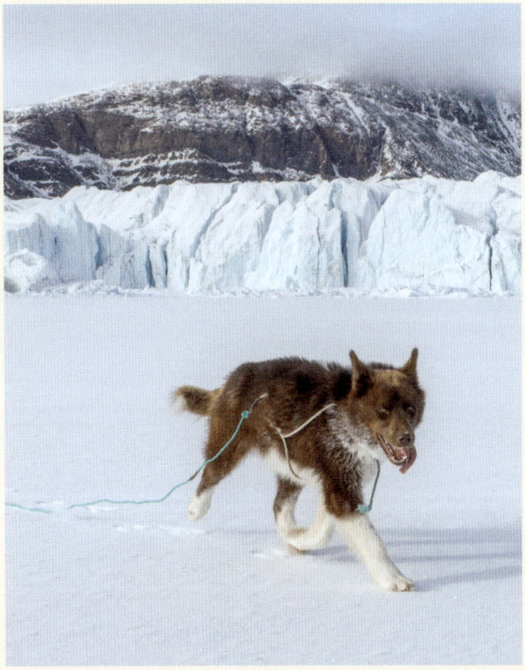

ABOVE RIGHT While most dogs sleep directly on the snow, dog houses are occasionally provided for a mother dog and her puppies.

RIGHT This pregnant dog came along for an overnight trip. She was not attached to the sled, so she cruised at her own pace. At some points she ran right in the middle of the pack, and other times she took it nice and easy, trailing far behind the sled. If her endurance is any indication, her pups are going to be ready to run as soon as they're born.

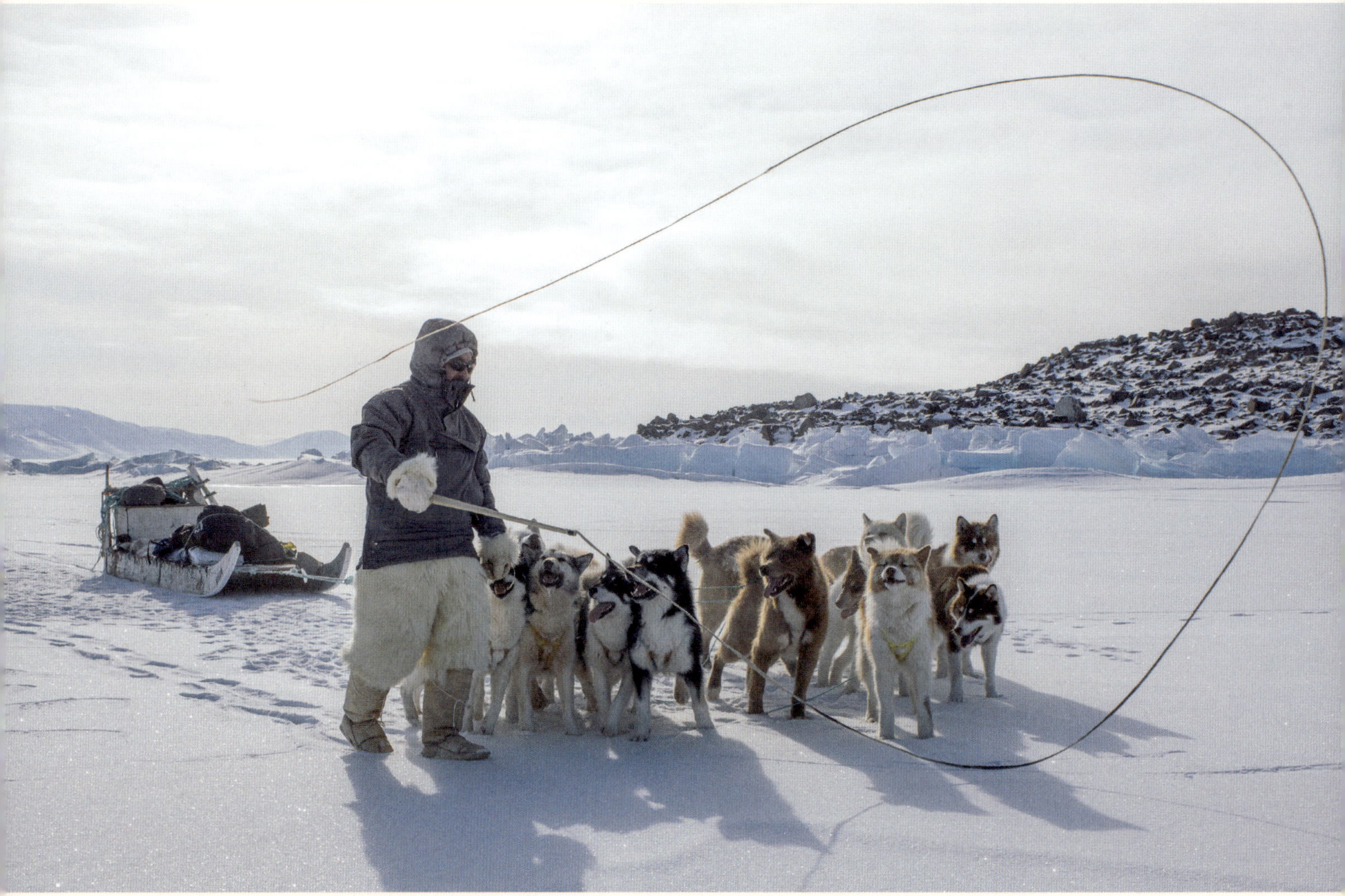

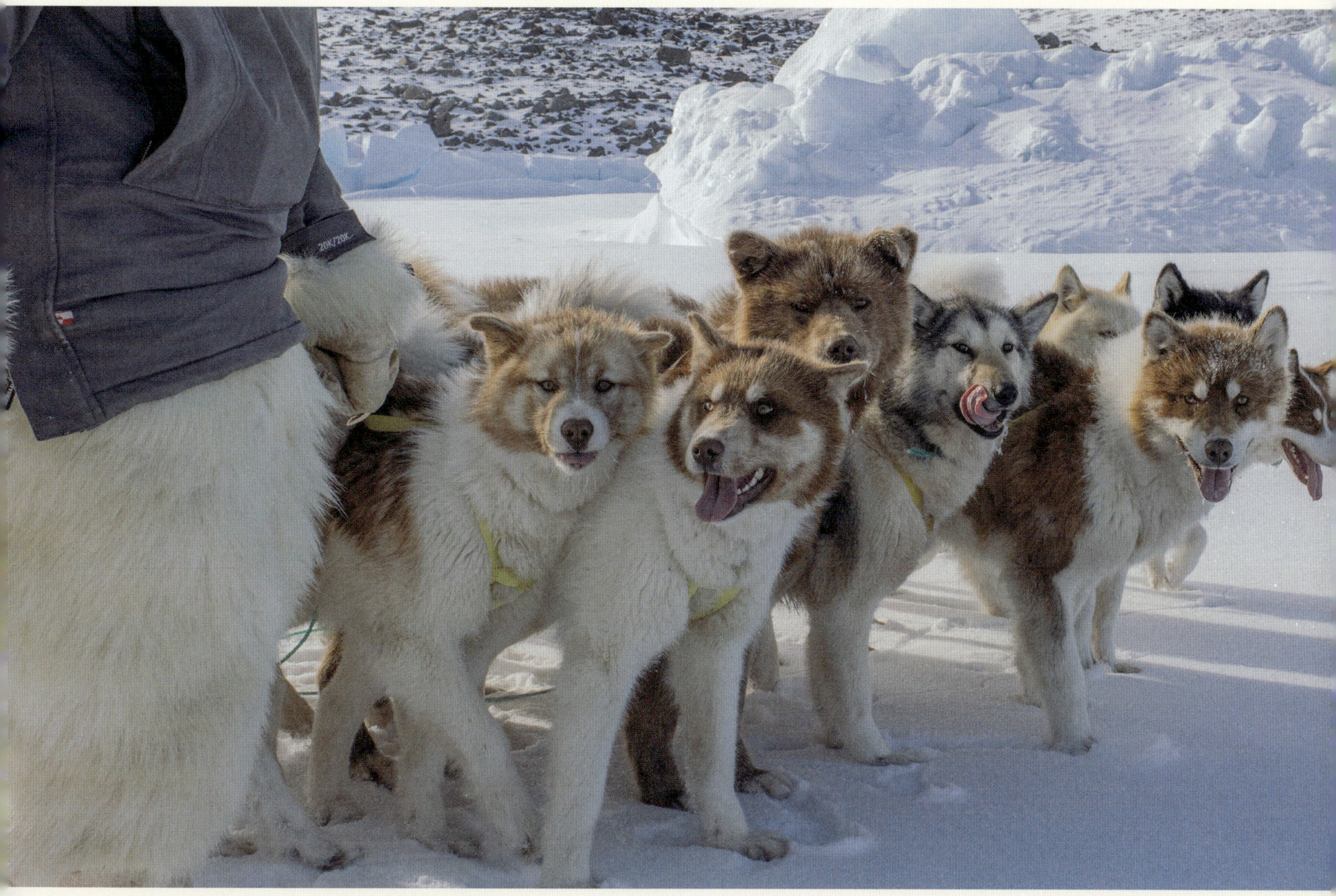

LEFT & ABOVE Hunters use the whip as a guide for the dogs. They will whip on either side of the team to shift the direction left or right. My guide, Markus, would walk with his team and nonchalantly whip across his peripheral. The dogs would walk alongside him, cognizant not to cross that invisible line.

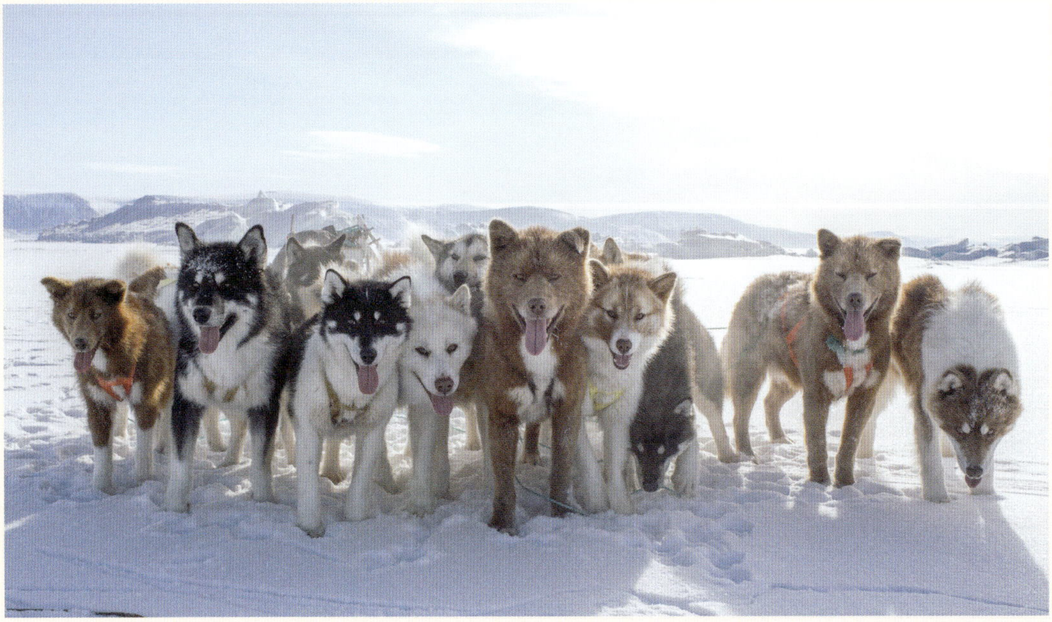

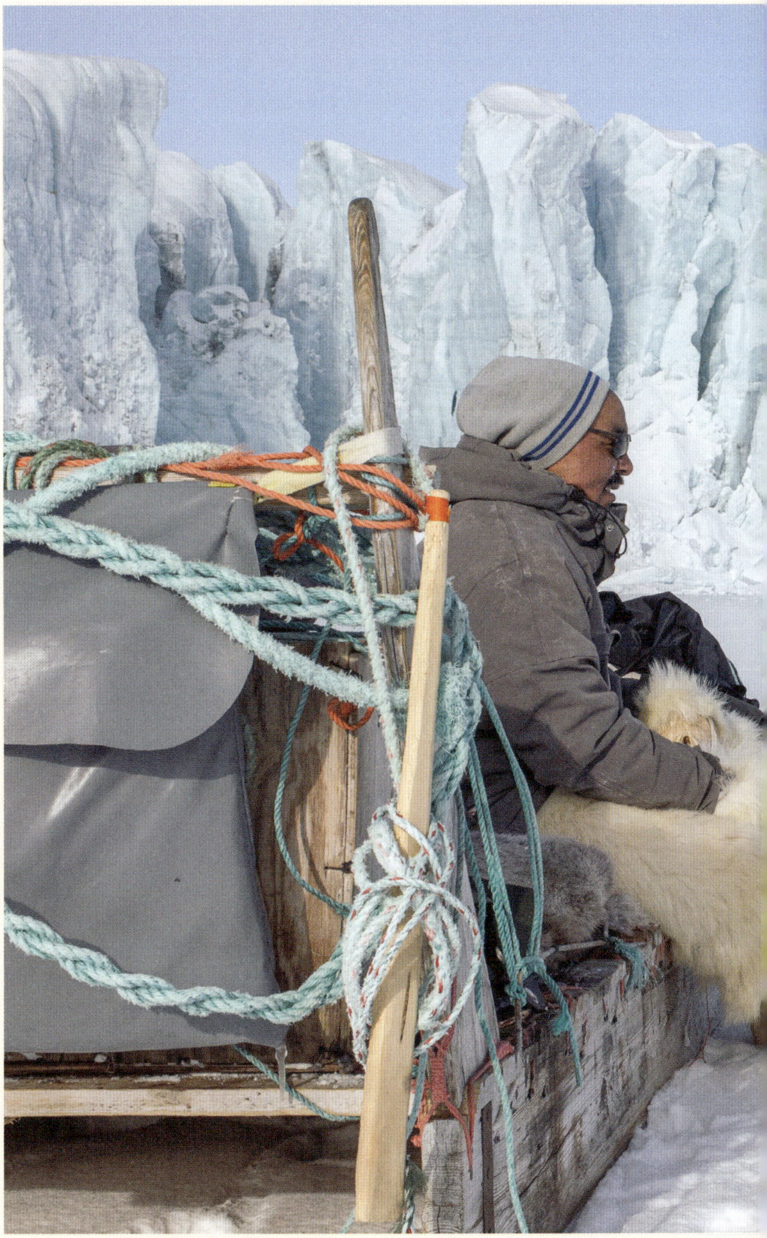

LEFT & BELOW When a target is spotted, the dogs must stay and wait while the hunter slowly treks toward the animal. During this trip, Markus saw two seals. One disappeared into the water before he could get a shot off. He shot at the other and missed. As soon as the dogs heard the gun fire, they immediately sprinted toward their owner with the sled dragging in their wake.

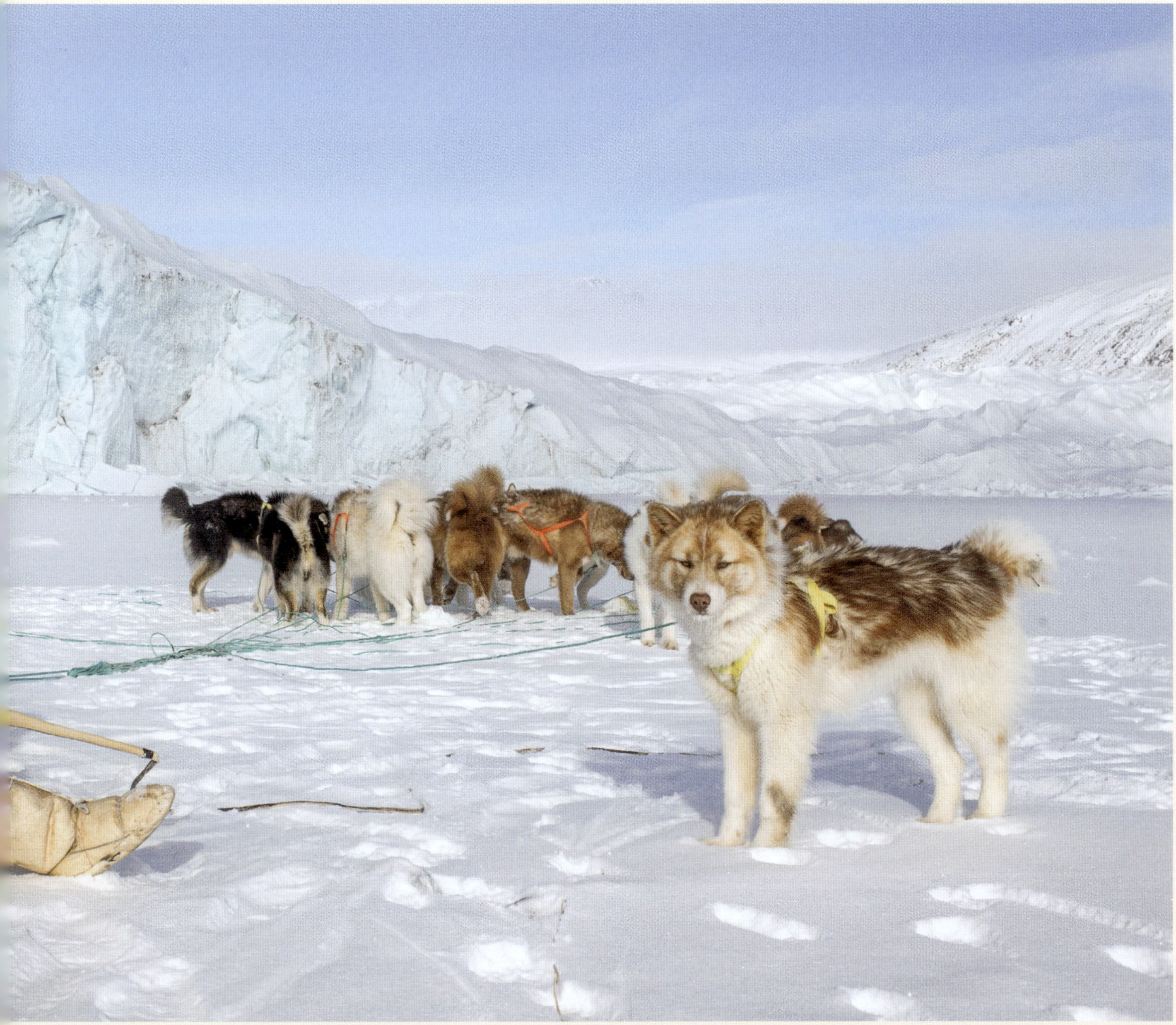

BELOW & RIGHT The town of Qaanaaq holds two annual sled races – one for hunters and one for kids. For the latter, there are multiple races, and with each, the participants get younger and the race gets shorter. By the end, a baby carrier on a sled was pushed over the finish line. It's never too early to get a child involved in sled dog racing in Qaanaaq.

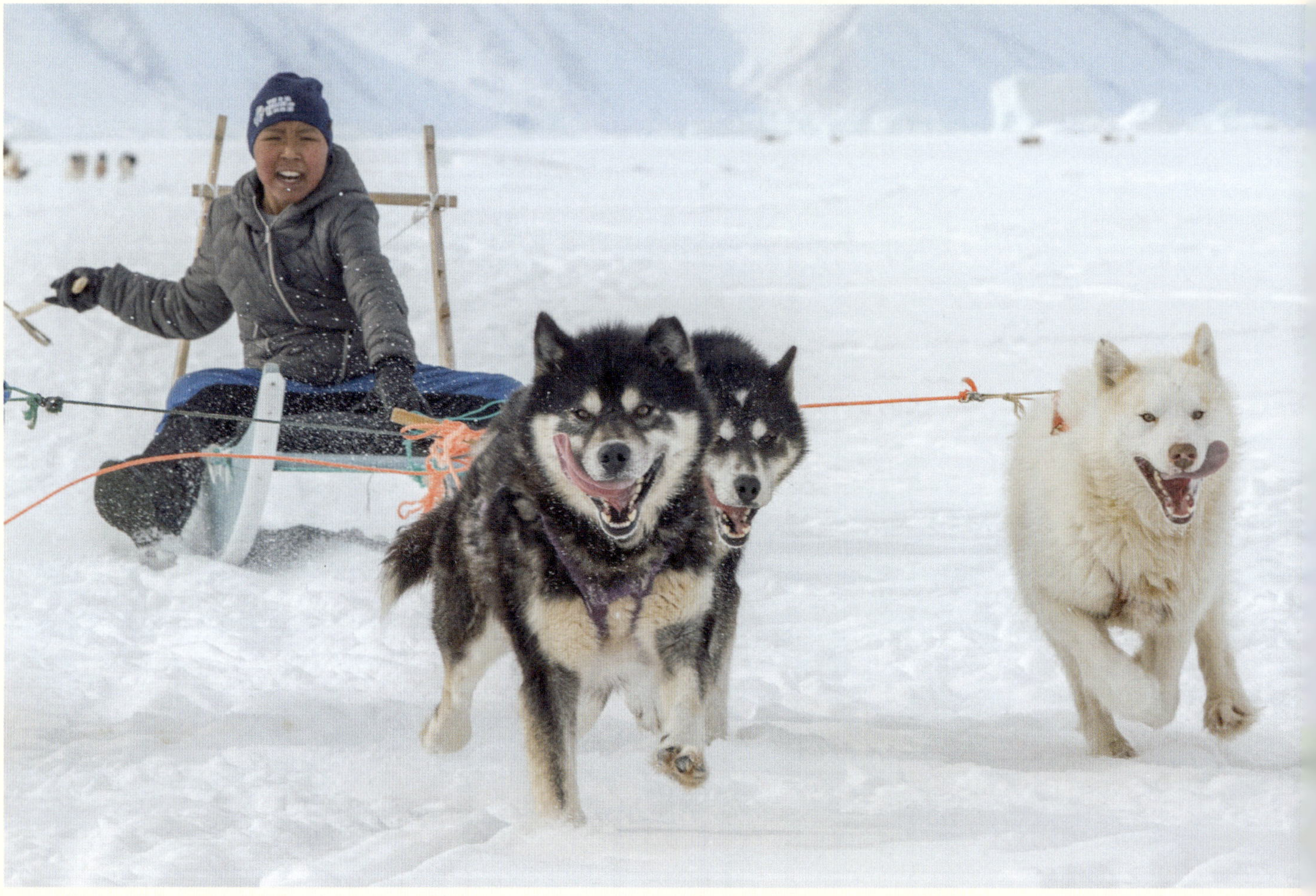

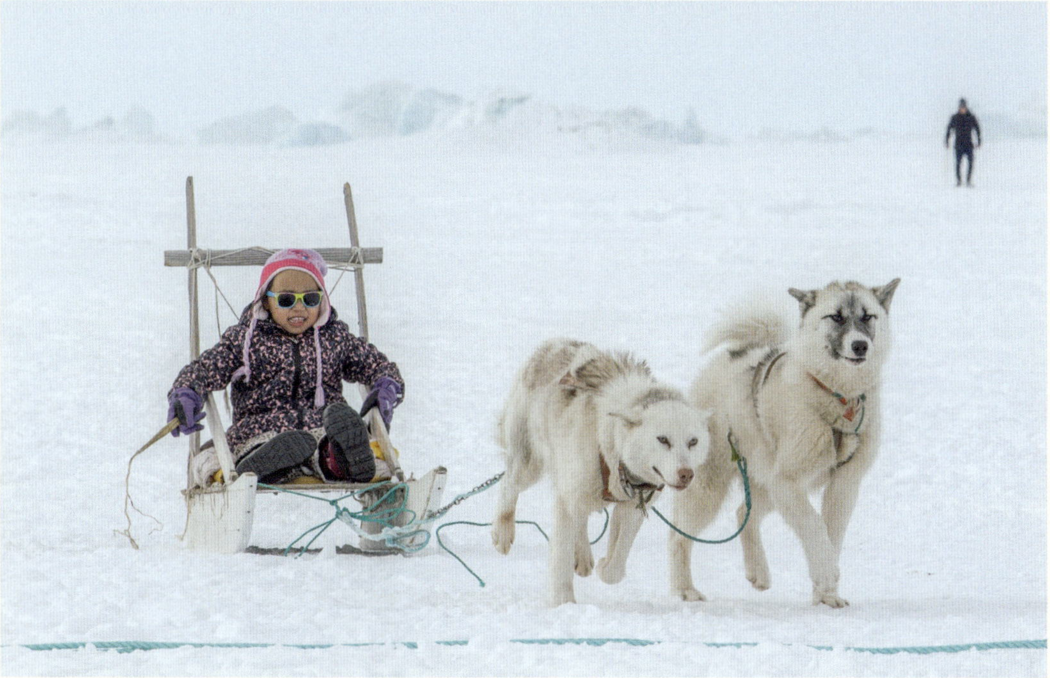

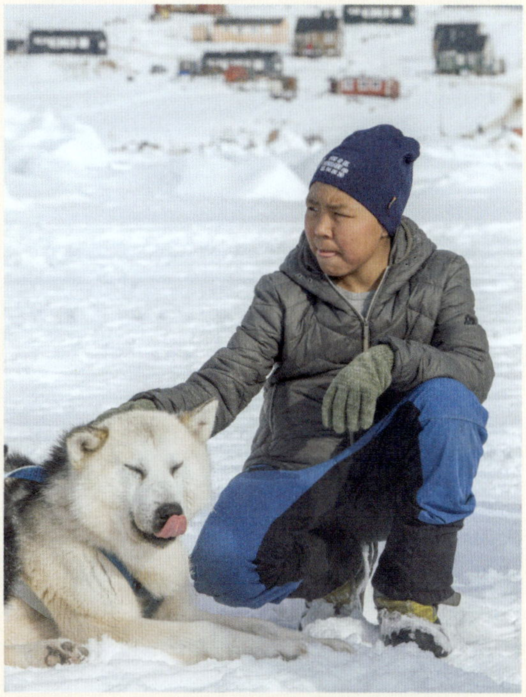

THIS PAGE I was lucky to go out on a hunt with Qillaq just days after he won the annual sled race in Qaanaaq. His team of dogs sped through the 40-kilometer race and won by a considerable margin. He credited his victory to his connection with his dogs, which was very apparent. In a culture that sometimes considers dogs as tools, he uses the word "love" for his team. He said love for and a connection to his dogs were necessary when he needed to stretch them at the end of race.

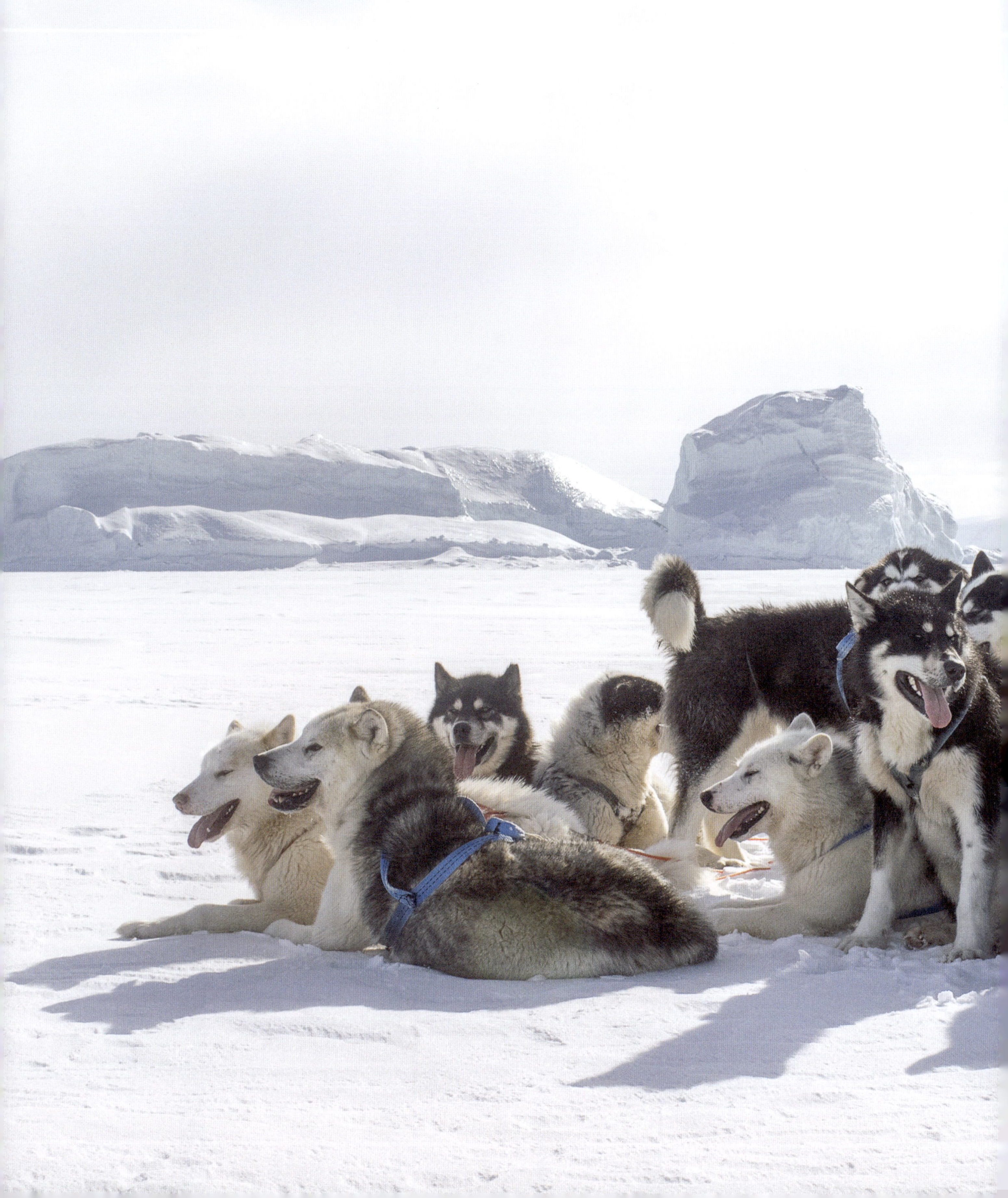

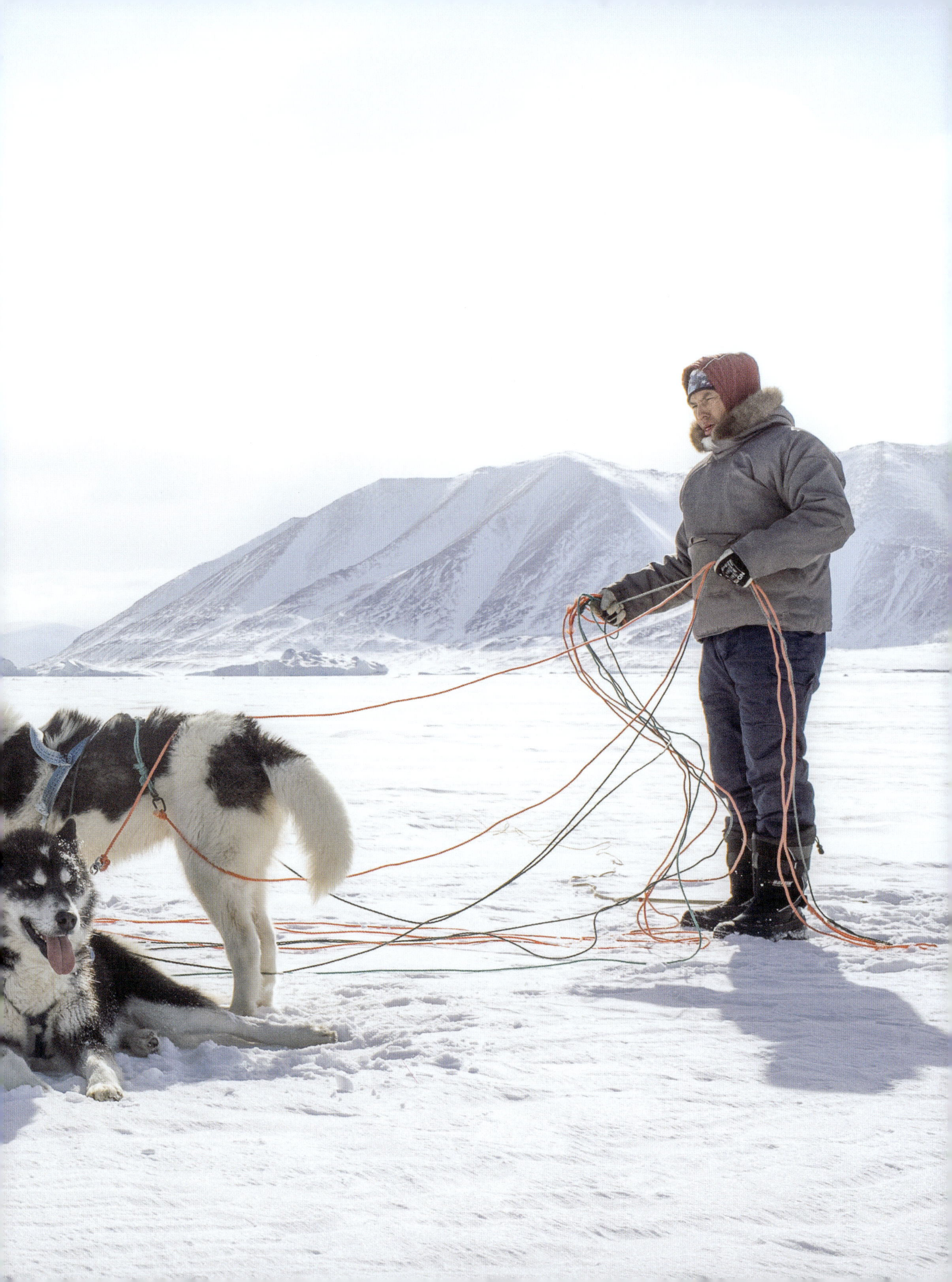

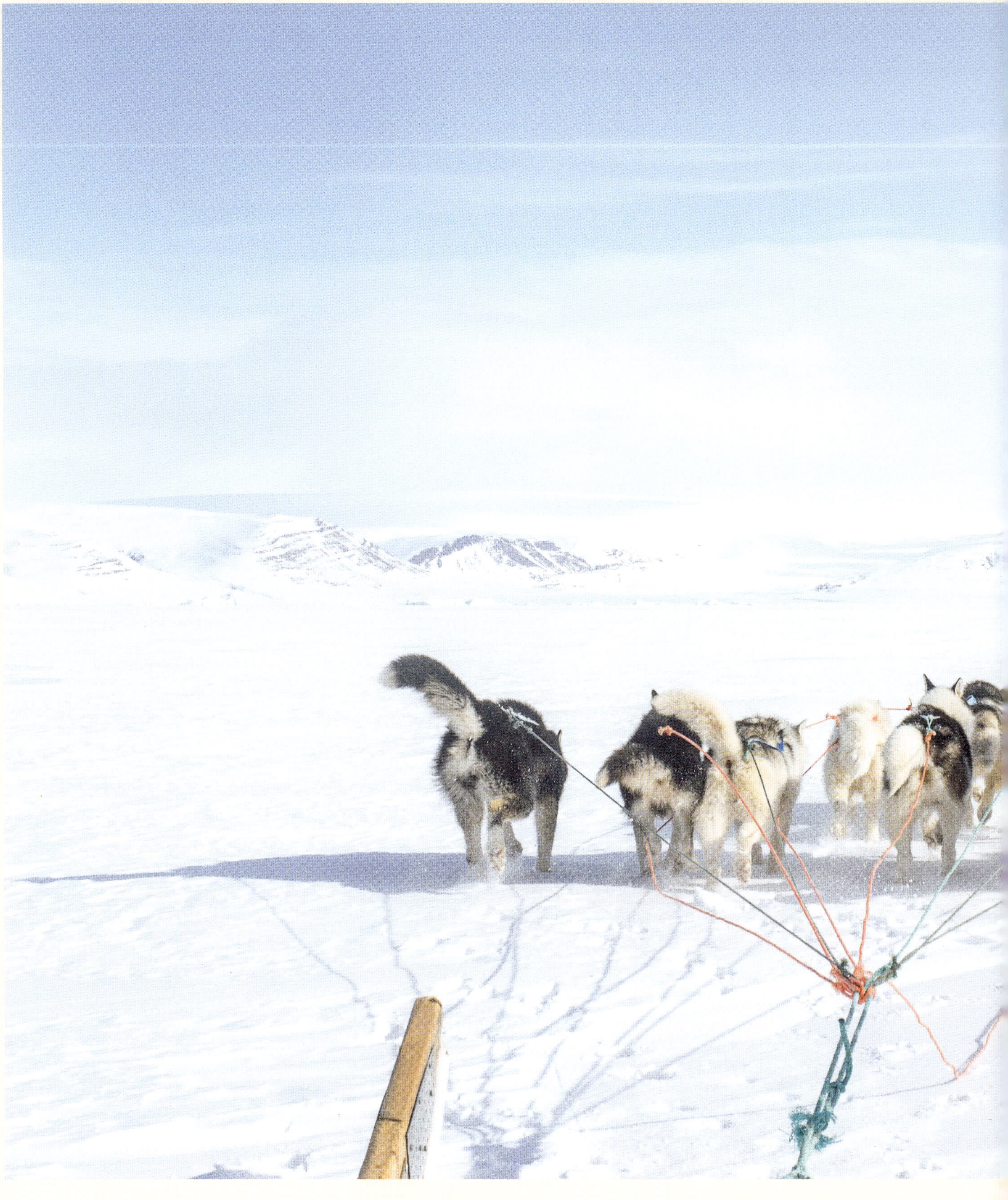

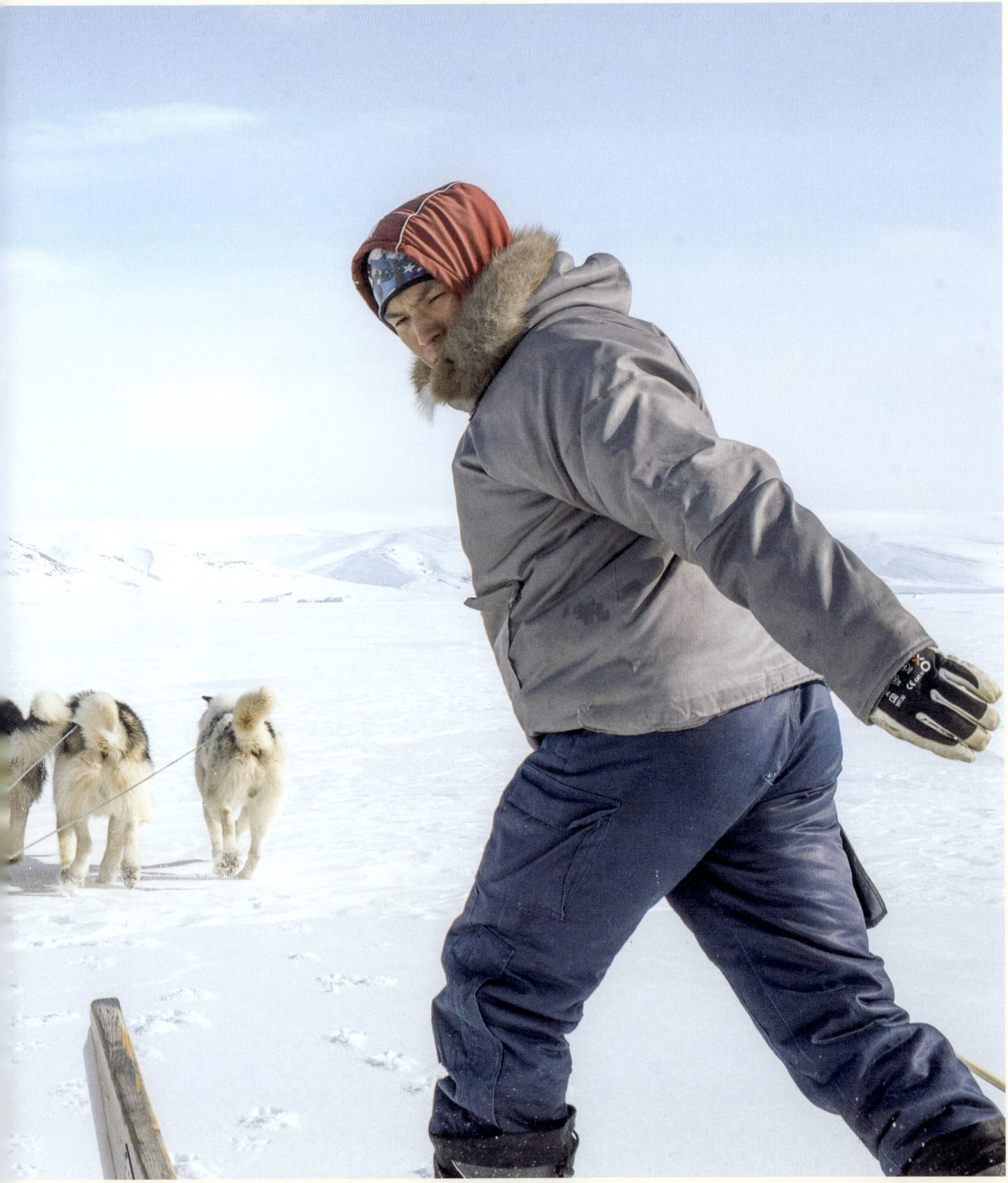

ABOVE The dogs are always anxious to run. Once they are told to go, they get moving fast so the hop on the sled has to be timed just right.

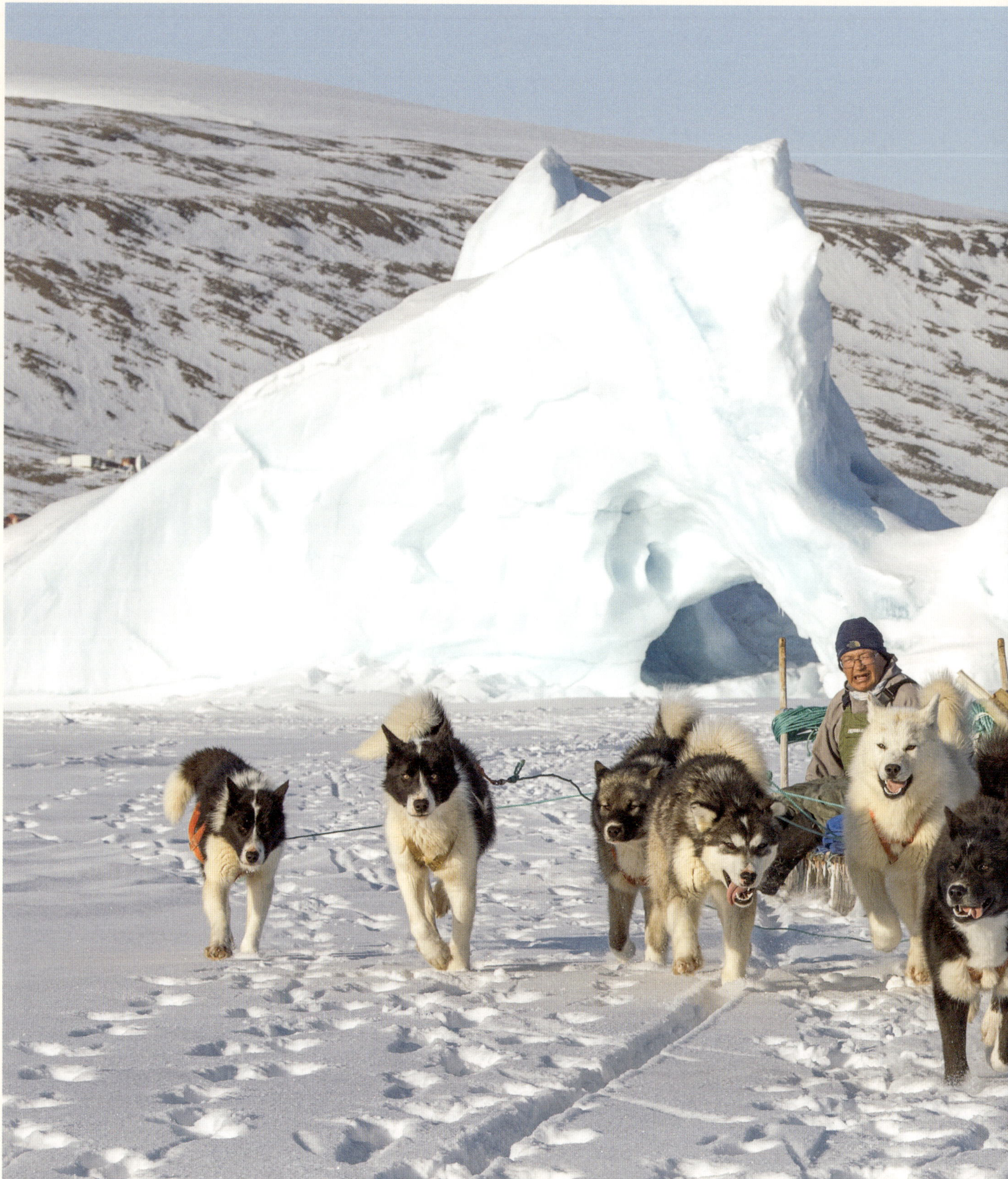

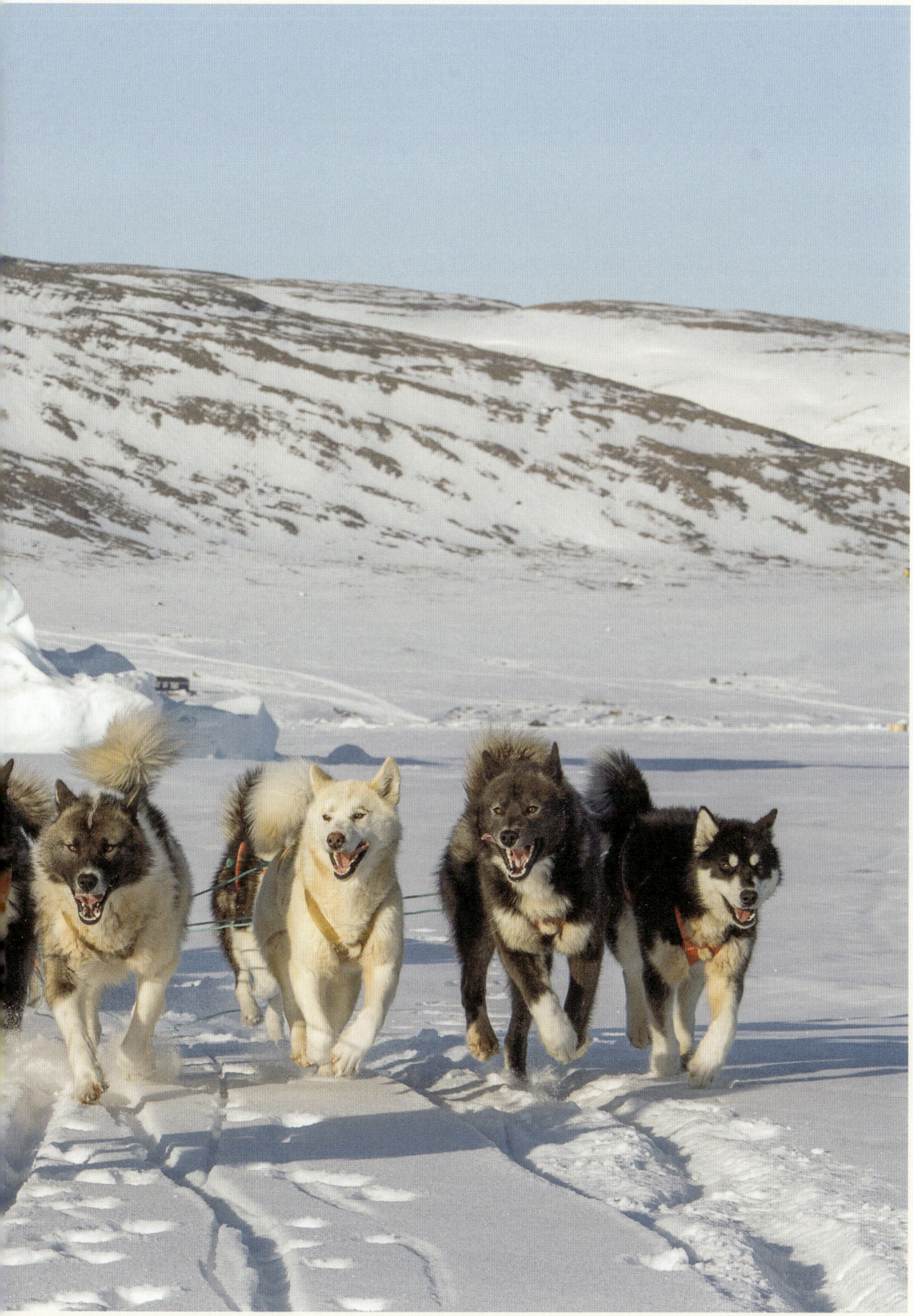

ABOVE Peter took me out with his dogs just for fun. It gave me the opportunity to photograph them as they ran toward me.

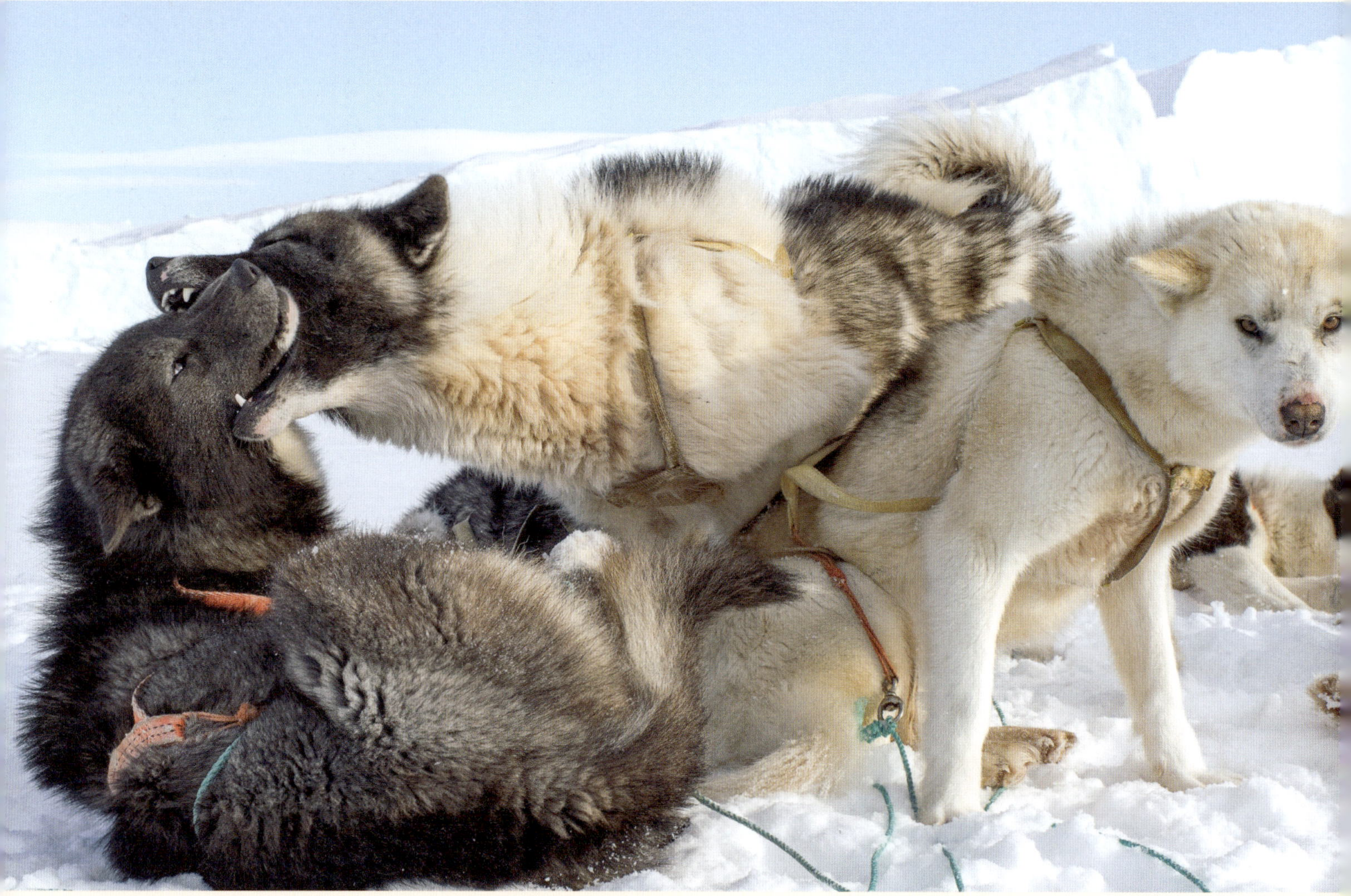

ABOVE & RIGHT The dogs all have their own agendas during running breaks. Some go right to sleep while others like to play for a bit. Once they all settle down, there are moments of absolute stillness in one of the purest and most beautiful environments in the world.

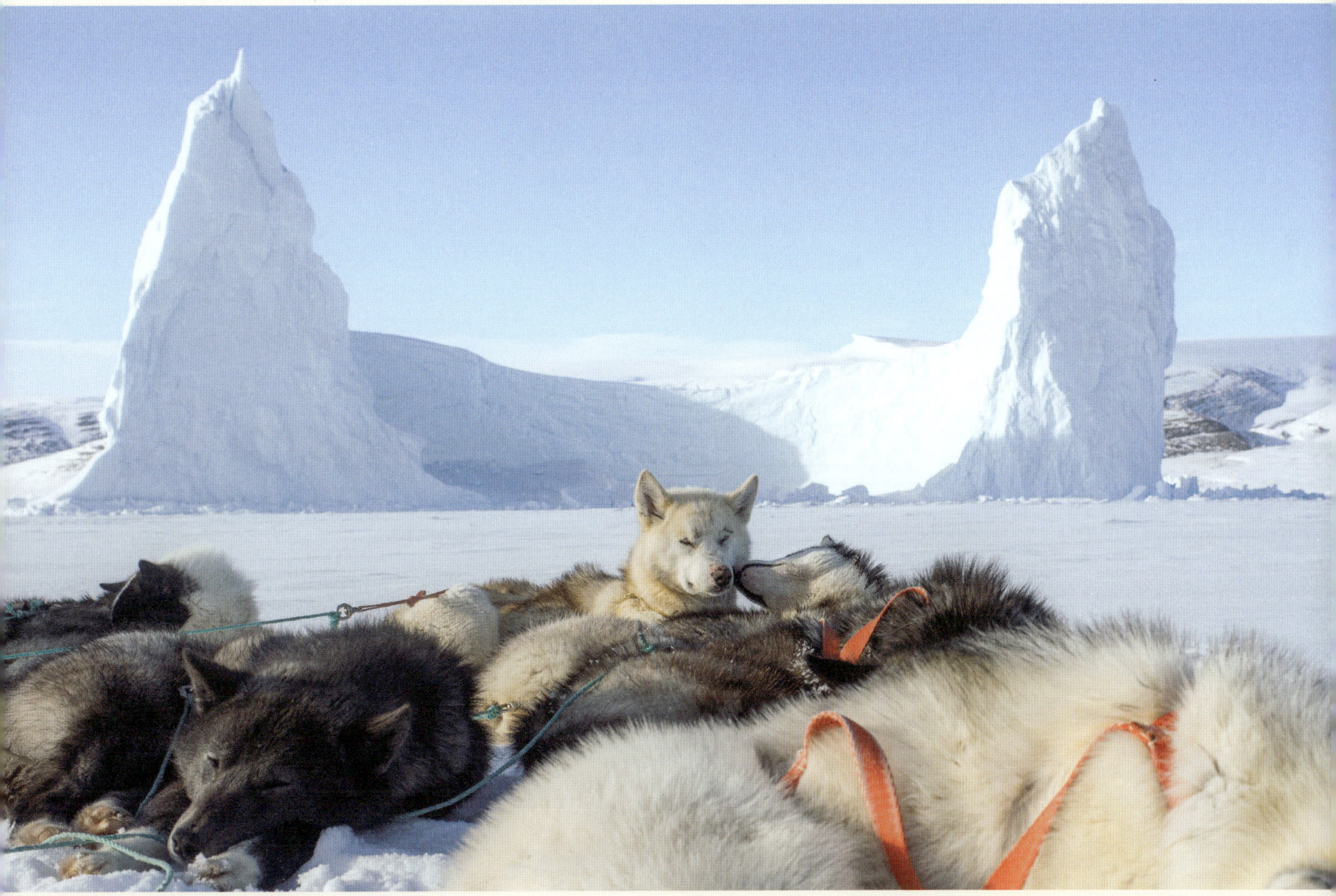

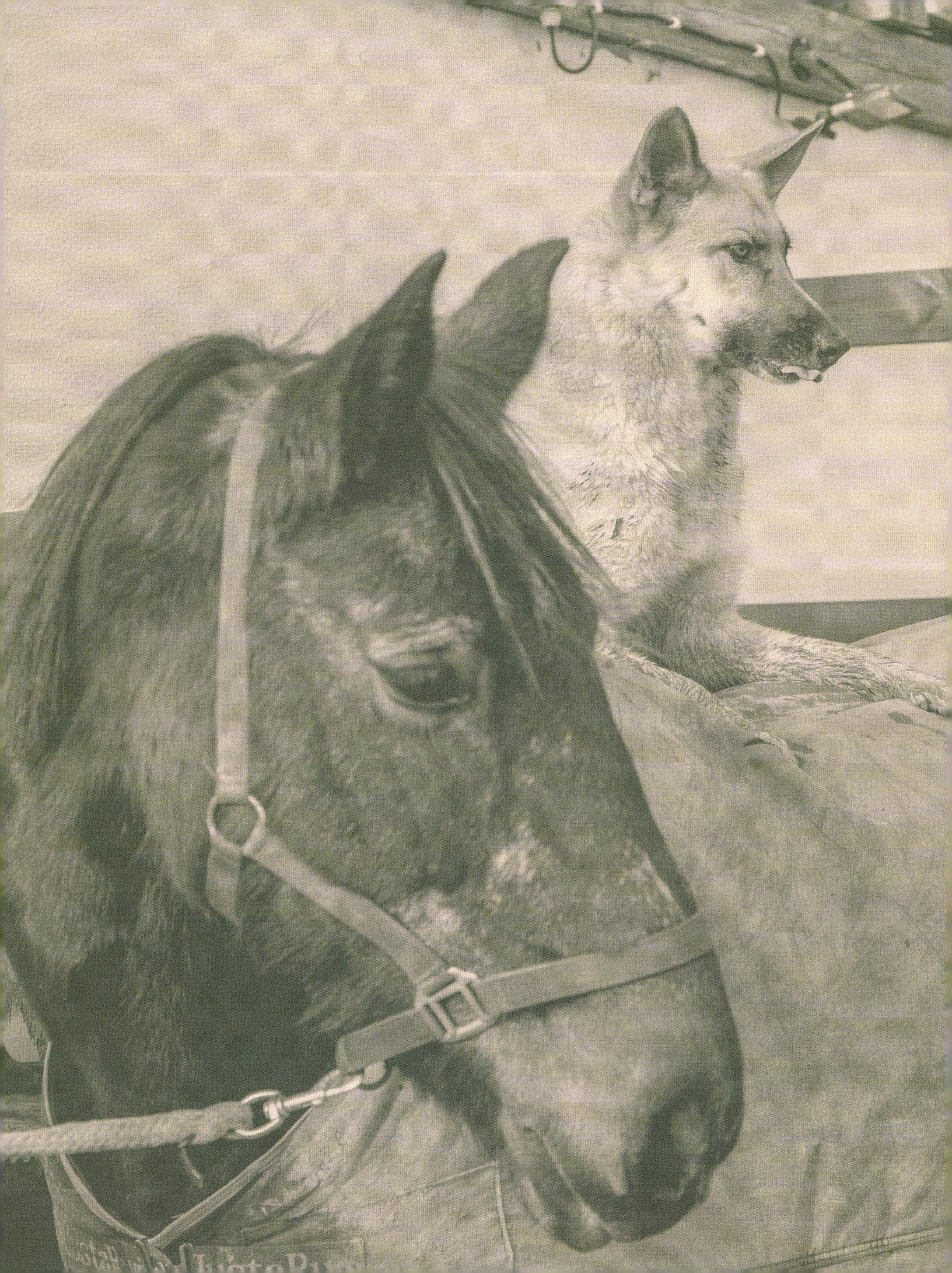

LOCATION	BREEDS	TASKS	SKILLS
North County Dublin, Ireland	Rhodesian Ridgeback and German Shepherd/ Belgian Malinois/Husky Mix	Playing, Befriending Riders, Complementing Horses	Sociability, Kindness, Awareness

EQUINE THERAPY DOGS

THERAPEUTIC HORSE RIDING can have a major physical and emotional impact on people with physical, cognitive, or emotional needs. In North County Dublin, The Royal Stables provides this service, giving everyone the chance to feel a little royal.

While horses are the main drawcard, the team at The Royal Stables has two dogs that provide complementary assistance during therapy sessions. Having two types of animals provides varied therapy, and it's sometimes easier for people, especially children, to approach the dogs. They can even act as a bridge between the humans and horses.

I visited the property to photograph two dogs, Bruce and Robin, and learn more about their work. They both help in unique ways. Bruce is a steadying presence during sessions, and the ridges on his back provides a unique sensory touch for the horse riders. Robin has helped visitors work through panic attacks by lying with them, offering a gentle presence to help them feel grounded.

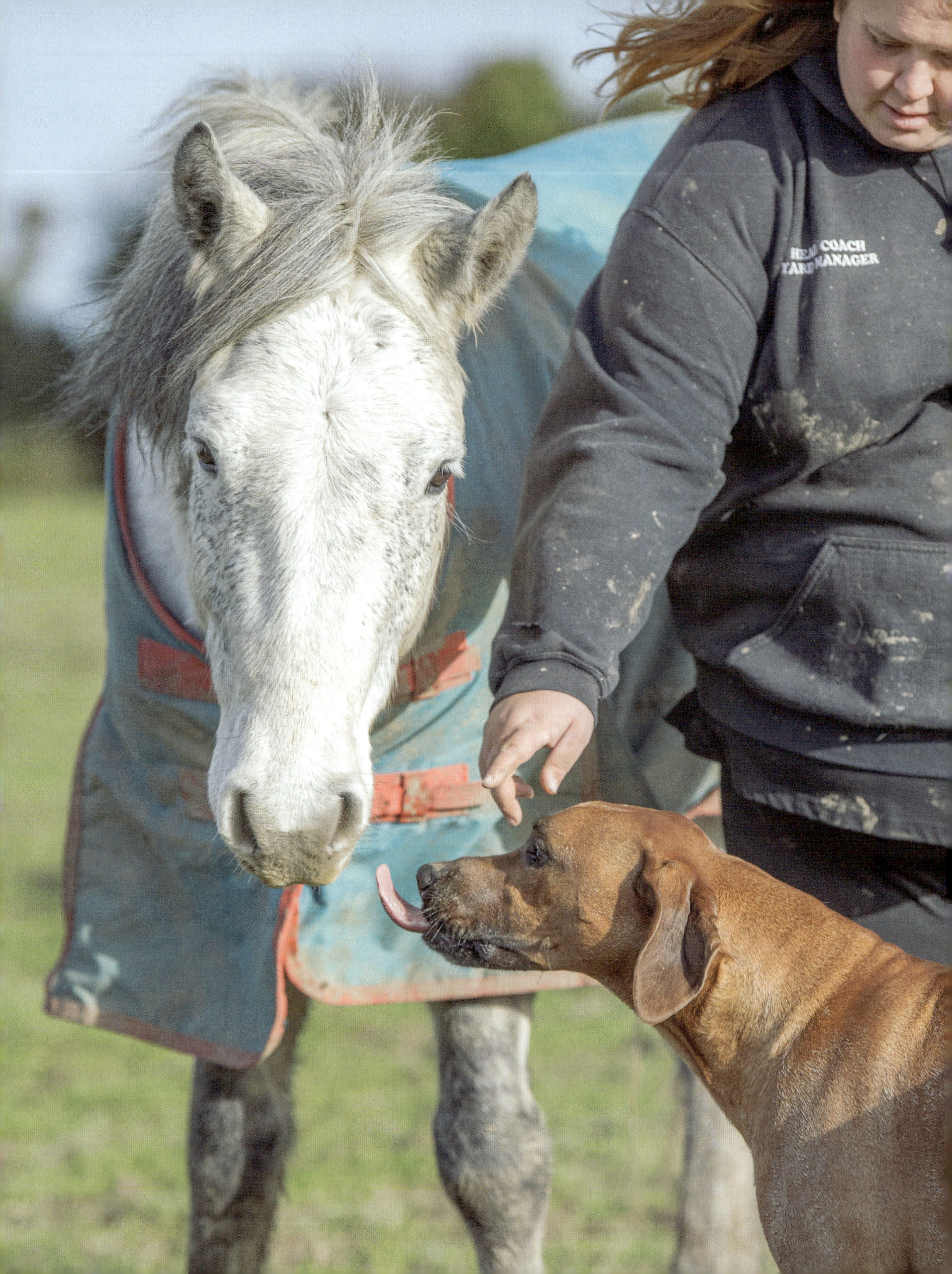
COACH
MANAGER

The beauty of Bruce and Robin's work is that they don't do anything completely out of the ordinary for a dog. They follow basic commands, coexist with the horses, and, most importantly, provide comfort merely through their presence.

LEFT Bruce is a Rhodesian Ridgeback and Robin is a German Shepherd mix. Both breeds fall under Ireland's restricted breed list, which means owners need to follow special precautions when handling these dogs in public. Many countries have similar laws, but Bruce and Robin are a great example of how responsible owners can get the most out of these breeds.

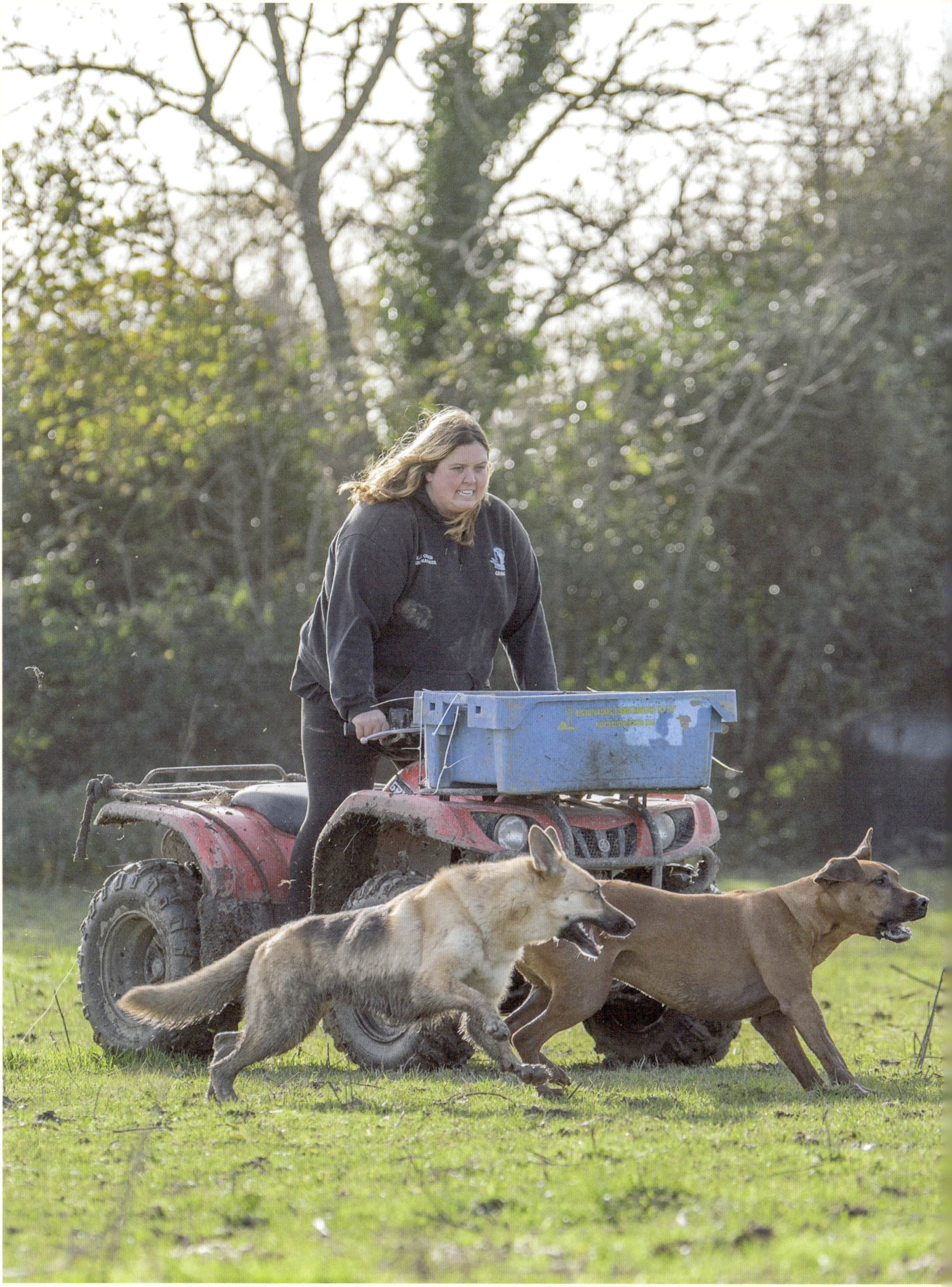

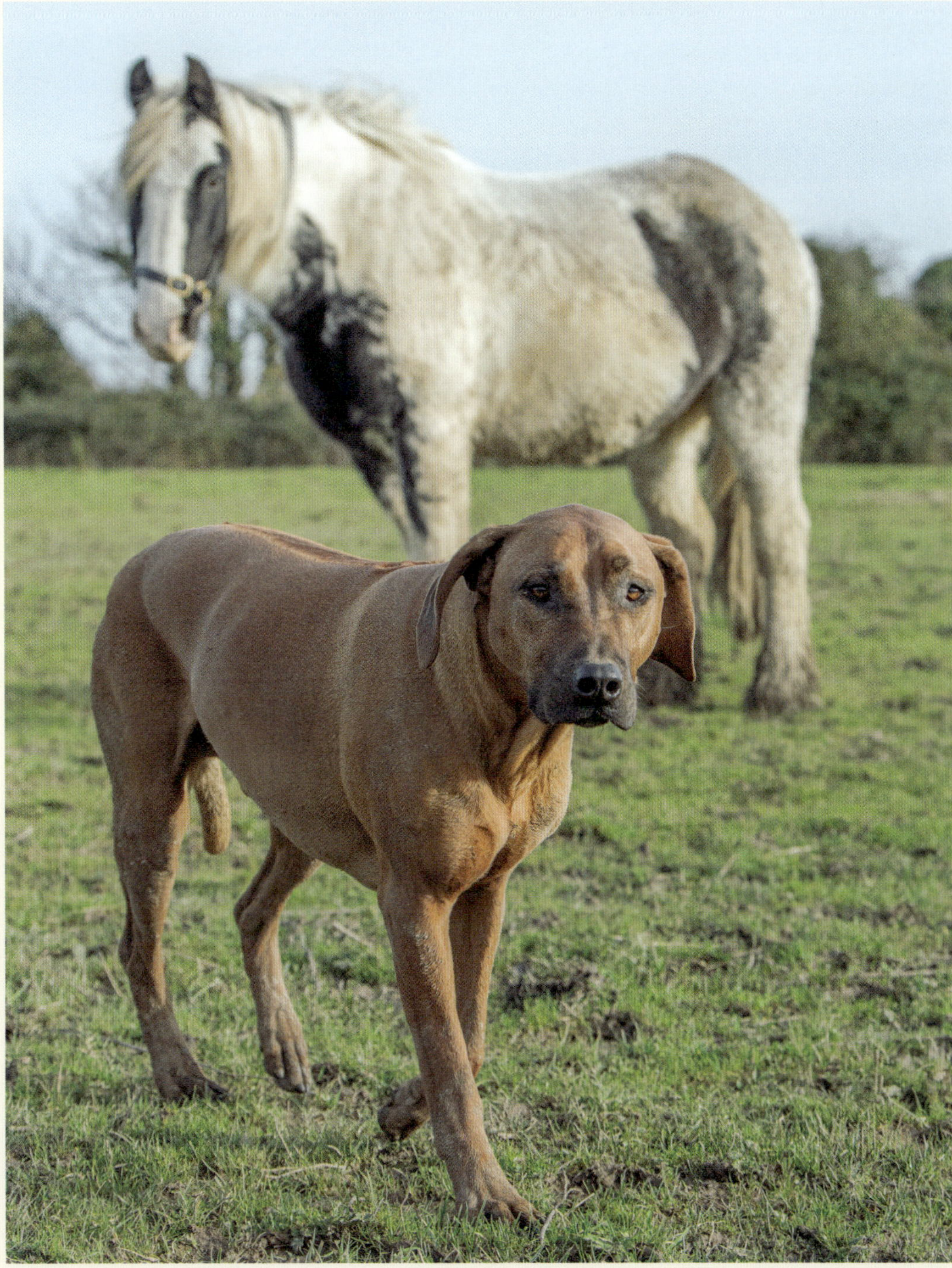

LEFT & ABOVE The Royal Stables is owned by Georgia Lillis, a wonderful human who uses her adoration of horses and dogs to promote kindness. She recognized the dogs' ability to work alongside horses during therapeutic sessions and found that some people are drawn to the dogs and make a deep connection with them.

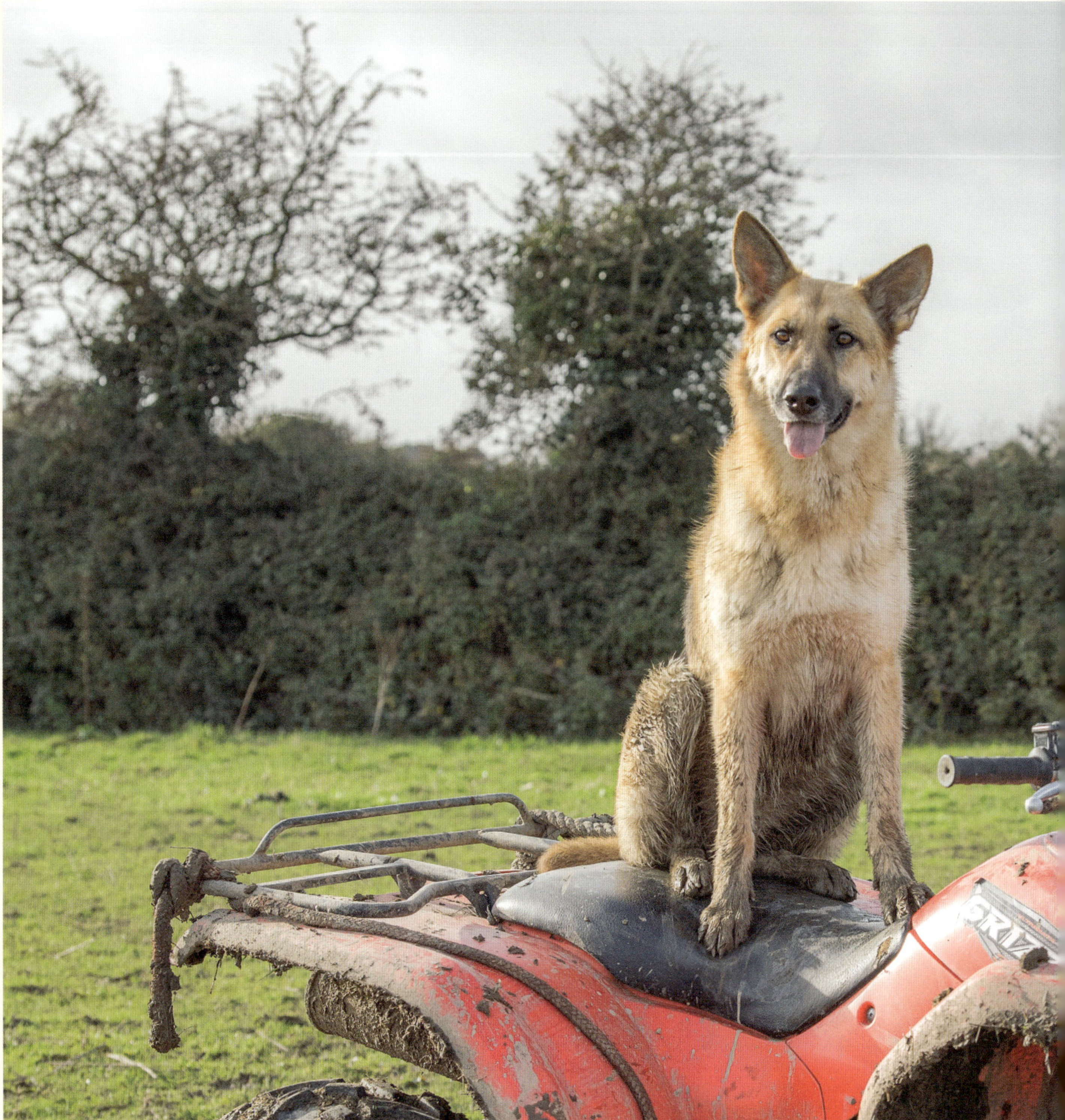

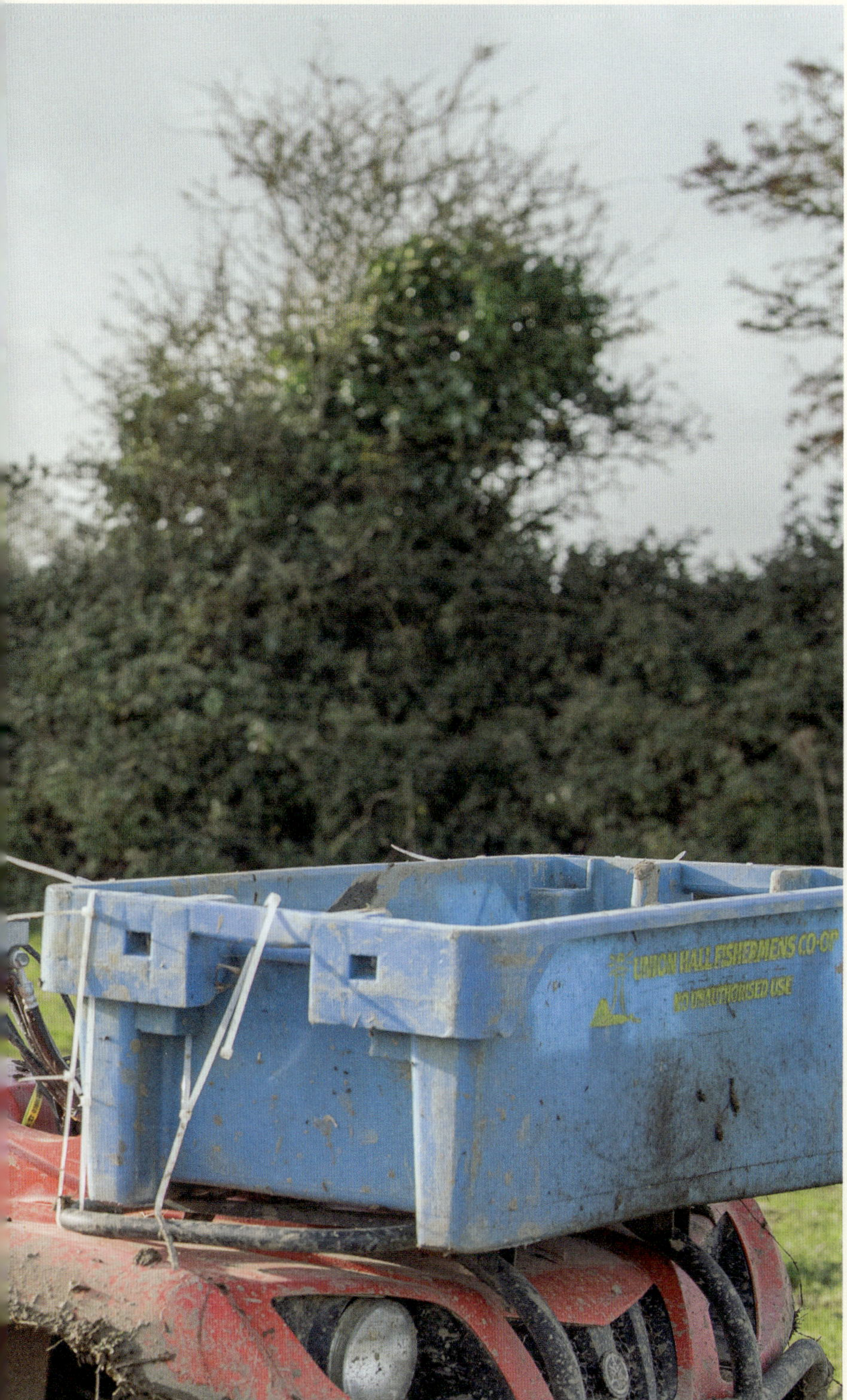

ABOVE & NEXT PAGE The beauty of Bruce and Robin's work is that they don't do anything completely out of the ordinary for a dog. They follow basic commands, coexist with the horses, and, most importantly, provide comfort merely through their presence. They also have plenty of fun running around the paddock with their equine pals.

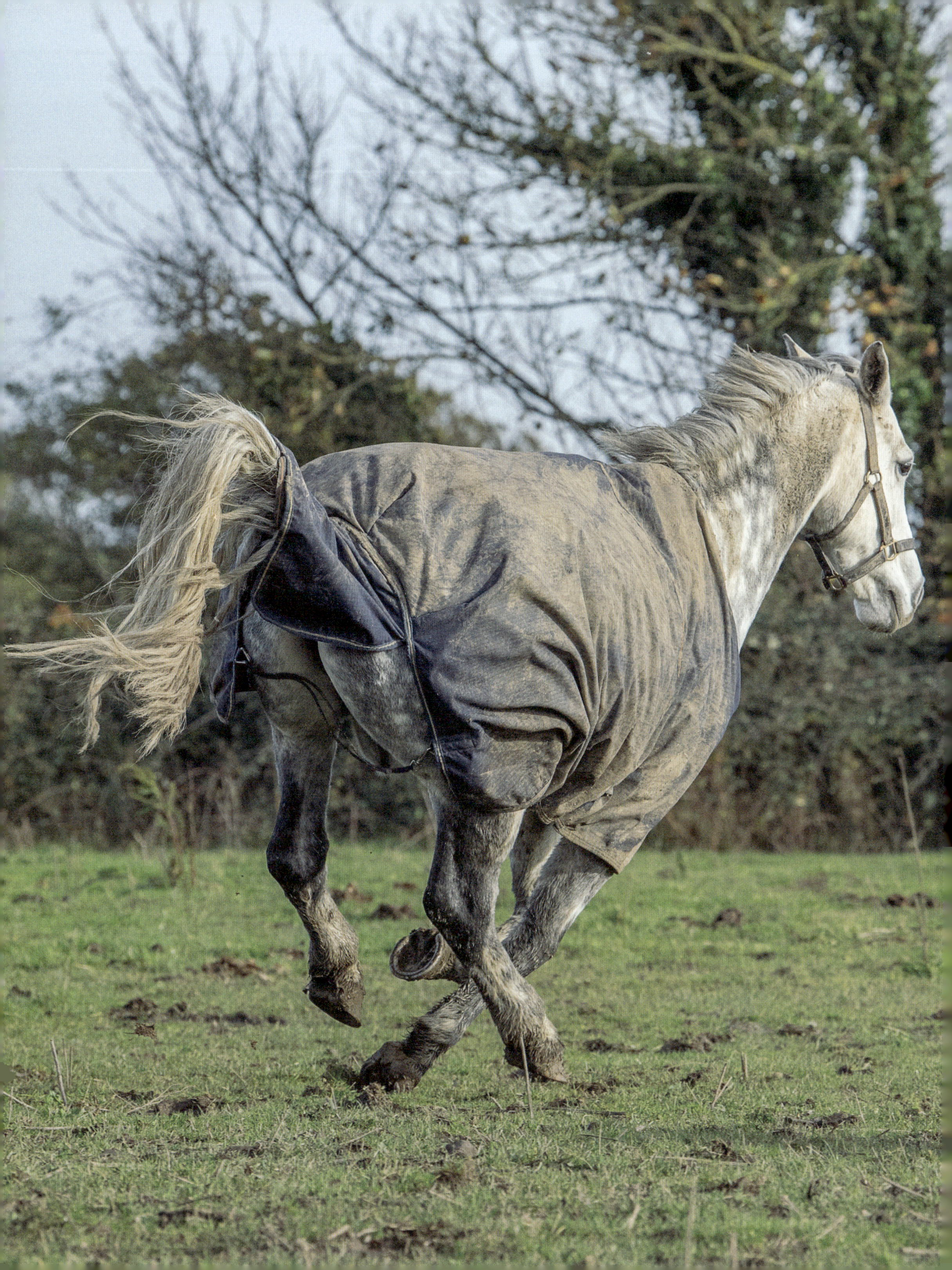

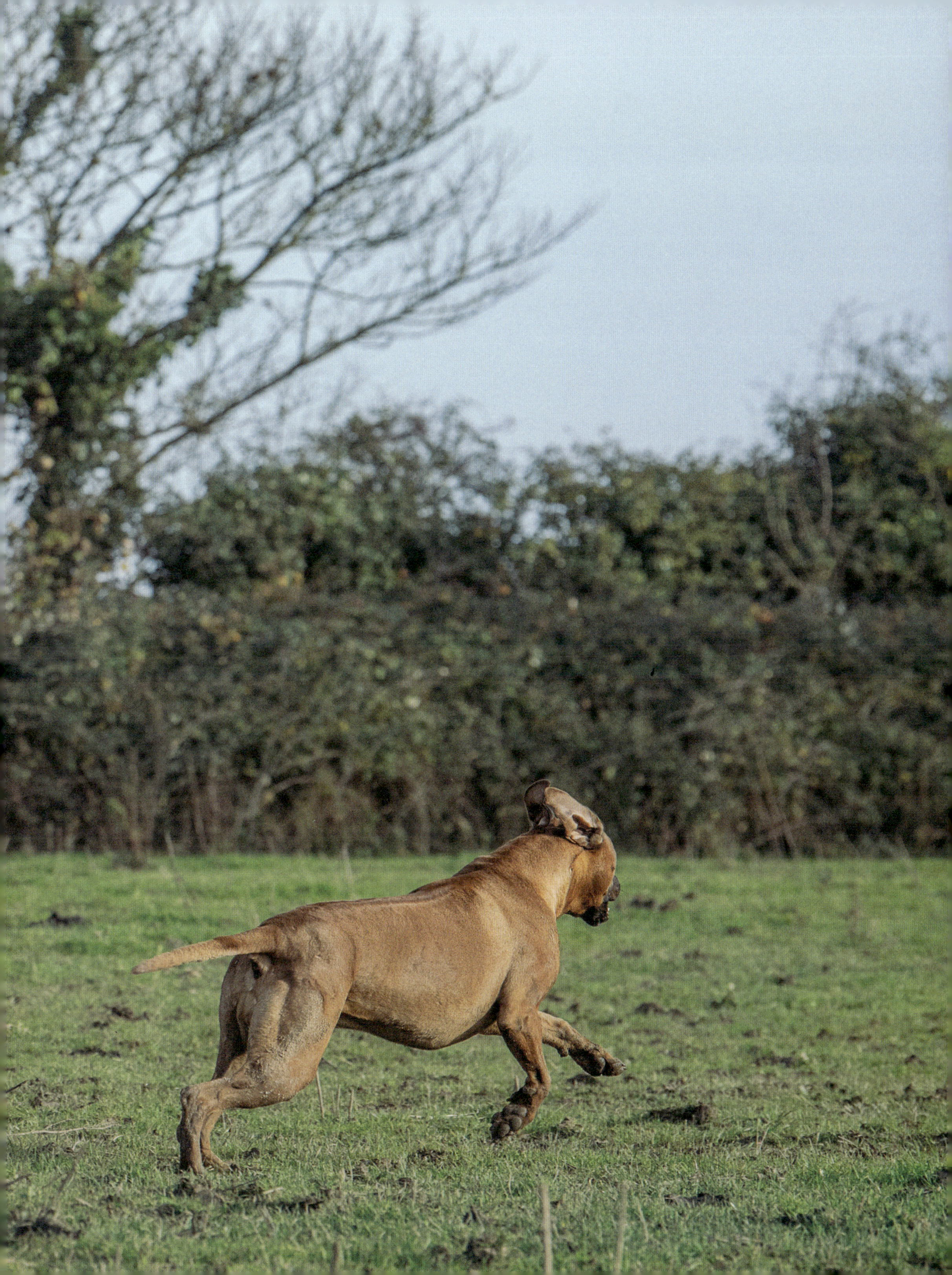

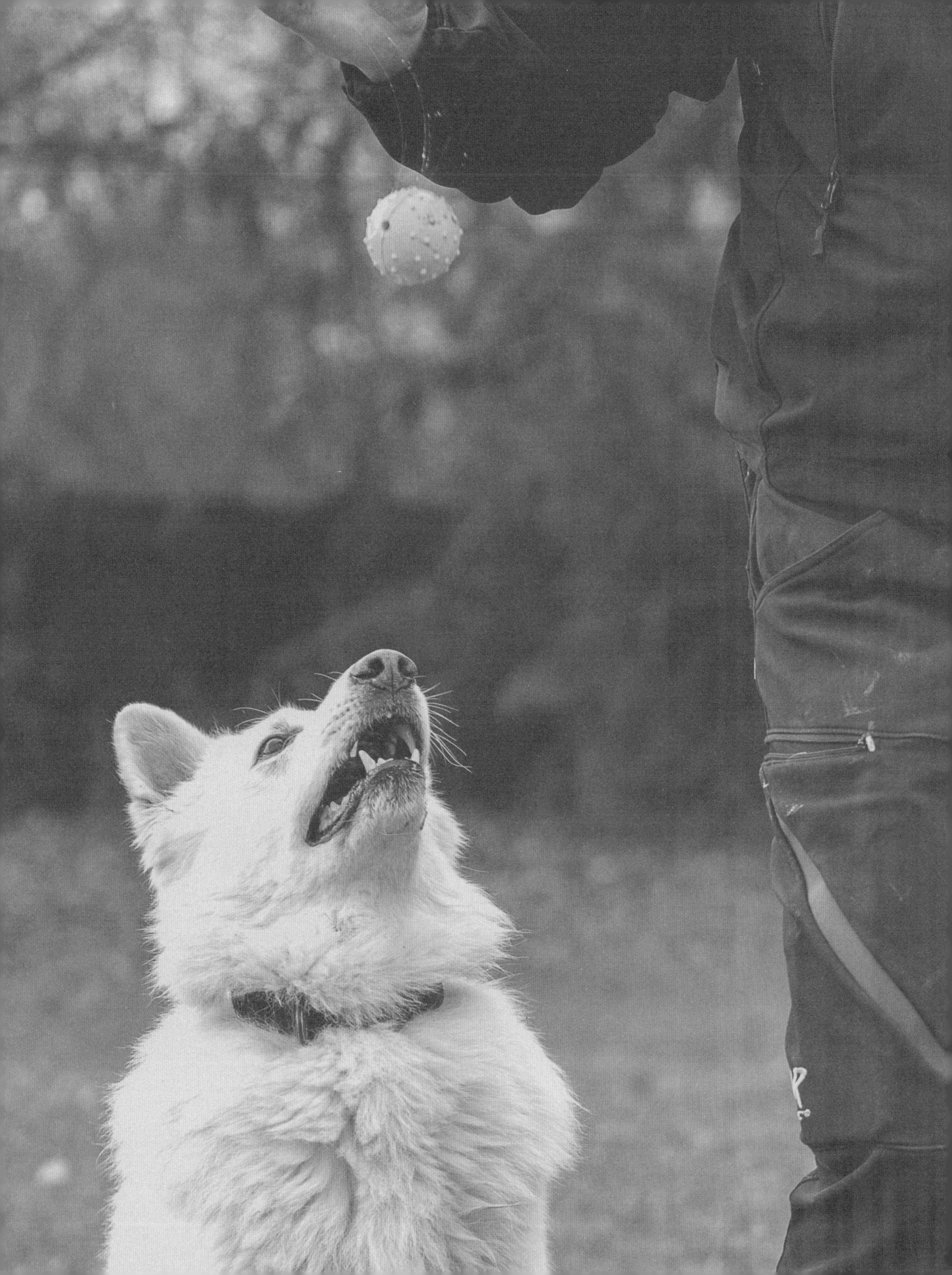

LOCATION	BREEDS	TASKS	SKILLS
Nuremberg, Germany	German Shepherd, White Swiss Shepherd, Doberman, and Schnauzer	Obeying, Tracking, Guarding	Memory, Obedience, Jaw Strength

WORKING DOG TRAINEES

PEOPLE OFTEN USE THE PHRASE "born to do this job," and for working dogs, that rings true. Working breeds have been bred with traits and instincts that allow them to excel at jobs including herding, guarding, and transportation. The high energy required for these tasks means that these dogs need mental and physical stimulation, so formal training is beneficial for both dog and owner. But like any worker, human or canine, it pays to have a good mentor, and that's where an experienced dog trainer makes a massive difference.

When I began traveling to photograph dogs, my first destination was Germany, and my first visit was to The Police and Protection Dog Club Nuremberg-West e.V. Founded in 1951, today the club stands for modern, practical dog training.

Specifically, it specializes in IGP Training (Internationale Gebrauchshundeprüfung Training), which highlights working breeds' abilities in tracking, obedience, and protection. This training can be used to hone skills for dogs who have actual jobs, like police dogs, or for those whose owners work with them as a hobby.

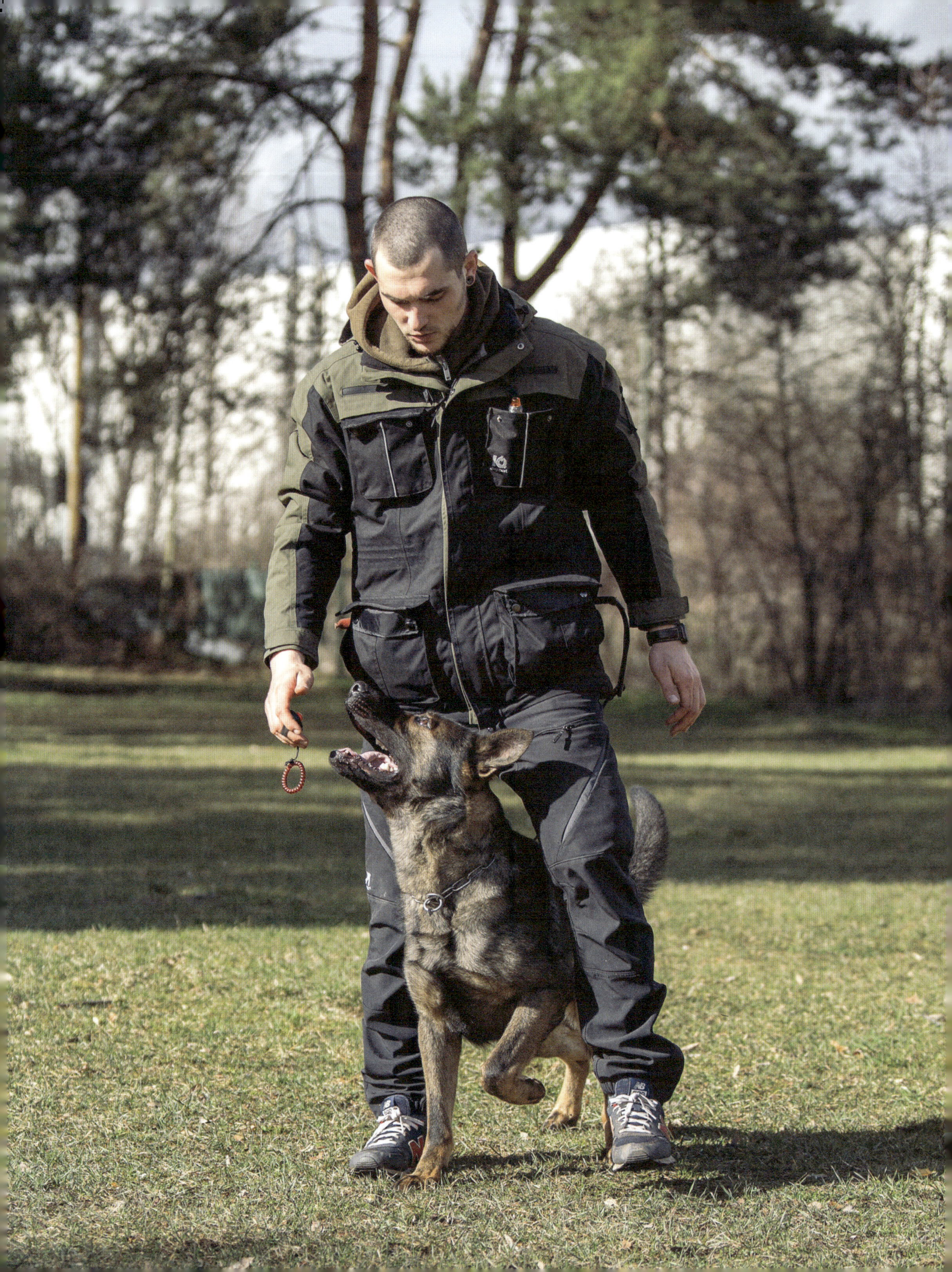

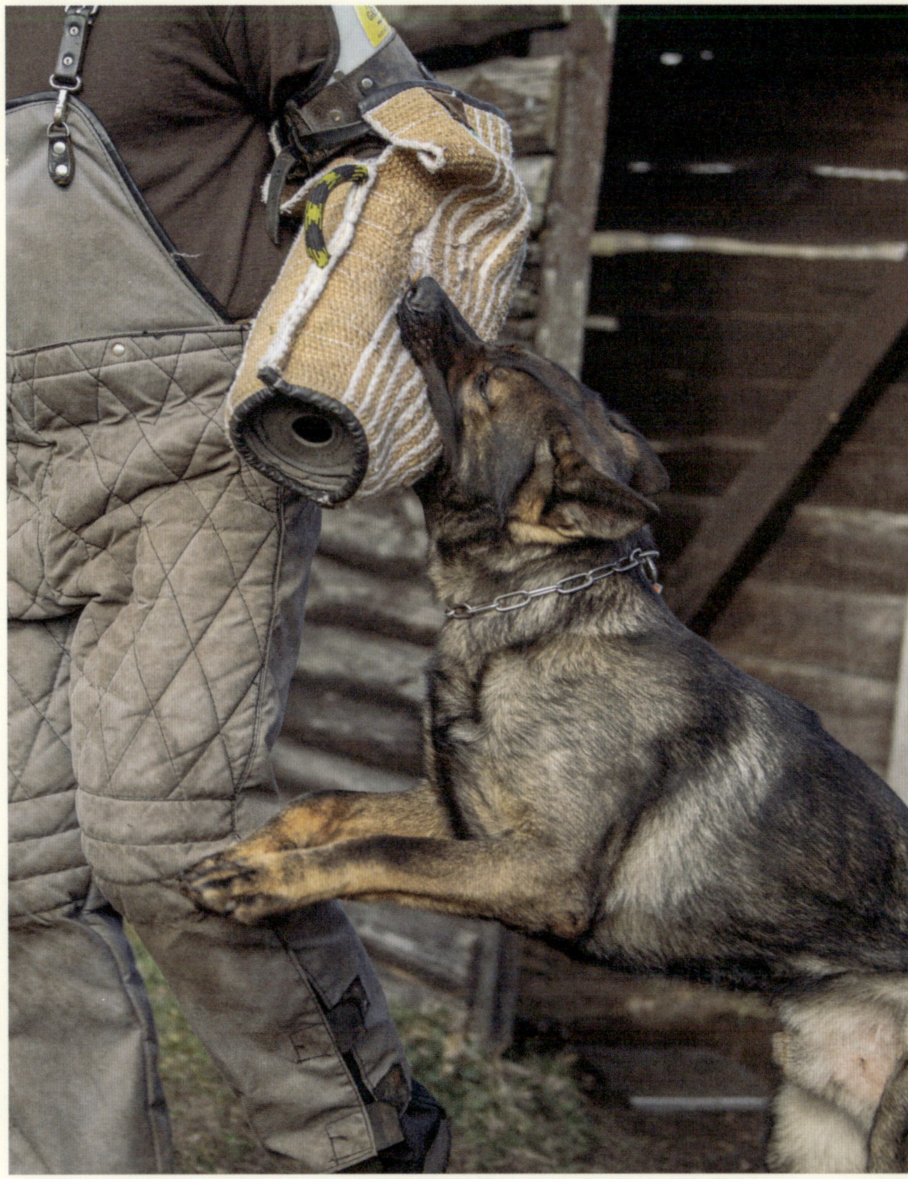

105

LEFT The First Chairman of the club, Dominic Götz has a deep appreciation for working dogs and their capabilities. For both sport and obedience training, he provides expert guidance, fair training conditions, and a strong community where teamwork and passion for the sport come first.

ABOVE Bitework was fun for everyone – the trainers, the dogs, and especially the dog photographer, who had never seen this type of work up close. The bitework photos and videos that captivate the internet can be a bit misleading; it sometimes appears that dogs are recklessly attacking and biting trainers, but the reality is much more controlled and intentional.

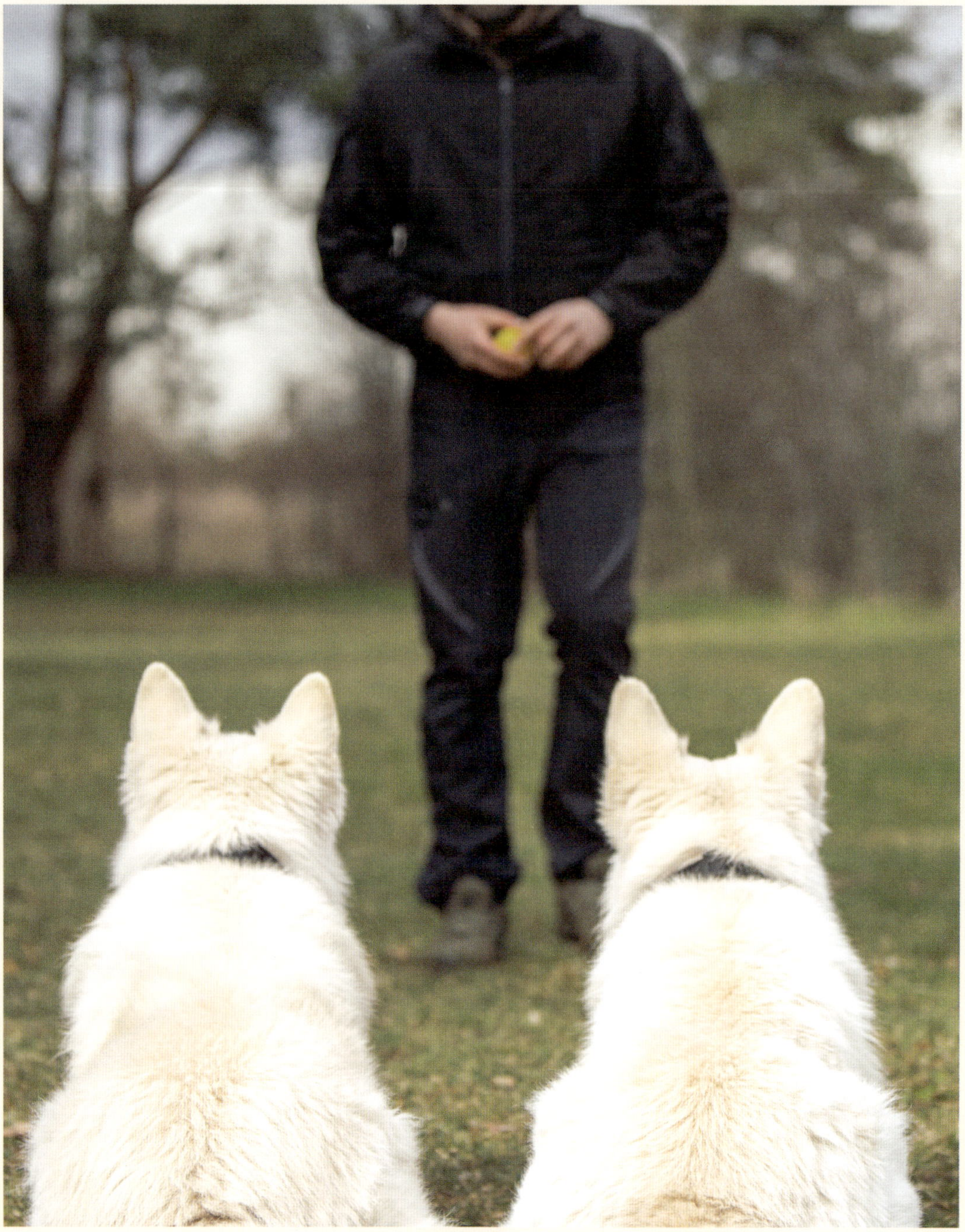

ABOVE & RIGHT In any effective training, there is a prize at the end for the dog. Do a good job? Get the reward. For these matching White Swiss Shepherds, their reward of choice was a rubber ball. They followed commands with eyes locked until their owner released the balls and let them play.

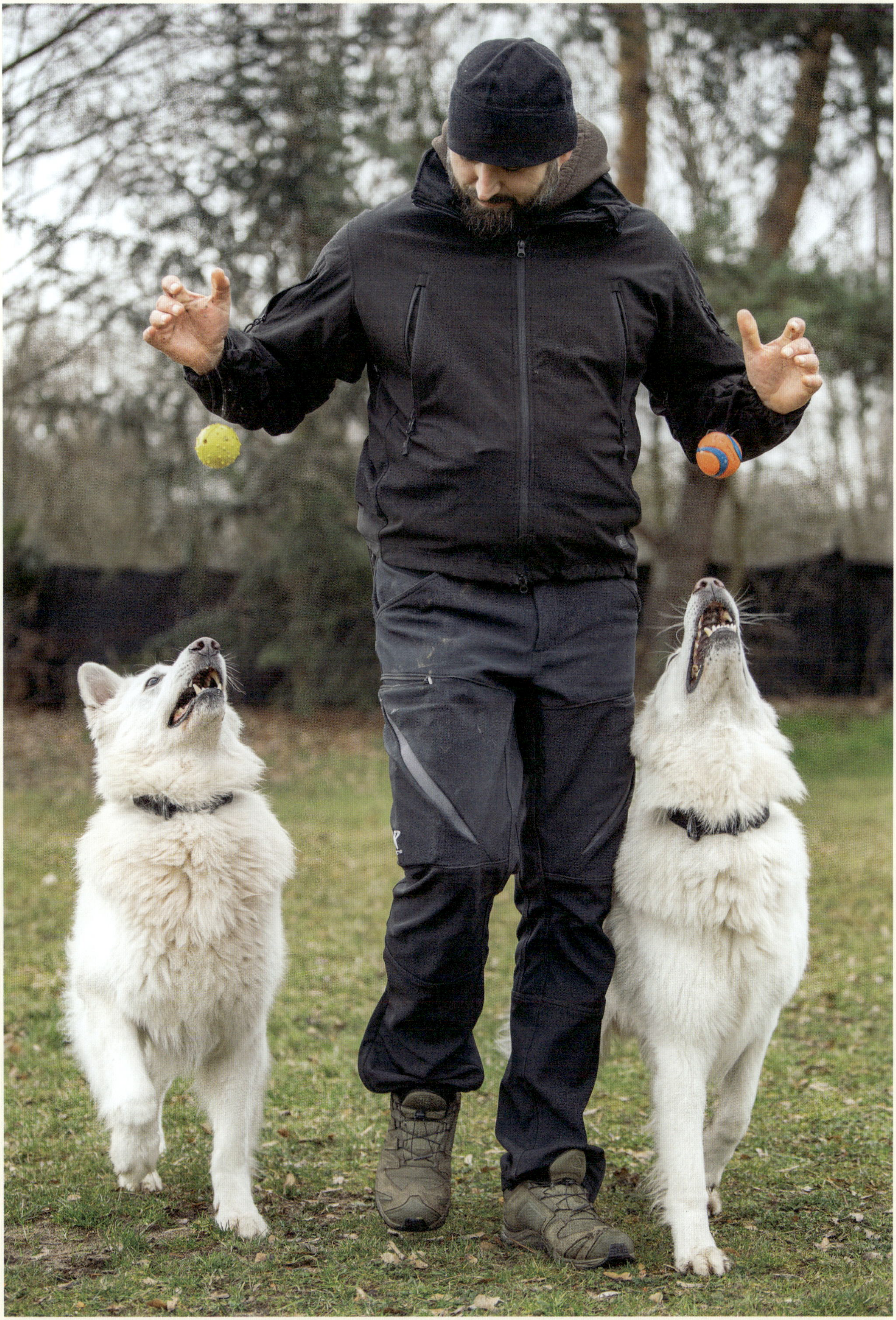

BELOW LEFT & RIGHT Owners and working dogs act as a unit during training sessions. I hadn't brushed up on my German dog training terminology prior to this photoshoot, but it wasn't hard to understand the commands. With just a single, quick word, the dogs would immediately take their position next to, or between the legs of, their owners. The two would walk in lockstep with the dog's eyes often looking up, fixated on their owner, waiting for the next command.

RIGHT Dominic's training journey started with his Doberman, Ulysse di Altobello. He unfortunately passed away in 2024, but he helped Dominic hone his training skills and left a lasting, positive impression on everyone who worked with him.

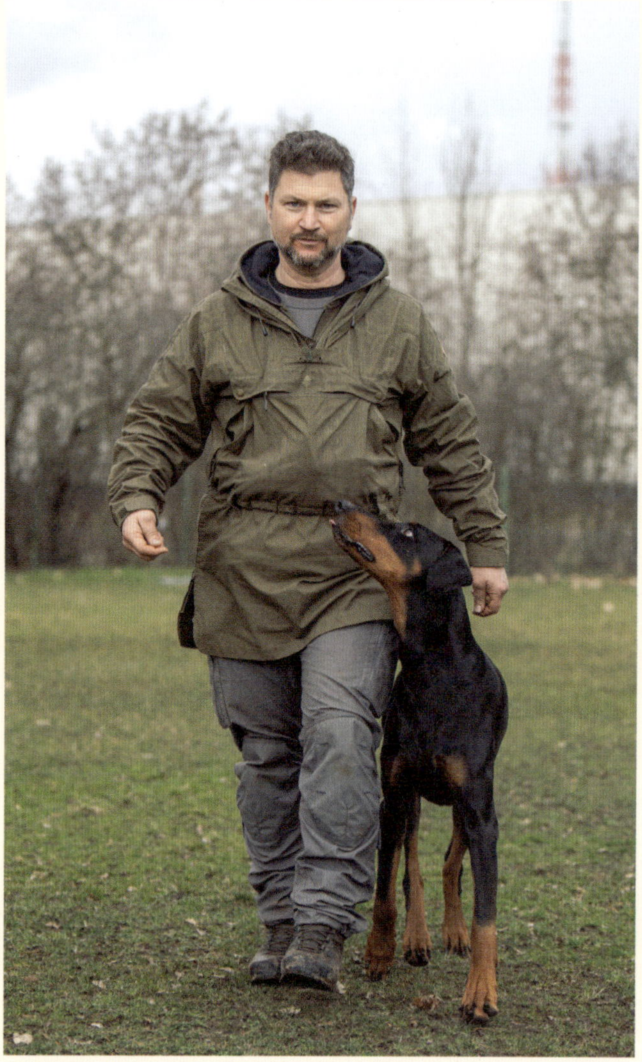

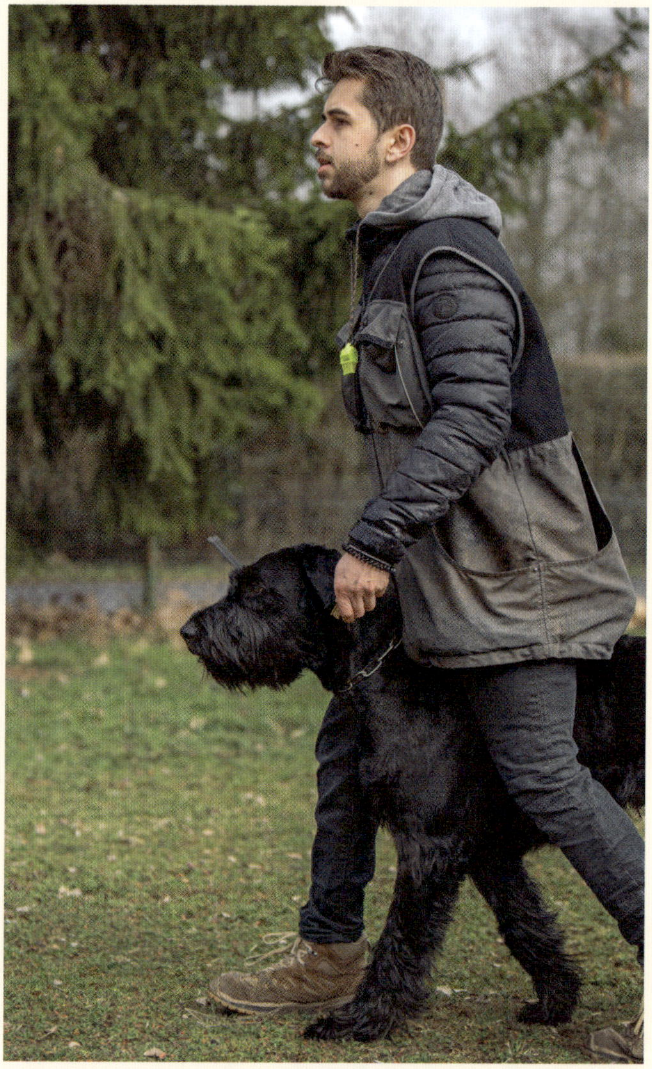

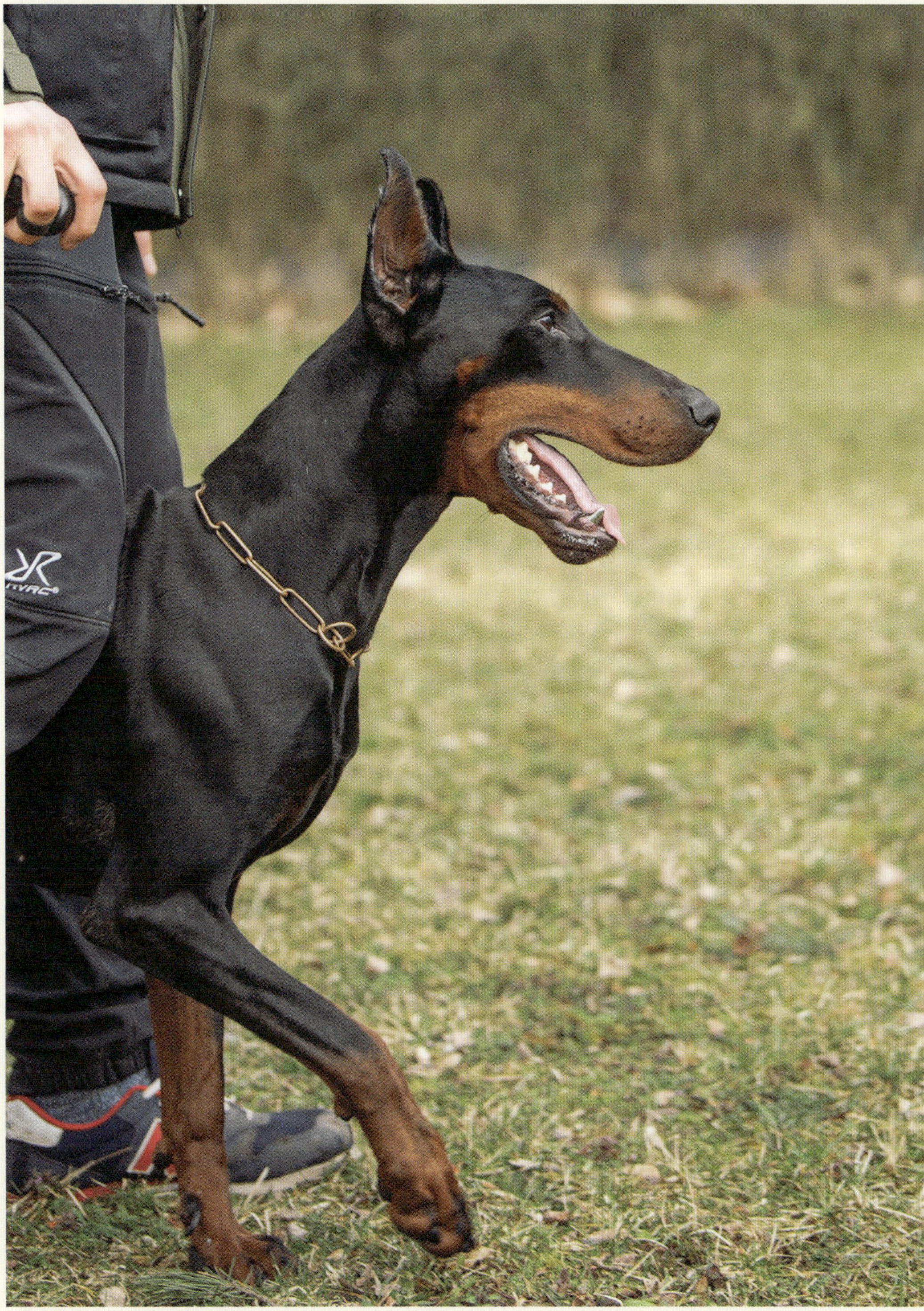

109

There is a sense of excitement for the dogs as soon as they see the bite sleeve or suit – they know they are going to put those jaws to work.

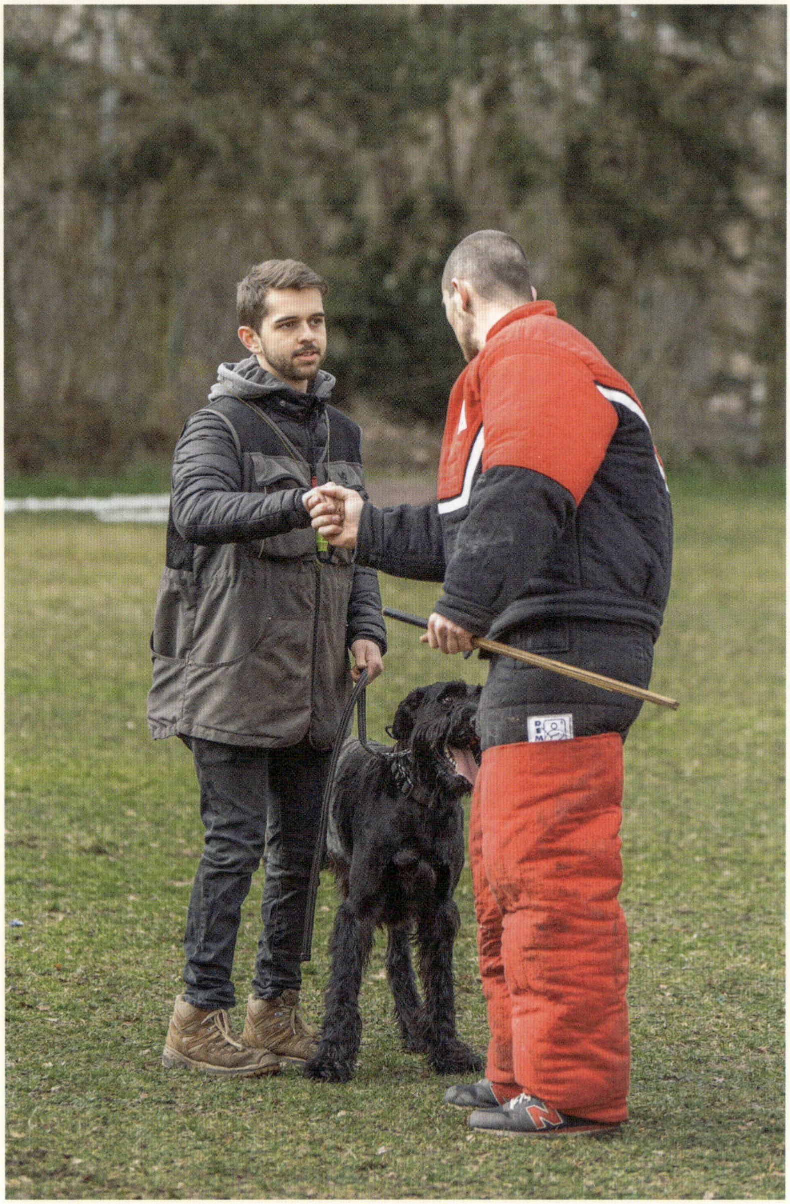

ABOVE There is a sense of excitement for the dogs as soon as they see the bite sleeve or suit – they know they are going to put those jaws to work. They've been trained to only latch onto the bitework gear, and only once the command is given. Here, the trainers started the session by shaking hands and seemed to make an agreement along the lines of, "My Schnauzer is going to bite you as soon as I tell him to." "Okay, deal."

RIGHT Once the dog latches on, that grip isn't letting up for anything other than the command to release. Dominic could calmly pet the dog's head without any worry that his hand would get bitten, since these dogs are only trained to bite the suit. After seeing this, I couldn't leave without giving it a try. The guys let me put on a jacket and we gave a German dog a bite of American meat.

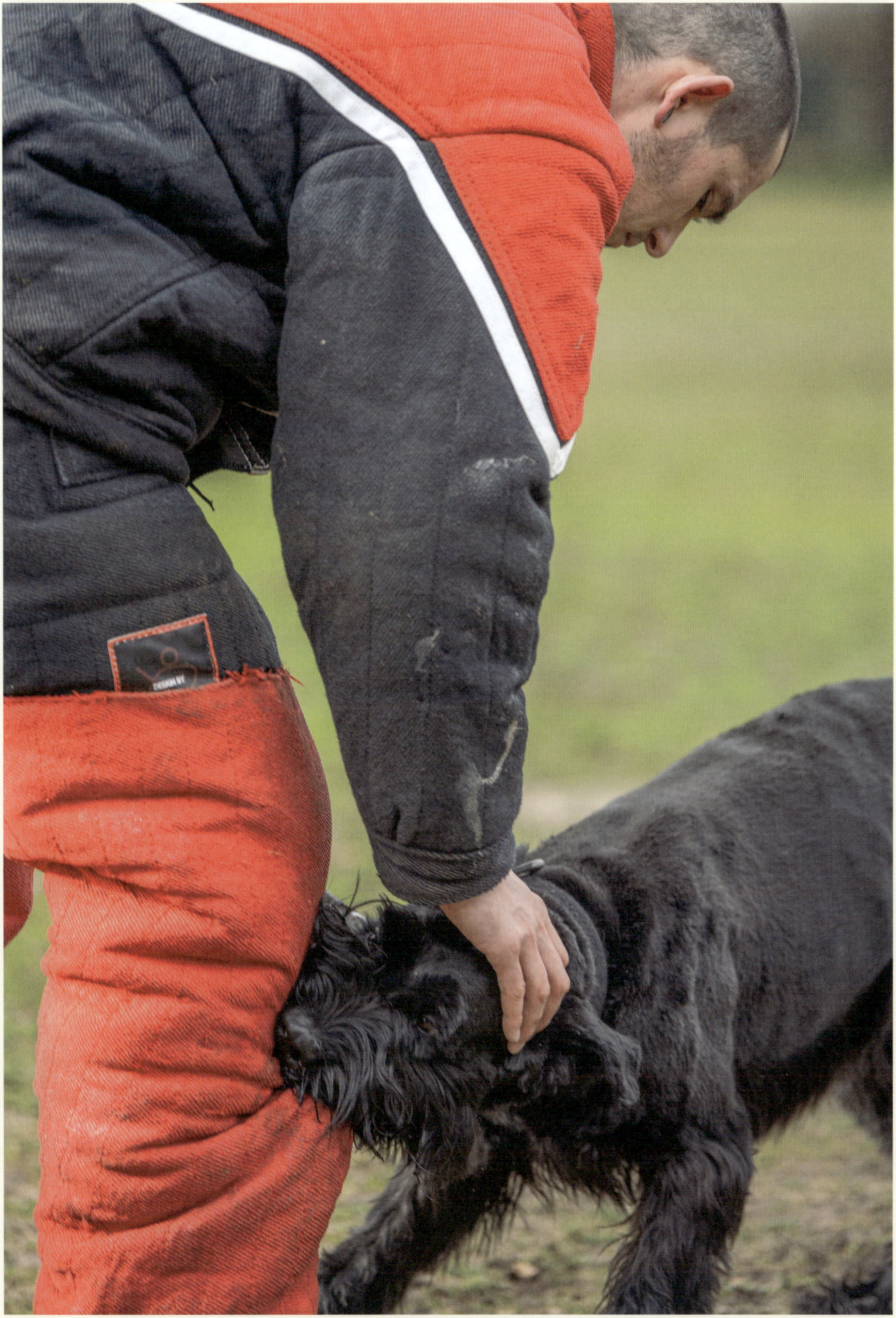

111

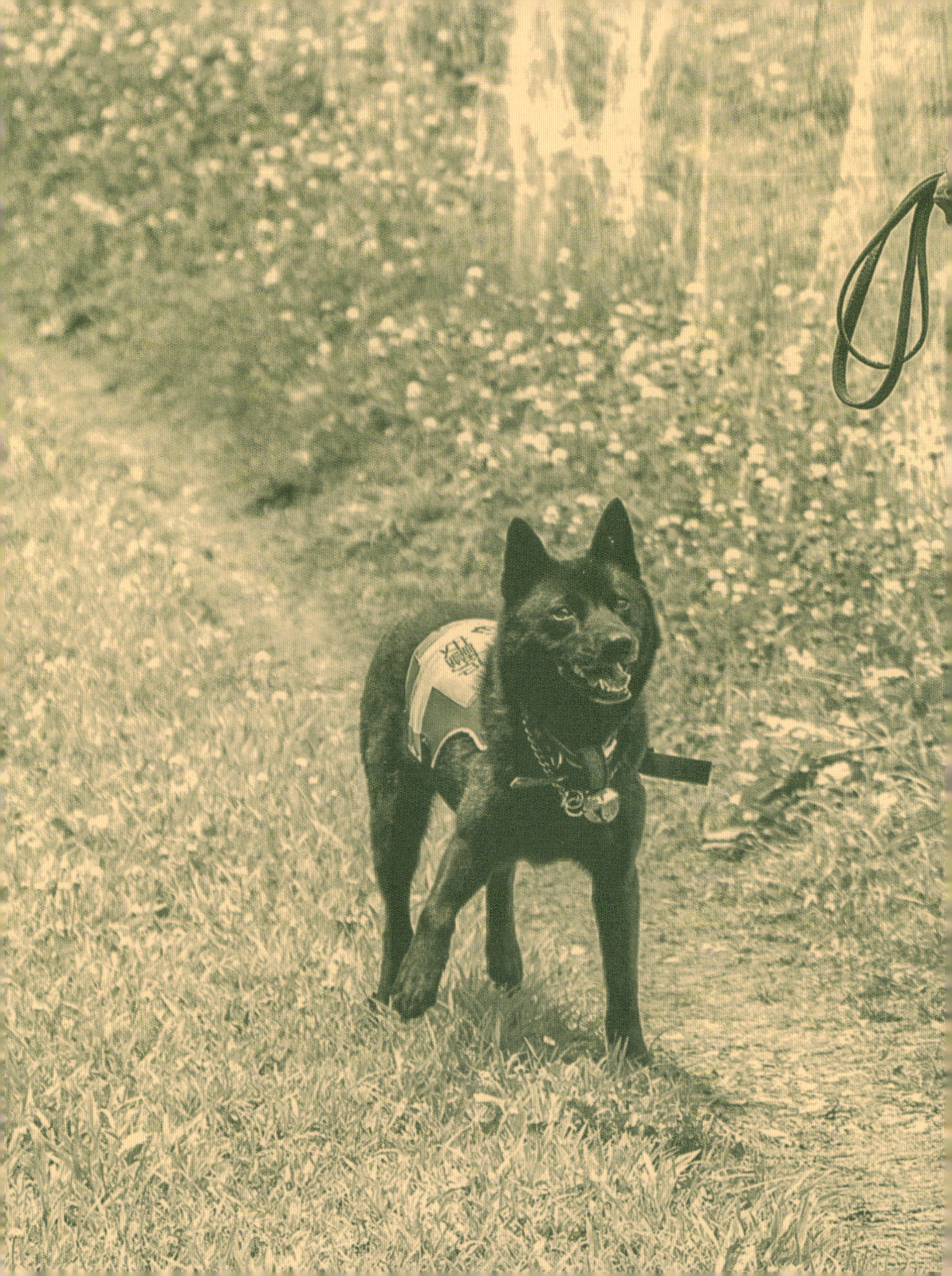

LOCATION	BREEDS	TASKS	SKILLS
Azumino, Japan	Border Collie and Kai Ken	Chasing, Intimidating, Guarding	Drive, Speed, Recall

MONKEY DOGS

AZUMINO IS A RURAL, farming community in Japan's Nagano Prefecture. In this town, there is an intelligent nuisance that loves to feast on crops: monkeys. In addition to running a dog-training school, Takahiro Isomoto works for a number of farmers who hire him, and his dogs, to chase monkeys away from their properties.

Mr. Isomoto owns a Border Collie and a Kai Ken. He described the latter as fearless, which gives the dog a good temperament to chase after monkeys. But Mr. Isomoto made it clear that there is no intention for the dogs and monkeys to engage in any physical altercation, which is why his dogs have elite recall skills. Their only goal is to chase the monkeys away from the properties where they appear.

Border Collies are revered workers all over the world, while the Kai Ken breed is native to Japan. They were traditionally used as hunting dogs, so they have a strong prey drive. Protective and fiercely loyal to their owners, they are highly trainable as workers.

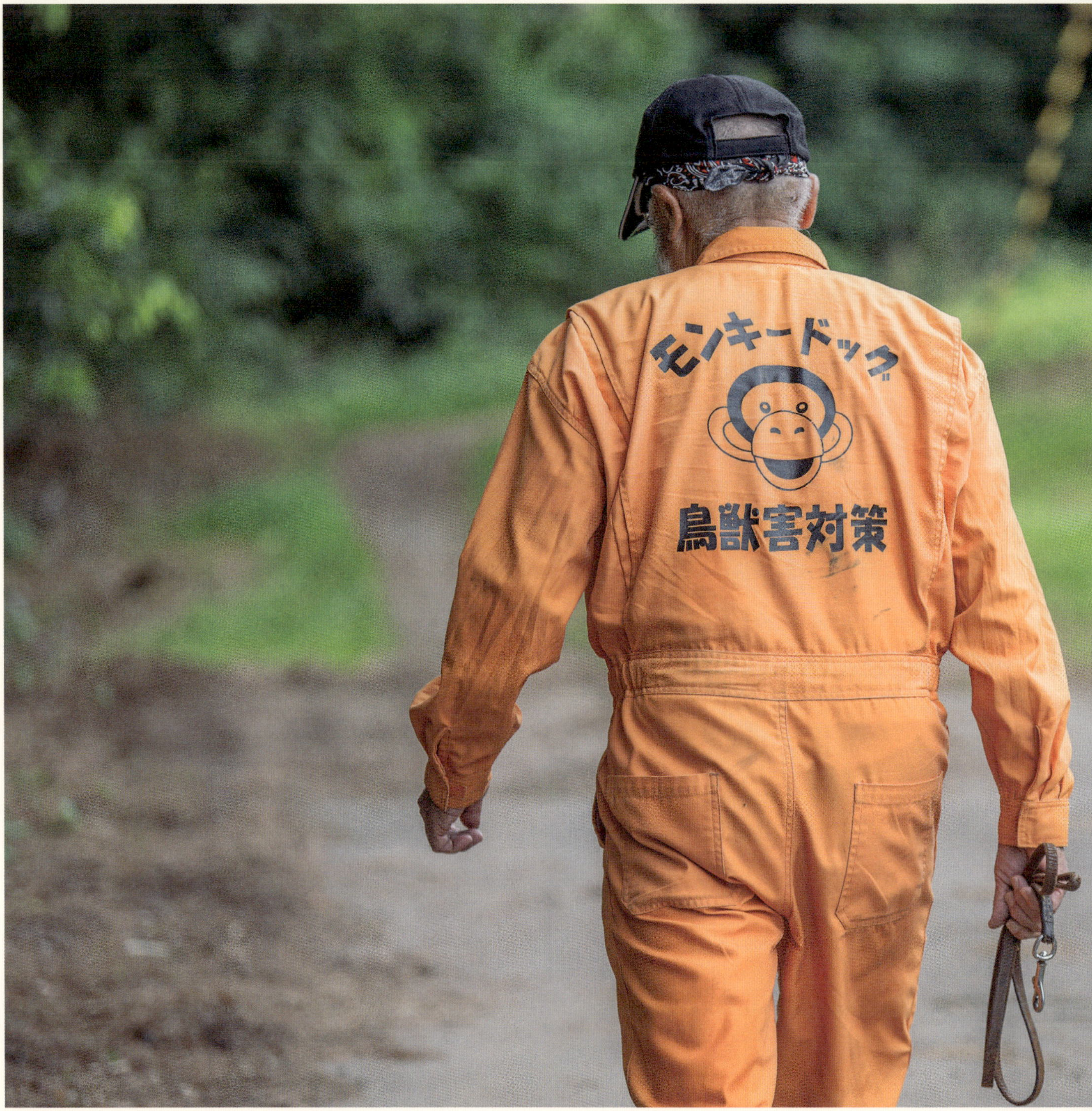
モンキードッグ
鳥獣害対策

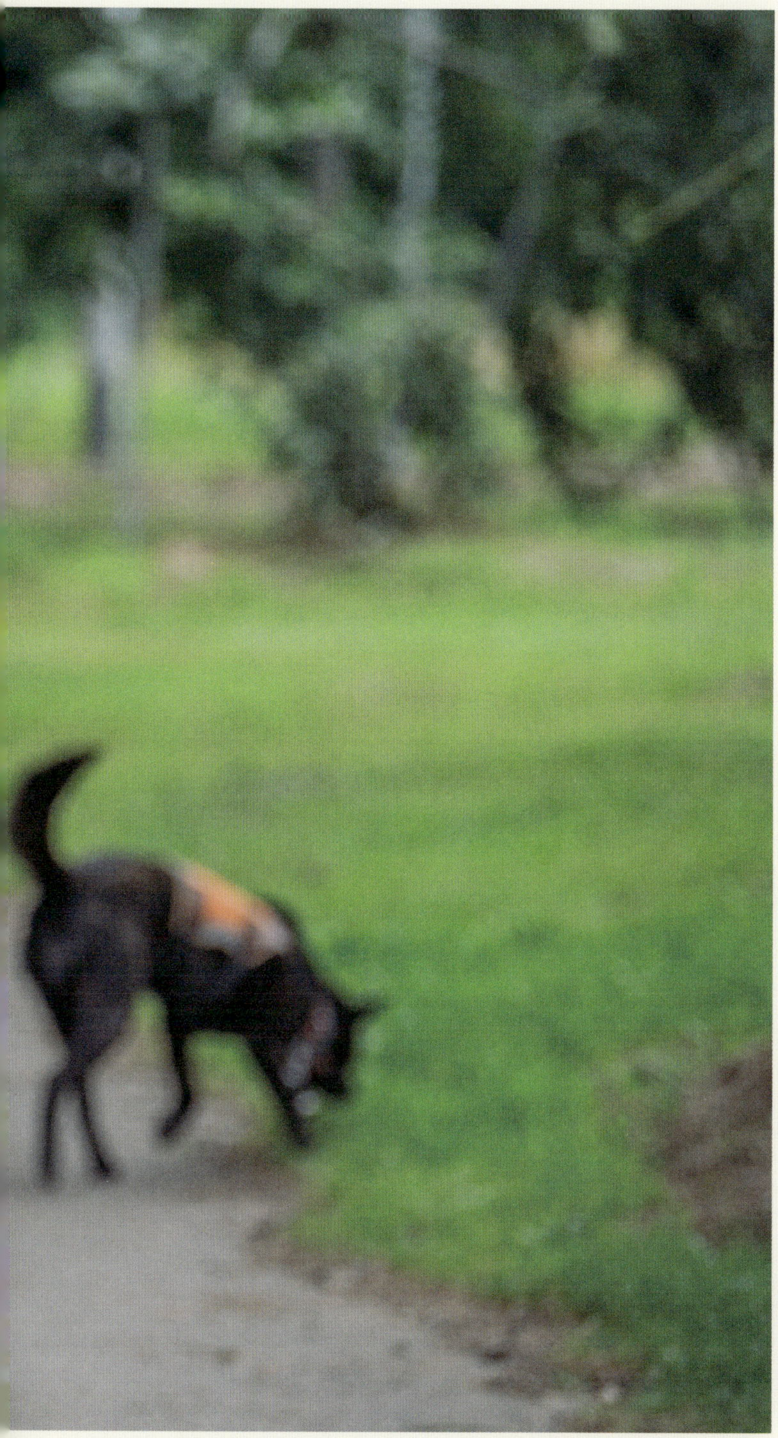

ABOVE Mr. Isomoto took me to different areas where there had been monkey sightings, including a farm. While there, he showed me remnants of crops that had been eaten by monkeys. The monkeys were not on the property when we arrived, but Mr. Isomoto still surveyed the area with his dog.

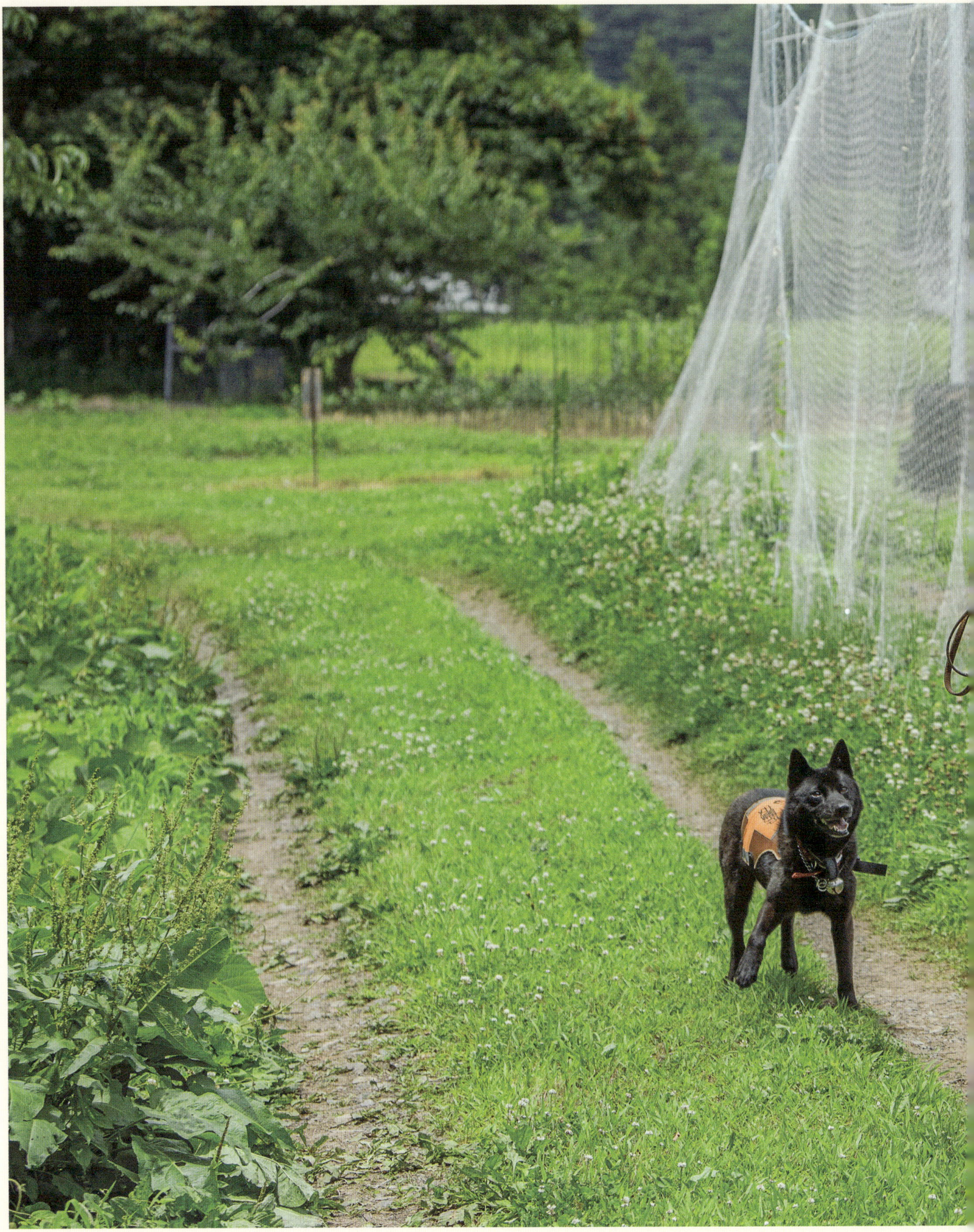

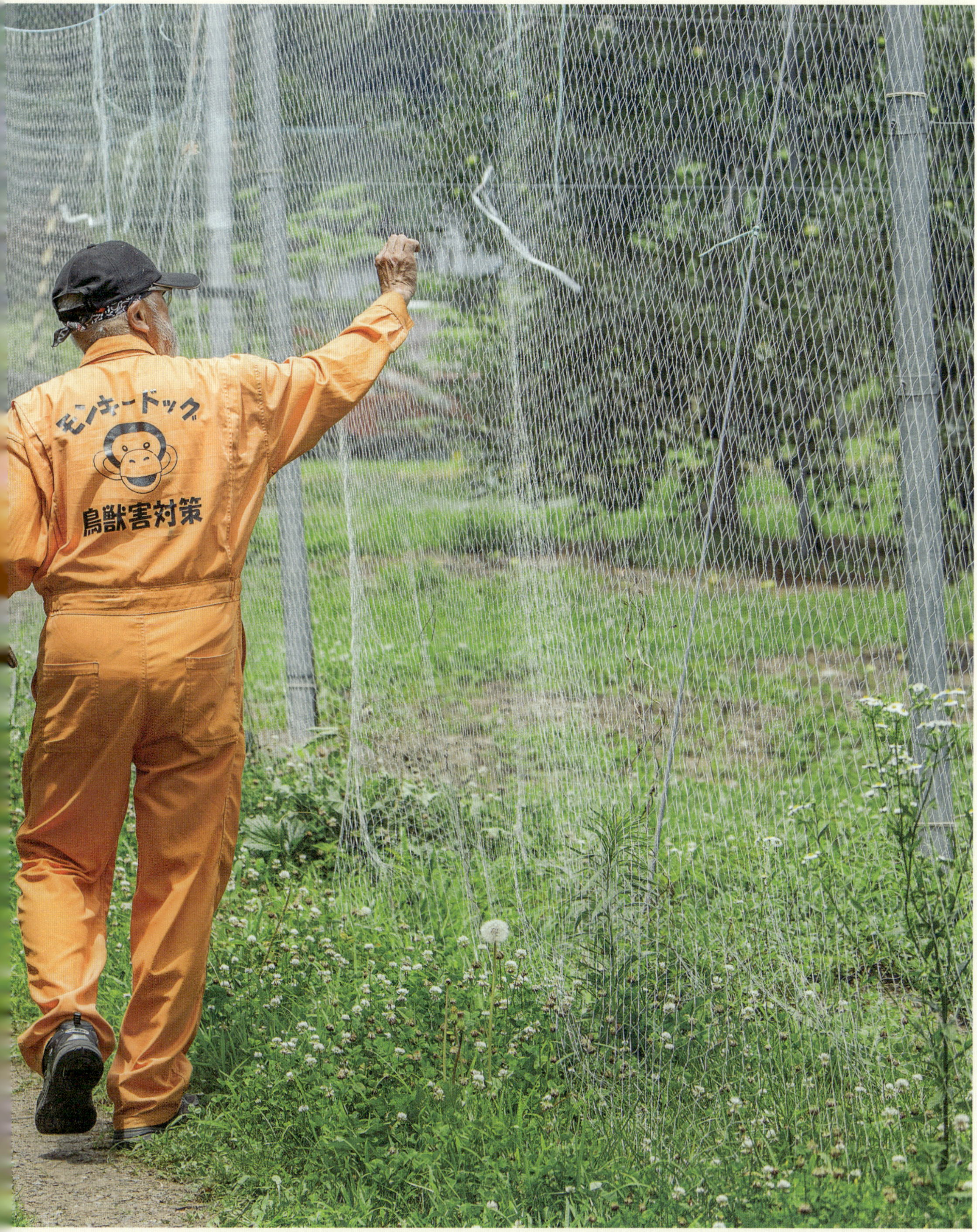

ABOVE Dog hair is spread around the property to leave the scent of dogs around the crops. Mr. Isomoto also provided a bag of dog hair to this farmer to spread around his crops to protect them at a later date.

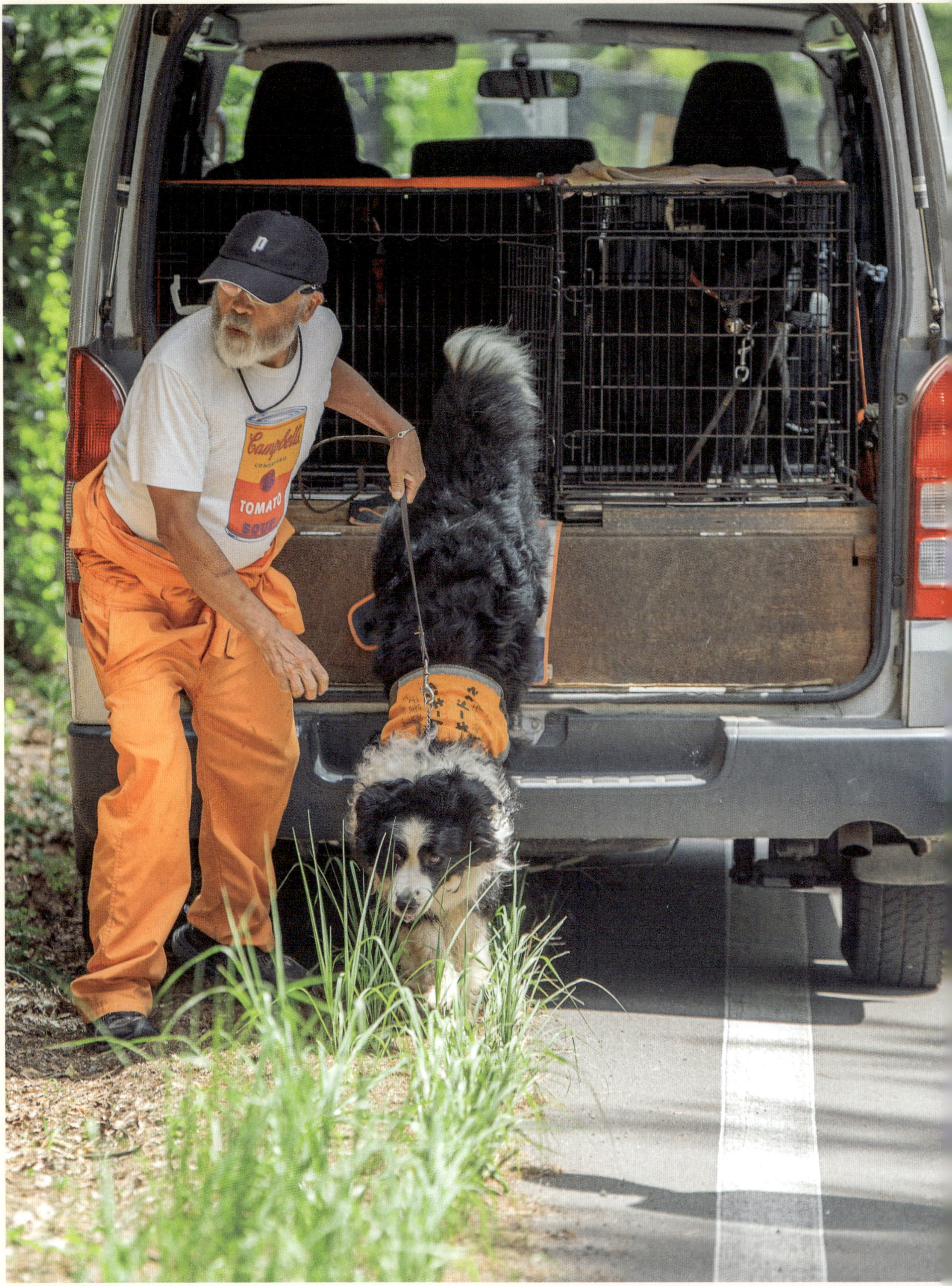
Campbell's
TOMATO

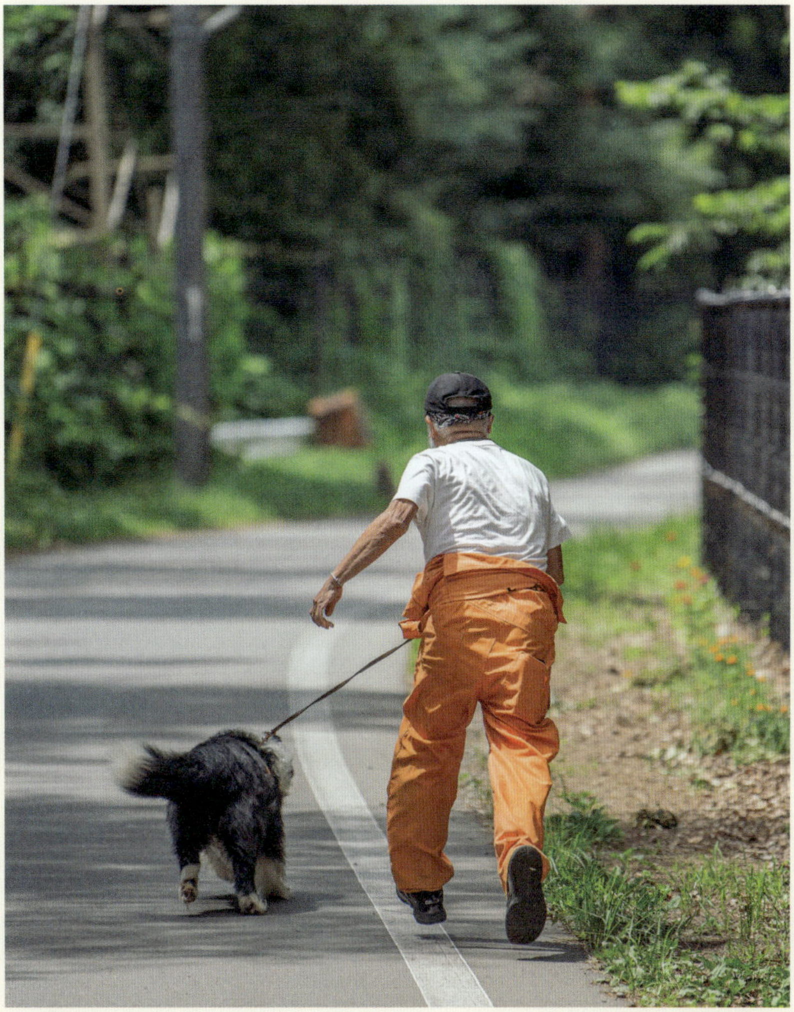

LEFT Monkeys are smart, and the local ones recognize this signature orange jumpsuit. In order to show me how his dogs work, Mr. Isomoto pulled the top of his jumpsuit down in an attempt to hide from the monkeys, but they quickly noticed him and started running toward the river.

ABOVE Mr. Isomoto is in great shape and full of enthusiasm. He took off toward the monkeys along with his Collie and ran up the street until every last monkey made its way into the forest. Once the coast was clear, Mr. Isomoto set off fireworks as a final deterrent. He knows that if farmers catch any monkeys, they are likely to kill them, so his role is important to keep the two parties away from each other.

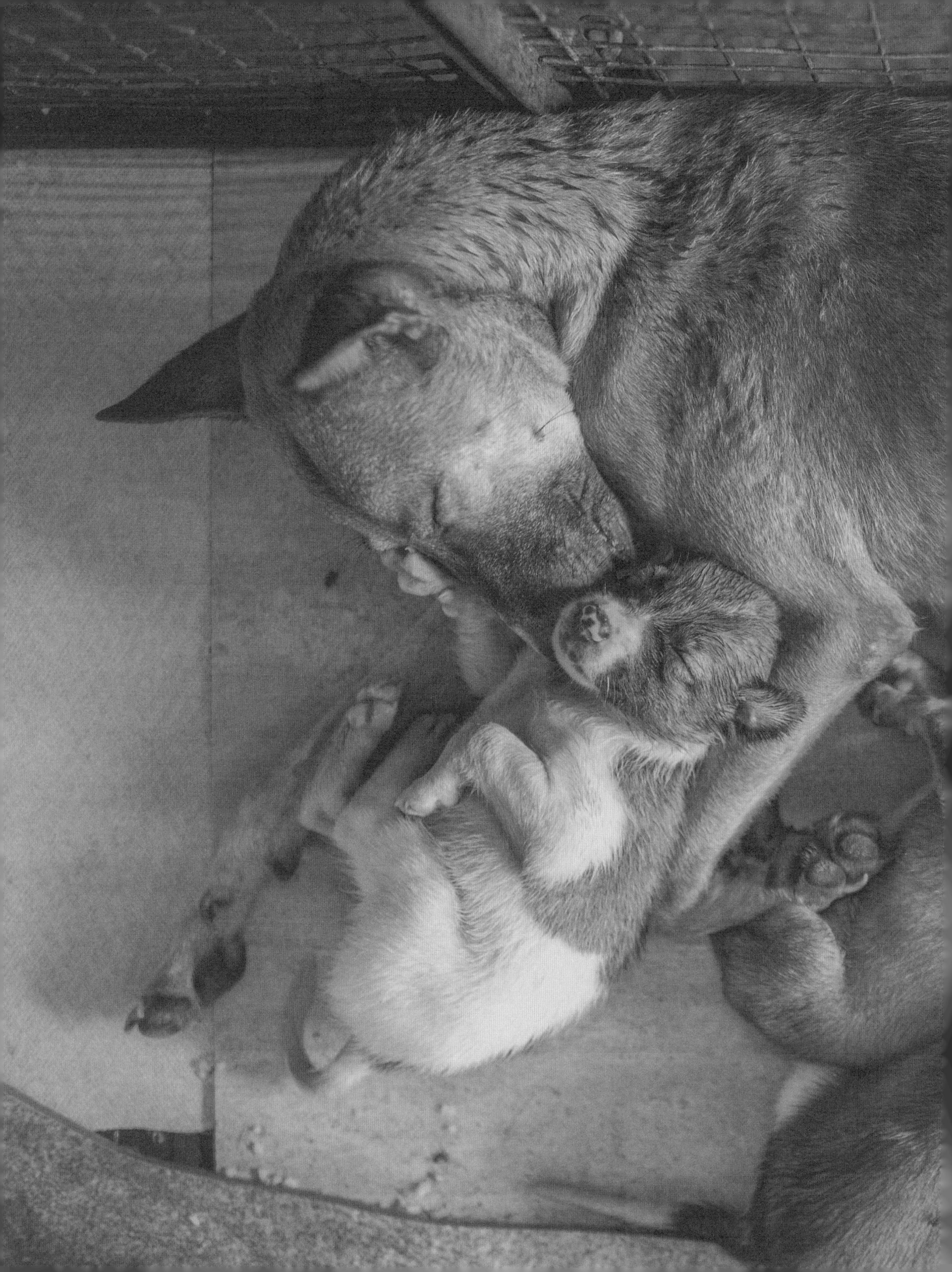

LOCATION	BREEDS	TASKS	SKILLS
Ireland, India, Germany, and Japan	Indian Street Dog, Labrador, German Shepherd, and Shiba Inu	Feeding Guarding Puppies, Educating	Love, Guidance, Protection

MOTHER DOGS

EVERYONE KNOWS THAT being a mother is perhaps the hardest job in the world, and that is certainly true for dogs. After all, let's be honest about dogs dads: They're deadbeats. Dog dads are long gone by the time the pups are born, leaving mother dogs to raise the kids on their own. Minding even one puppy is hard enough, and dogs multiply that by the size of their litters.

In my travels, I have come across many mother dogs. Some were bred for their puppies, while others were rescues given care and support as they raised their offspring. The common thread among them all: They were a force, willing to do anything for their pups.

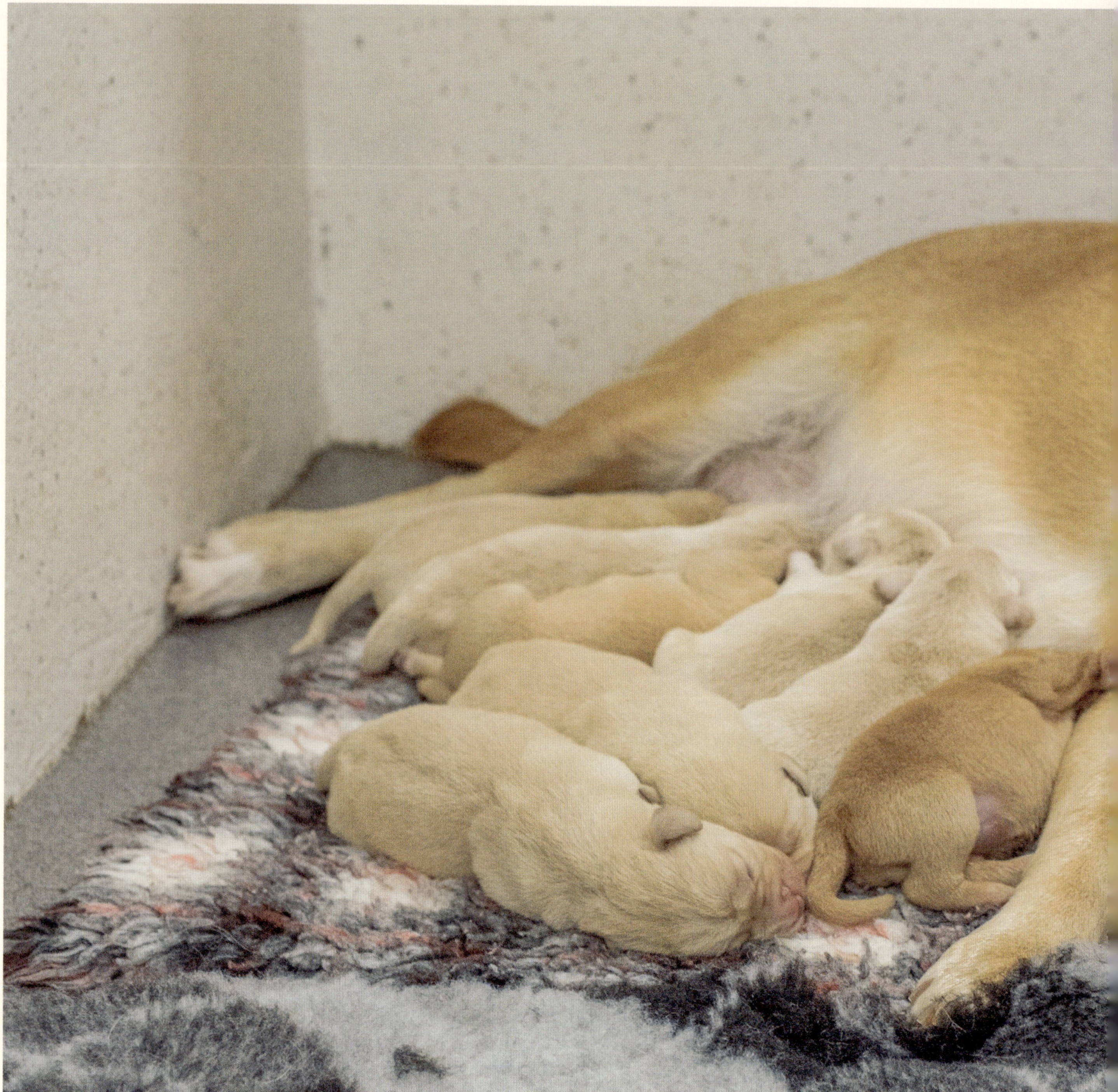

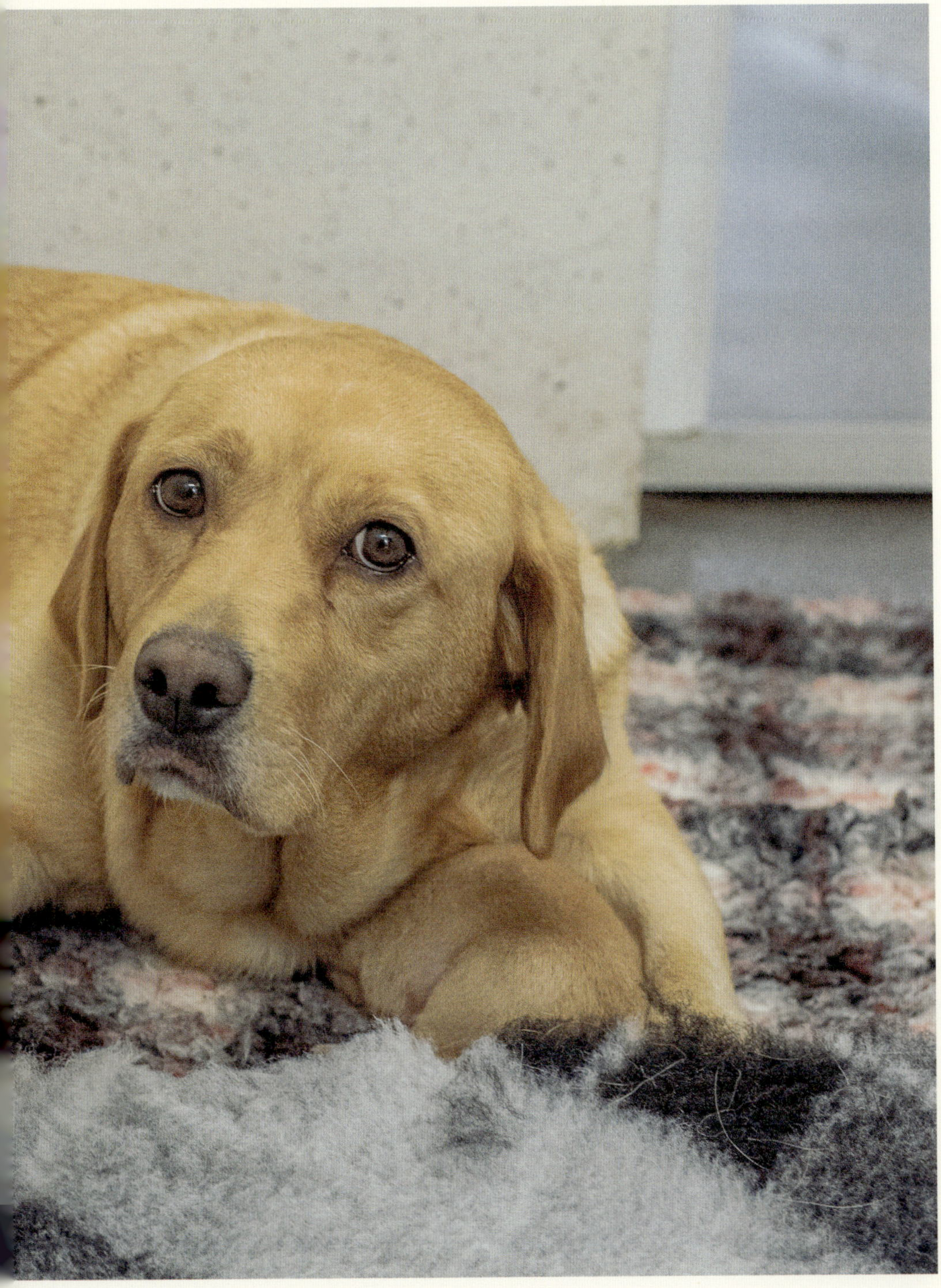

ABOVE I could feel the pure exhaustion behind the eyes of this mother at Limerick Animal Welfare in Ireland. That's a lot of mouths to feed.

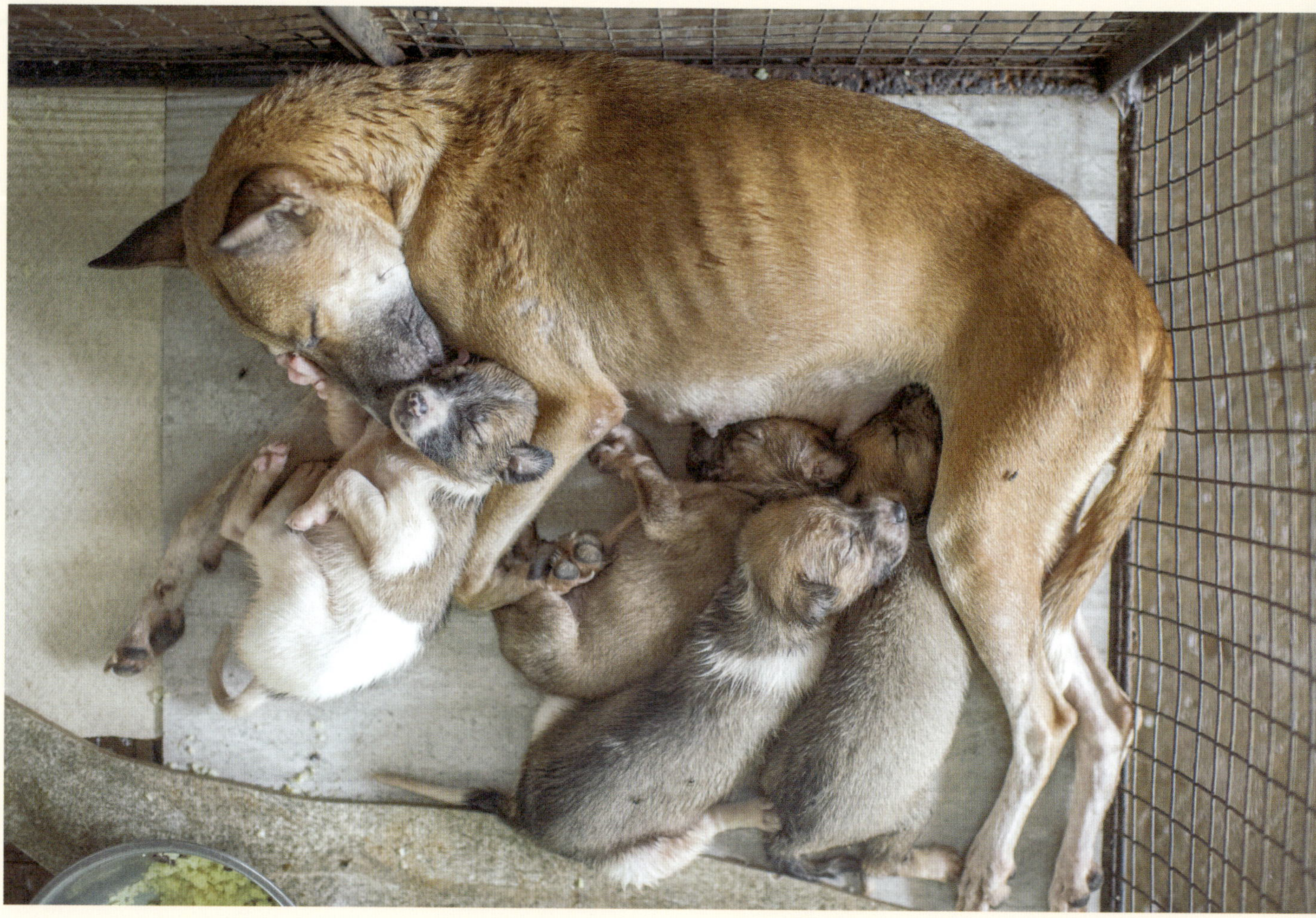

ABOVE The odds are stacked against street puppies in India, but on their side, they have the care, protection, and sheer determination of their mothers. This dog and her litter were rescued by People for Animals in Goa, India. The care dogs like these receive in the shelter dramatically increases their chances of survival. But even as their situation improves, the care of a mother dog never wavers.

RIGHT When I visited Nagler See Kennel in Pfeffenhausen, Germany, owner Agathe Rank had ten German Shepherds, including puppies from two recent litters. The protective mother dog, Lotus, watched while one of her puppies wrestled with a puppy from another litter to make sure things didn't get out of hand.

... being a mother is perhaps the hardest job in the world, and that is certainly true for dogs.

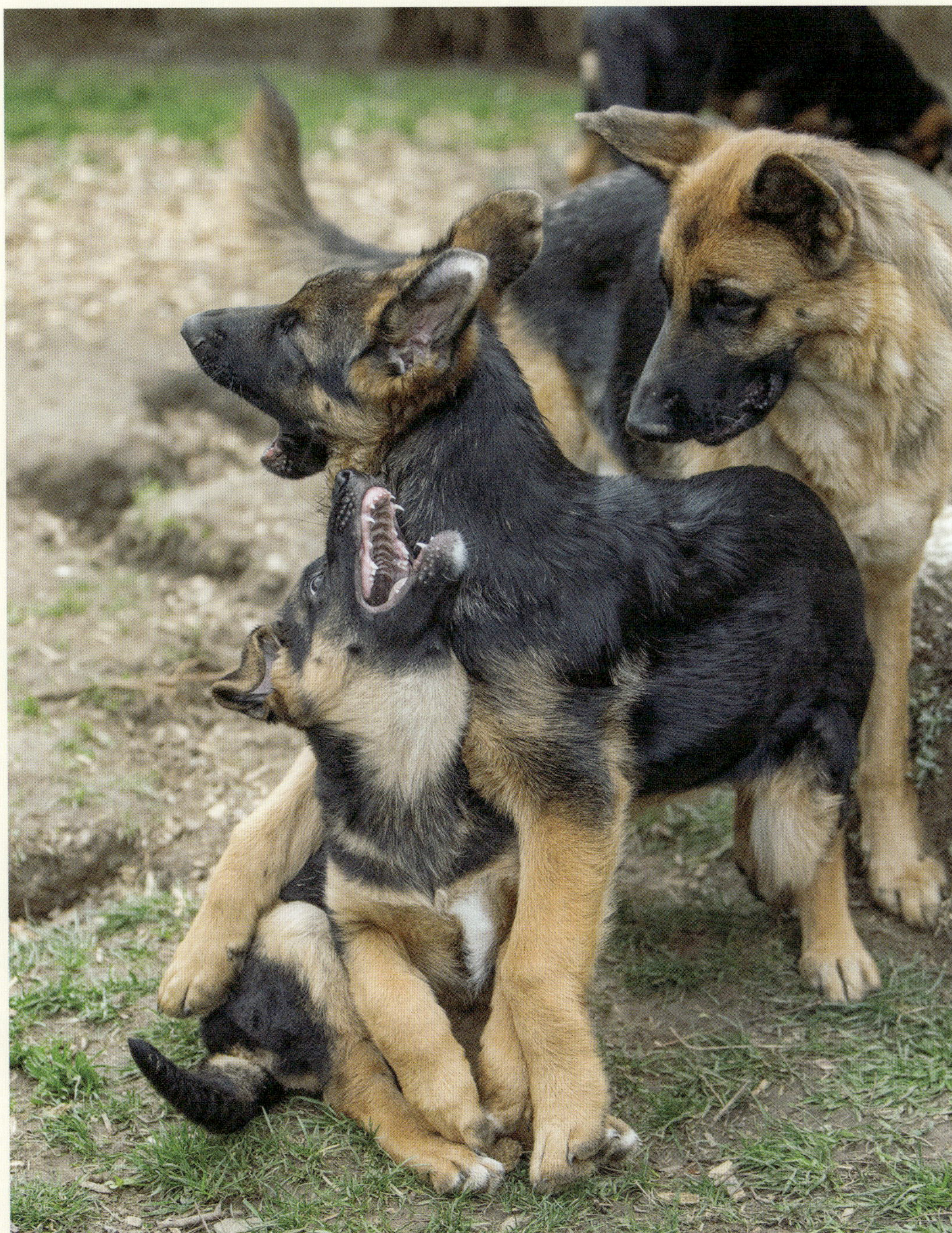

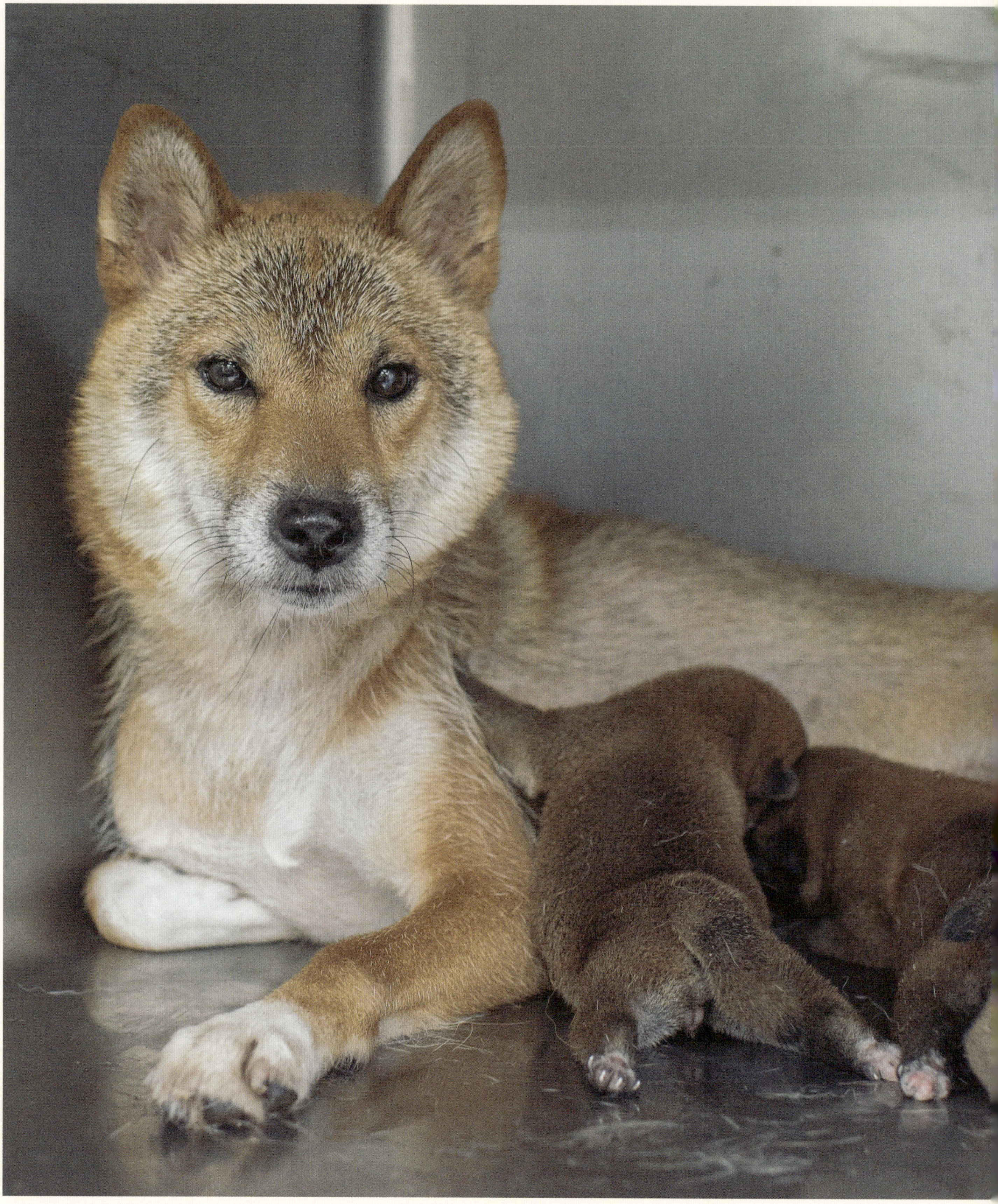

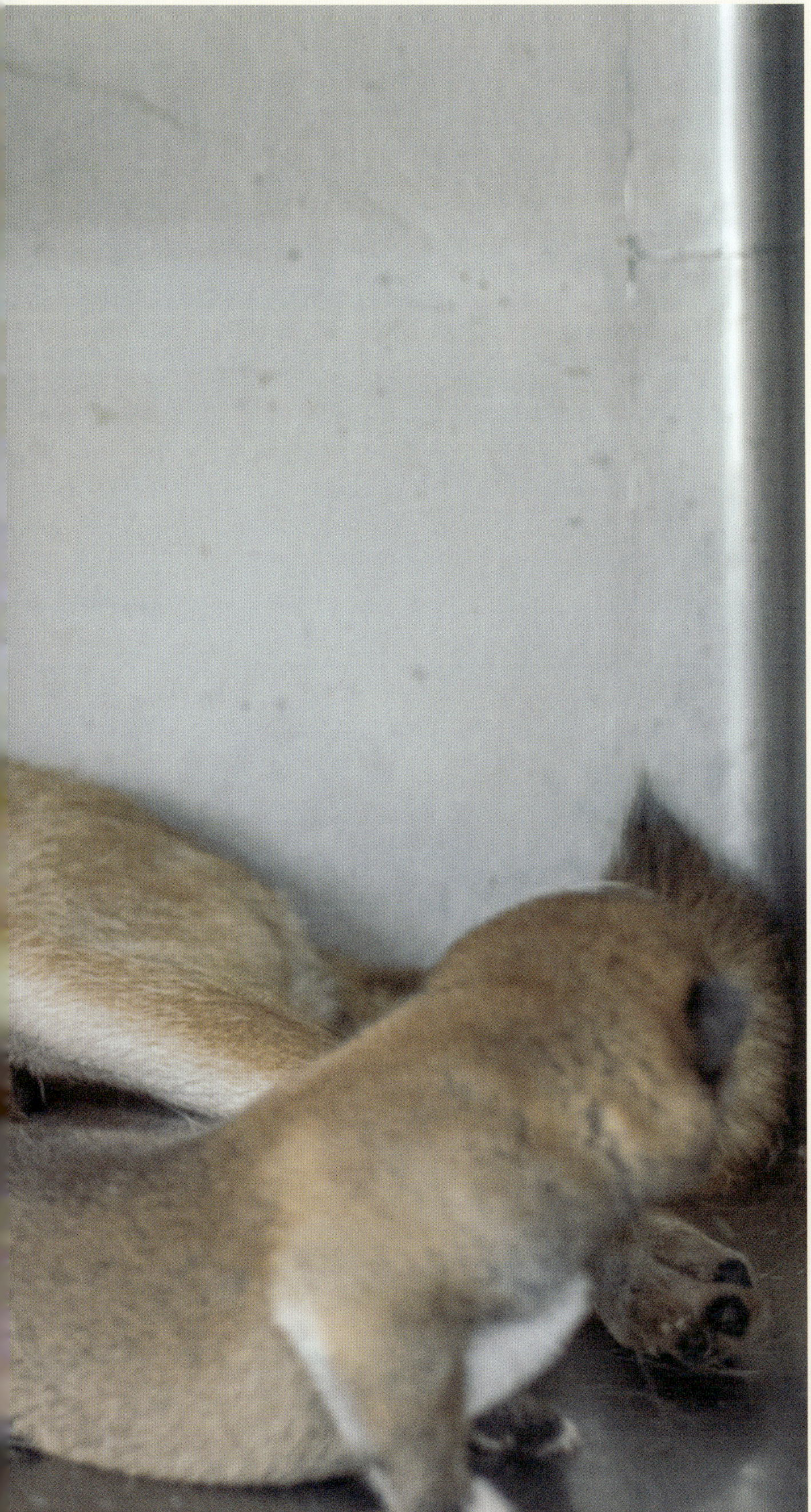

ABOVE The Shinshu Shiba Inu had six-day-old puppies and was very suspicious of me, a stranger with a camera. Mother dogs are extremely protective, and this dog did not take her eyes off me during our entire interaction

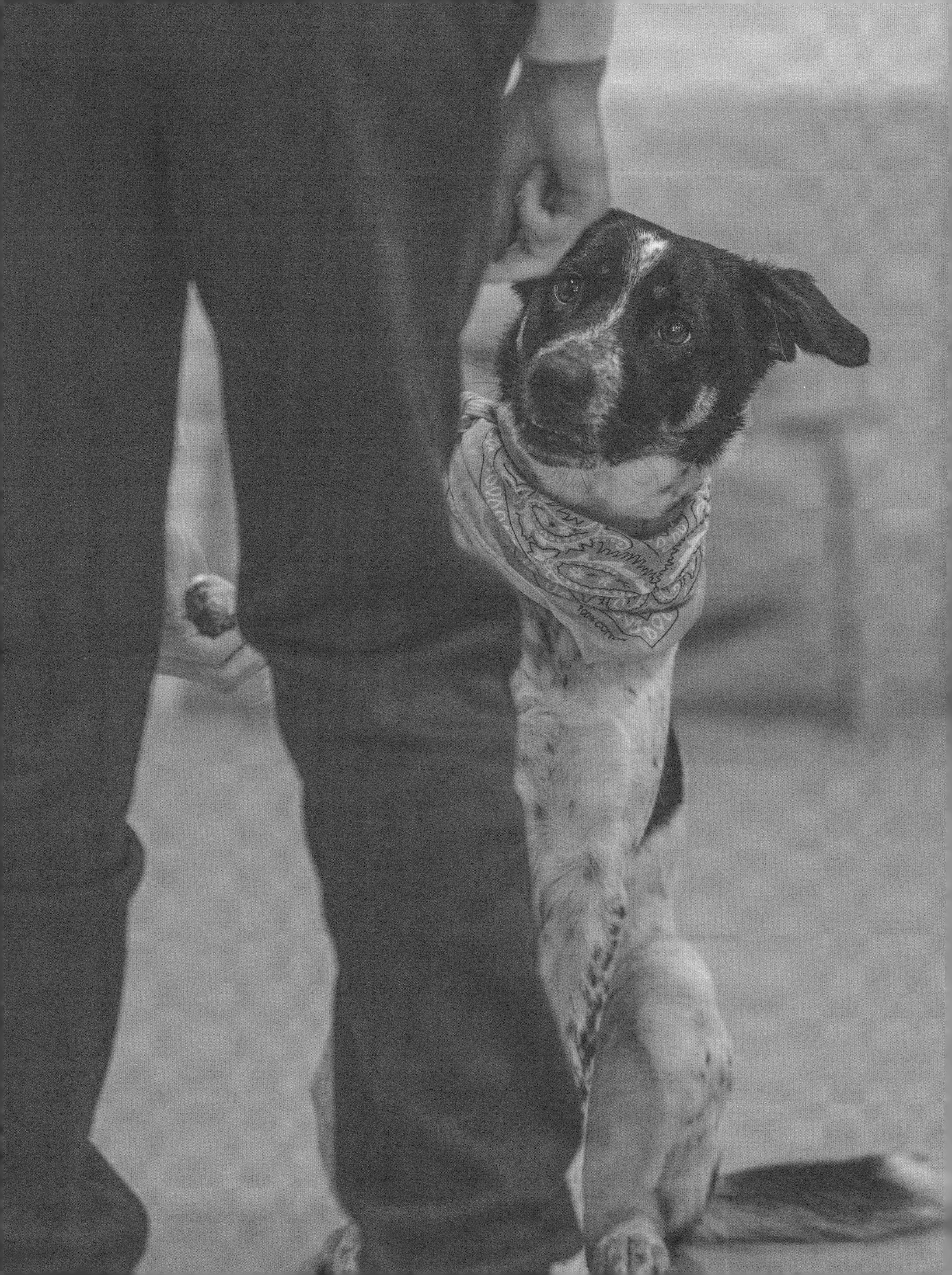

LOCATION	BREED	TASKS	SKILLS
Cascais, Portugal	Border Collie	Training, Playing Games, Grooming	Sociability, Enthusiasm, Docility

SCHOOL THERAPY DOGS

ASSOCIAÇÃO MÃO GUIA is an organization that works with dogs to provide therapy sessions in classroom settings. Their mission promotes social inclusion, with a particular focus on people who have disabilities.

I was lucky to attend a classroom session with children at a school near Cascais, Portugal. Poppy, a Border Collie and therapy dog, was there to entertain the children and teach them emotional, social, and cognitive skills through training sessions and games. Associação Mão Guia trains a number of different breeds, each with temperaments and training that allow them to excel in a school environment.

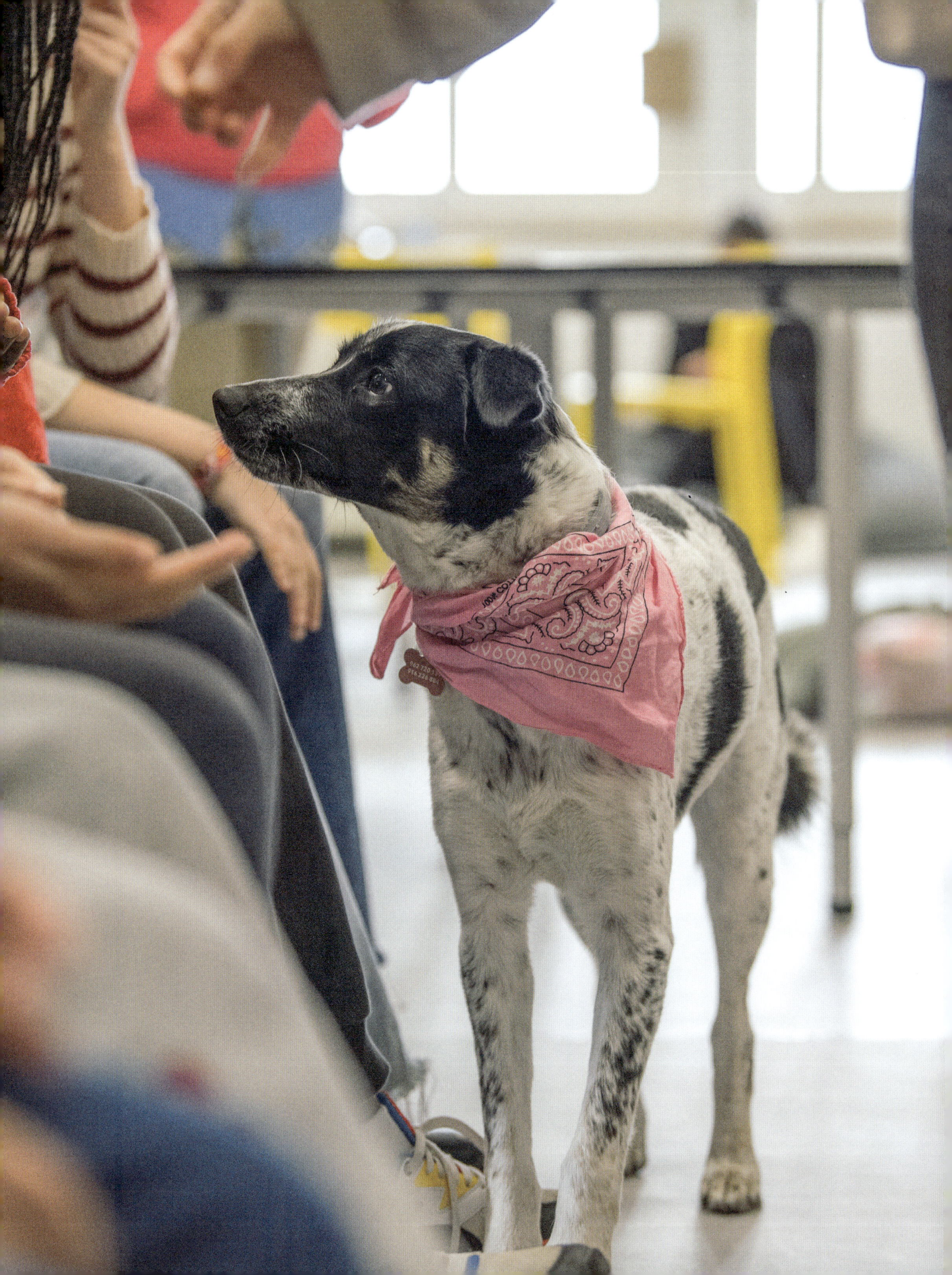

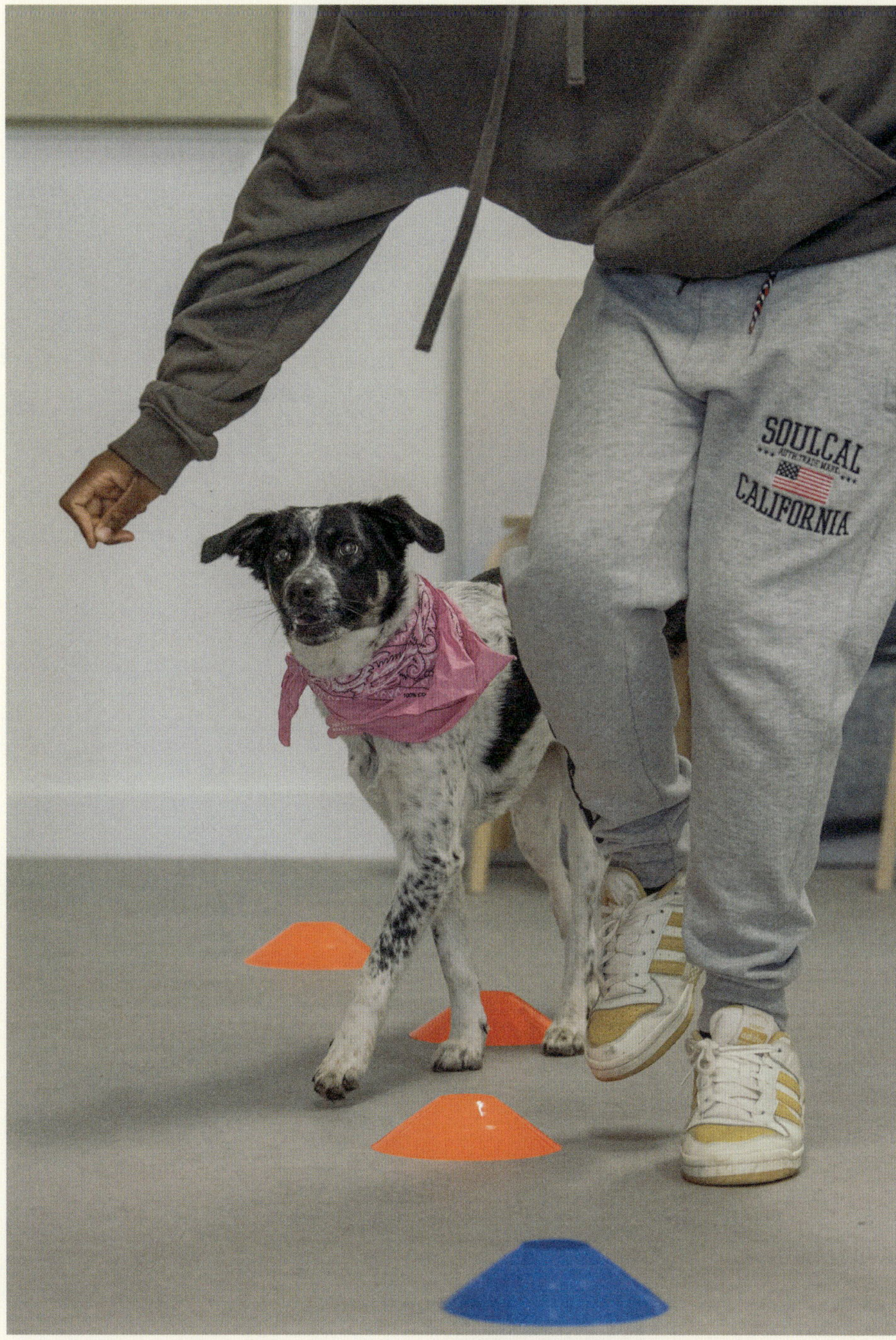

LEFT When Poppy showed up, there was a sense of excitement and order in the classroom. The students quickly lined their seats up in a row and sat patiently while Poppy provided greetings and received scratches.

ABOVE The students took turns working Poppy through a number of exercises, including a weave between cones. Her footwork was excellent, and I wouldn't be surprised if she ends up on Portugal's national team. The entire session was a tremendous amount of fun. Both the kids participating and those observing were engaged and enjoying the excitement.

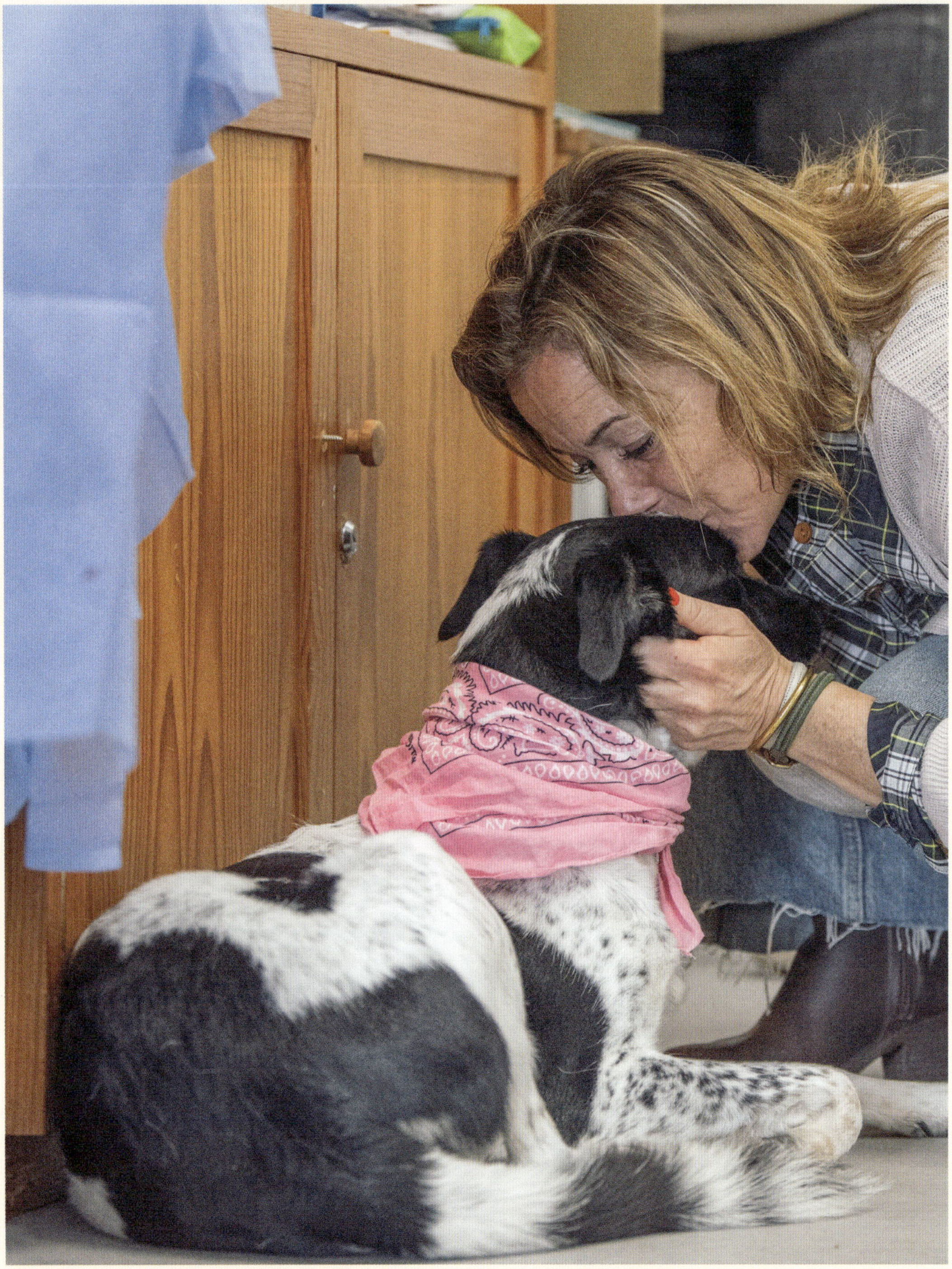

ABOVE Maria teaches students with disabilities. She recognizes and appreciates the positive impact of a therapy dog in the classroom, so she took time to thank Poppy for stopping by.

RIGHT Poppy finished her visit with a grooming session. It was a relaxing and calming way to end a wonderful session for everyone involved, Poppy included.

When Poppy showed up, there was a sense of excitement and order in the classroom.

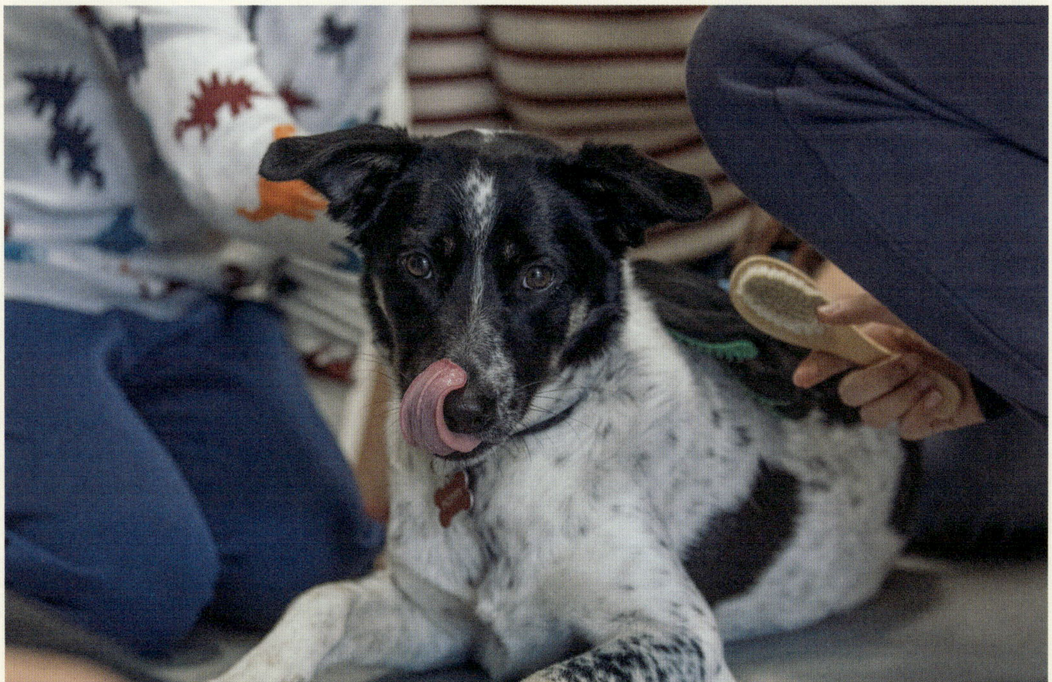

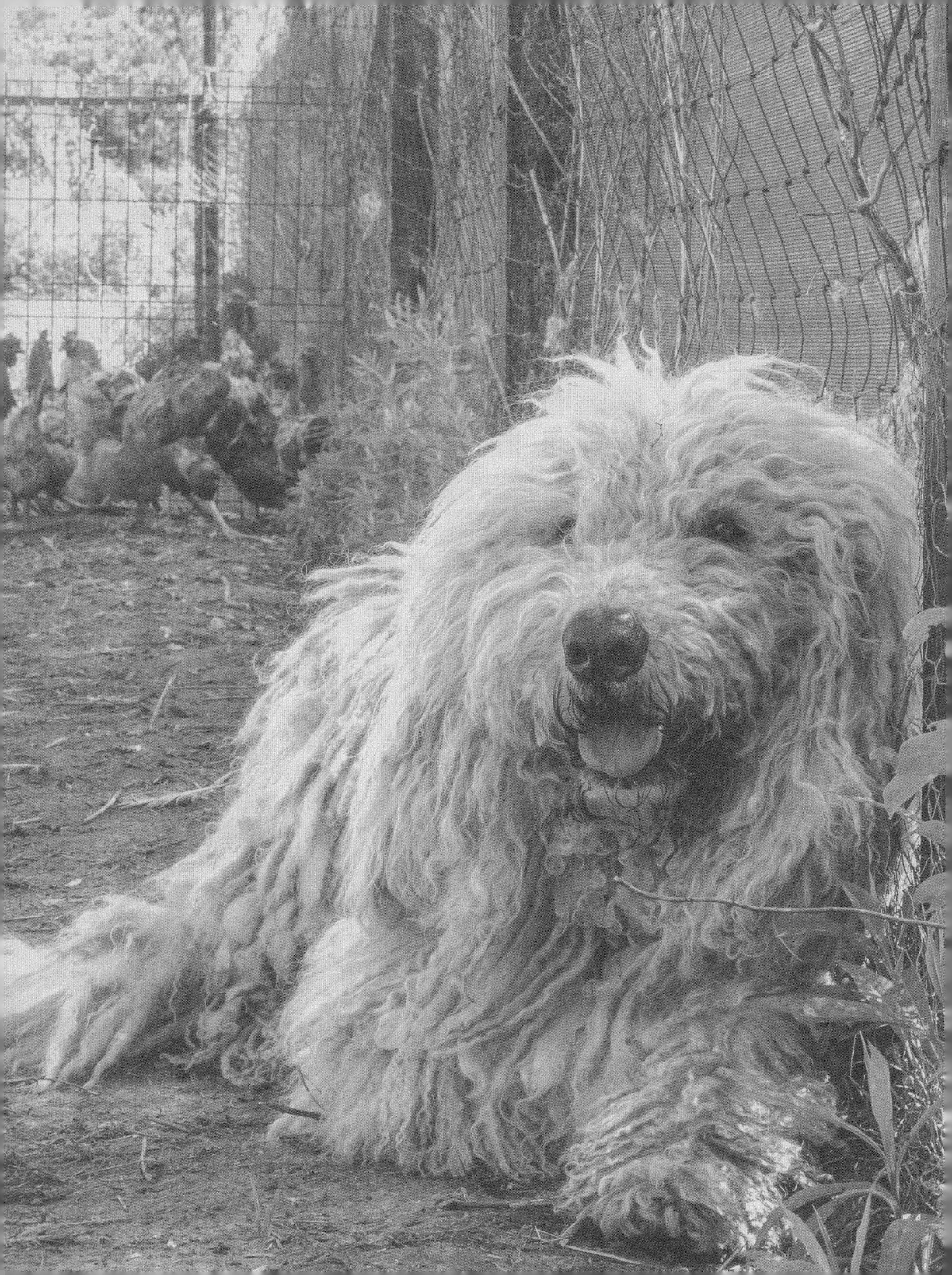

LOCATION	BREEDS	TASKS	SKILLS
Higashihiroshima, Japan, and Tahitótfalu, Hungary	Komondor and Jōmon Shiba Inu	Alerting Wards and Owners, Guarding, Keeping Watch	Intimidation, Threat Assessment, Confidence

GUARDIAN DOGS

I HAVE FOUND THAT GUARDIAN DOGS come sized big and small, with extreme variances in their coats. But what these dogs have in common is a history of breeding for the protection of both humans and livestock. Guardian dogs are carefully raised with those they are trained to protect, which helps them distinguish between the pack and predators.

In Japan, the Jōmon Shiba Inu is an extremely rare breed. They are very loyal and vigilant, and have been historically used as guards in farming communities. They alert their pack to dangers and are willing to go up against much larger animals to protect their charges.

Komondors, also known as Hungarian Sheepdogs, make good silent protectors who are docile but very independent. The breed makes decisions based on instinct without needing human direction. They will stand up to wild boar and even have the awareness to recognize hawks circling in the sky.

The common theme I recognized between these breeds is a fierce connection to their owners and a hesitation to welcome newcomers into their territory without a thorough evaluation.

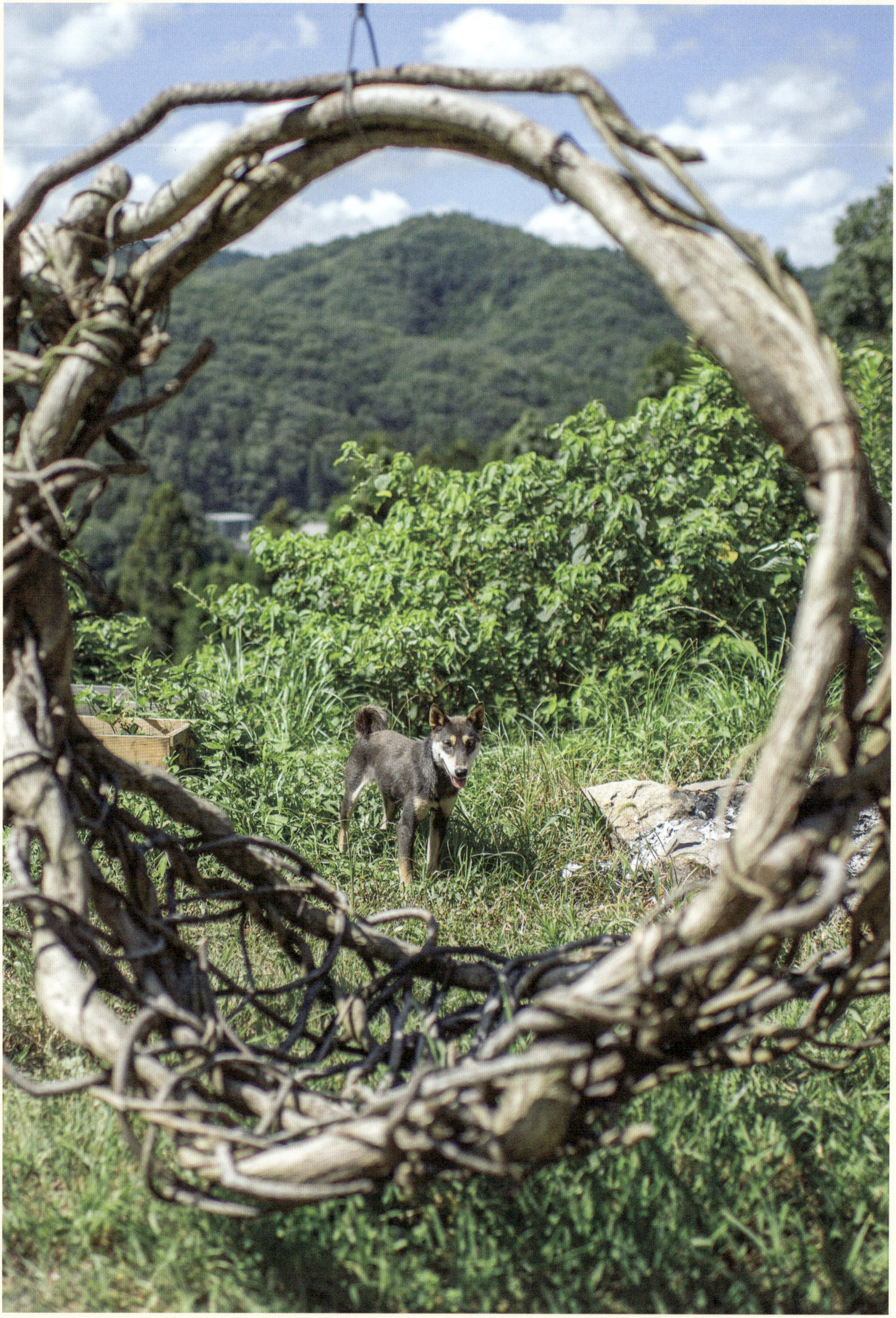

LEFT & BELOW The Jōmon Shiba Inu is extremely rare and found almost exclusively in Japan. The Nagira family in Hiroshima Prefecture have preserved this breed as an ode to the Jōmon period, when there were no wars in the country. The family lives in a very rural area, so the dogs act as protection against wild animals, such as boar. The Nagiras have a great deal of respect for nature, and the dogs help them maintain balance while living within it.

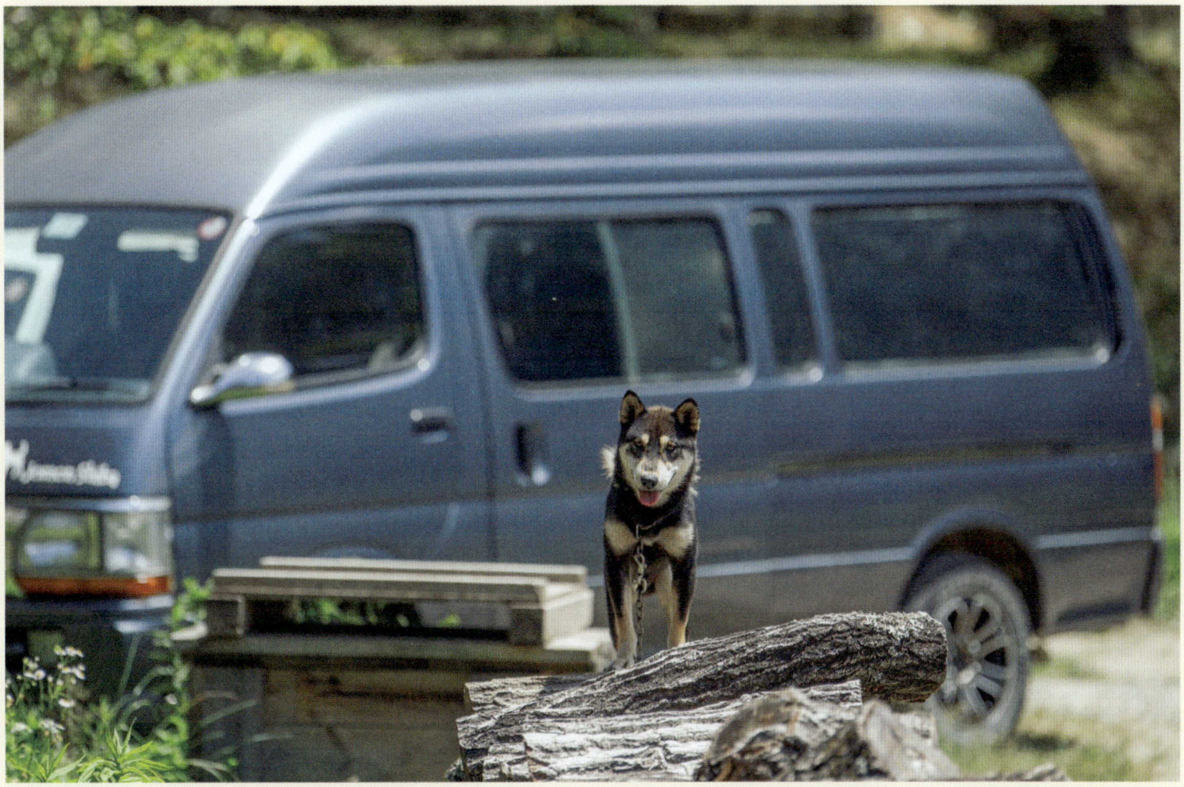

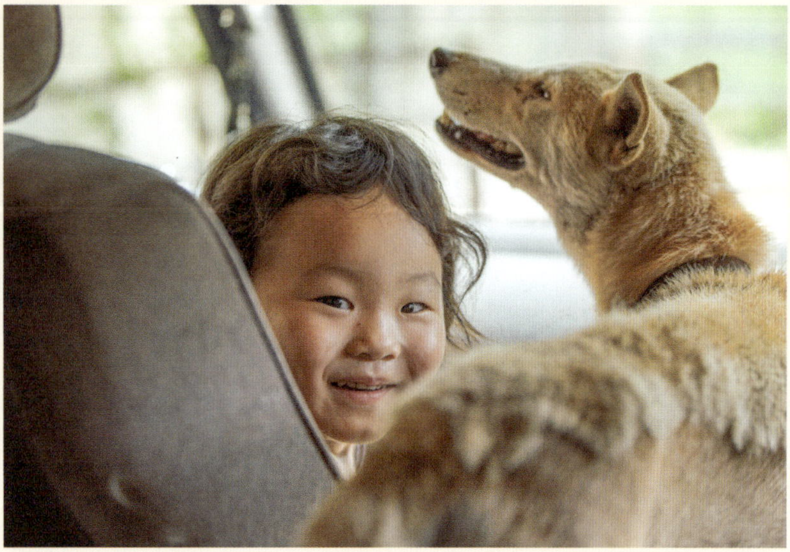

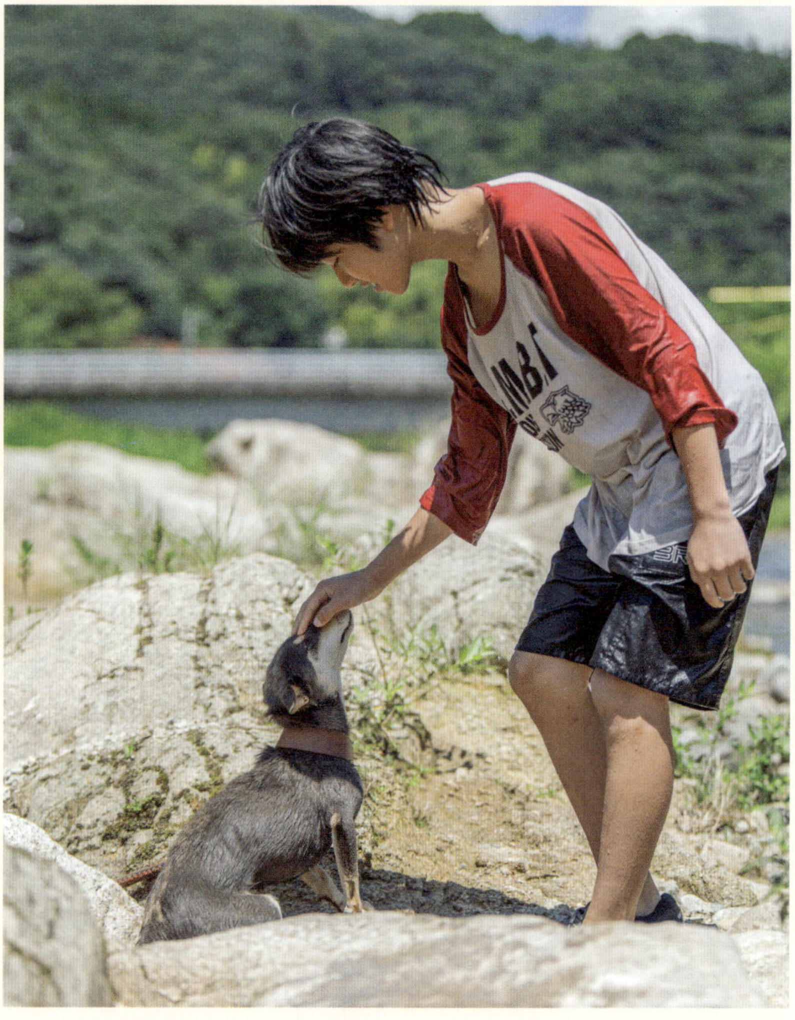

ABOVE & RIGHT These dogs were very timid around new people, but that is not the case at all around the Nagira family. The children adore these dogs, and the admiration is reciprocated. Mr. Nagira described the dogs as "beasts" around animals, as they would do anything to protect their family.

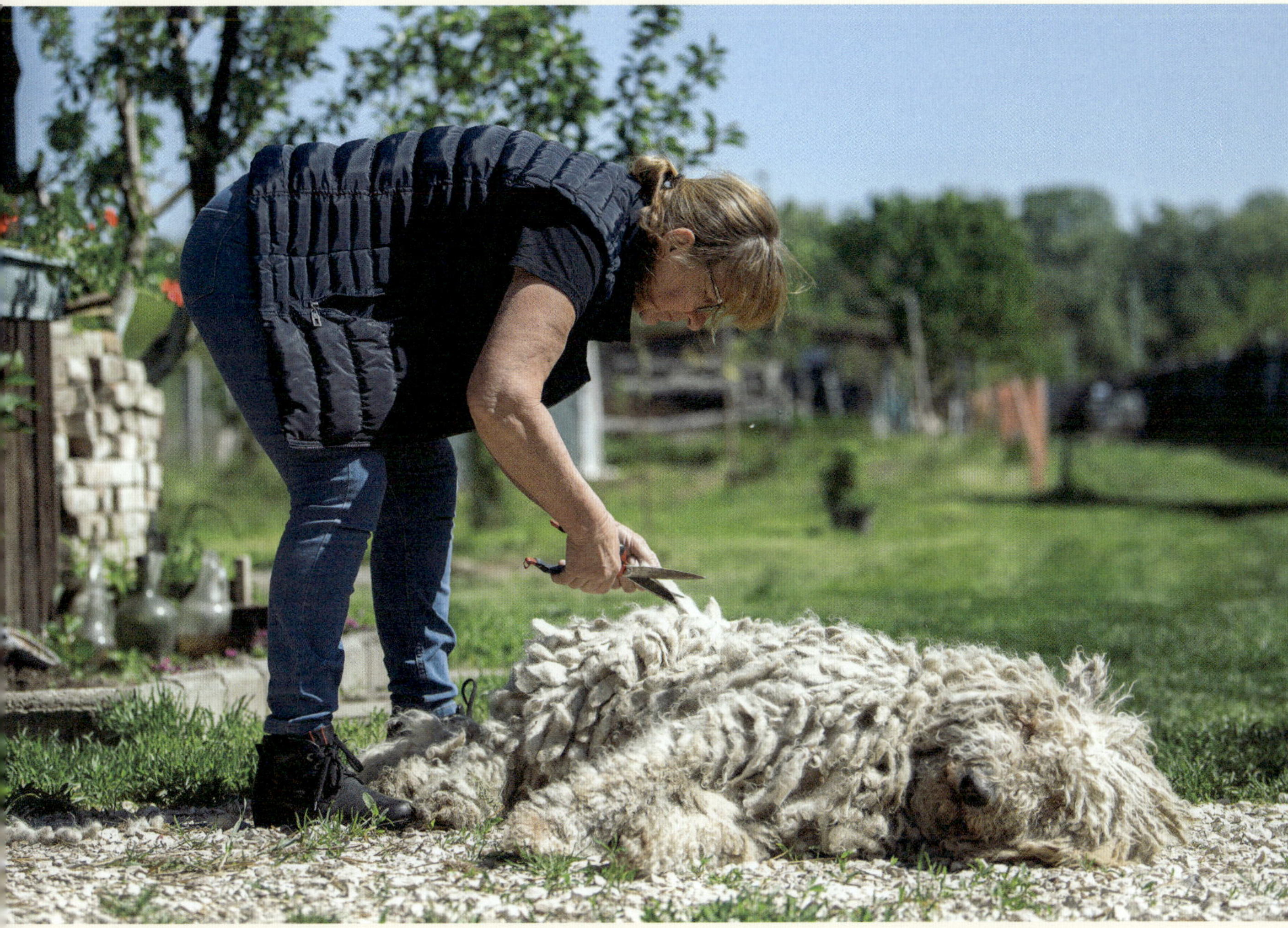

ABOVE Ágnes Lőrinczyné Velencei is an owner, breeder, and lover of Komondors. When I visited, she had six dogs who looked after her chickens and geese. Owning this furry breed requires her to moonlight as a groomer.

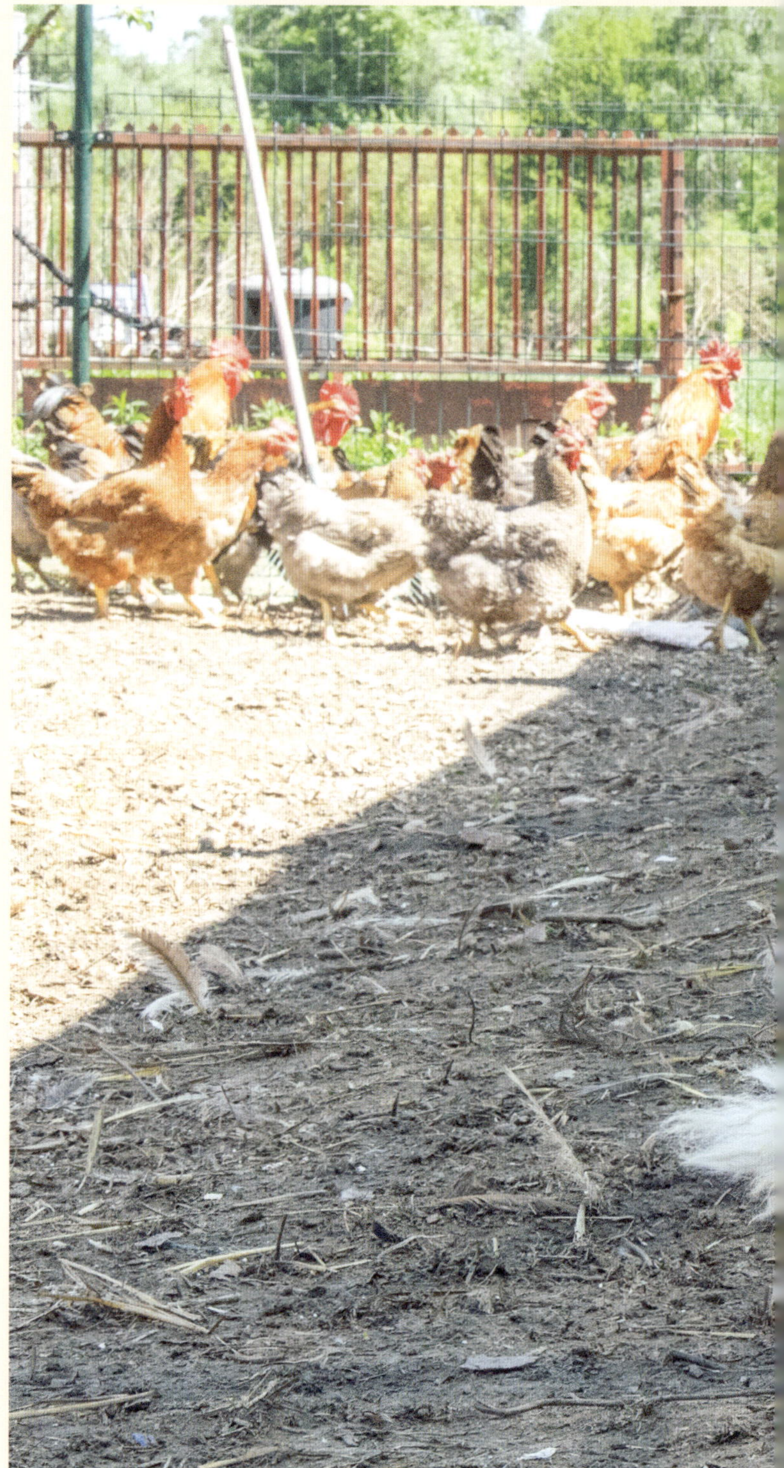

140

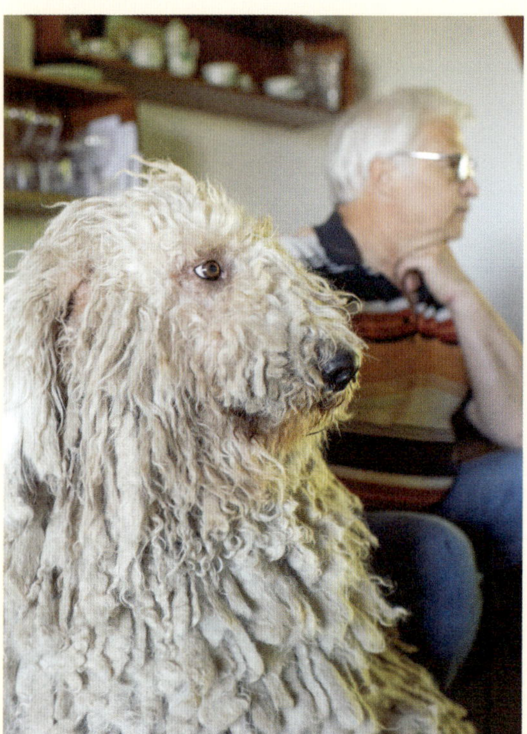

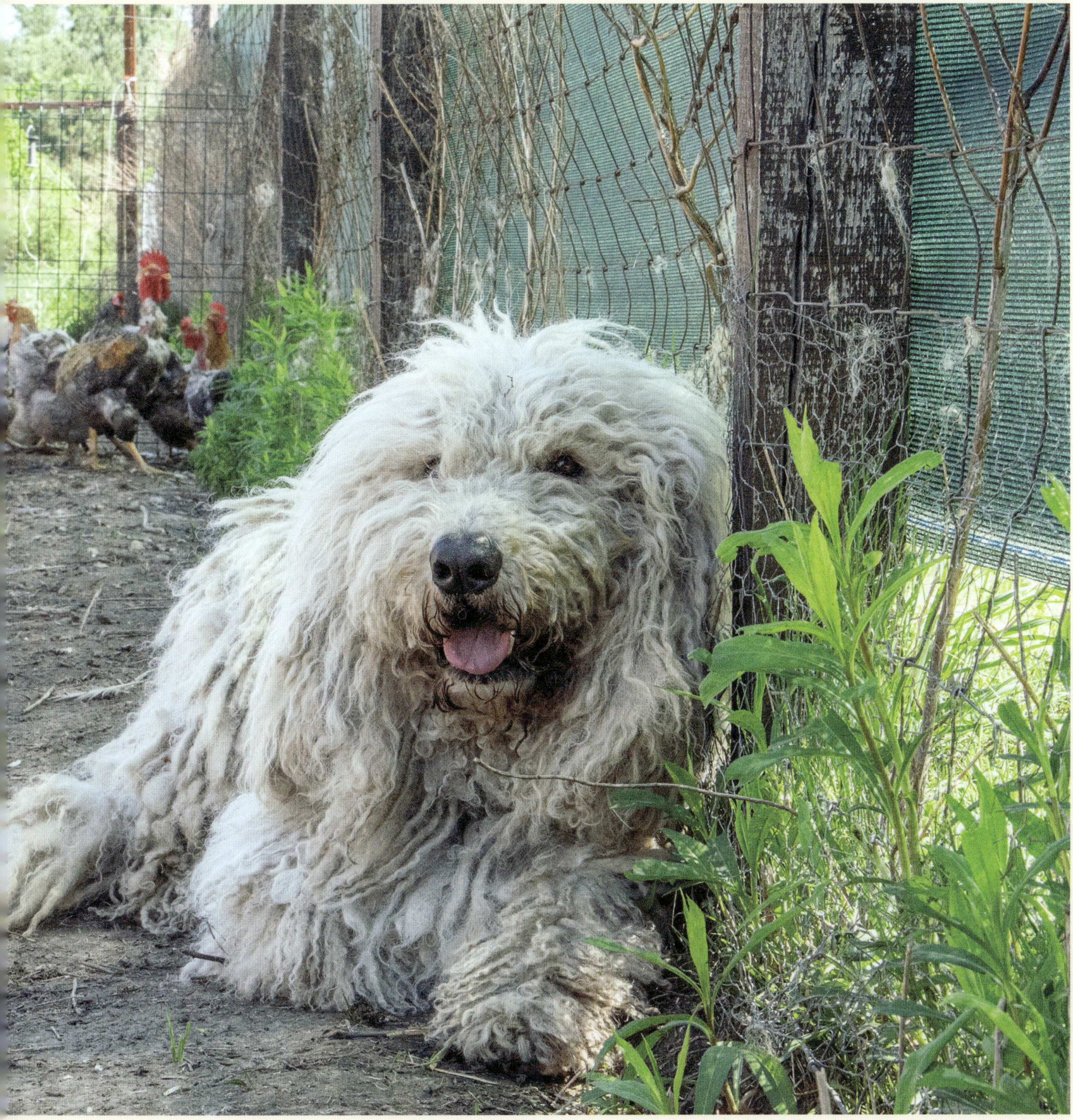

LEFT Working Komondors traditionally live outside, with a coat that can bear the elements, but some like to find their way inside and do their best impression of a mop.

ABOVE Overall, Komondors are pretty docile. They are silent protectors who are very independent. It doesn't seem like the dogs would be able to see much through their thick bangs, but they have a unique ability to detect predators from a distance, including birds of prey flying overhead.

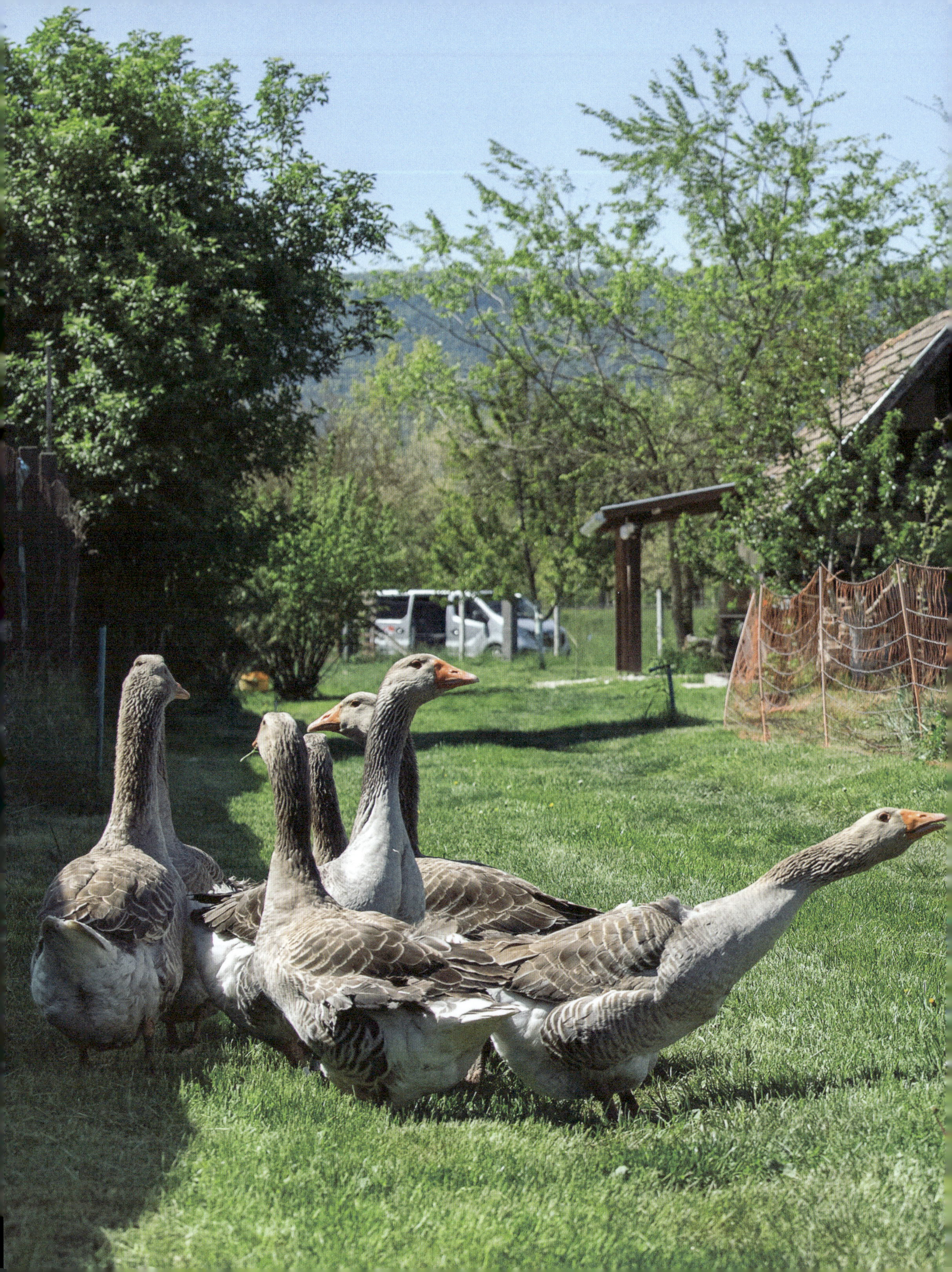

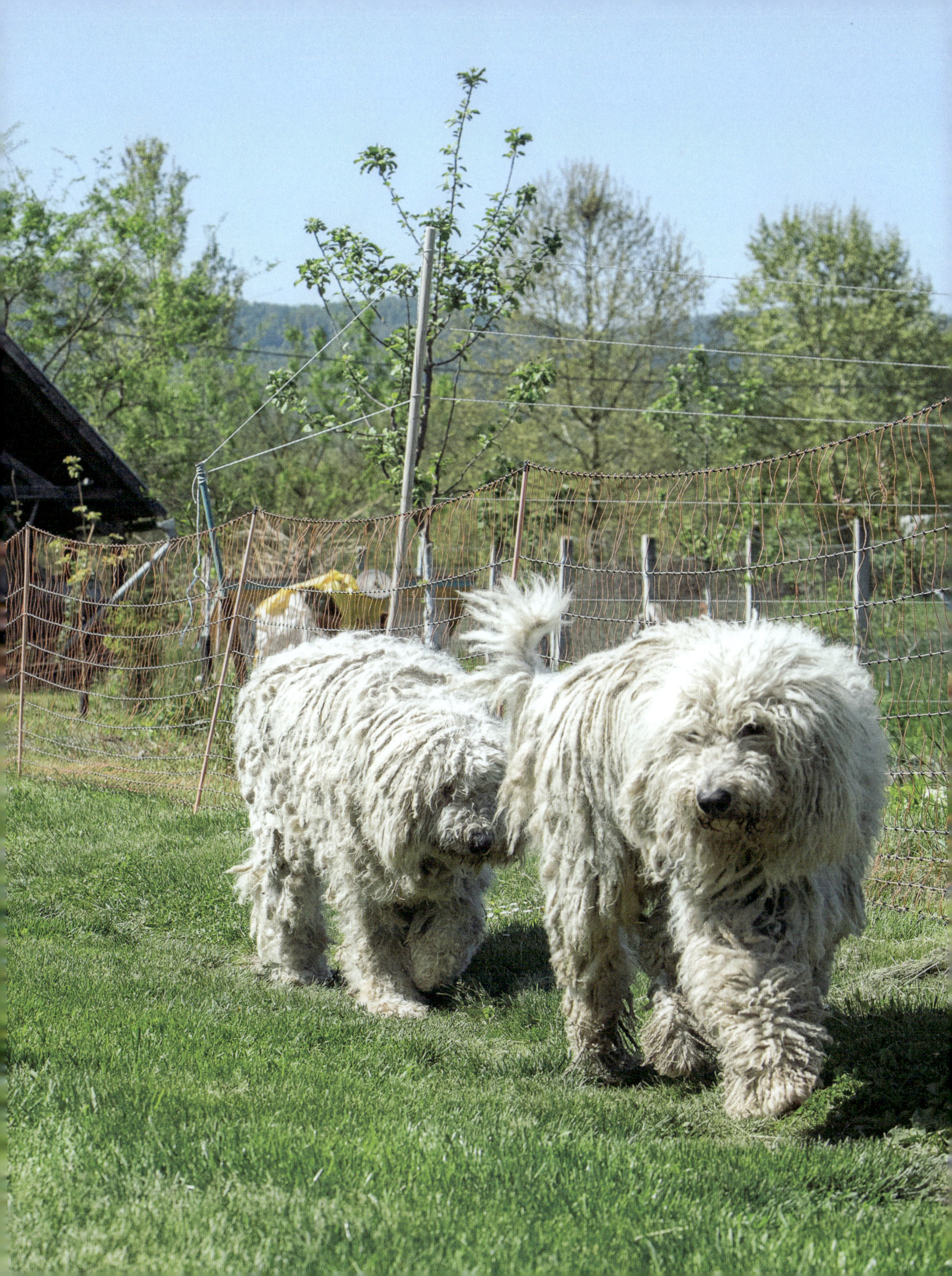

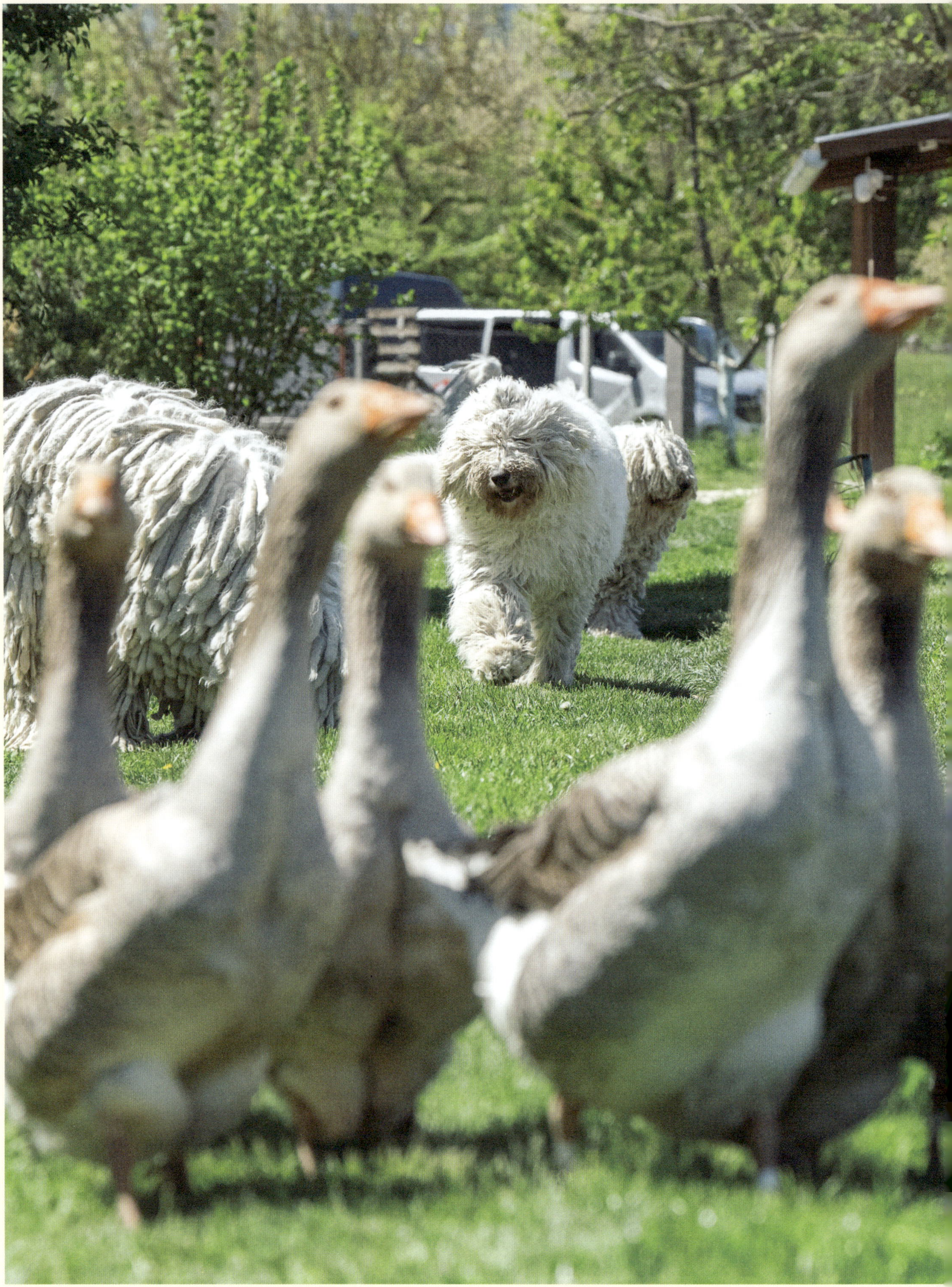

PREVIOUS PAGE & LEFT The geese that the Komondors protect are ingrates. They charged and hissed at the dogs as they walked by, not recognizing nor appreciating the protection provided. The dogs, for their part, were unfazed by the bird threats hurled their way.

BELOW Gabi is Ágnes's granddaughter. She also has a deep love and appreciation for the breed, along with an excellent grasp of the English language, so she acted as a translator during my visit. She shows the family's Komondors at dog shows across Europe and has earned a stockpile of trophies and ribbons.

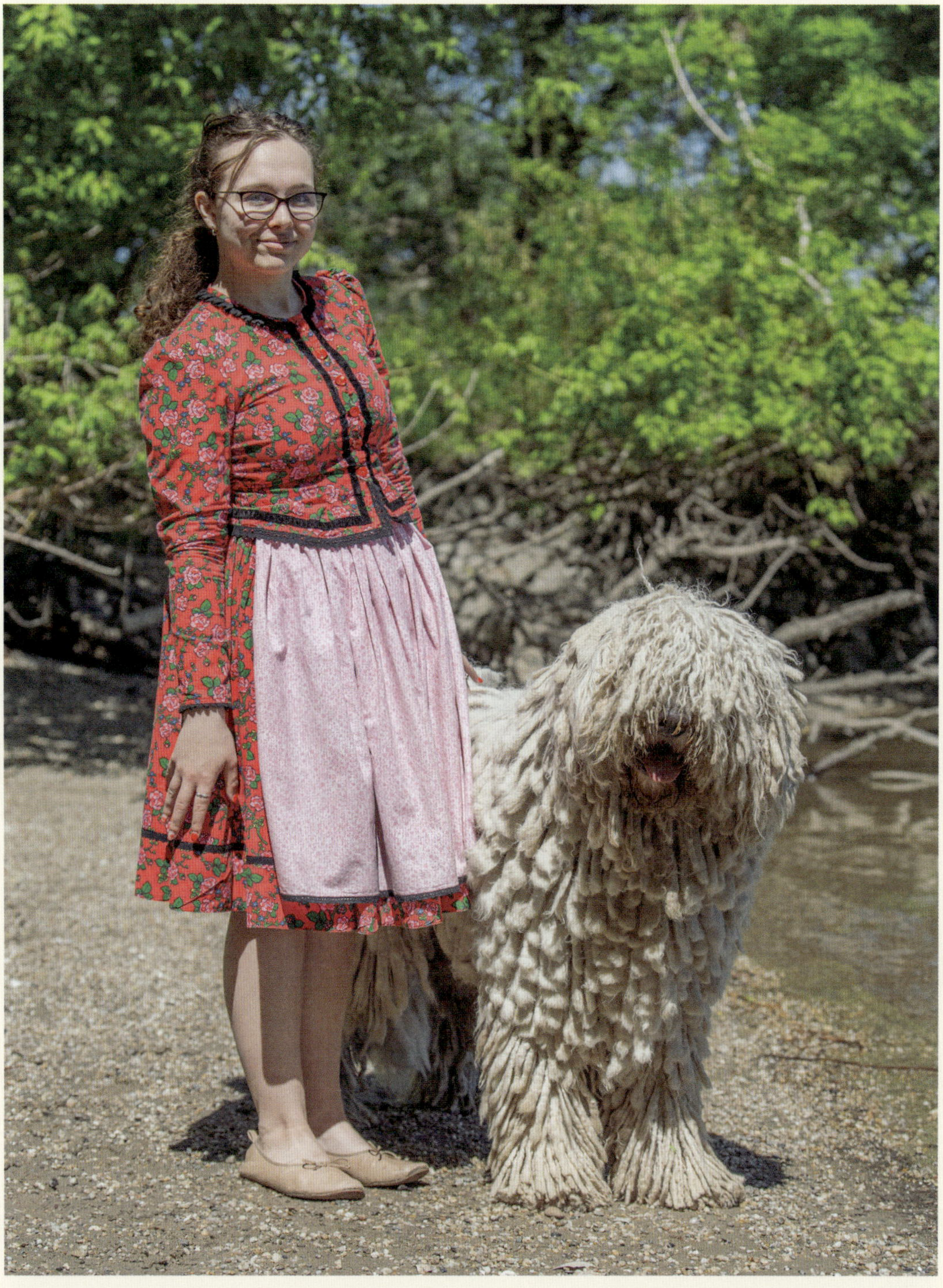

It doesn't seem like the dogs would be able to see much through their thick bangs, but they have a unique ability to detect predators from a distance, including birds of prey flying overhead.

RIGHT This was the photo I dreamed of. When given the opportunity out in the open, the dogs really enjoyed running. The massive Komondors barreled toward me, their cords swinging with every step. It was like the album cover of Beck's *Odelay* come to life.

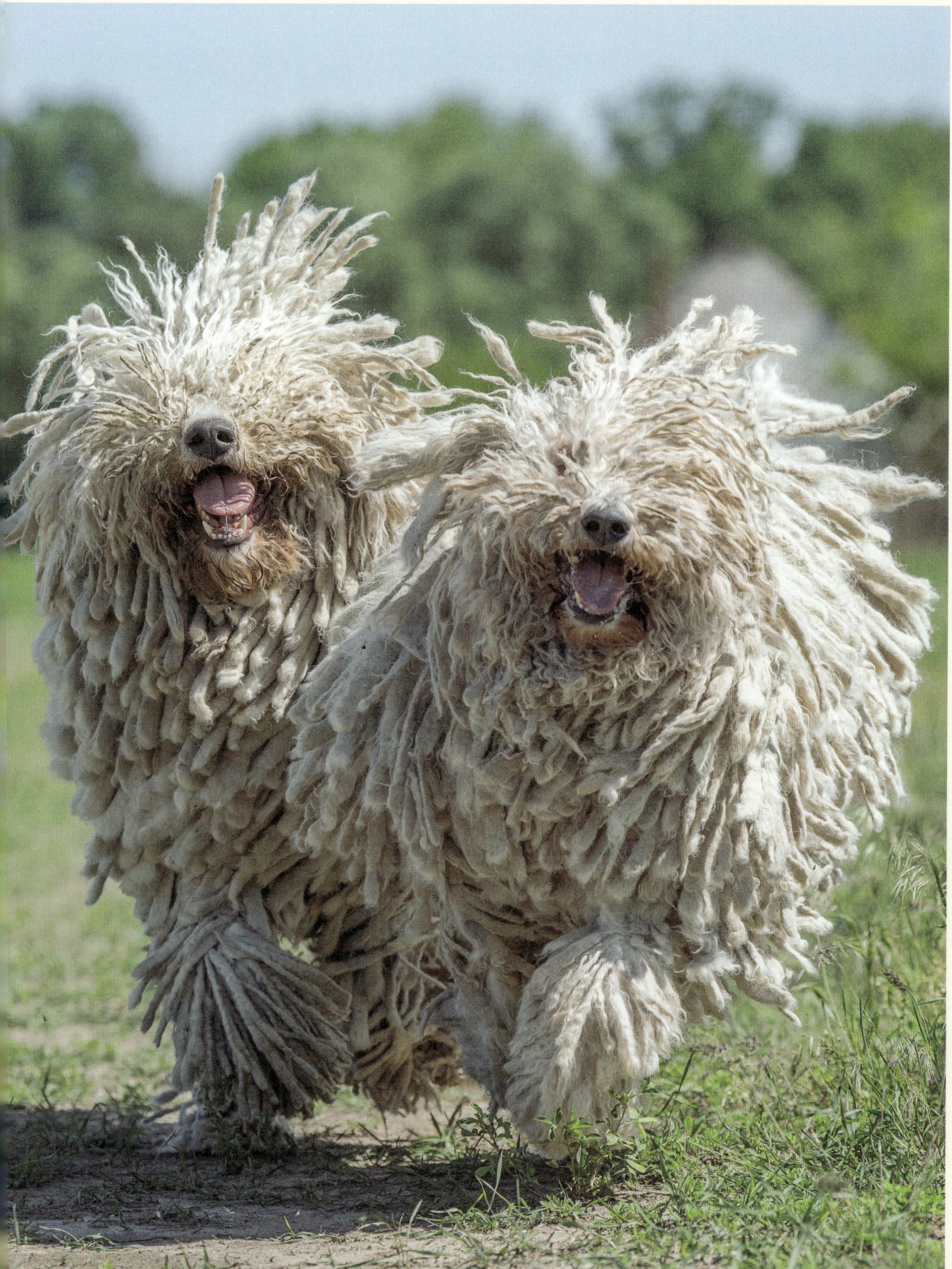

147

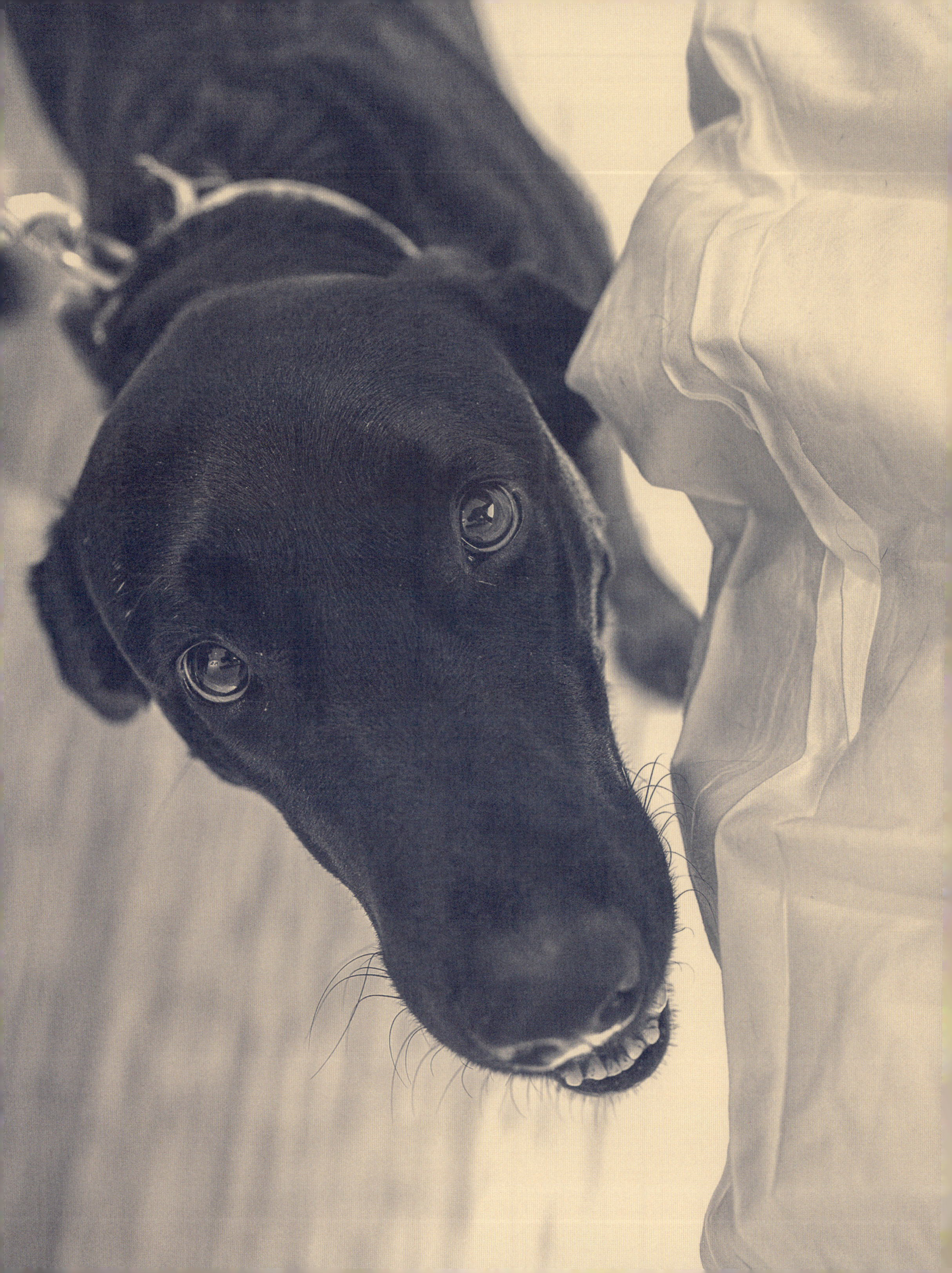

LOCATION	BREED	TASKS	SKILLS
Paris, France	Labrador	Detecting Scents, Identifying Bugs, Alerting Handler	Sense of Smell, Drive, Thoroughness

BED BUG DETECTION DOGS

I'M NOT MUCH INTO FASHION, but I did take notice of the news out of Paris in 2023 when citywide bedbug infestations coincided with Fashion Week. Naturally, I figured out a way to connect this news story to dogs when I made my first trip to France two years later.

Bedbug infestations can be a prolonged, daunting problem. They can also be a PR nightmare for hotels. That is why numerous businesses rely on dogs to do routine checks to make sure buildings are clear of the microscopic menaces.

I met with Thierry Hassid and his dog, Pedro, who work for a company called Cynoscan to detect bedbugs. Many breeds can be used for this work, including Labradors, who do an excellent job as they have a strong scenting ability, are highly trainable, and have the endurance to search entire buildings.

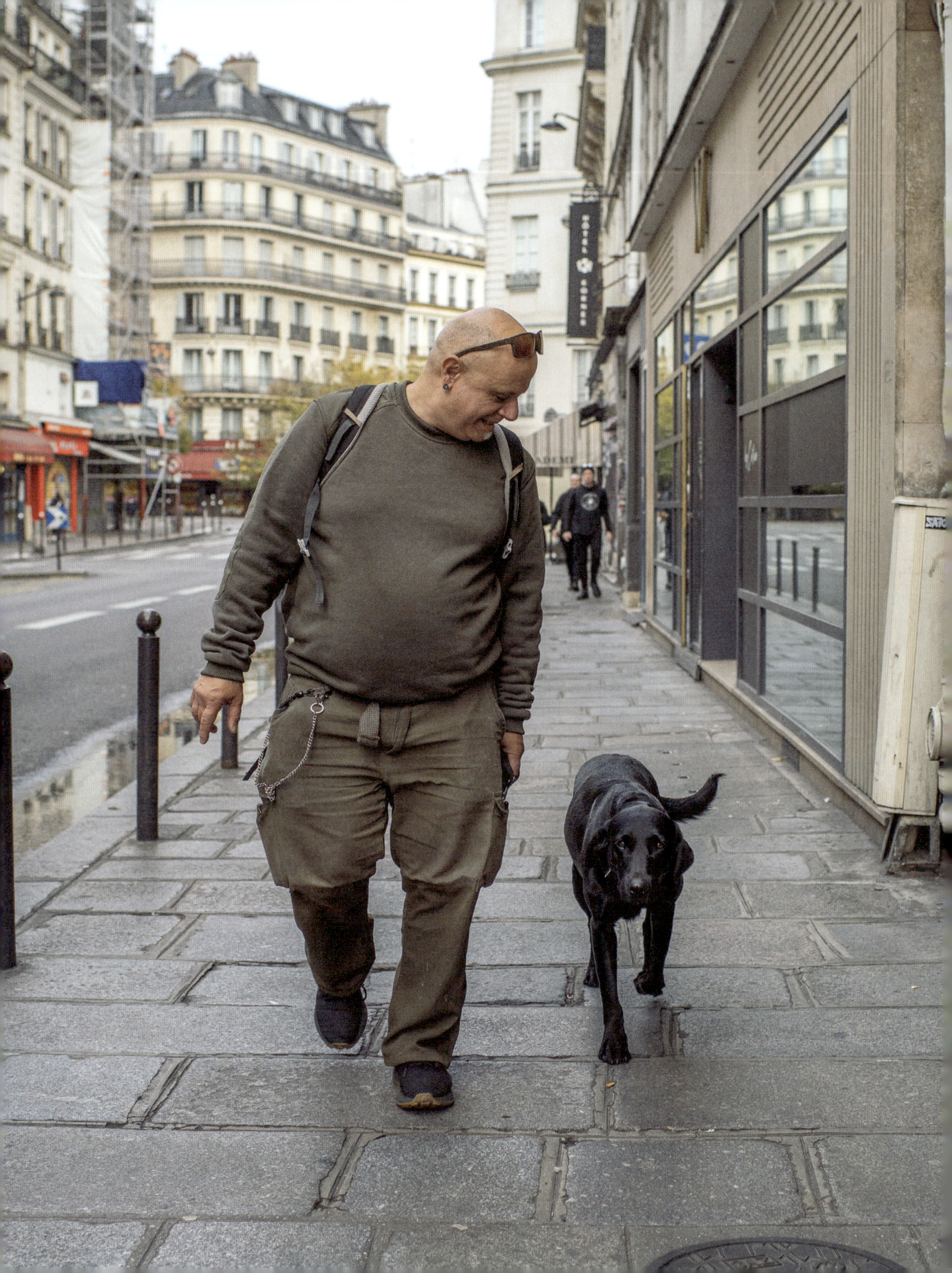

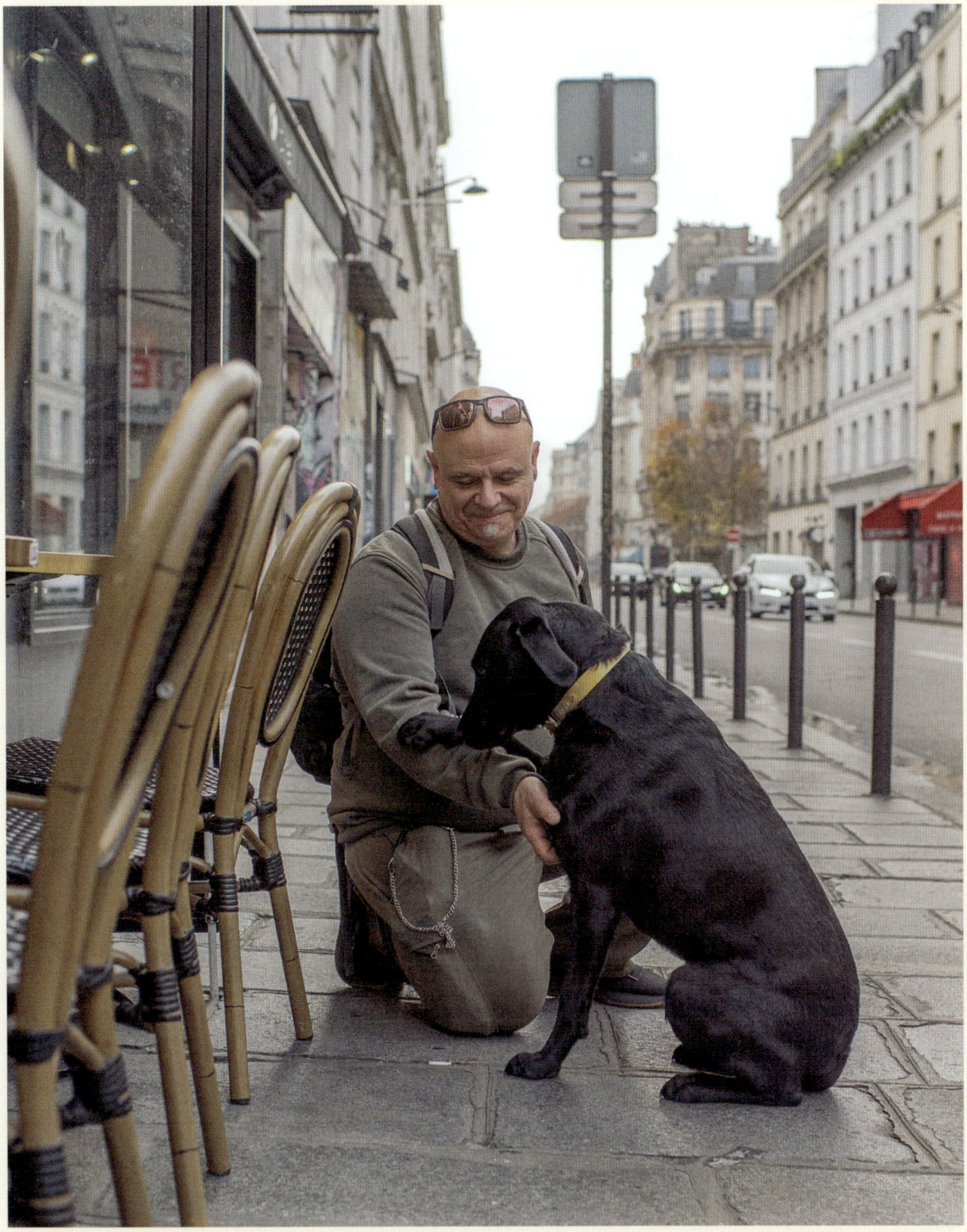

LEFT & ABOVE Thierry and his dog are a team with a very special relationship. Thanks to their bond, Pedro is rarely is on a leash unless he is working.

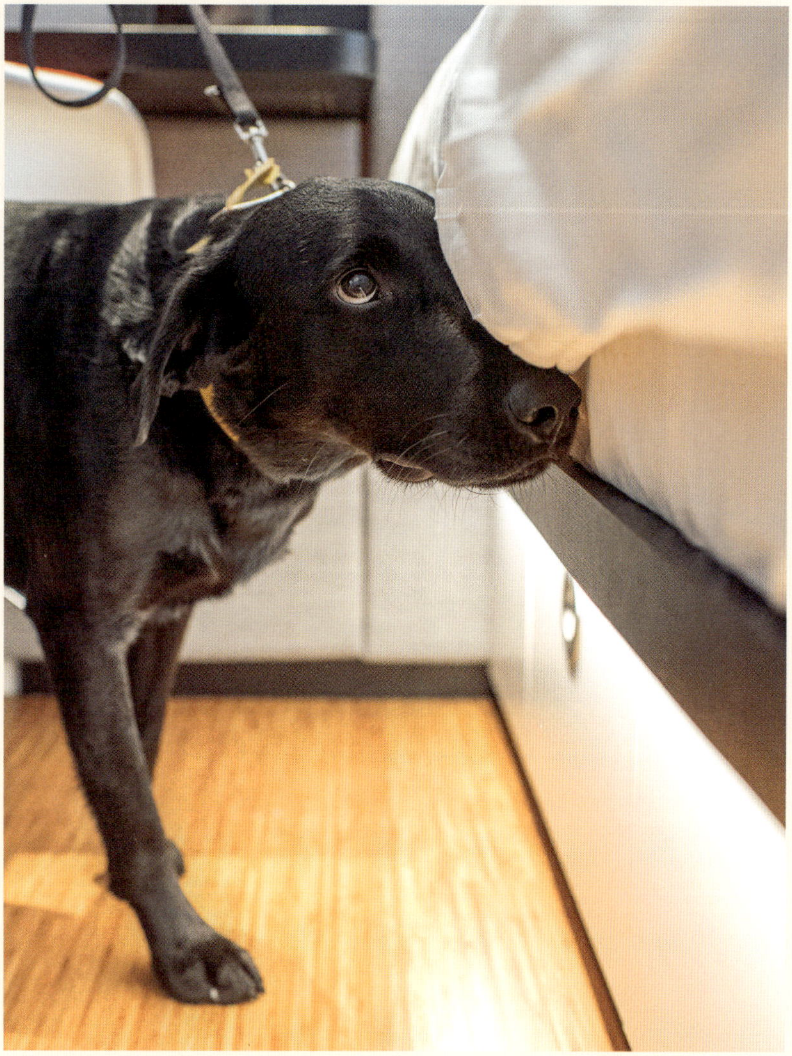

ABOVE Bedbugs are a challenging target because they are highly mobile. When the leash goes on and it is time to work, Pedro feverishly sniffs around the room on the hunt for his target. While many dogs sit when they find bedbugs, Pedro points his nose and becomes immovable until he is rewarded for his detection work. Luckily, I never witnessed him doing this while he sniffed around my hotel room.

RIGHT After scanning the room, the leash comes off and Pedro quickly gets out of work mode. If bedbugs were detected during the scan, Cynoscan recommends companies that exterminate them via heat, cold, chemicals, or a combination of the three. The benefit of having a dog detect an infestation is that the exact area where bugs reside is identified, so treatments can be targeted.

When the leash goes on and it is time to work, Pedro feverishly sniffs around the room on the hunt for his target.

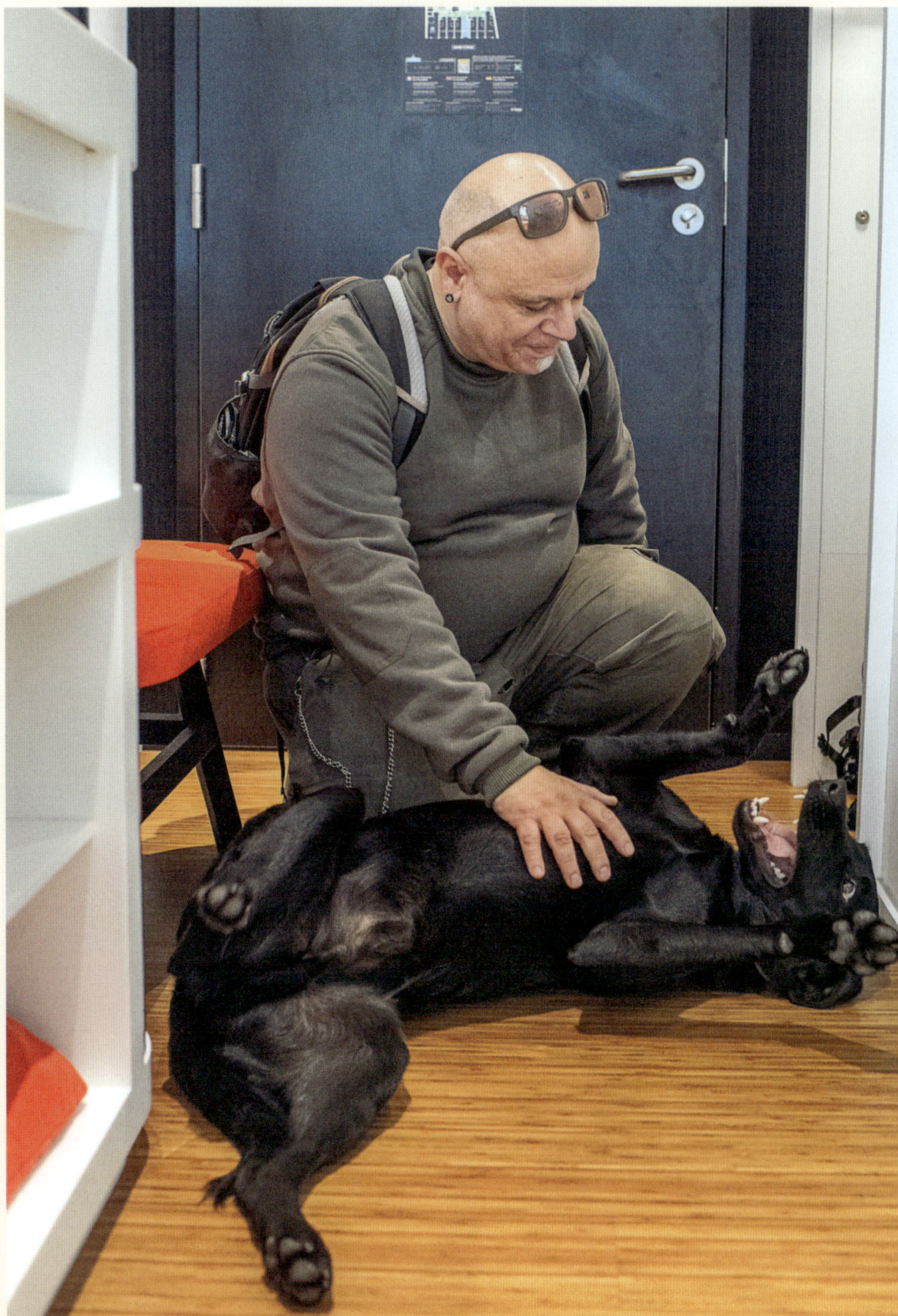

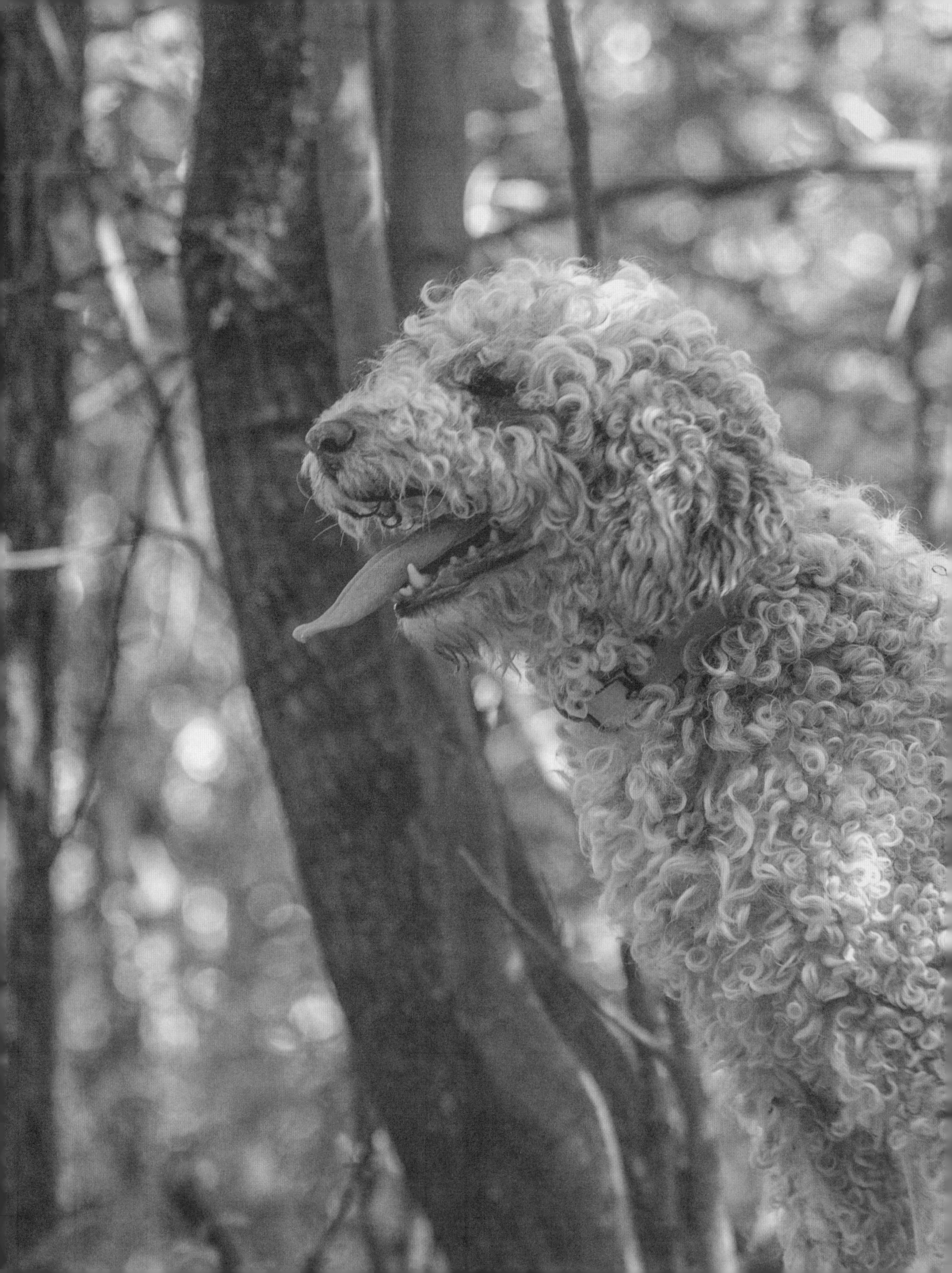

LOCATION	BREED	TASKS	SKILLS
San Miniato, Italy	Lagotto Romagnolo	Detetcing Scents, Digging, Retrieving	Sense of Smell, Agility, Endurance

TRUFFLE DOGS

TRUFFLE HUNTING, a job once reserved for pigs, has gone to the dogs – literally.

A specialty ingredient in Italian cooking, truffles are fungi that grow underground. Given their rarity, they are very valuable in the culinary world. Traditionally, pigs were used to search out truffles, but truffle hunters have found that dogs are much easier to manage than pigs, cause less destruction to forests, and are less likely to eat the truffles.

In the Tuscan town of San Miniato, family-run Tartufi Nacci has been hunting and selling truffles for decades. The Naccis love bringing guests along for hunts with their dogs, Birba and Maya. Birba is a Lagotto Romagnolo, a breed that specializes in truffle hunting. These dogs have a thick, curly coat that provides protection while running through the forest. Those curls can sometimes cover their eyes, but that's okay because the real work is being done with the nose.

BELOW Riccardo, dressed the part to go hunting, owns Tartufi Nacci alongside his wife, Monica. Their two dogs, Maya and Birba, are expert hunters and on the scent as soon as they hop out of the car and into the forest.

RIGHT Riccardo showed off his speed whenever he saw digging. Had he waited too long, there's a good chance this truffle would have ended up in Birba's stomach.

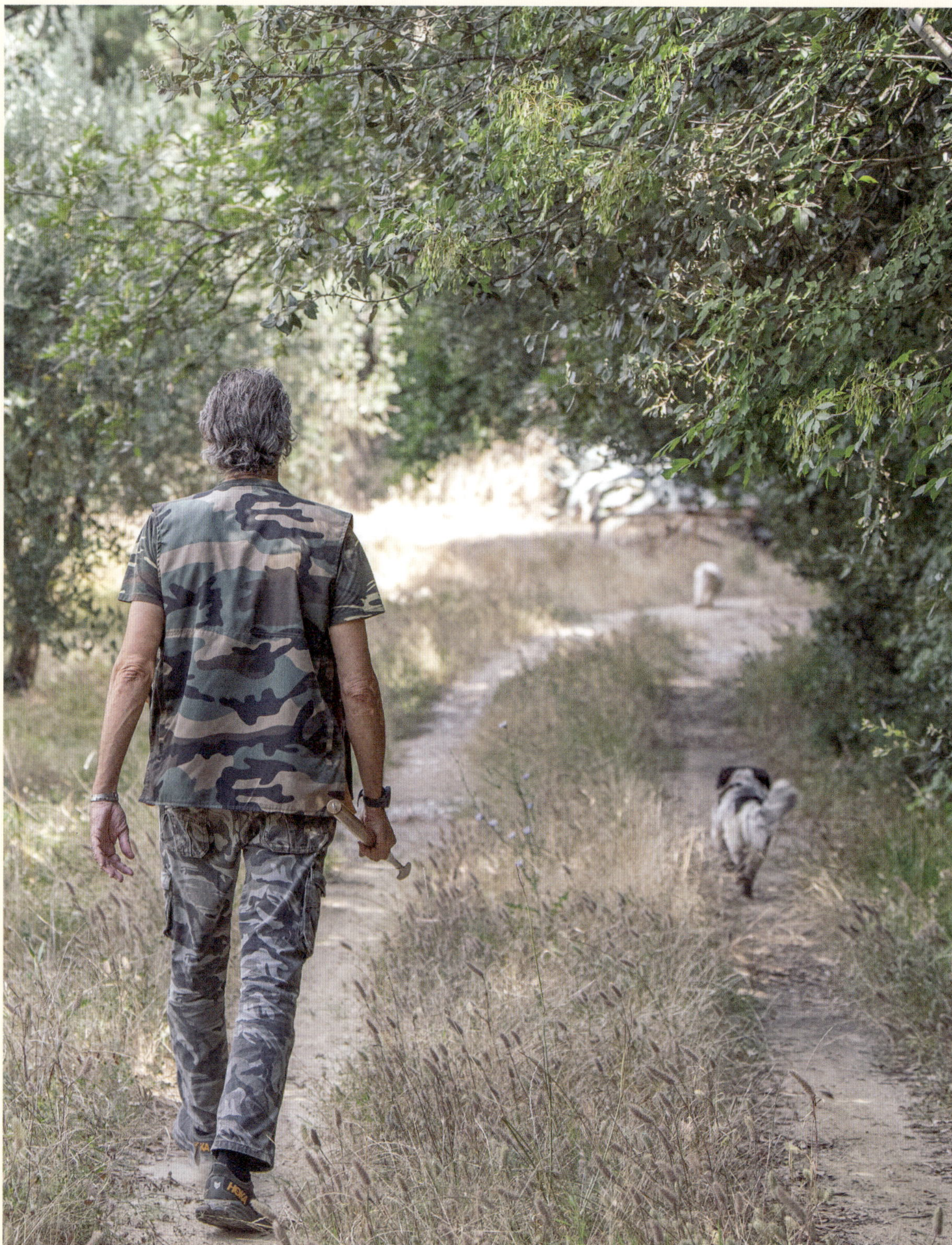

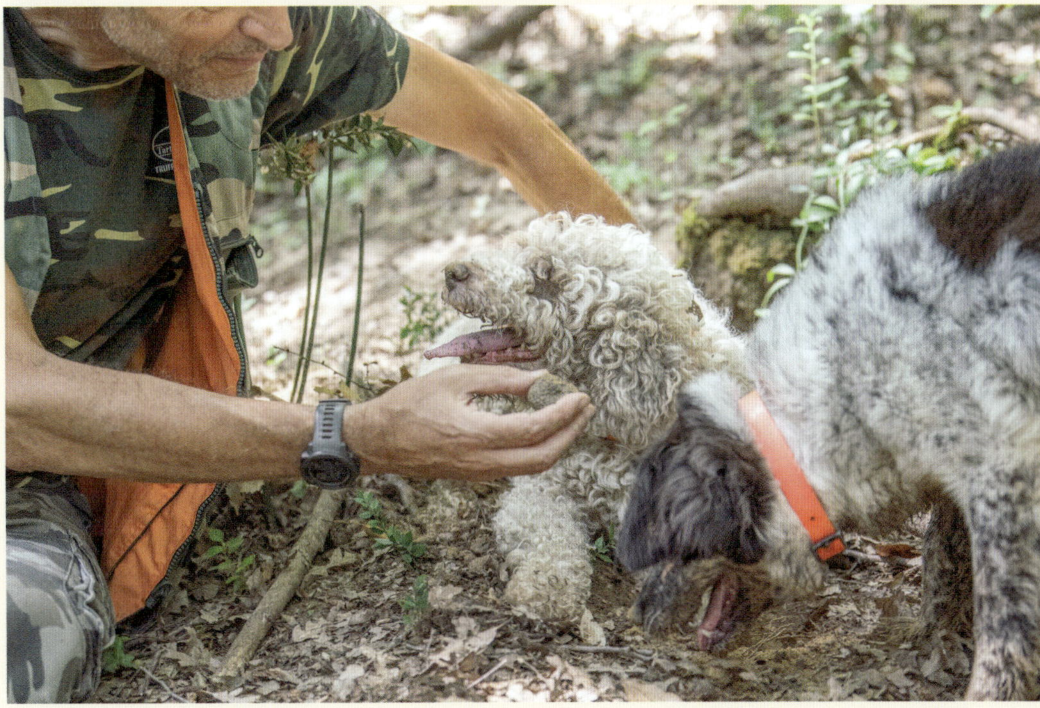

The dogs furiously run around the forest with their noses to the ground. Once they stop and start digging, that's when the adrenaline hits and it's a dash to meet them at their target.

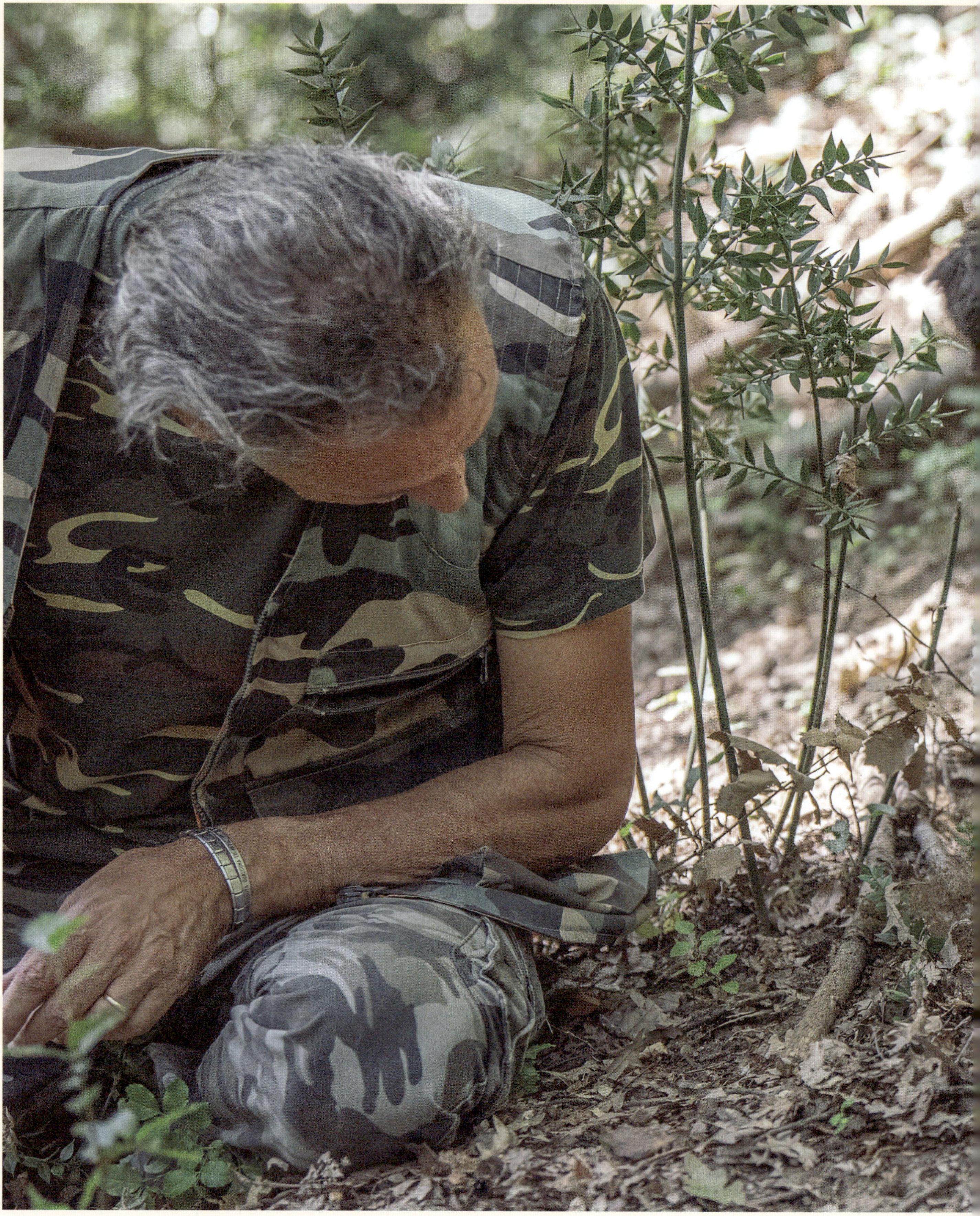

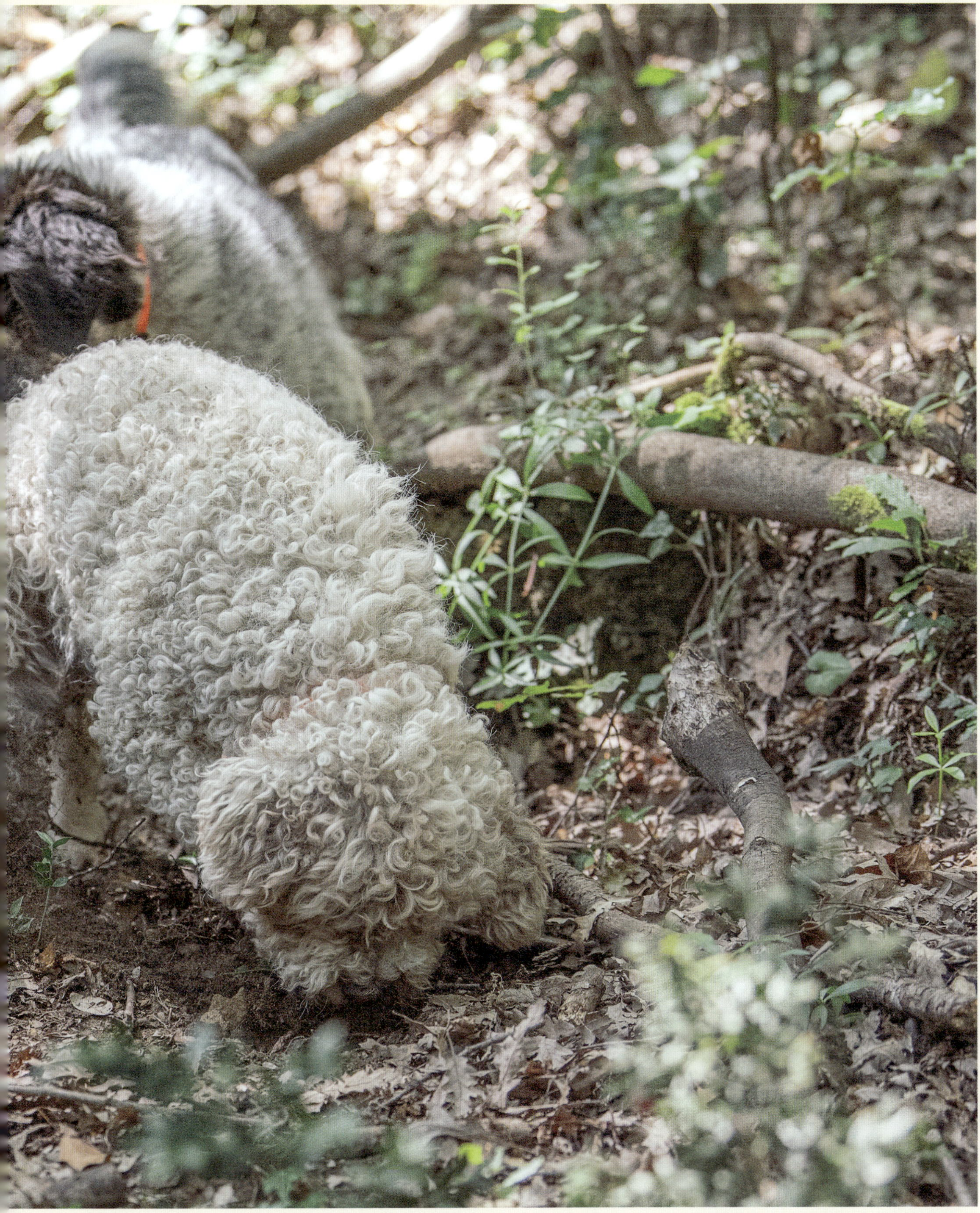

ABOVE You want to feel a rush? You don't need to go skydiving, or ride a motorcycle, or bet a week's paycheck on a single roulette spin. Just go truffle hunting. The dogs furiously run around the forest with their noses to the ground. Once they stop and start digging, that's when the adrenaline hits and it's a dash to meet them at their target.

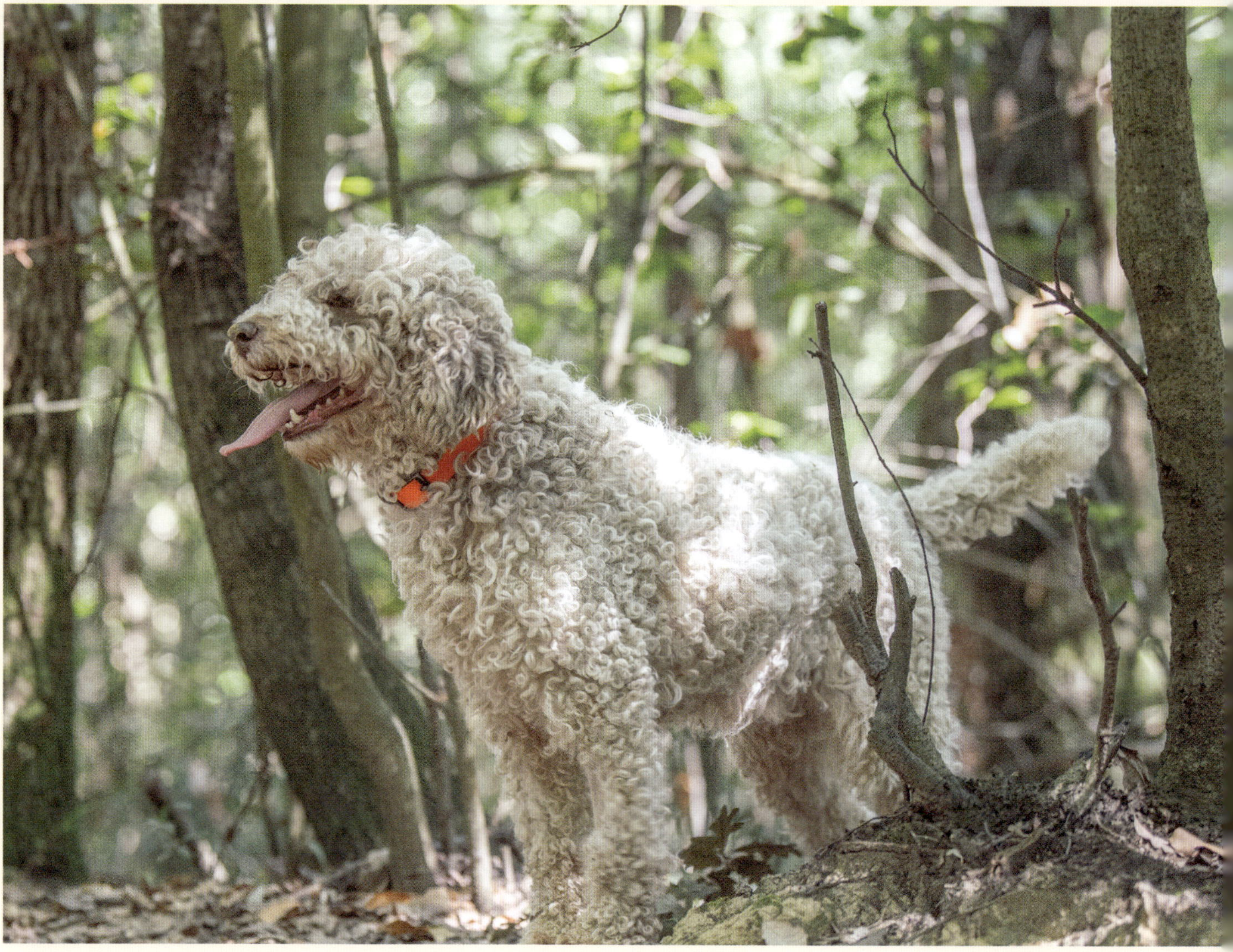

ABOVE Birba was all over the forest during our hunt – weaving between trees, diving into holes, and collecting mud on her nose as she feverishly sniffed.

BELOW Eyes on the prize, and for good reason. Italian truffles are exceptional, and our tour ended with a tasting of these freshly dug-up delicacies. Thanks Birba and Maya!

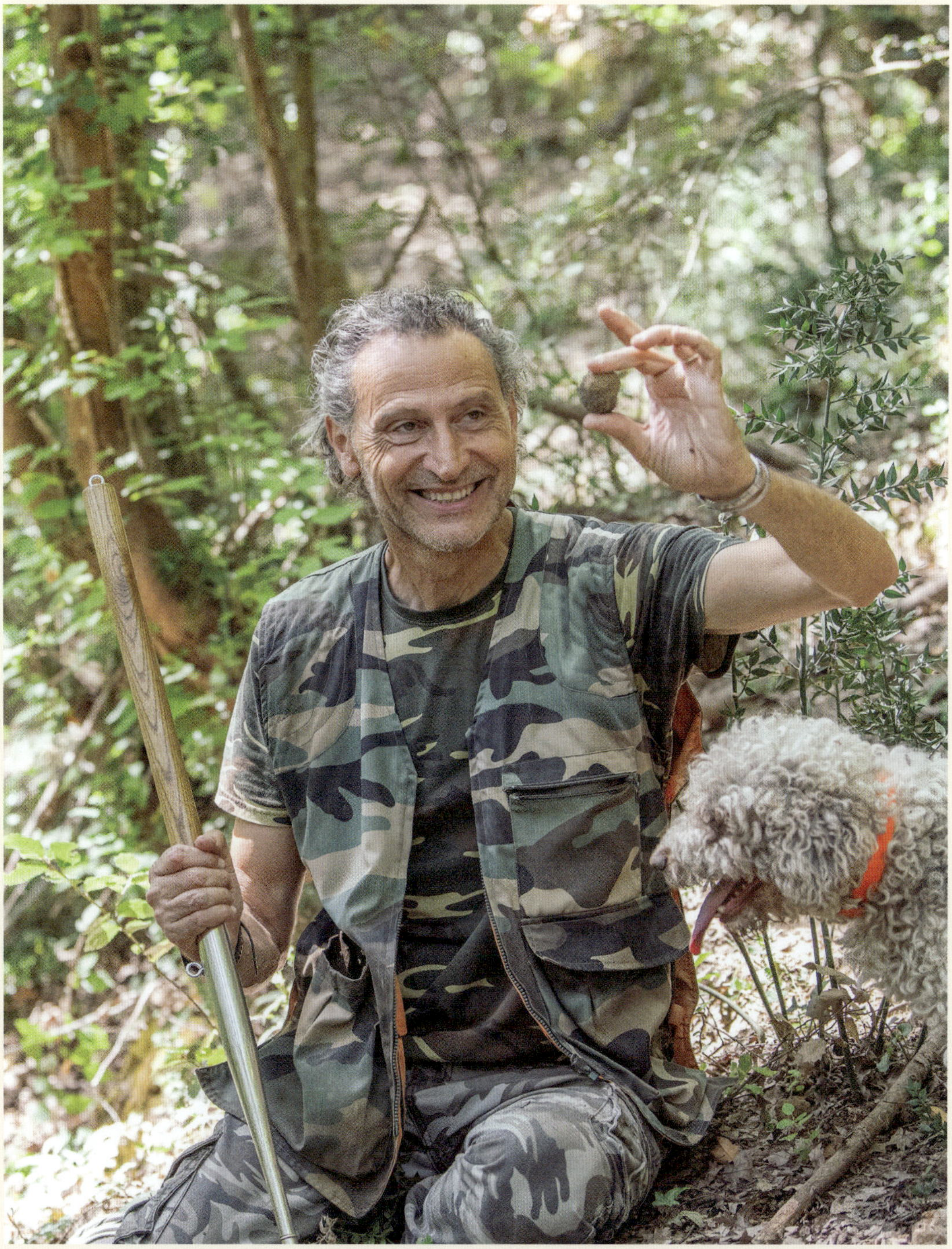

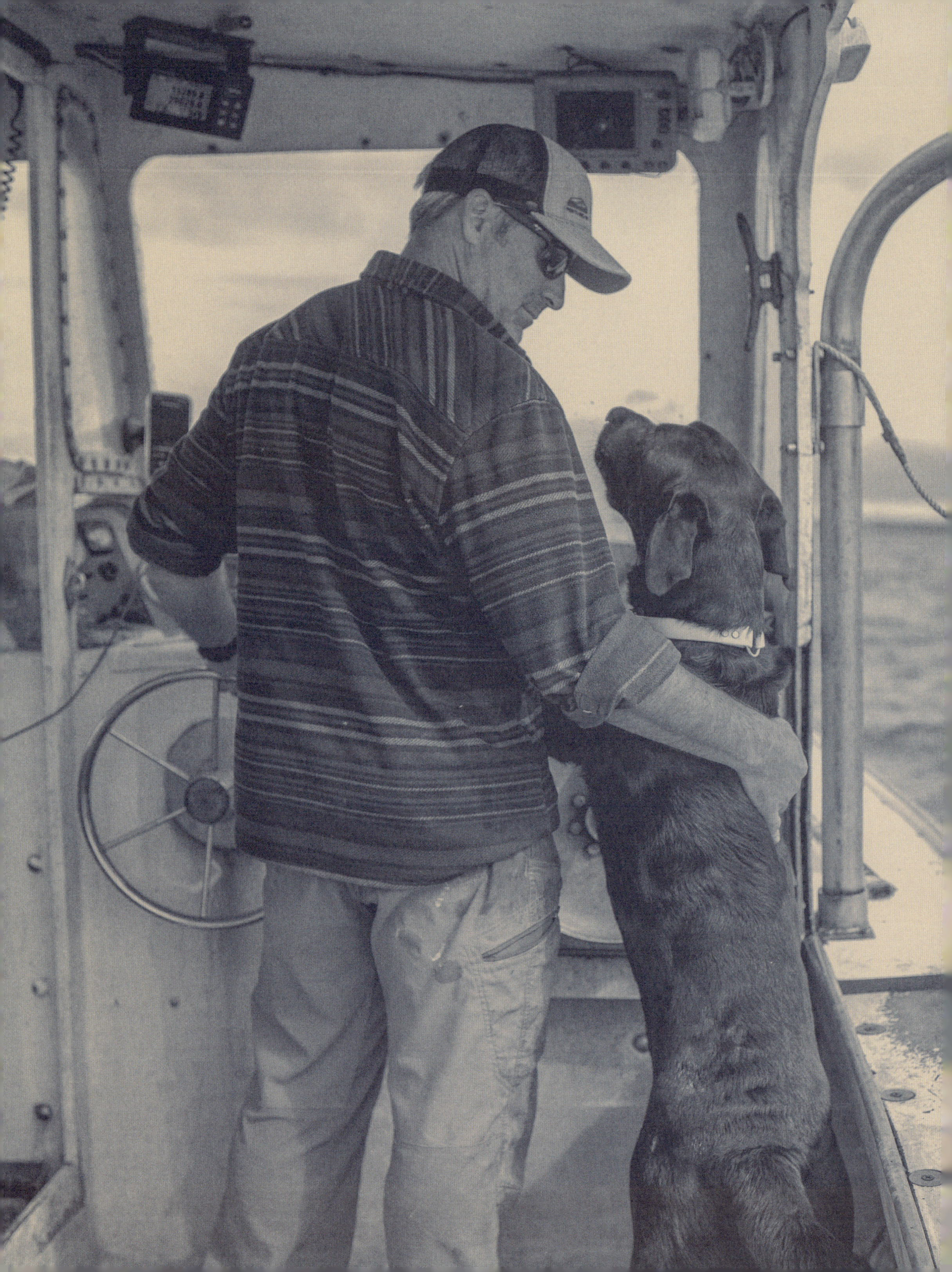

LOCATION	BREED	TASKS	SKILLS
Maine, USA	Labrador	Cleaning Deck, Providing Companionship, Boat-Themed Tricks	Balance, Enthusiasm, Sea Legs (x4)

LOBSTER BOAT DOGS

THERE IS A LONG HISTORY of dogs tagging along on fishing boats. Working on the water can be a solitary experience, so the companionship of a dog makes long working hours much more manageable and enjoyable. In the area of Maine where I took these photos, several fishing vessels regularly have dogs aboard.

During my time there, I spent one morning on the water with Eric and his Labrador, Briggs, to photograph their unique working relationship. Briggs is the perfect boat dog: happy and high-energy, and equipped with excellent Labrador swimming skills if he ever ends up in the water.

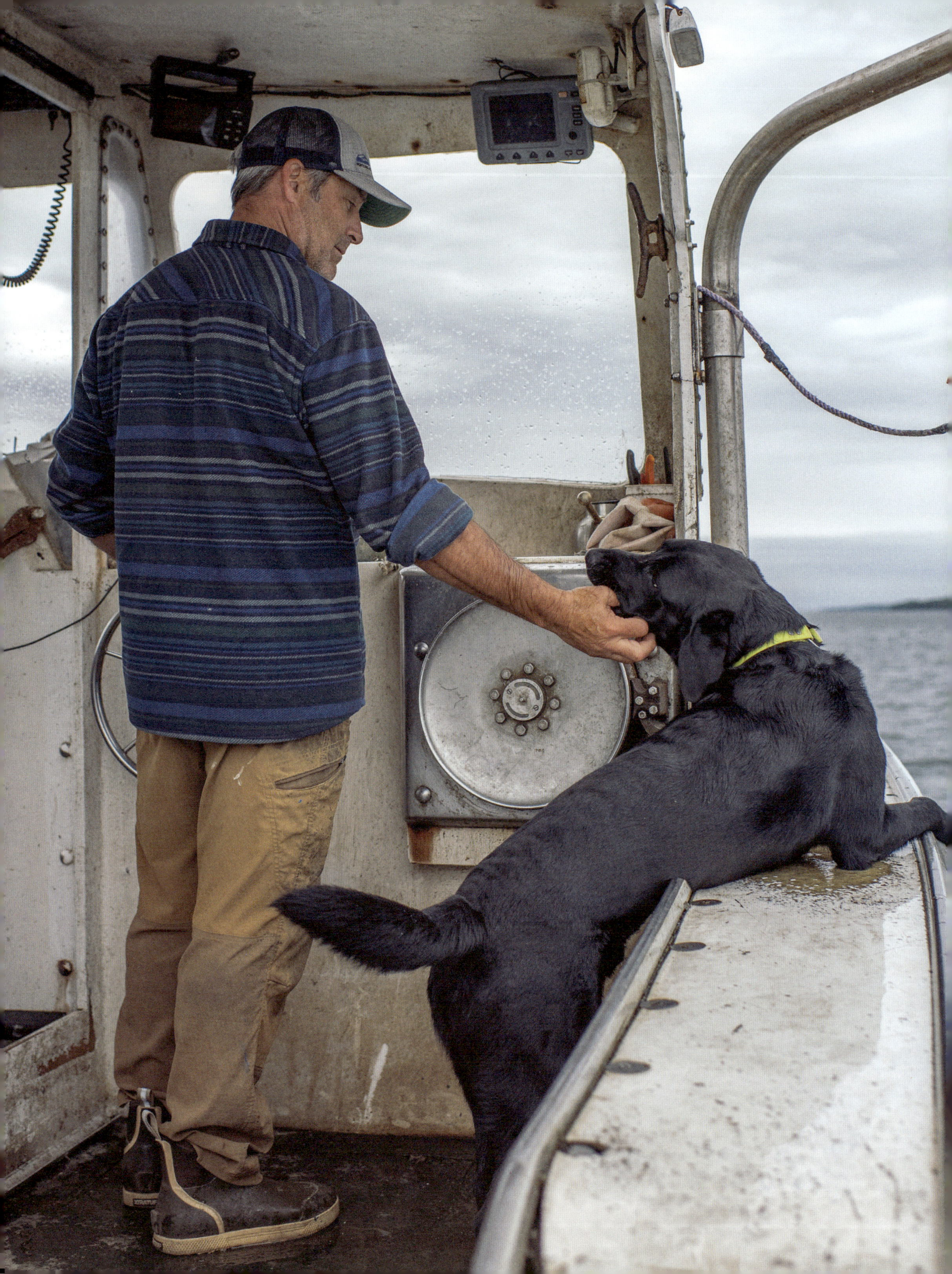

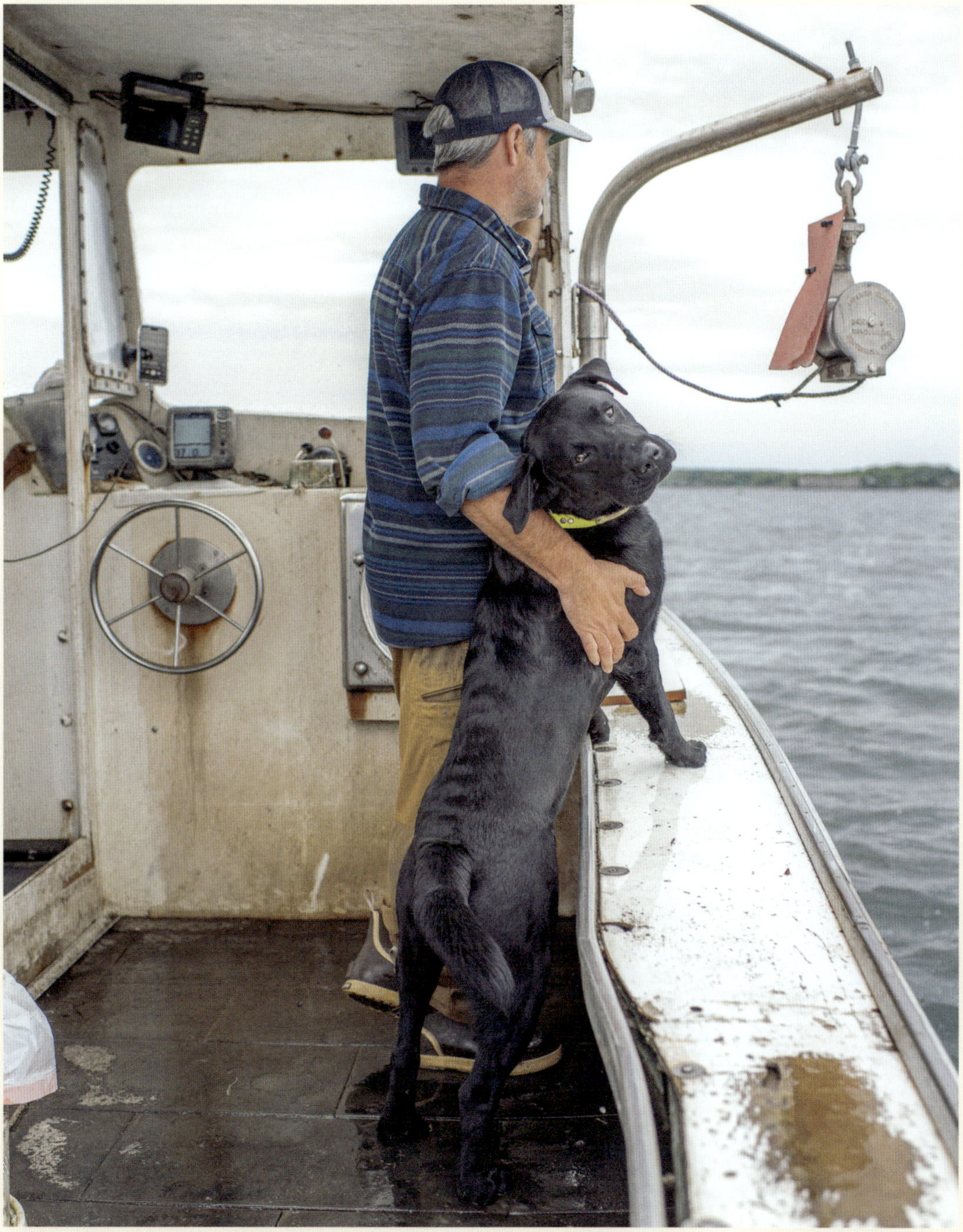

LEFT & ABOVE Eric is a lifelong Mainer who started his own lobster company, E.A.T. Lobster, out of Scarborough. He docks his boat and sets his traps just off the coast of Portland. He built his impressive business from the ground up without prior lobstering experience. As a one-man show, he'd be alone on the boat if it weren't for his first mate, Briggs.

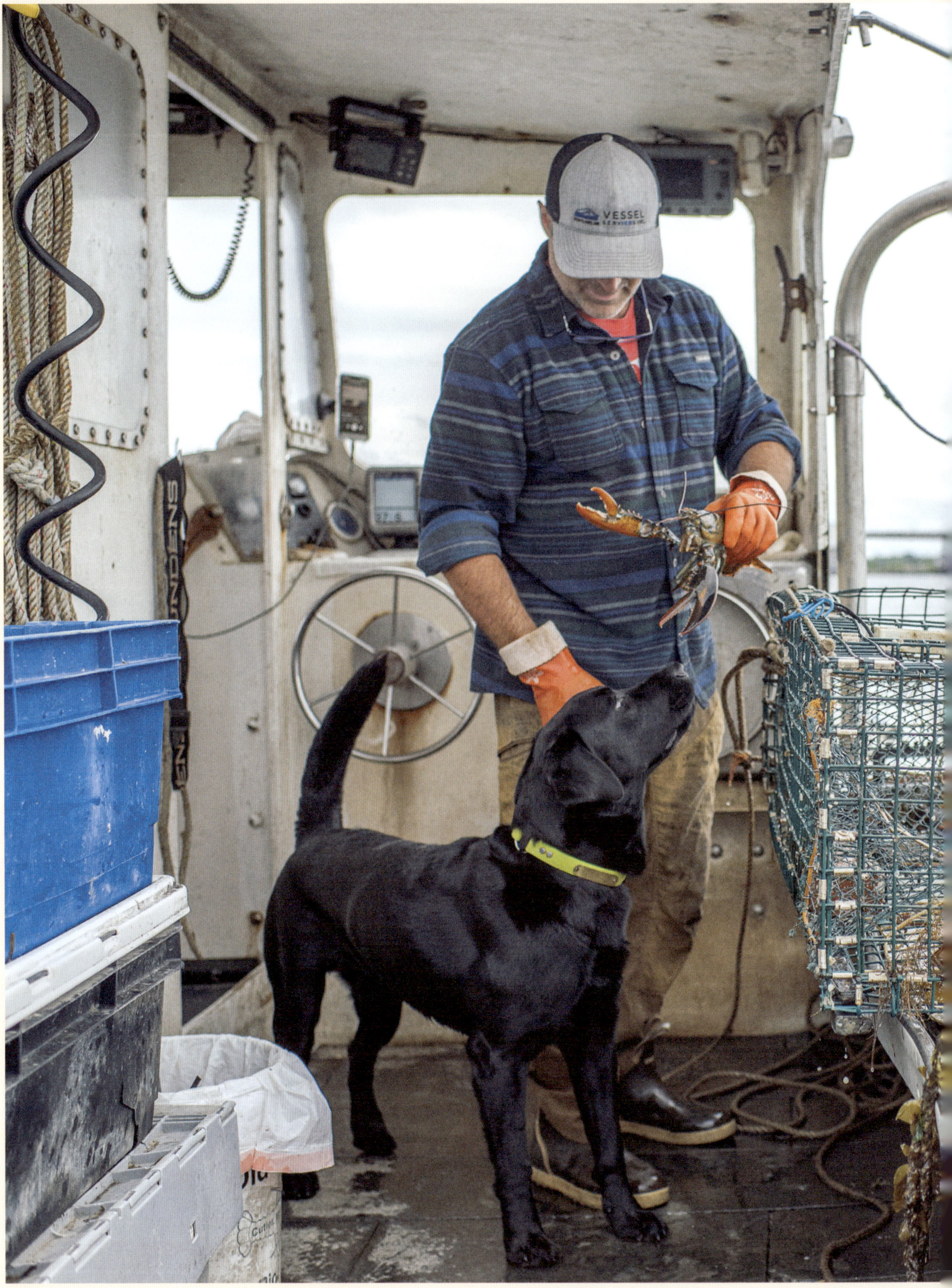
VESSEL

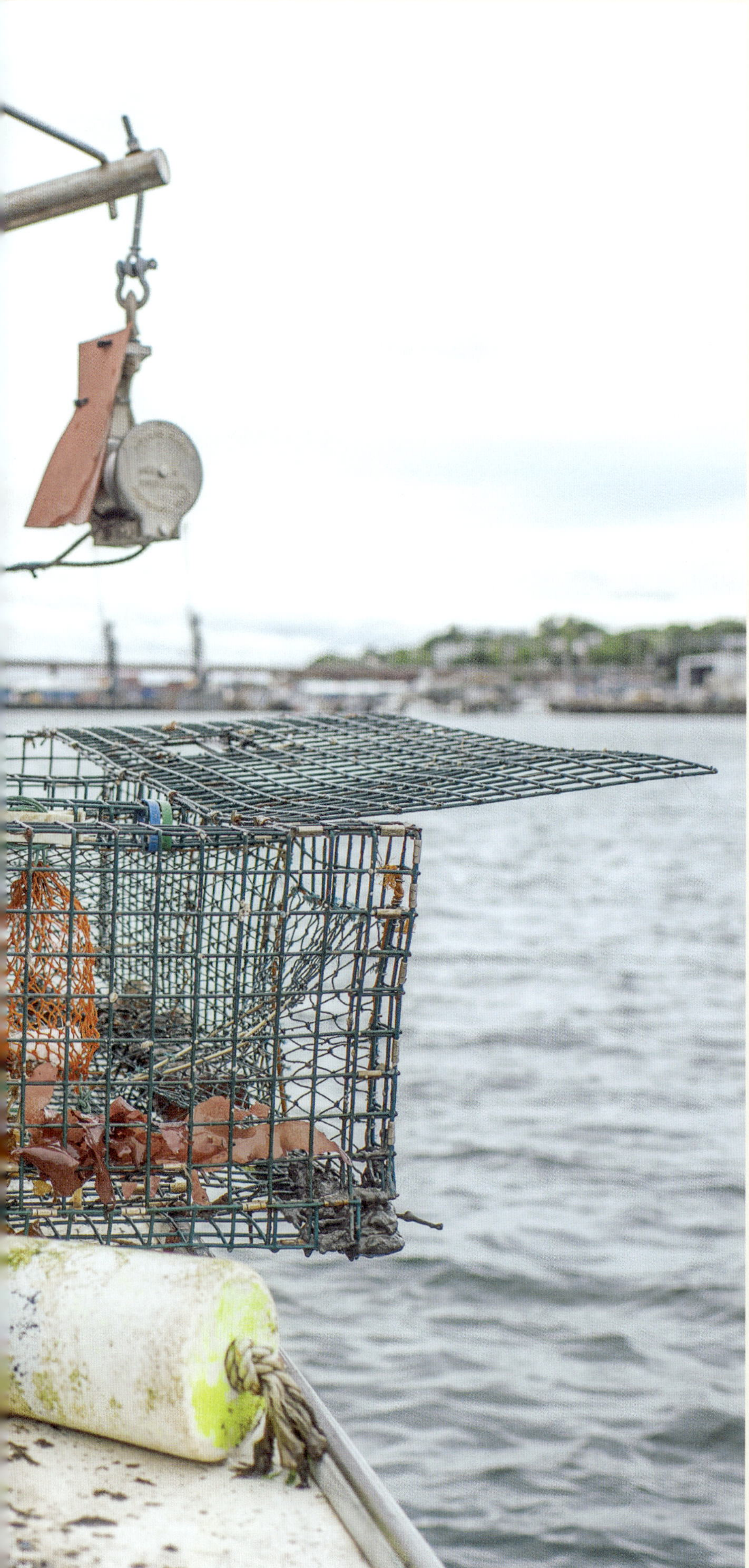

LEFT Briggs is always available to provide product inspection for any lobster coming on board. He shows a genuine curiosity toward the crustaceans and gives them a thorough sniff. All sorts of things come out of those traps, and when a rogue claw ends up on the deck, Briggs is happy to eat it up.

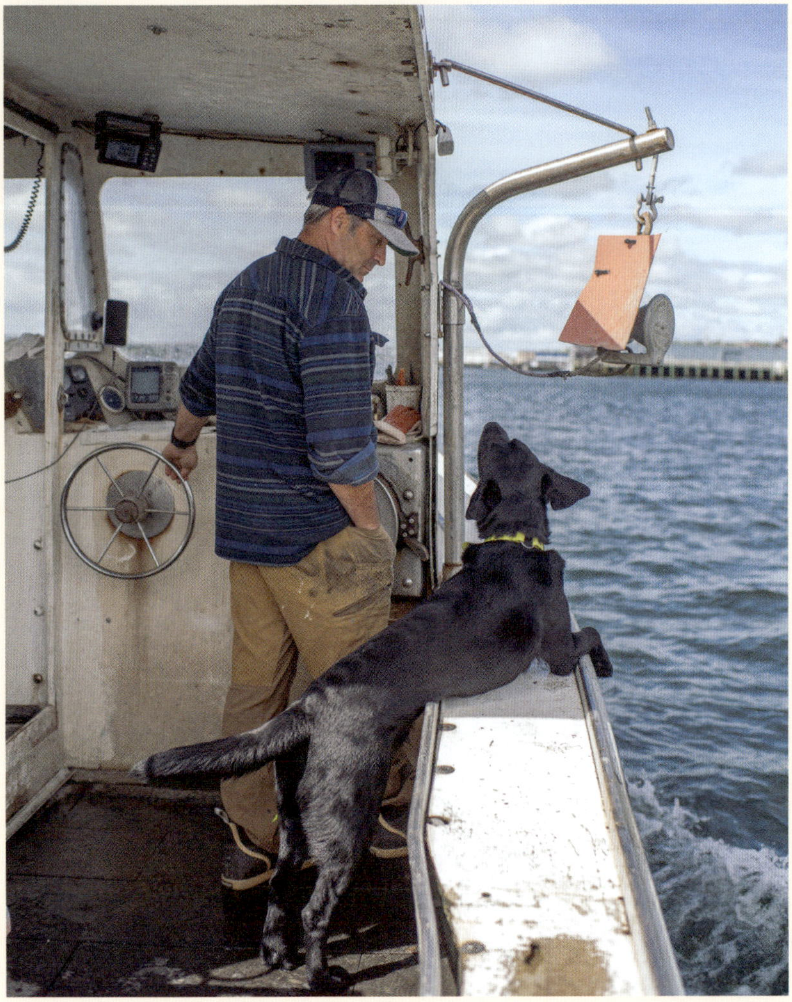

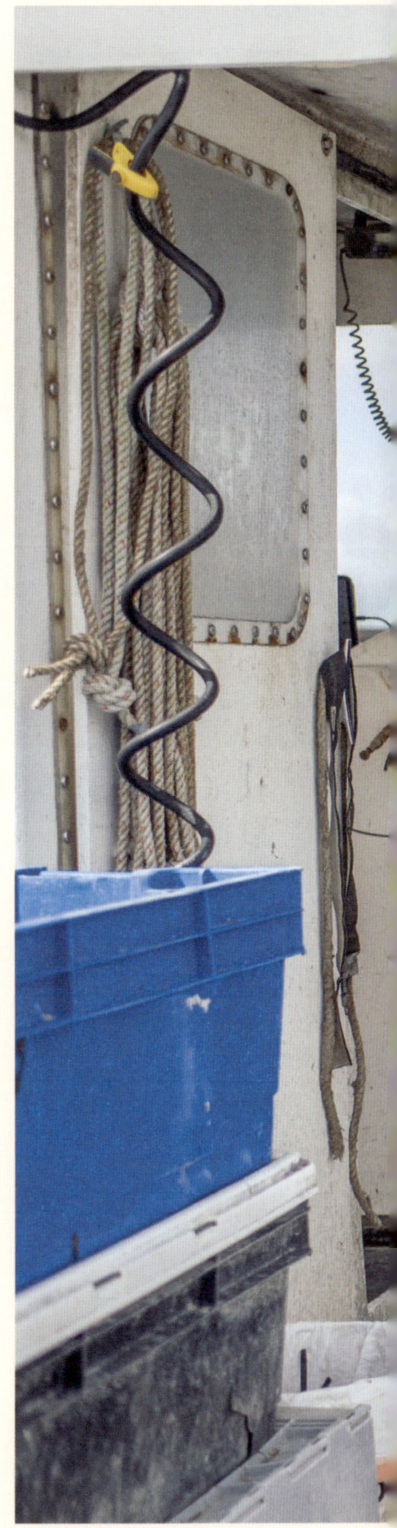

ABOVE & RIGHT If you ask Briggs to "Drive the boat," he will hop up right next to the steering wheel, and he will look out into the distance whenever you say "Lobster!" His working commands are more fun than necessary, but what he does best is provide a positive presence on the boat. Eric and Briggs have an incredible bond and both love spending their days together.

... what Briggs does best is provide a positive presence on the boat. Eric and Briggs have an incredible bond and both love spending their days together.

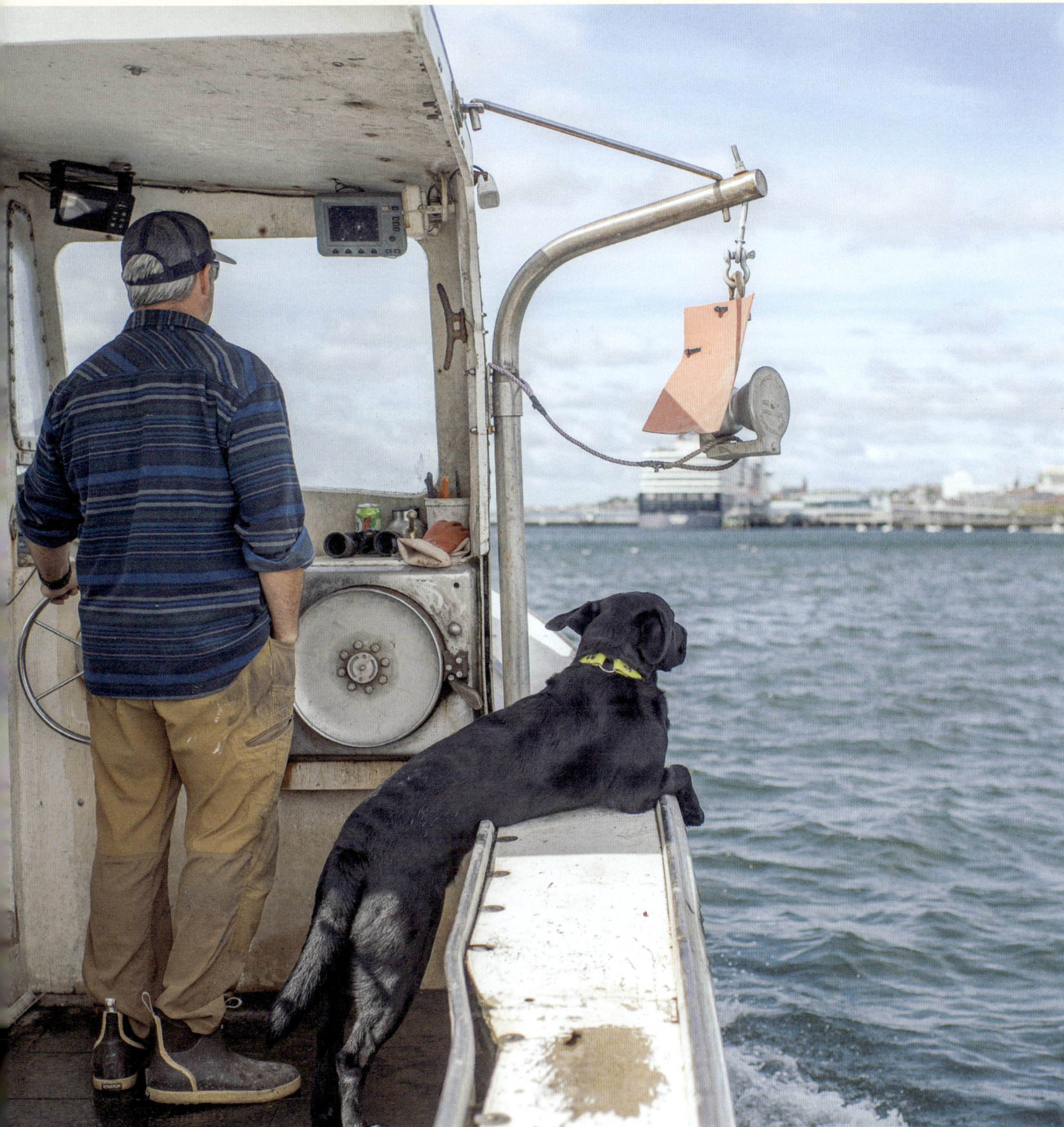

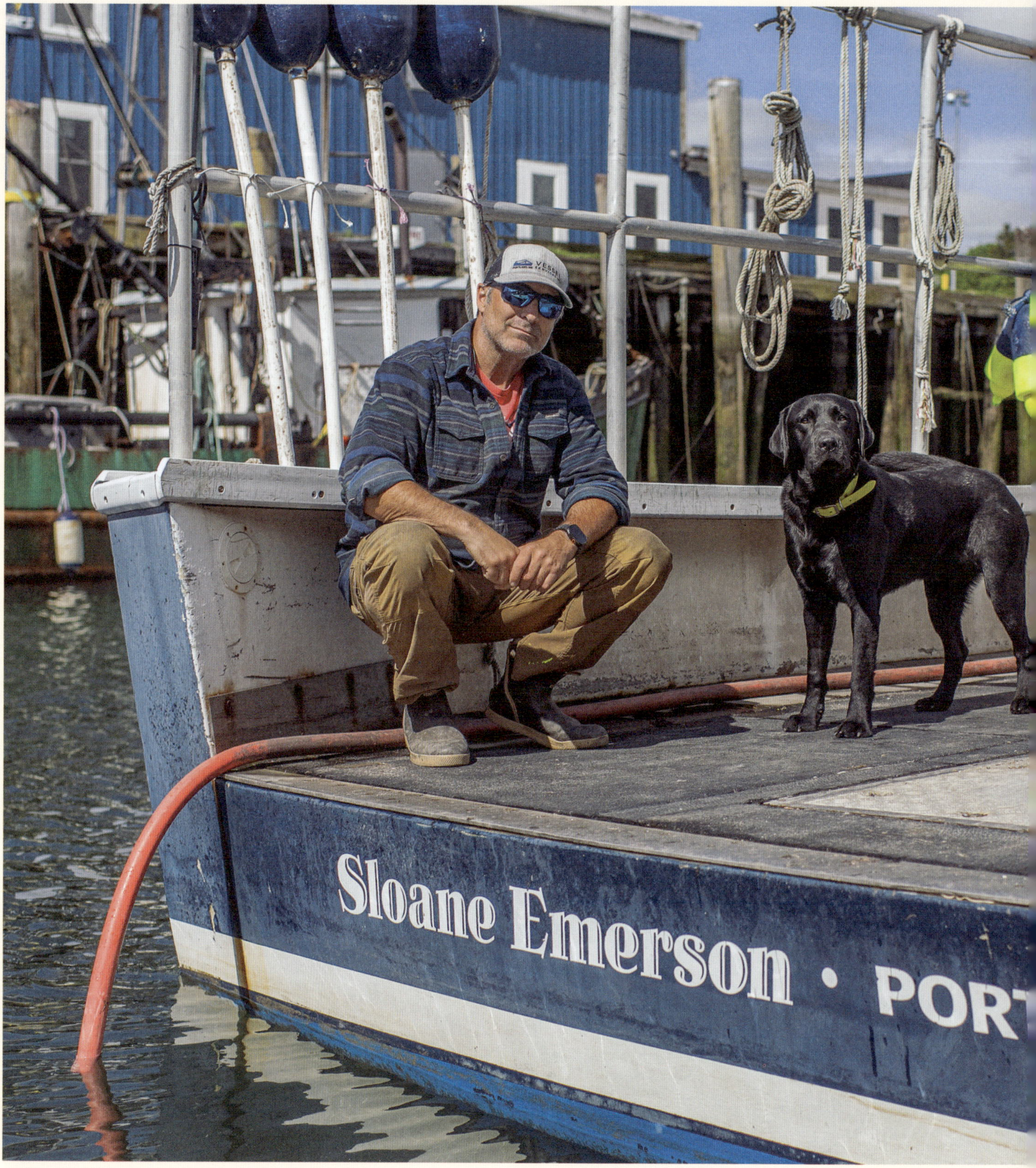
Sloane Emerson · PORT

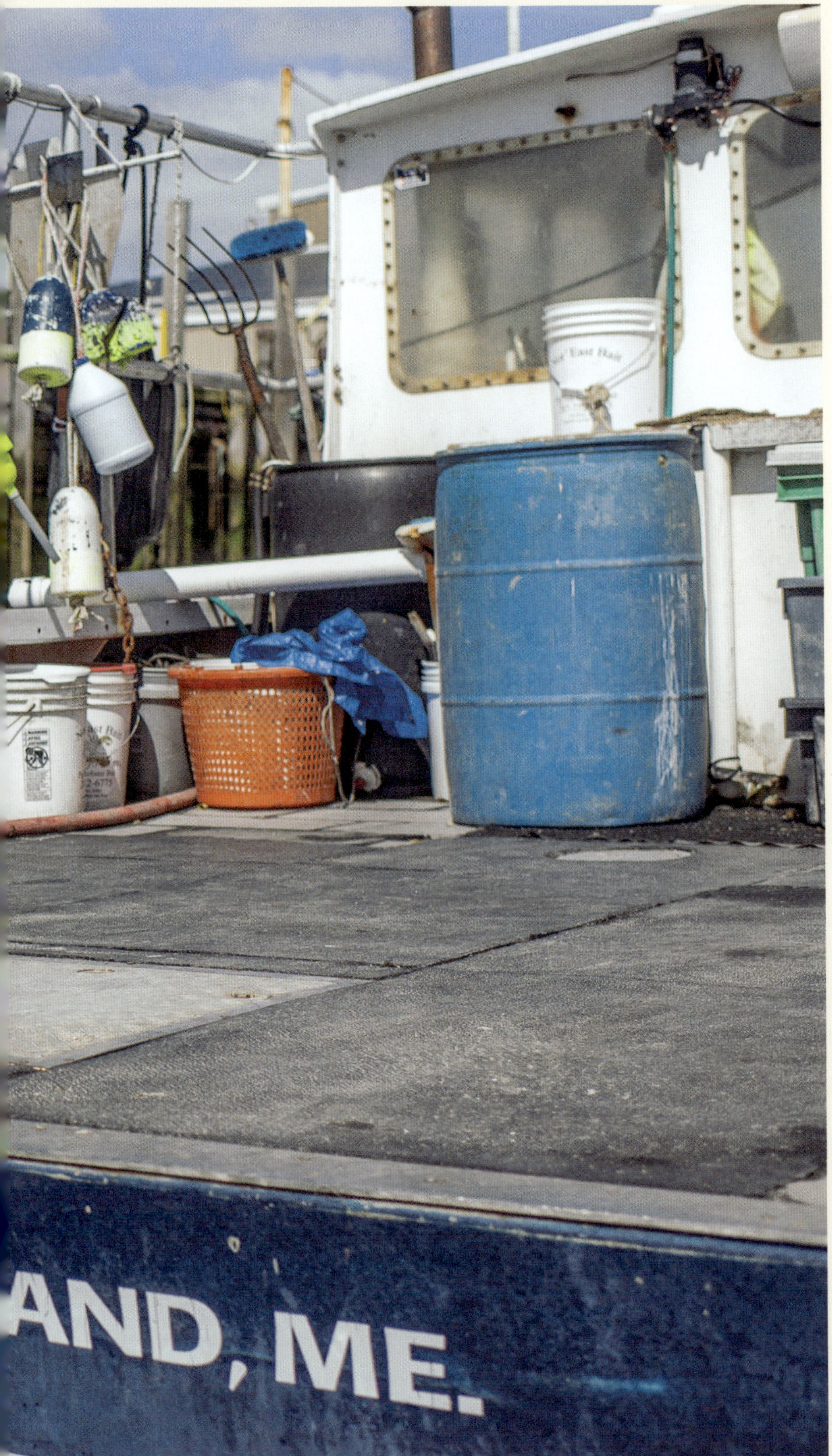

ABOVE The best lobster roll I had while in Maine was made by Captain Eric with meat that he caught. A trip to E.A.T. Lobster will get you fantastic lobster and an enthusiastic greeting from the good boy, Briggs.

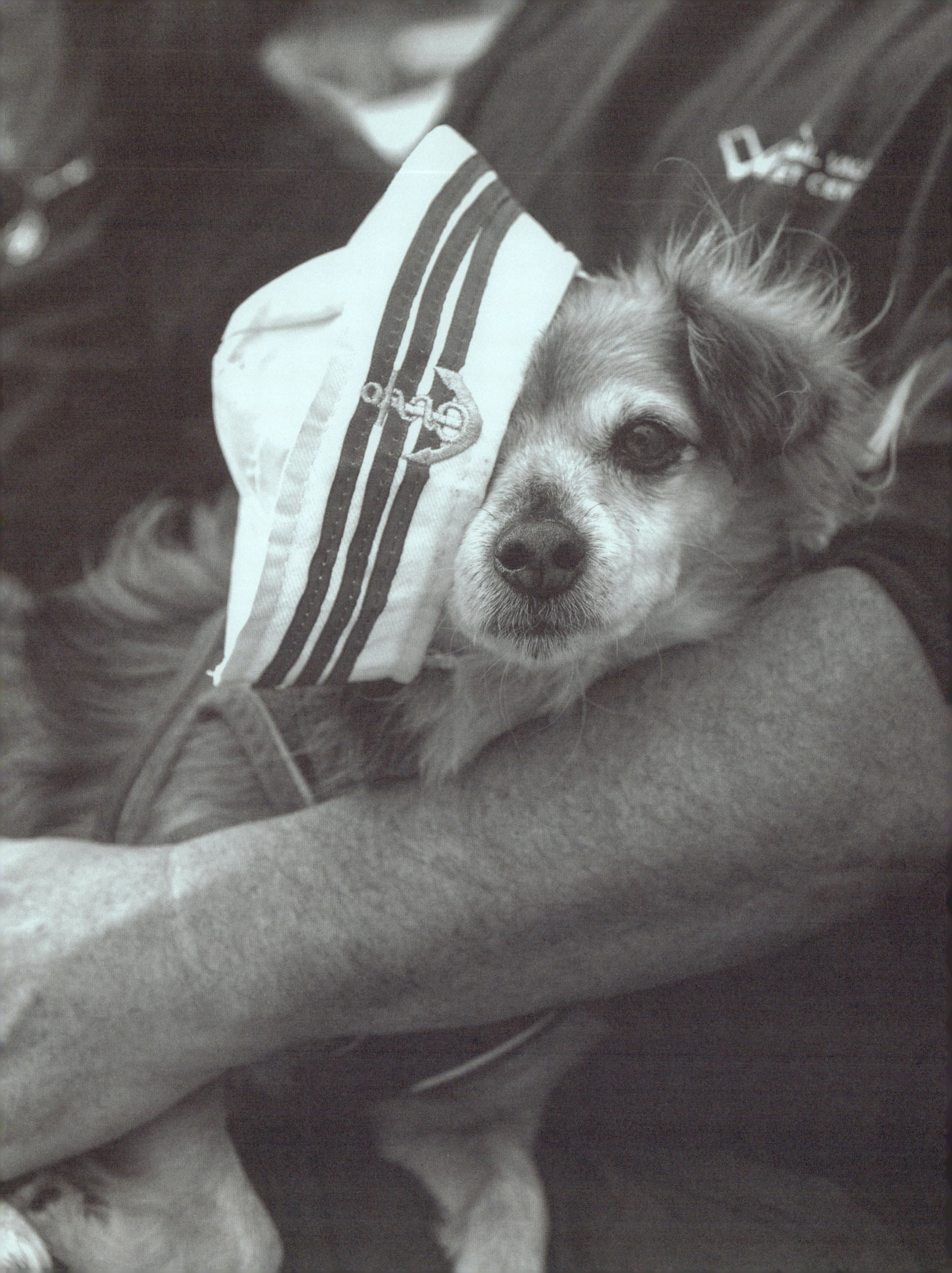

LOCATION	BREED	TASKS	SKILLS
Amsterdam, Netherlands	Romanian Street Dog	Hanging with Guests, Posing for Photos, Wearing Captain Hat	Docility, Holdability, Sociability

TOUR BOAT DOGS

THERE ARE MANY WAYS to see Amsterdam: by foot, bike, or boat. There are numerous canal tours that show off the beauty of this capital city, but one has found a way to stand out with its offering.

Pixie works as a tour guide in Amsterdam. She is an easy-going rescue dog from Romania who brings the perfect vibe alongside her owner, Lee, who offers canal tours with Those Dam Boat Guys tours. Pixie joins the tours as co-captain and is a hit with guests. While there's no specific breed that specializes in this type of work, Pixie's temperament pairs perfectly with anyone who boards her boat.

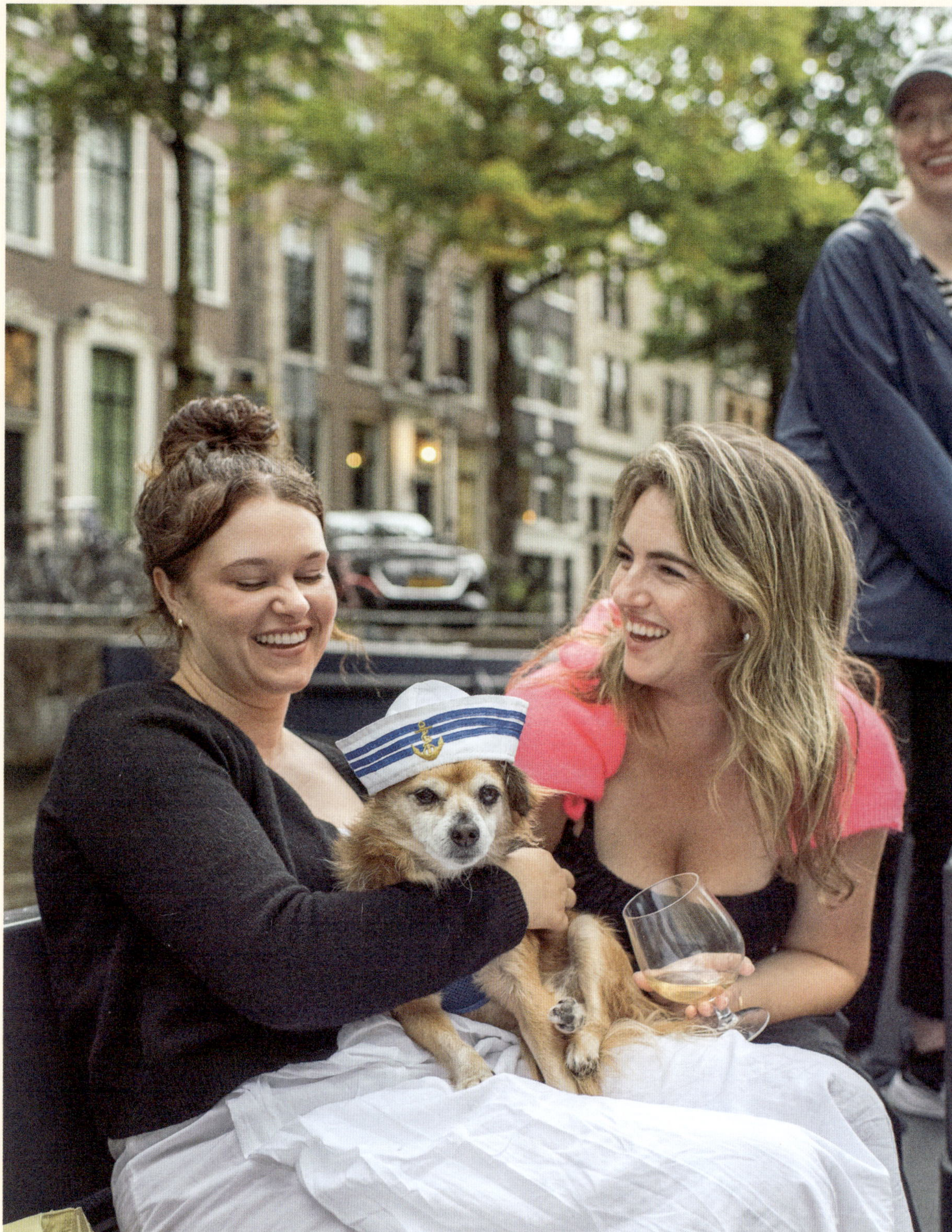

ABOVE Guests love to pass Pixie around, and she happily takes turns sitting on everyone's lap. While drinking alcohol is allowed during tours, Pixie refrains from drinking on the job.

RIGHT Pixie dresses the part for her job, with her dashing captain hat. Even when it falls sideways, she doesn't seem to mind. She's one of the most laid-back dogs I've ever met.

Guests love to pass Pixie around, and she happily takes turns sitting on everyone's lap.

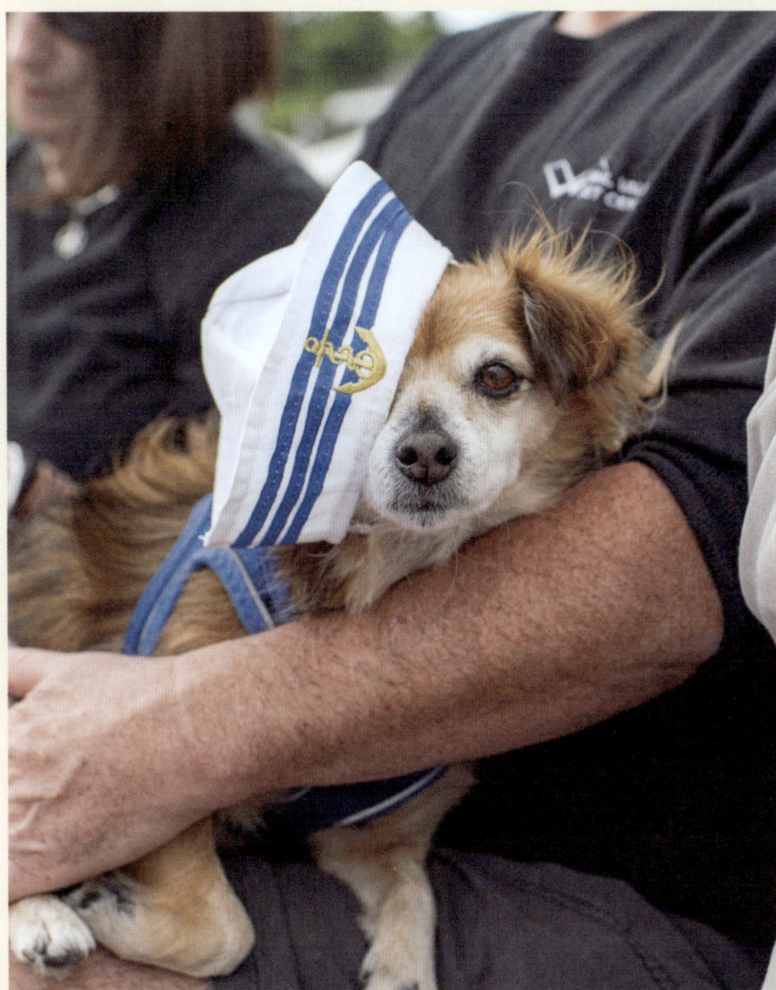

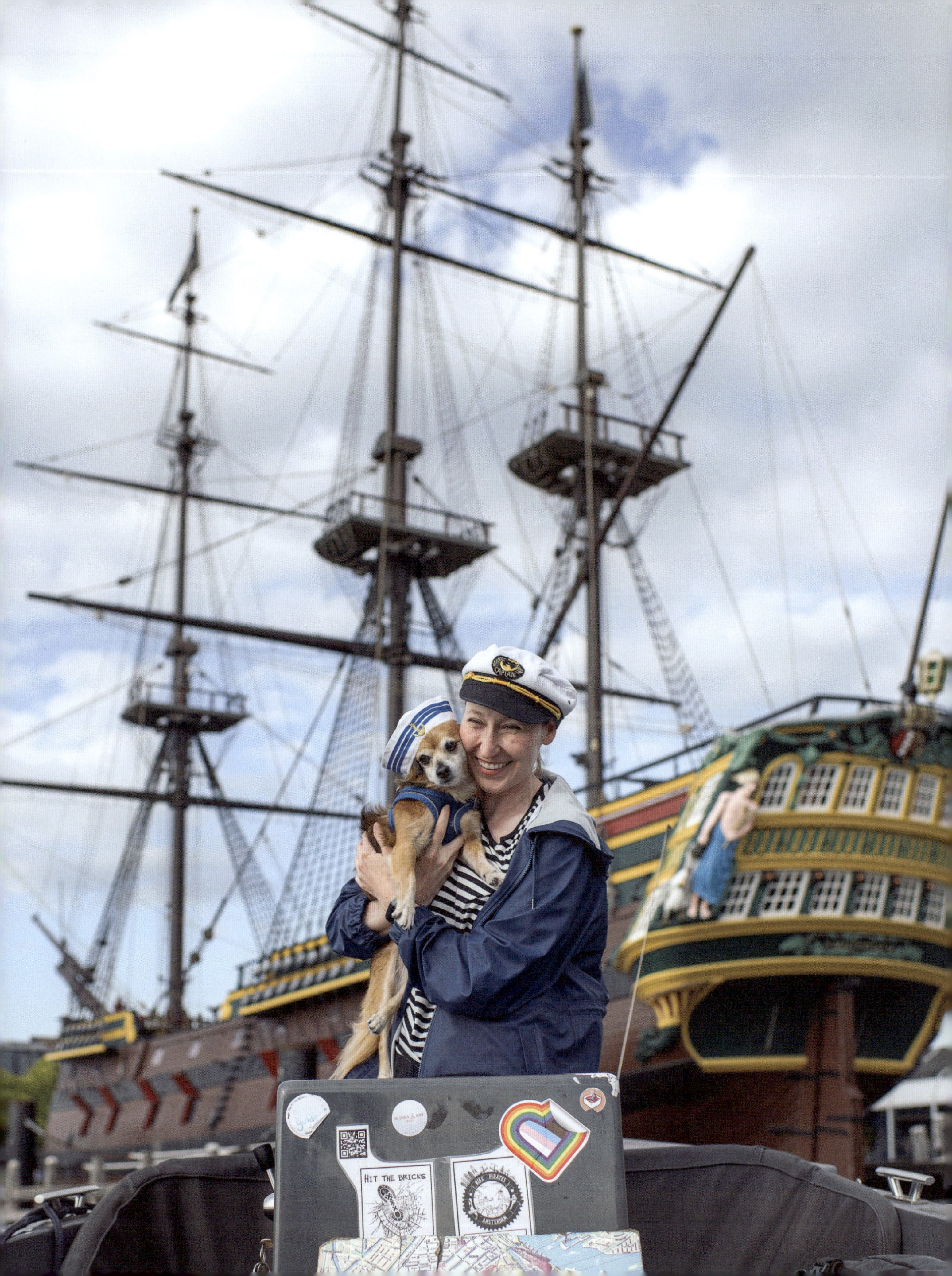
CAPTAIN
HIT THE BRICKS
BIKE PIRATES
AMSTERDAM

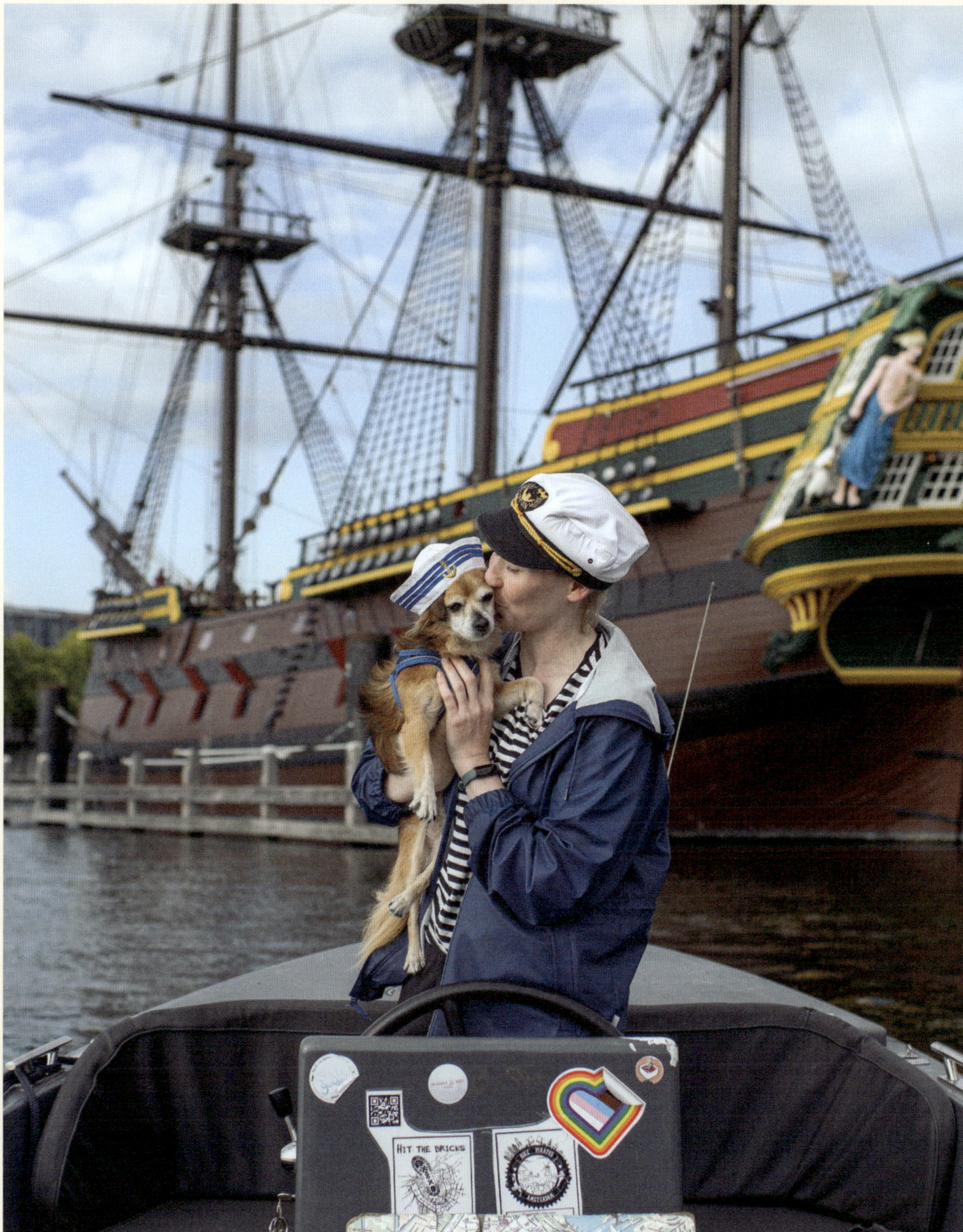

LEFT Pixie and Lee are an incredible pair, and their loving relationship is on display during every tour.

ABOVE Pixie spent the first few years of her life as a street dog in Romania. Her DNA was tested and the number one breed result was "Romanian Street Dog." From streets to ships, Pixie has lived an eventful life moving across Europe.

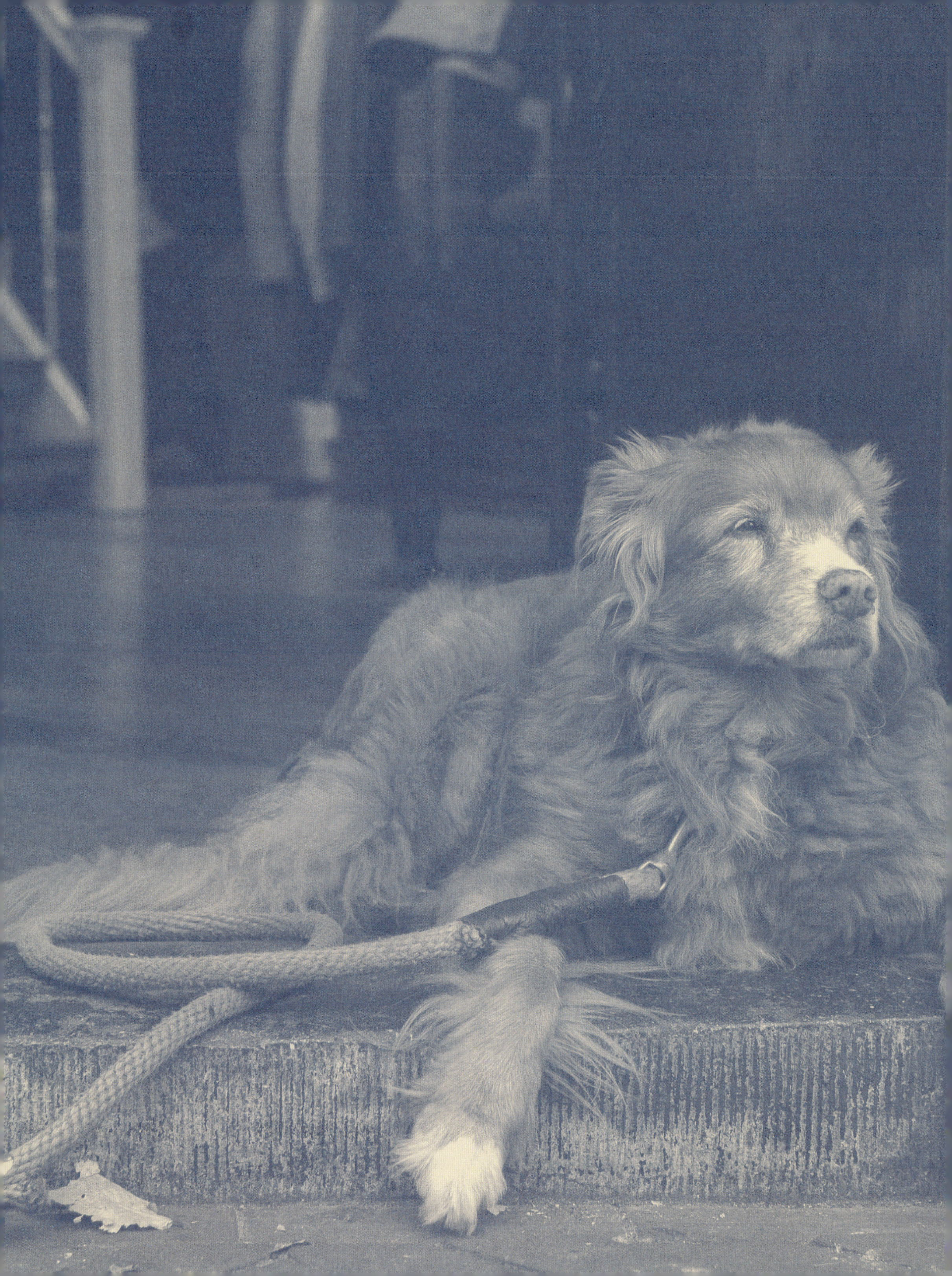

LOCATION	BREED	TASKS	SKILLS
Amsterdam, Netherlands	Toller, Vizsla, German Shepherd/ Belgian Malinois Mix, and Rescue	Greeting Guests, Generating Foot Traffic, Getting Photos Taken	Calmness, Sociability, Customer Service

RETAIL DOGS

AMSTERDAM IS AN INCREDIBLE CITY. The canals, the bikes, the tall, leaning houses, and a personal favorite of mine – the brown bars. There is a palpable ease here, so it's no surprise that it is a very dog-friendly city. You'll find plenty of them strolling through department stores, sitting in cafes, and riding public transportation.

Within a few weeks of moving to Amsterdam, I noticed something in the stores around my neighborhood. A few businesses had discovered a marketing hack – they keep a dog on the premises. It's ingenious, as it's an easy way to attract customers. And as for the people who are turned off by the dog employees? Those aren't the type of customers that any business would want.

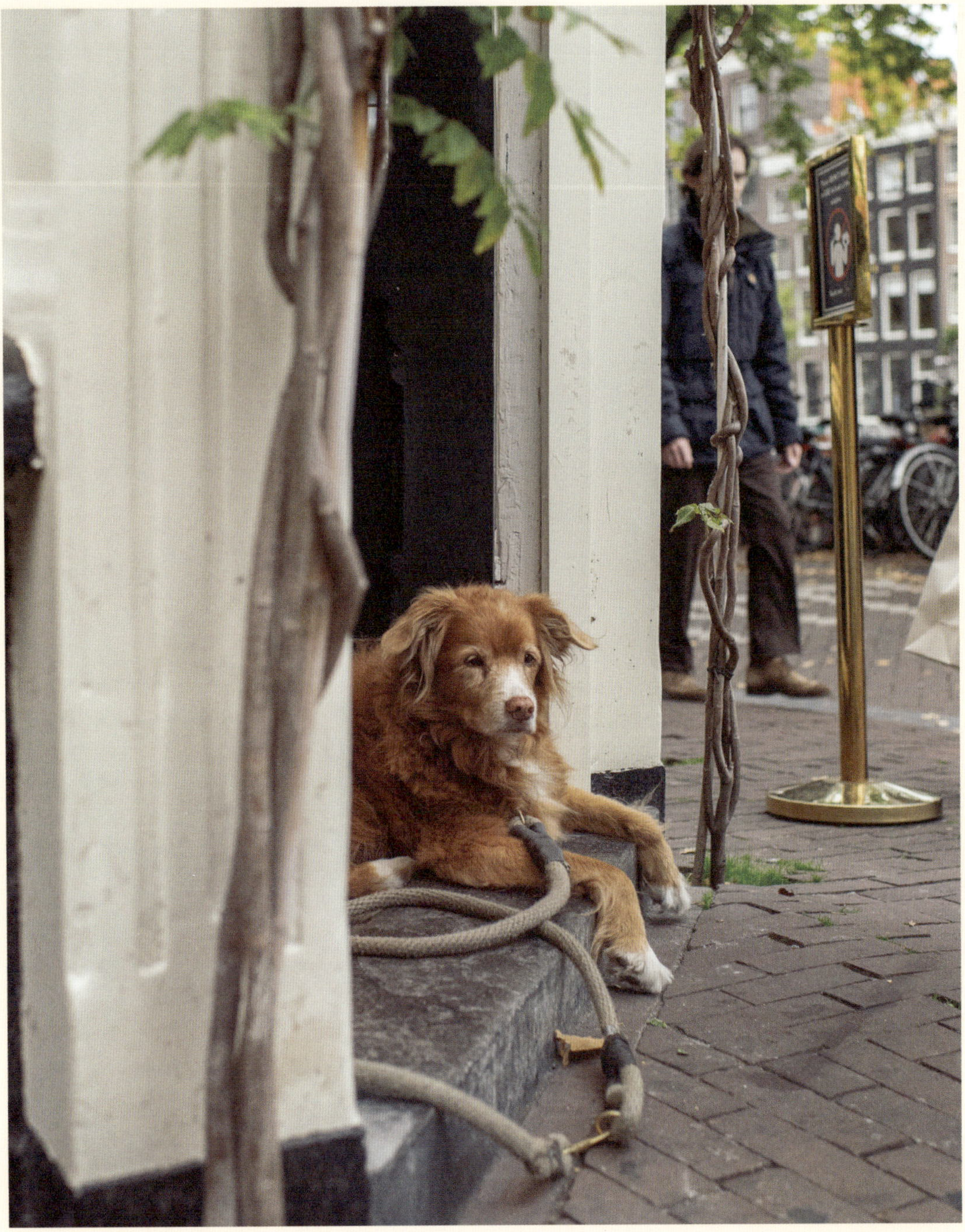

ABOVE & RIGHT Sam sits in the doorway greeting anyone who enters the clothing store Local Service. Many people who are shopping, waiting in line at the french fry shop across the street, or just strolling by, stop to snap a photo or offer a pat on the head. Sam has such a gentle, calm demeanor, and is an iconic member of the 9 Straatjes district of Amsterdam.

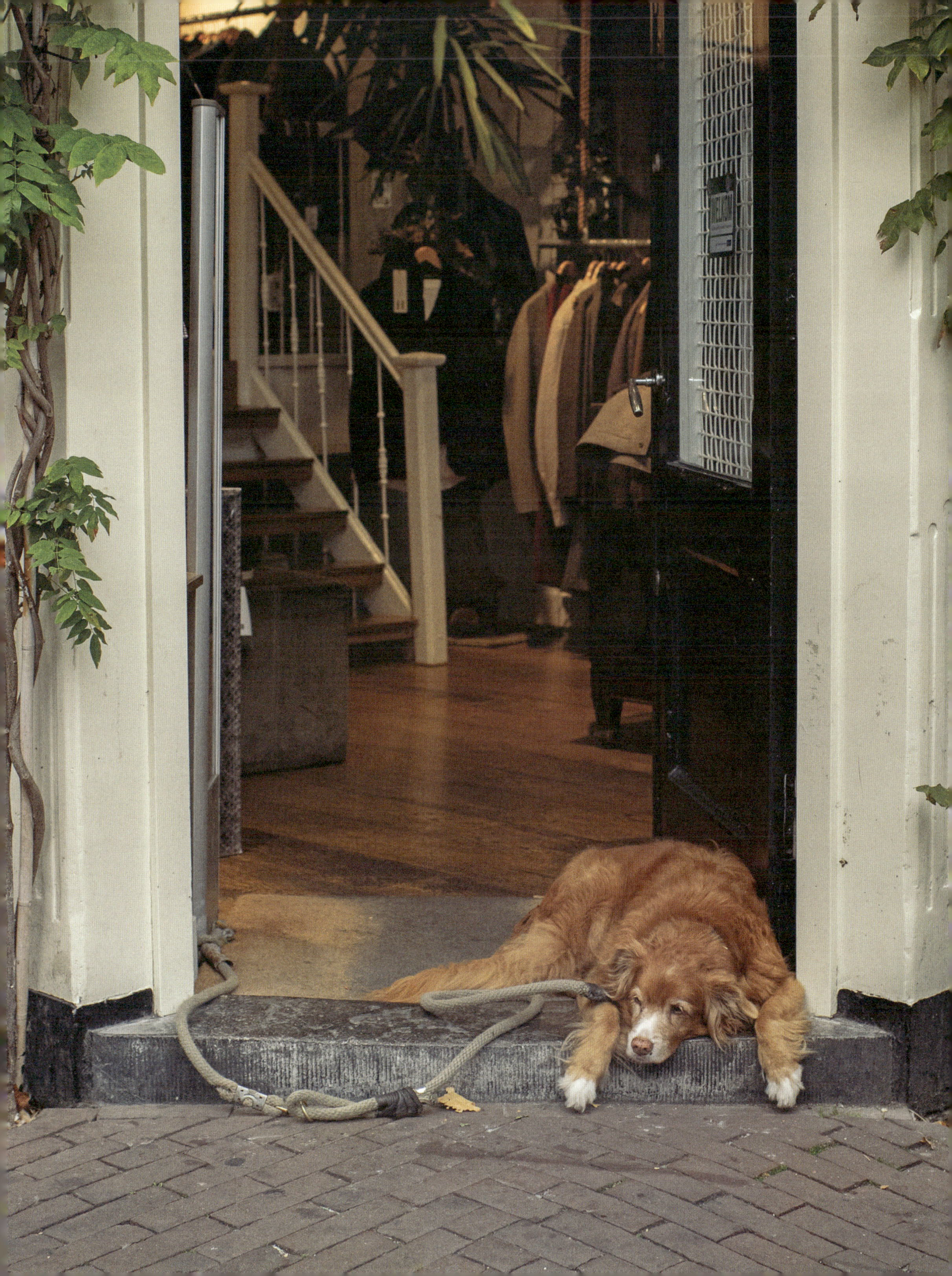

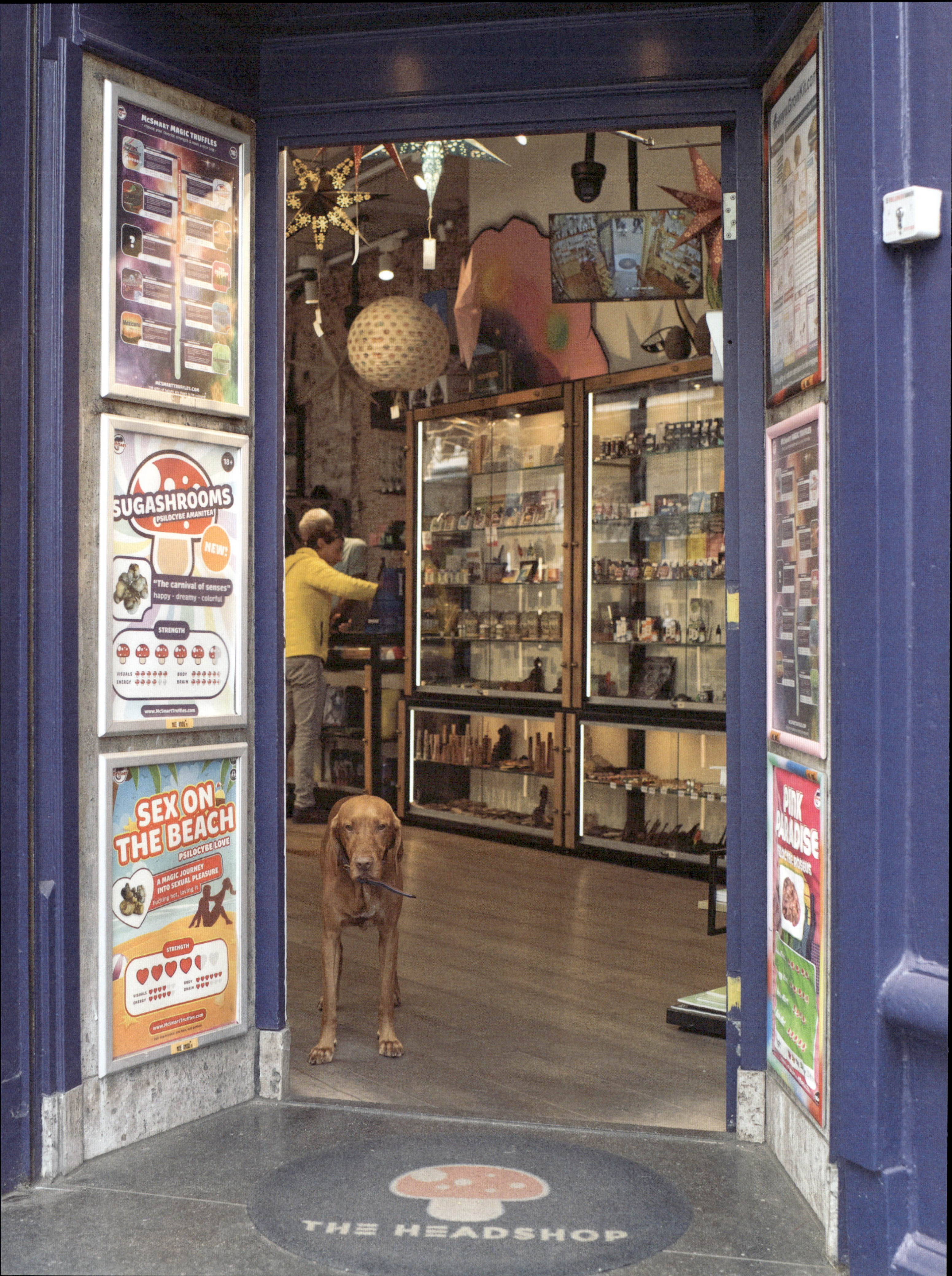
McSMART MAGIC TRUFFLES
18+
SUGASHROOMS
PSILOCYBE AMANITEA
NEW!
"The carnival of senses"
happy · dreamy · colorful
STRENGTH
www.McSmartTruffles.com
SEX ON THE BEACH
PSILOCYBE LOVE
A MAGIC JOURNEY INTO SEXUAL PLEASURE
STRENGTH
www.McSmartTruffles.com
PINK PARADISE
THE HEADSHOP

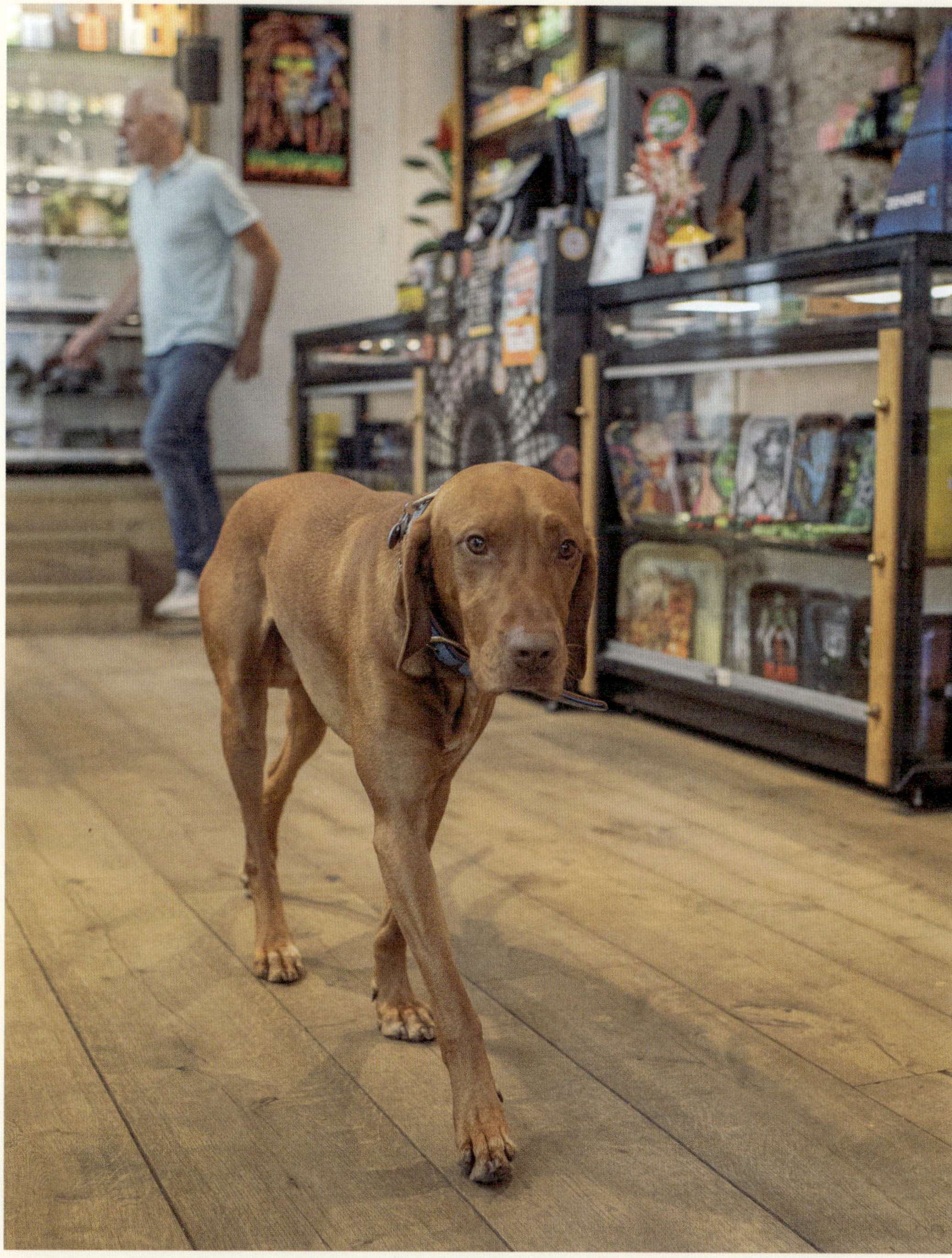

LEFT Amsterdam is known around the world for its coffeeshops – especially those that don't specialize in coffee. While there are many to choose from, I've only come across one with a stable dog presence: The Headshop Amsterdam.

ABOVE Jack accompanies his owner to work and hangs out at the store. He waits in the doorway, happy to welcome anyone off the street, then calmly follows shoppers around with his tail slowly wagging. His laid-back demeanor fits right in with the vibe of the store.

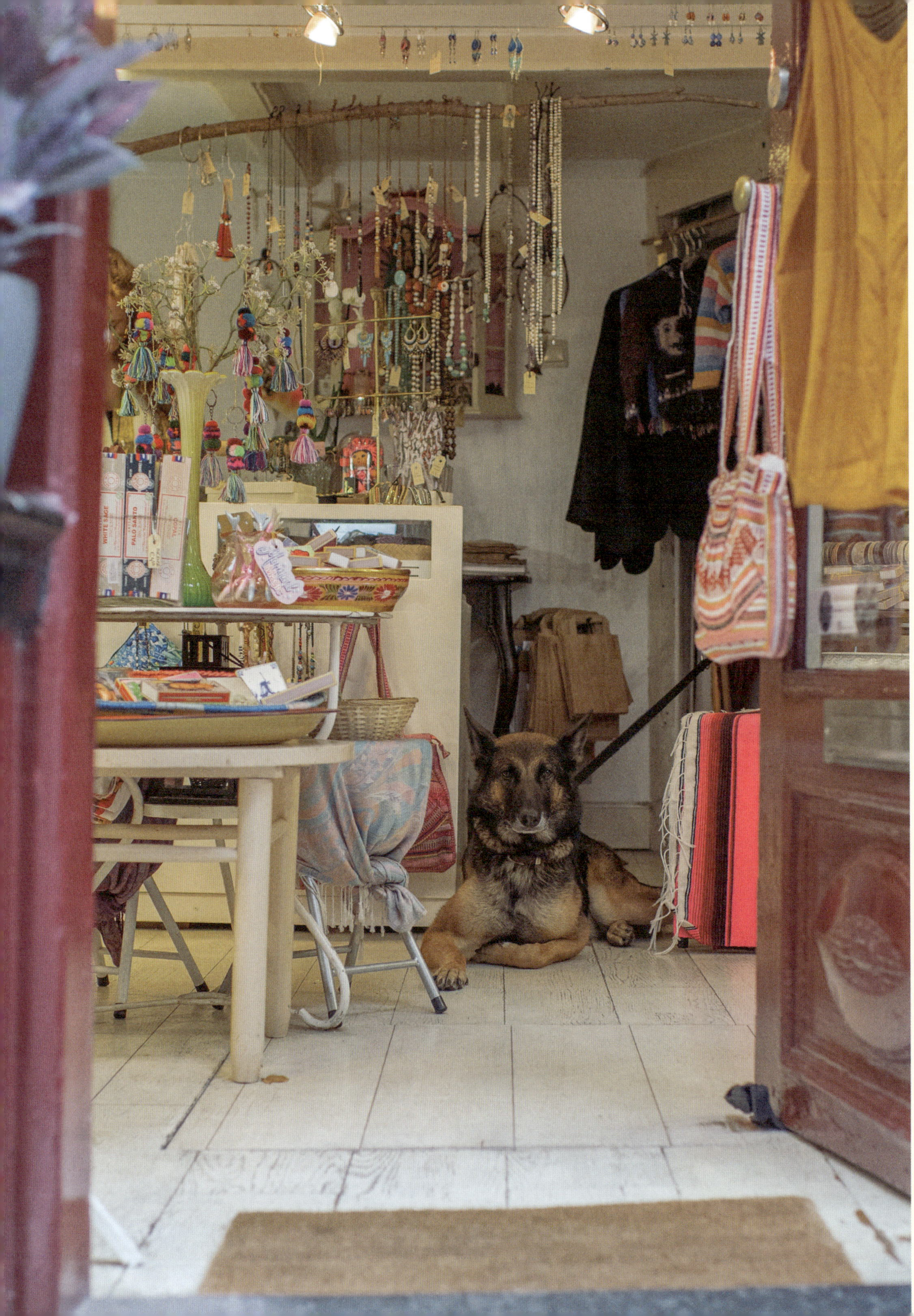

WHITE SAGE
PALO SANTO
COPAL

LEFT & BELOW meCHICas is a boutique offering jewelry in the heart of Amsterdam. Just as appealing as the unique product offerings is the greeting of the store dog. Lupi is a German Shepherd and Belgian Malinois mix – two breeds that are often used to guard properties. But Lupi was born with a bevy of friendly genes and loves to help the store owner, Debbie, greet customers from all over the world.

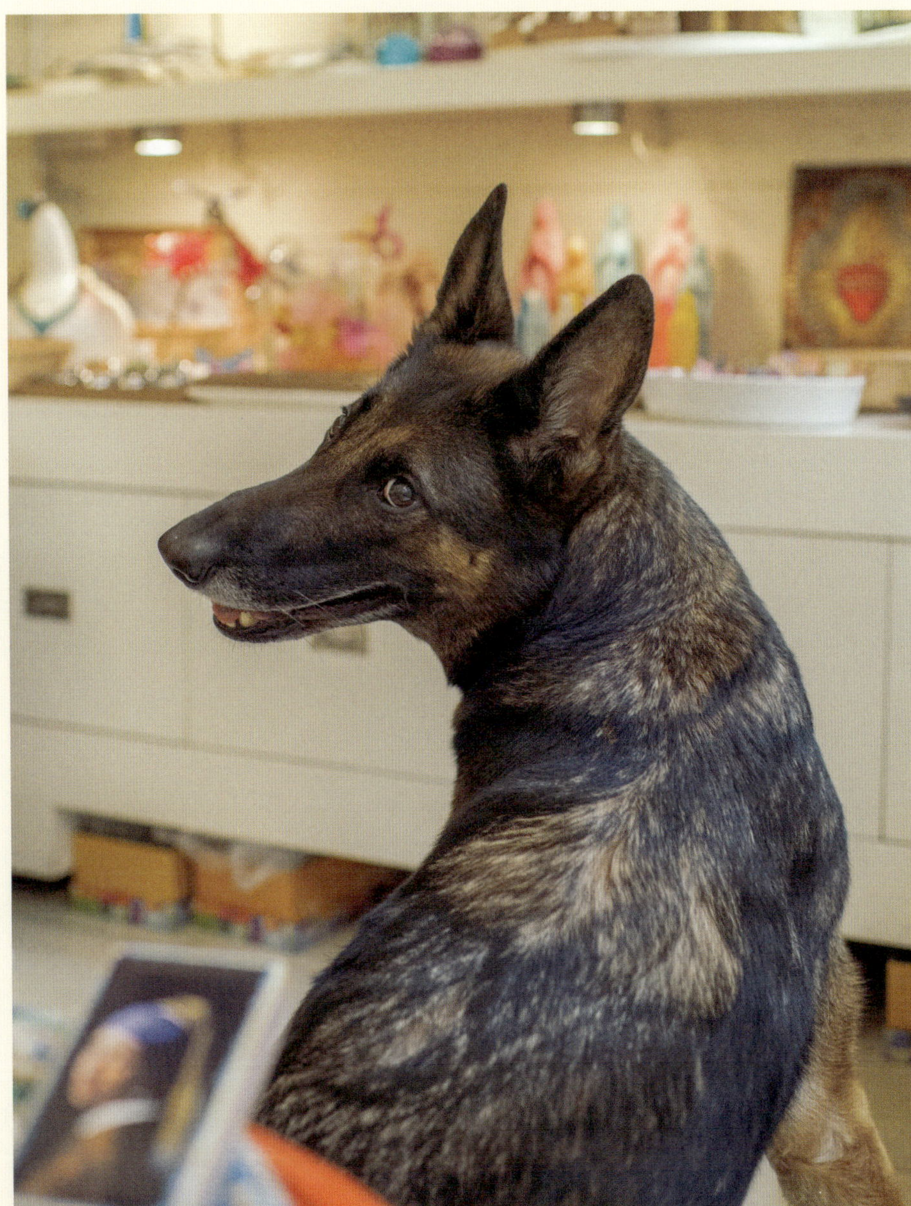

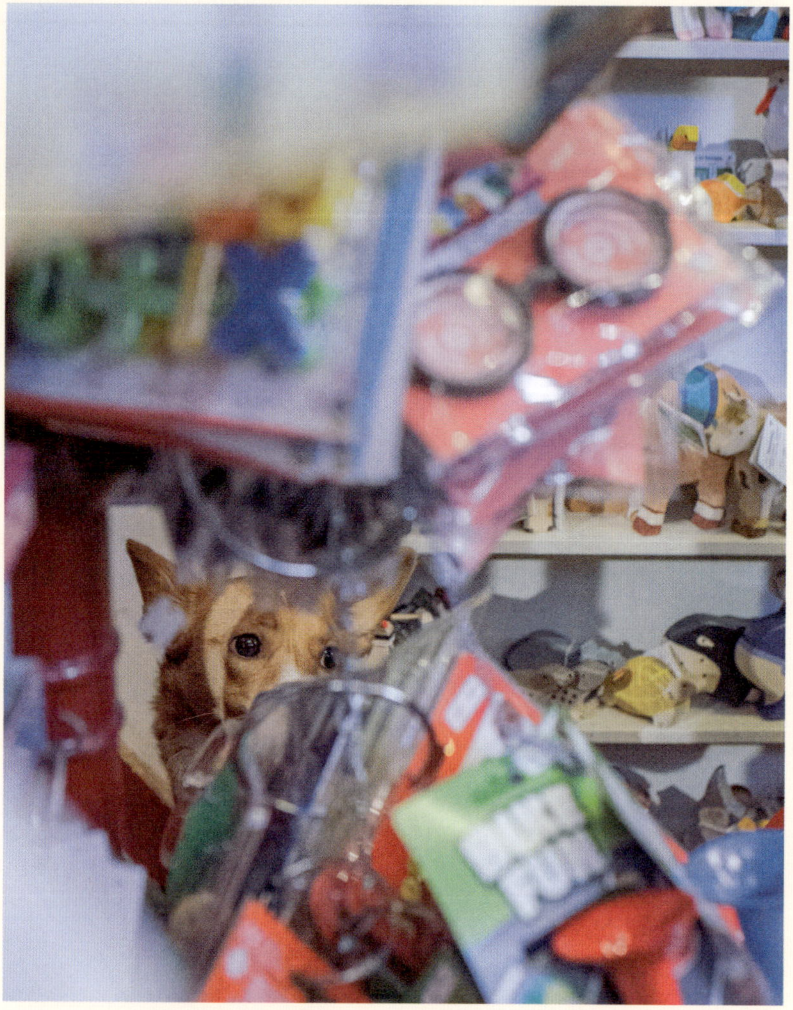

ABOVE & RIGHT Dobby is a rescue dog from Greece who accompanies his owner, Kiki, at the toy store Mechanisch Speelgoed, in Amsterdam's Jordaan district. Dobby is a sweet, gentle boy who has the perfect personality to interact with the children shopping in the store. When the aisles become packed, Dobby blends in with the toys to take a break from the crowd.

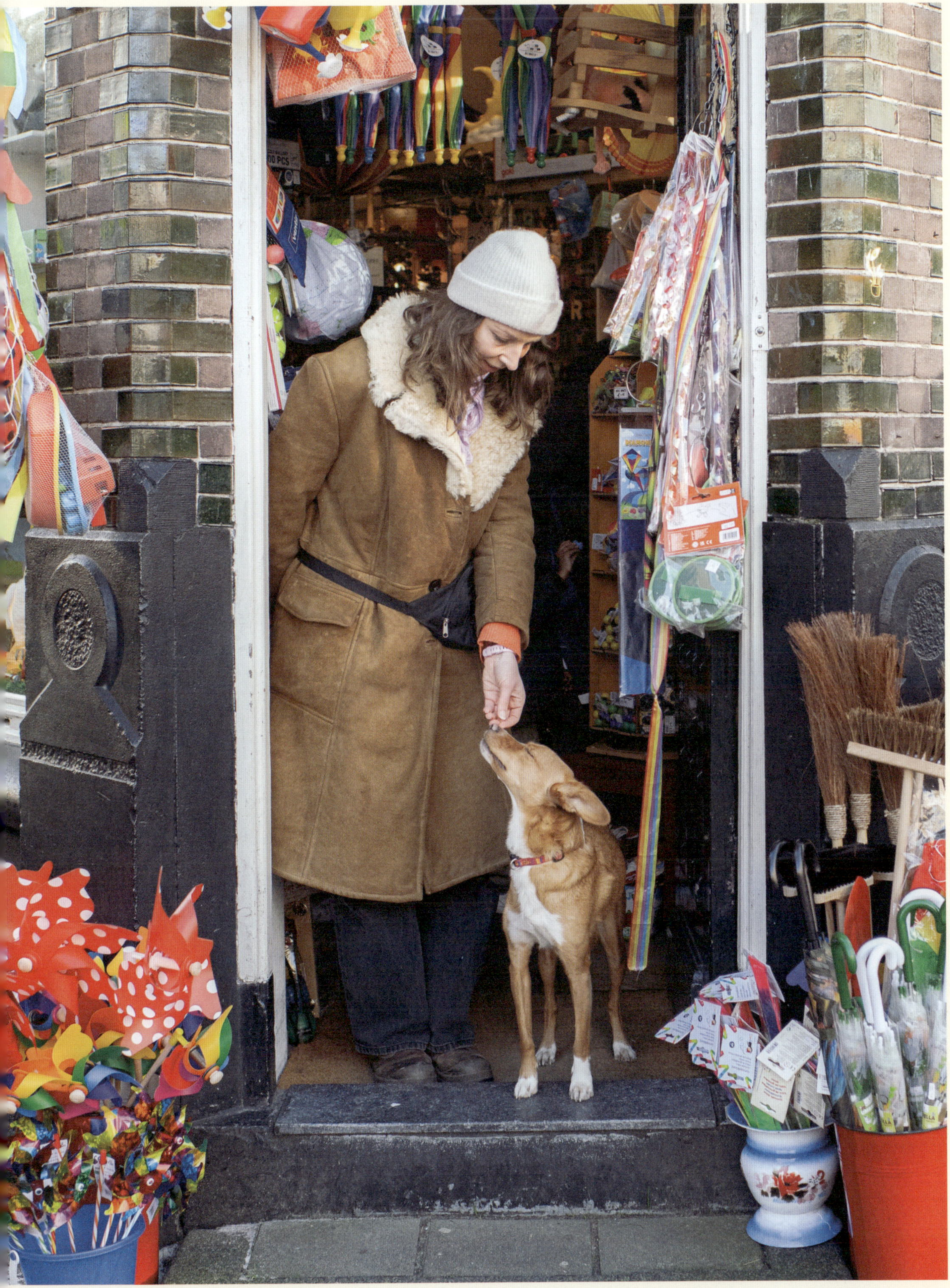

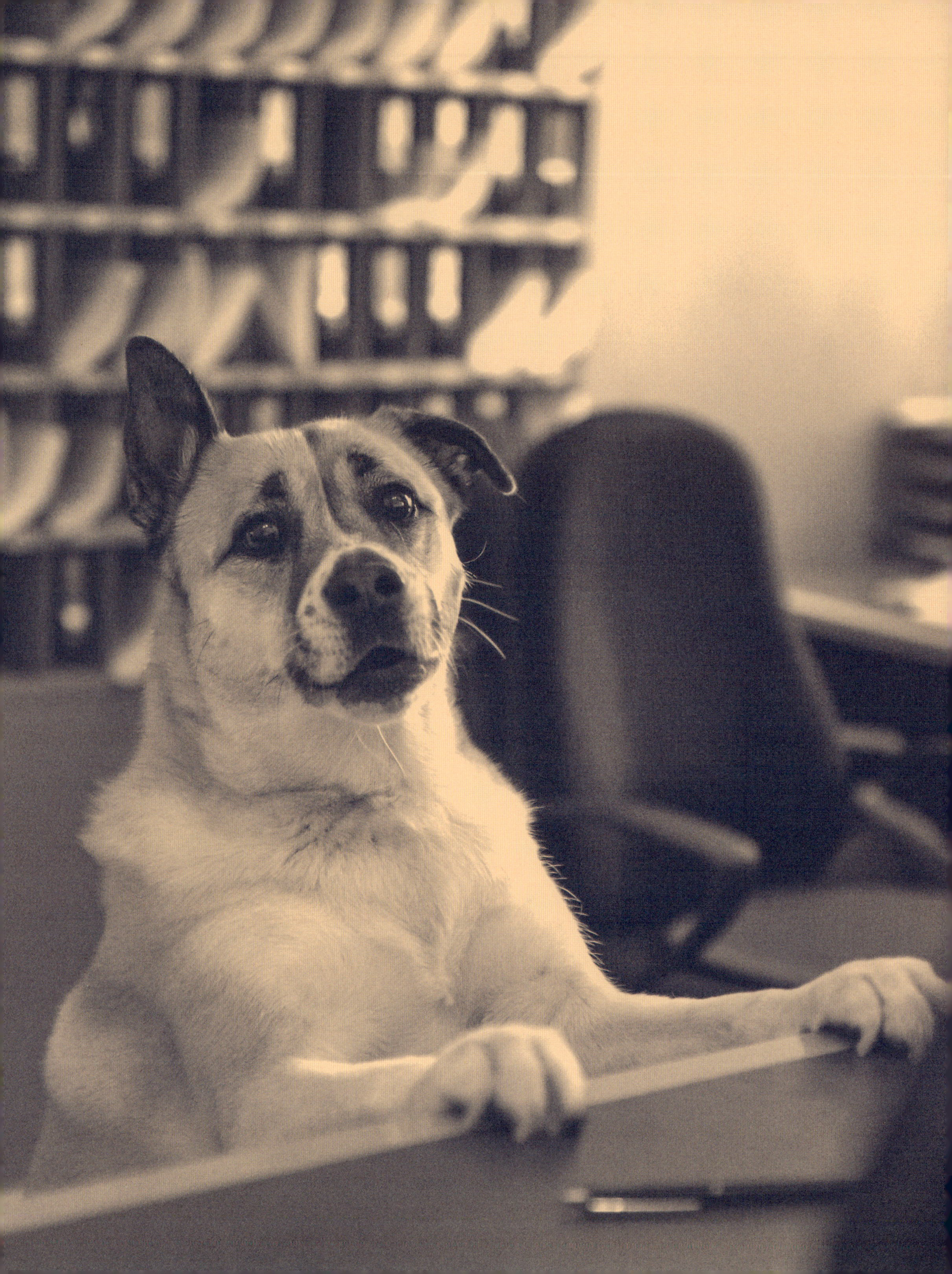

LOCATION	BREED	TASKS	SKILLS
Cologne, Germany	Akita/Husky Mix	Greeting Guests, Mingling in the Lobby, Providing Customer Service	Sociability, Manning the Desk, Calmness

HOTEL DOGS

DURING MY TRAVELS I've stayed in all sorts of lodgings – some nice and others not so nice, but that's life on a shoestring budget. Some were memorable for all the right reasons, including my hotel in Cologne, which began with a greeting from the hotel dog, Perla.

Dogs have become a major attraction for hotels globally, and, in some cases, people travel from all over the world to meet hotel dogs that have gained internet fame. I didn't know about Perla before I checked into her hotel, but she was a welcome surprise on my arrival.

Customer service is such an important part of the hotel industry, and there is no better greeting after a long day of travel than one from a dog working at reception. Any breed can excel at this job: They just need the right temperament to handle all the personalities that walk through the door.

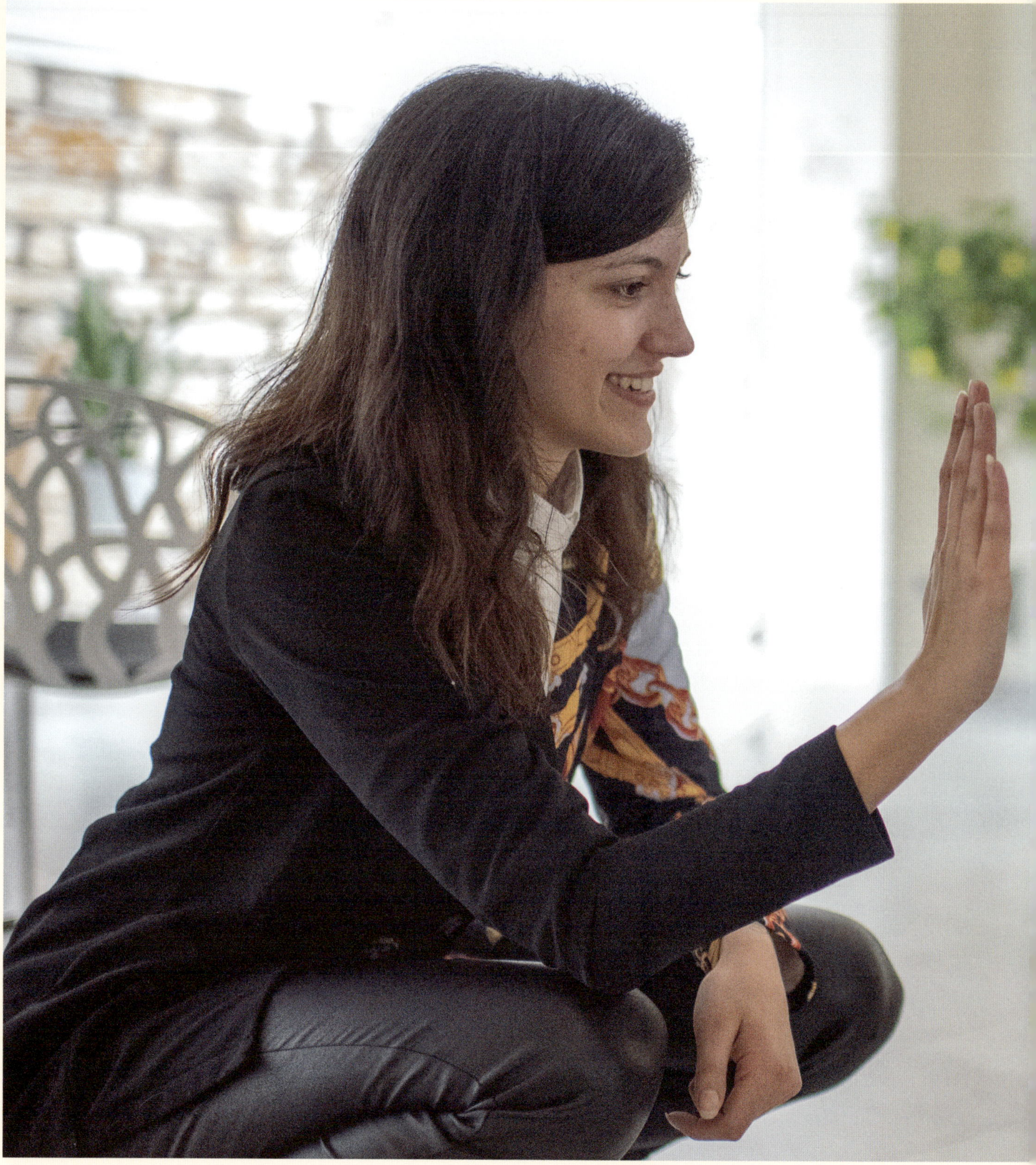

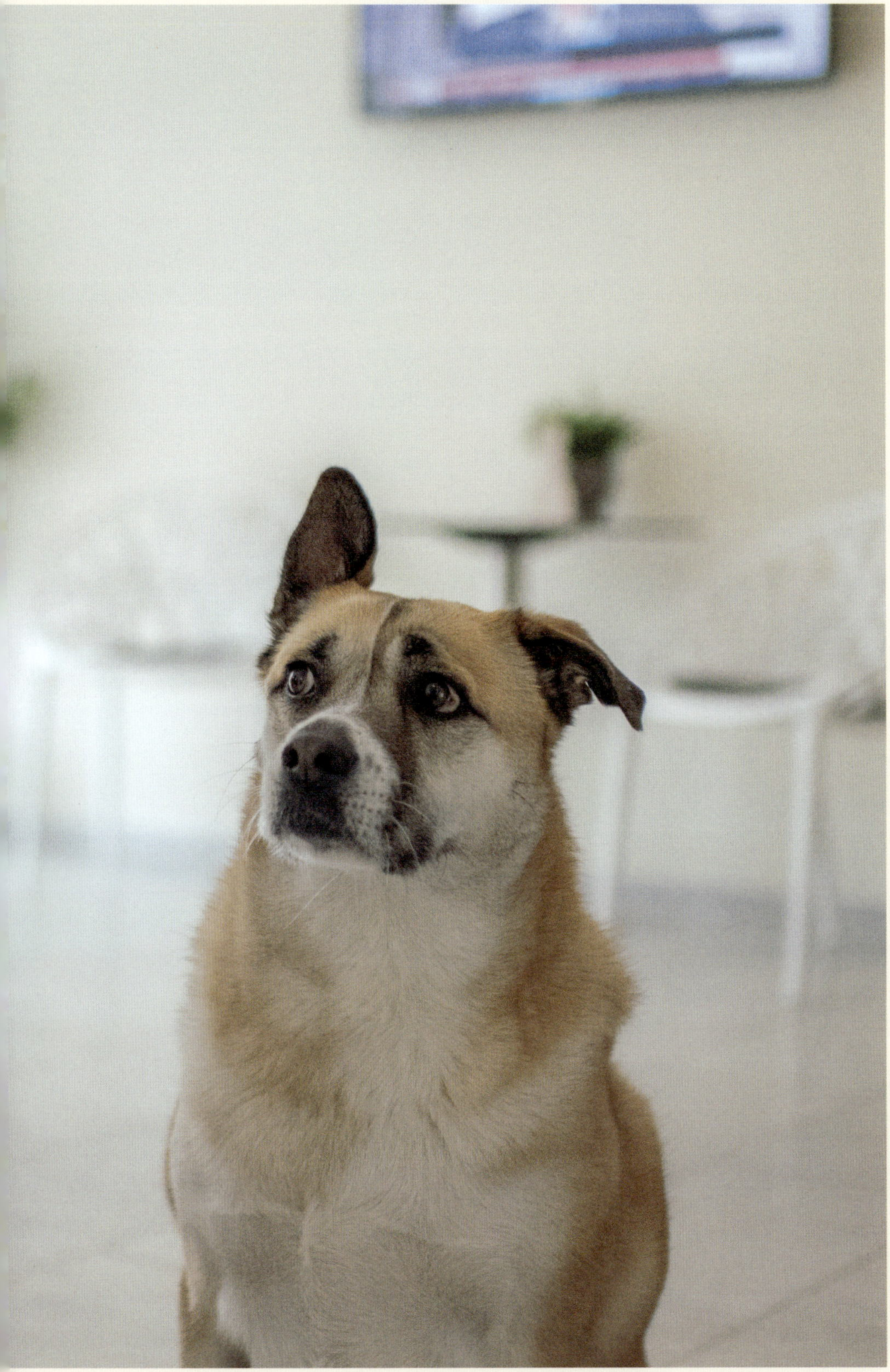

ABOVE Celina and Perla have a very special relationship and were a fun duo. This is serious work, though. Perla likes to confirm that all duties are done before celebrating with any high-fives.

Hotel dogs are the perfect employees to ask for a late checkout, primarily because they can't tell time.

RIGHT They say the customer is always right, but some customers don't like dogs, so, obviously, the customer can be very, very wrong. Perla was the perfect reception dog to handle difficult clientele, as she remained neutral toward all guests. If you wanted to approach her and give her a few pets, she would happily welcome you with gentle acceptance. As for guests who ignored her? She reciprocated the same indifference.

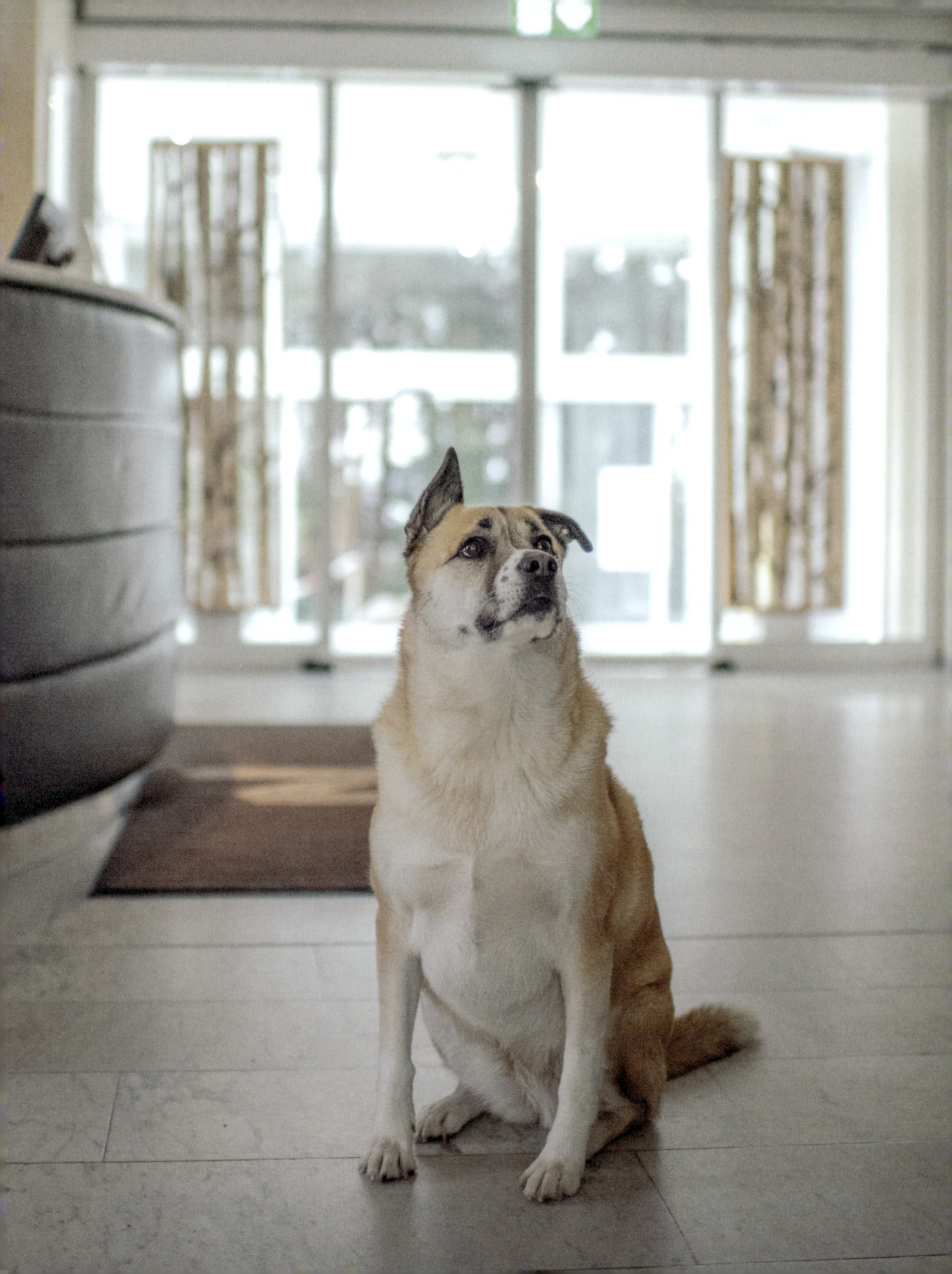

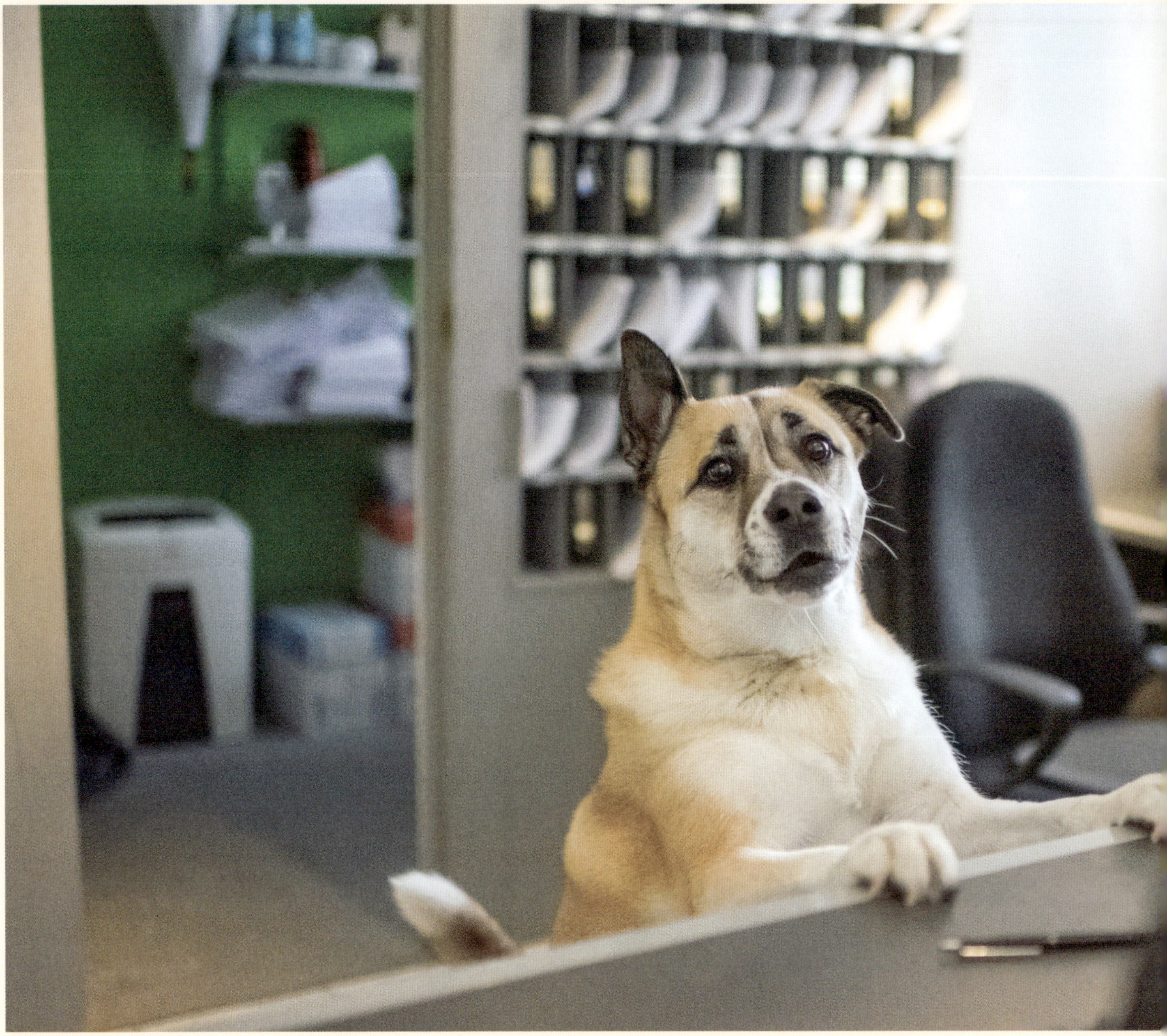

ABOVE Perla happily jumped up on the reception desk when Celina asked her to, and really made it believable that she knew how to work the computer. Hotel dogs are the perfect employees to ask for a late checkout, primarily because they can't tell time.

RIGHT Perla spent the first few years of her life living on the streets of Spain. She then ended up in an illegal, cramped holding facility until a rescue organization took her in and transported her to Germany. After a brief stay with a foster family, she finally made it to her owner, Celina. For a dog that lived through a chaotic adolescence, Perla does not show any of it in her behavior: She was extremely calm and kind.

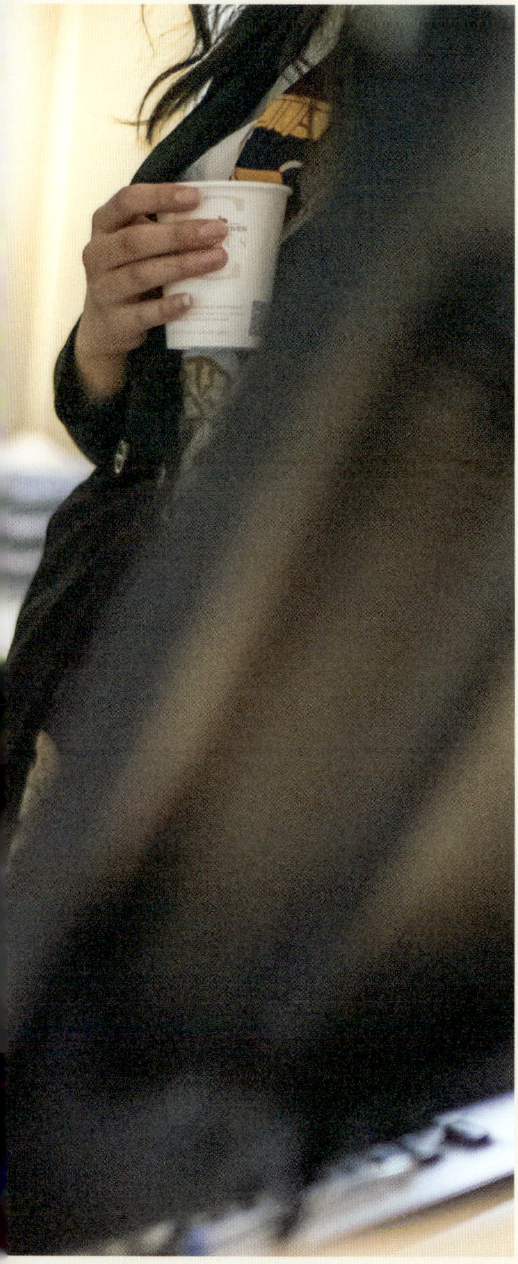

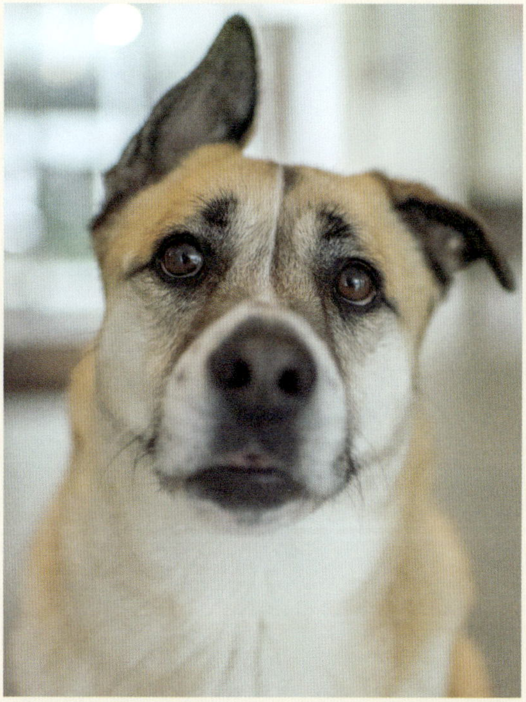

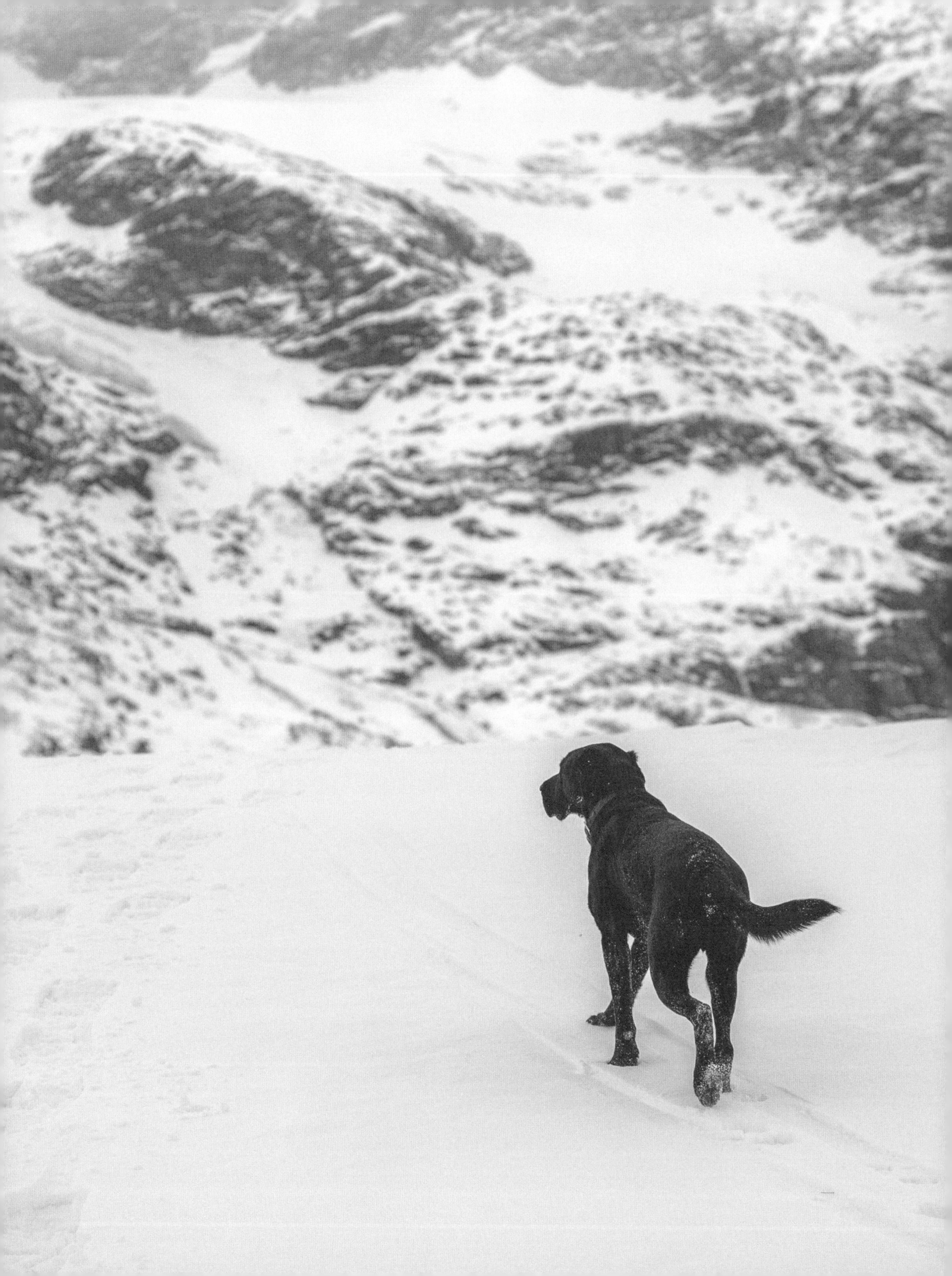

LOCATION	BREEDS	TASKS	SKILLS
Bernina Pass, Switzerland	Belgian Malinois, Golden Retriever, Labrador, and Border Collie	Digging, Scent Trailing, Identifying Targets	Endurance, Navigation, Hardiness

AVALANCHE RESCUE DOGS

WHEN AN AVALANCHE OCCURS and people are trapped in the snow, time is of the essence and rescue efforts begin immediately. The people, and the dogs, who participate in this line of work must be ready to act when an emergency strikes.

Rega is Switzerland's air rescue service. Rega co-founded Alpine Rettung Schweiz (ARS), an alpine rescue service that provides terrestrial rescue across the mountains, with a team that includes handlers and their dogs. After an avalanche, Rega sends out an alarm to all rescuers in the area so that available teams can assist as quickly as possible.

Handlers and their dogs regularly go through training sessions to prepare for avalanches. I traveled to the Bernina Pass in Switzerland, where over 30 handler–dog tandems were training. I witnessed many different breeds excelling, but what they all had in common was a strong working drive and the ability to handle the harsh winter elements.

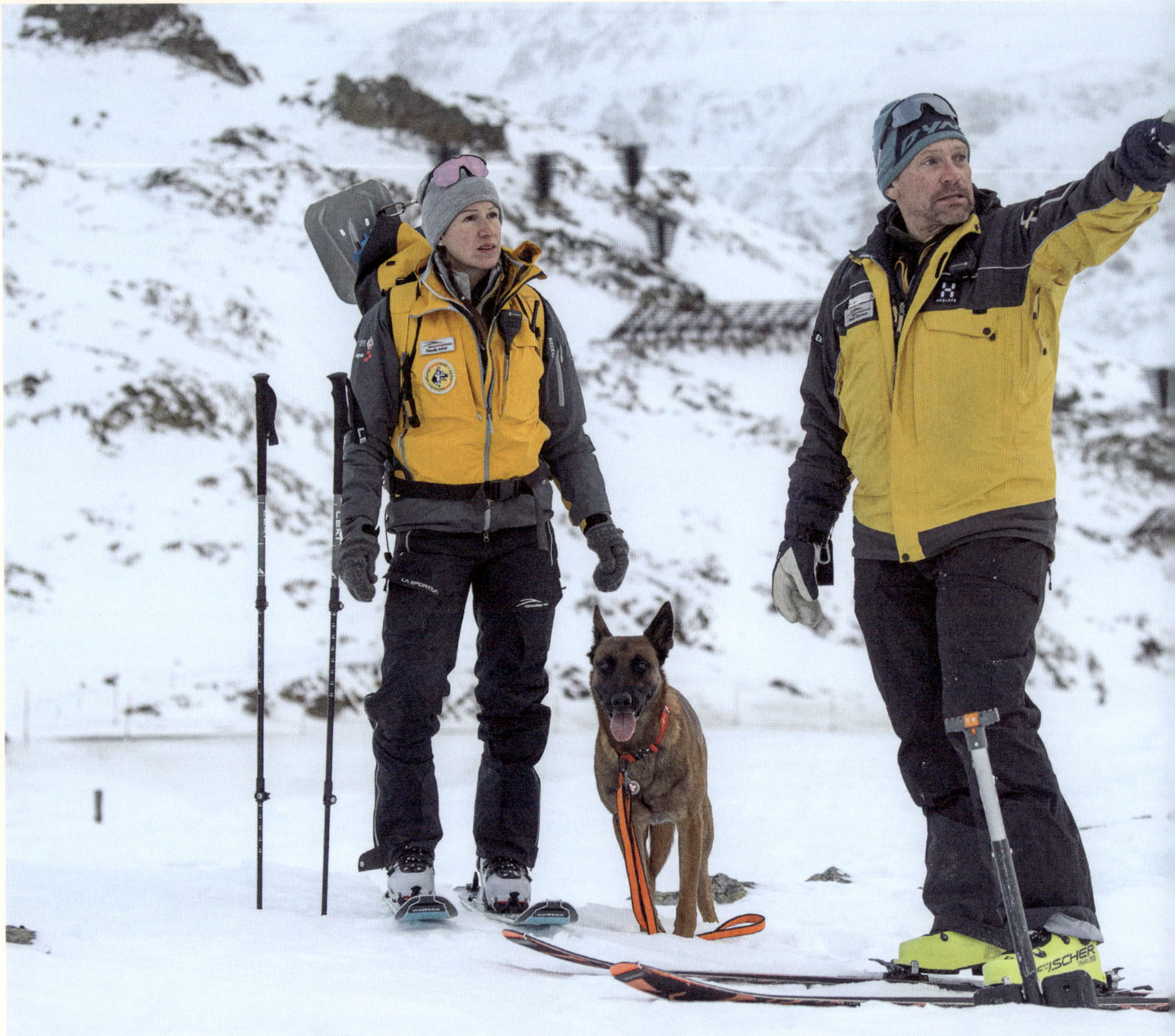

ABOVE The training was run by René, an experienced trainer and handler. He sets the scene, telling a story for the rescue – when the avalanche happened, how many people are reported missing, and the area where they are suspected to be trapped in the snow. Claudia took detailed notes of the mission, while her dog, Vox, patiently waited to go to work.

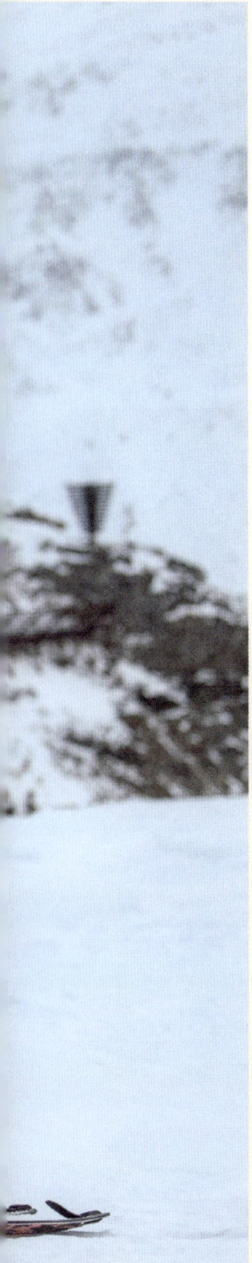

BELOW Some dogs will run off, scanning the area on their own, while others will look back to their handlers for guidance on where to go. Each relationship is unique, and the handlers must know how their dogs prefer to work.

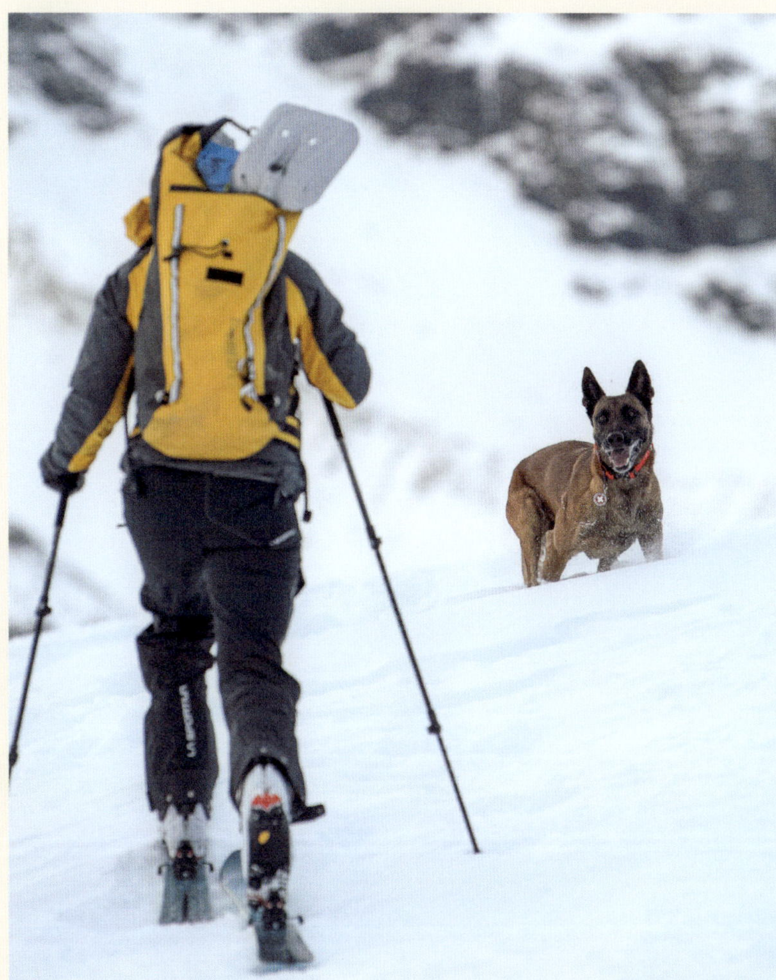

BELOW & RIGHT The dogs, and especially their noses, often lead the way. Scent from people trapped in the snow will slowly make its way into the air where the dog can smell it, with the snow's varying conditions influencing how quickly that scent rises.

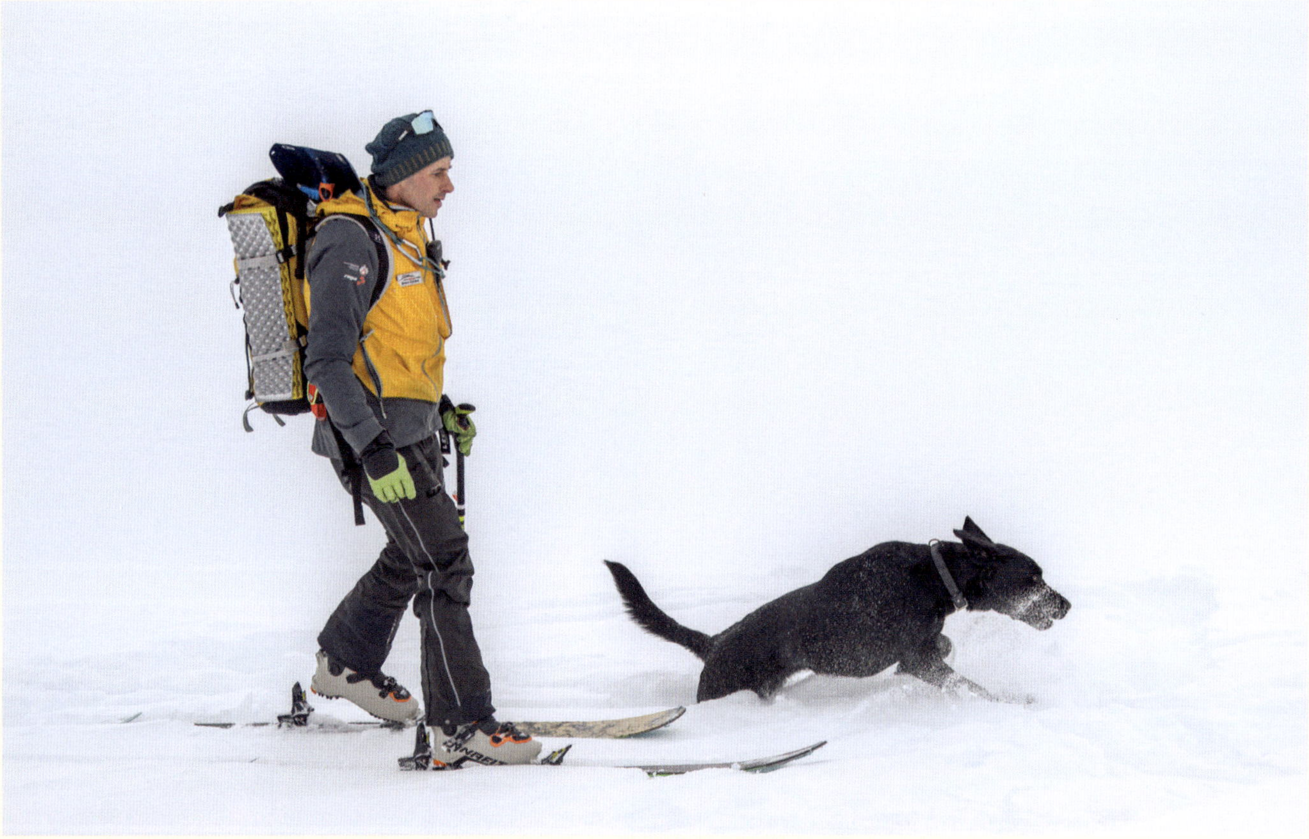

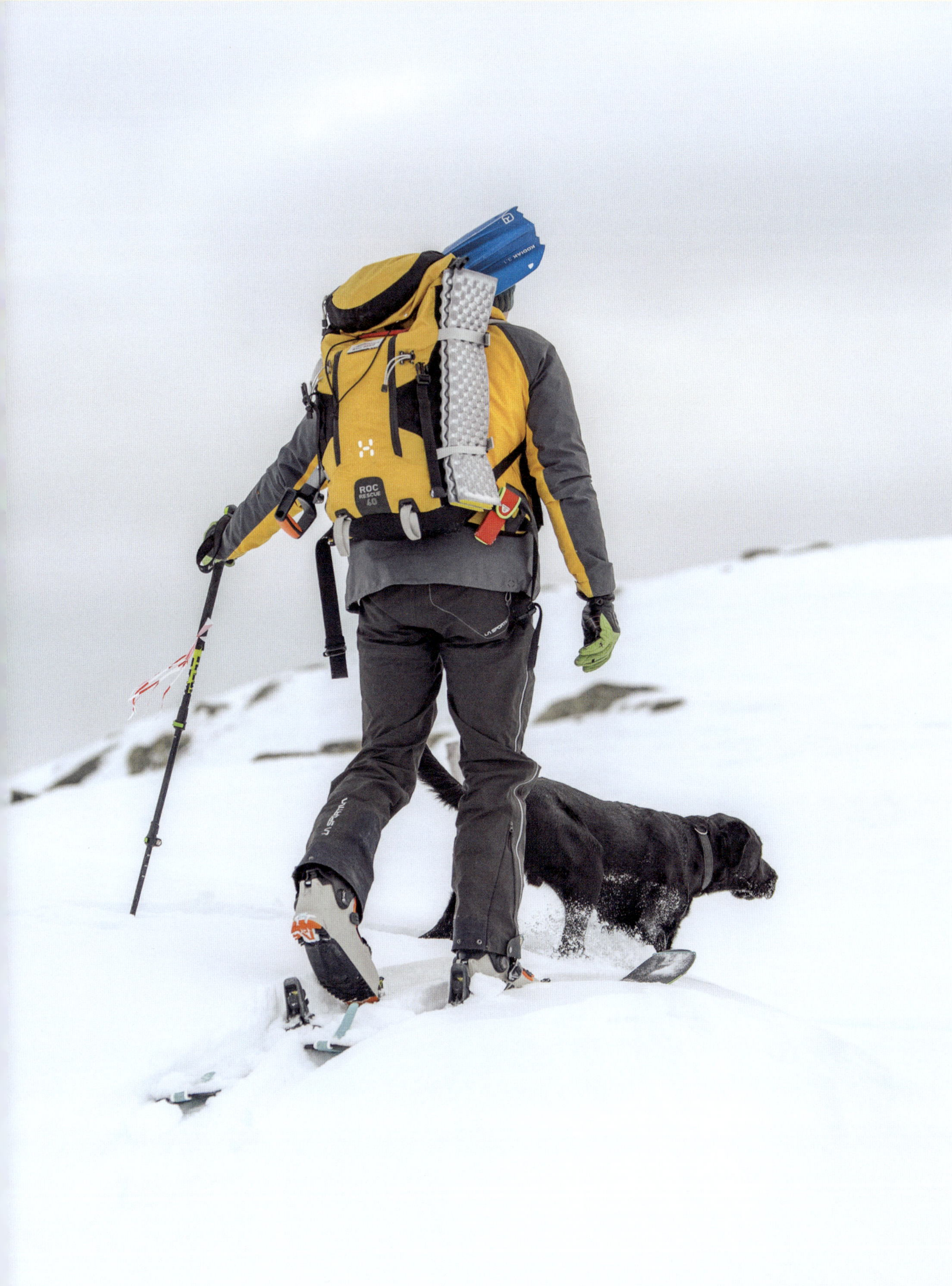
ROC
RESCUE
40

202

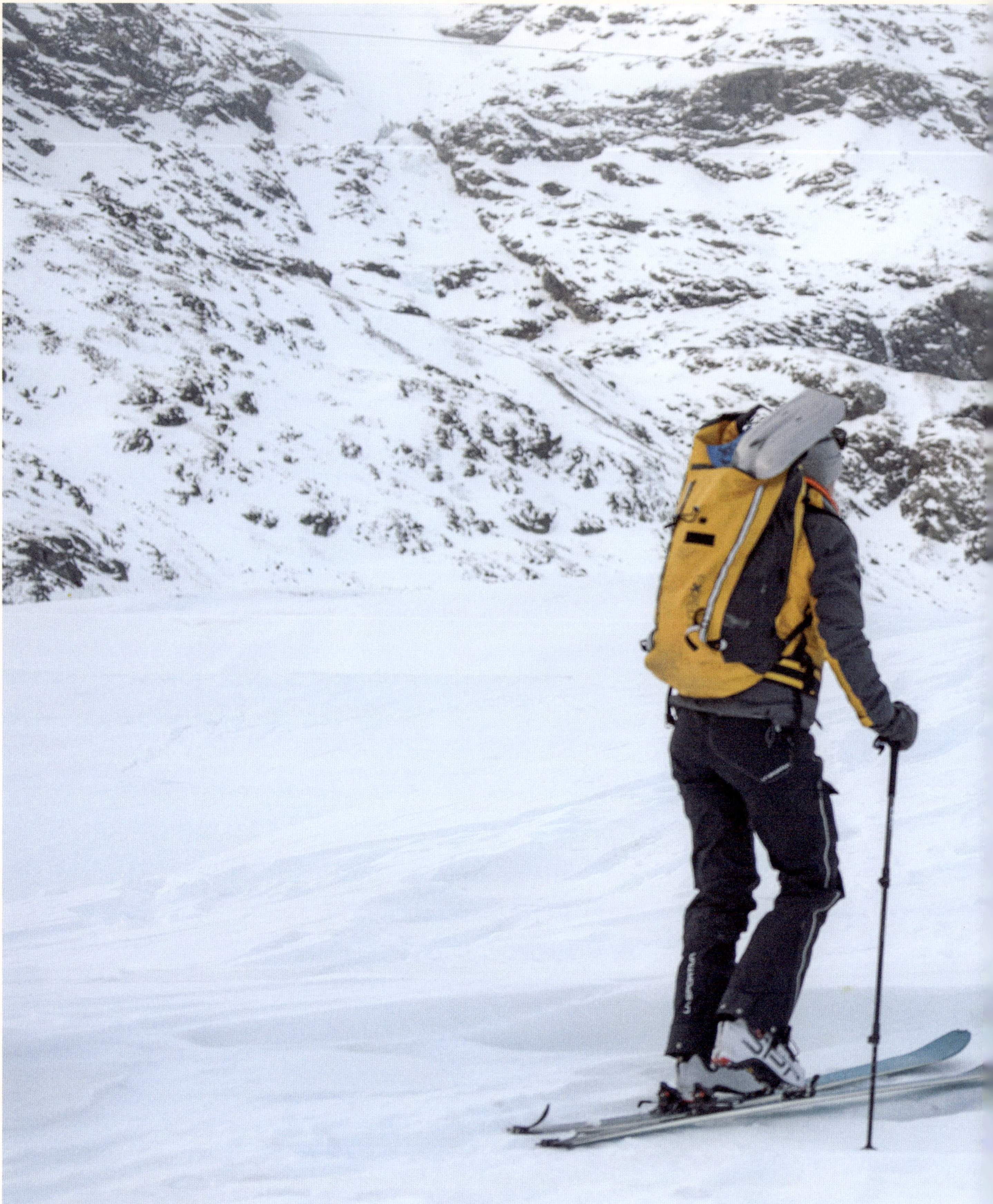

ABOVE Once the leash comes off, the dog is free to start searching the area. Dogs are used because they can cover much more ground than humans, and their powerful noses can lead them to people who are trapped, hidden from sight under the snow.

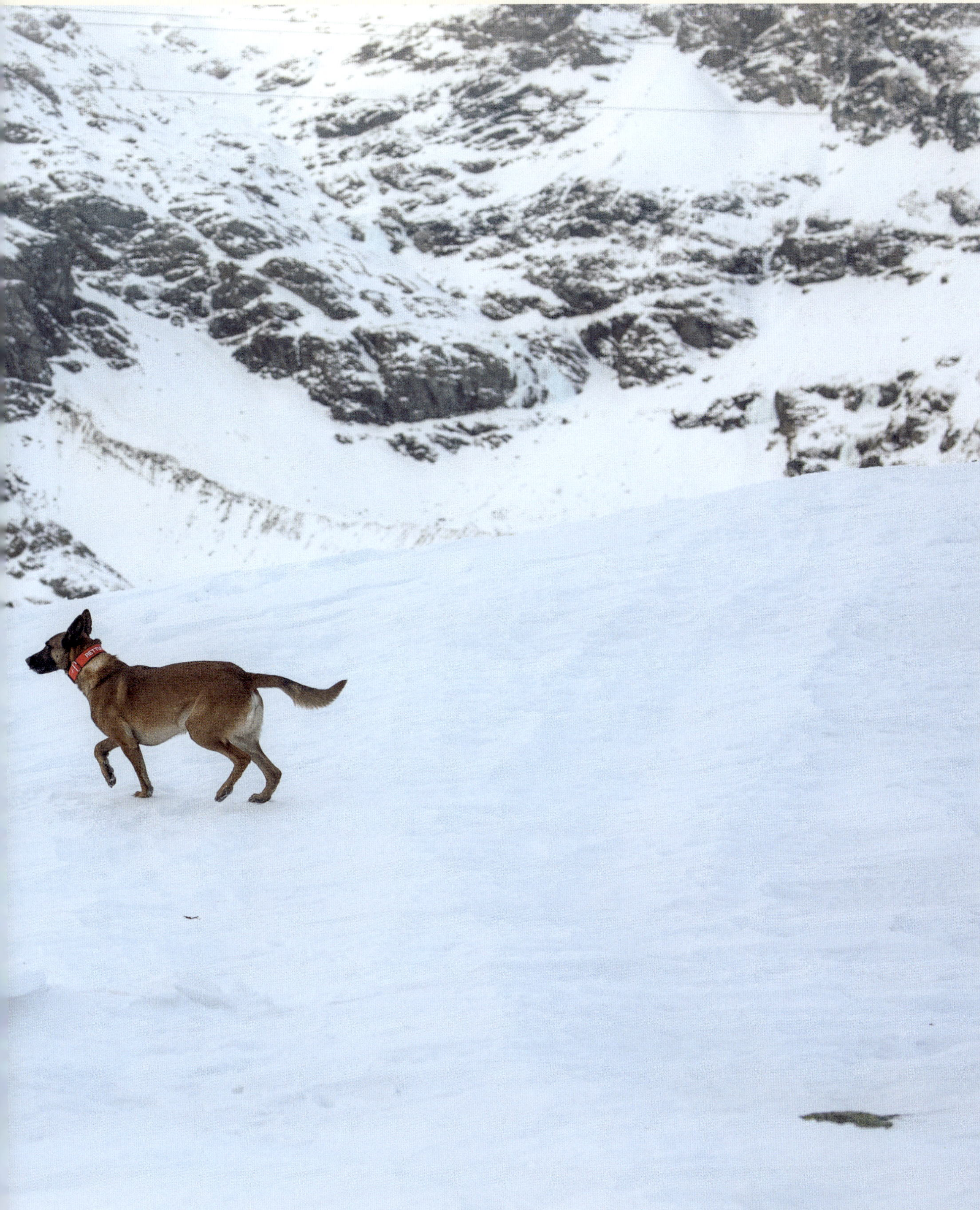

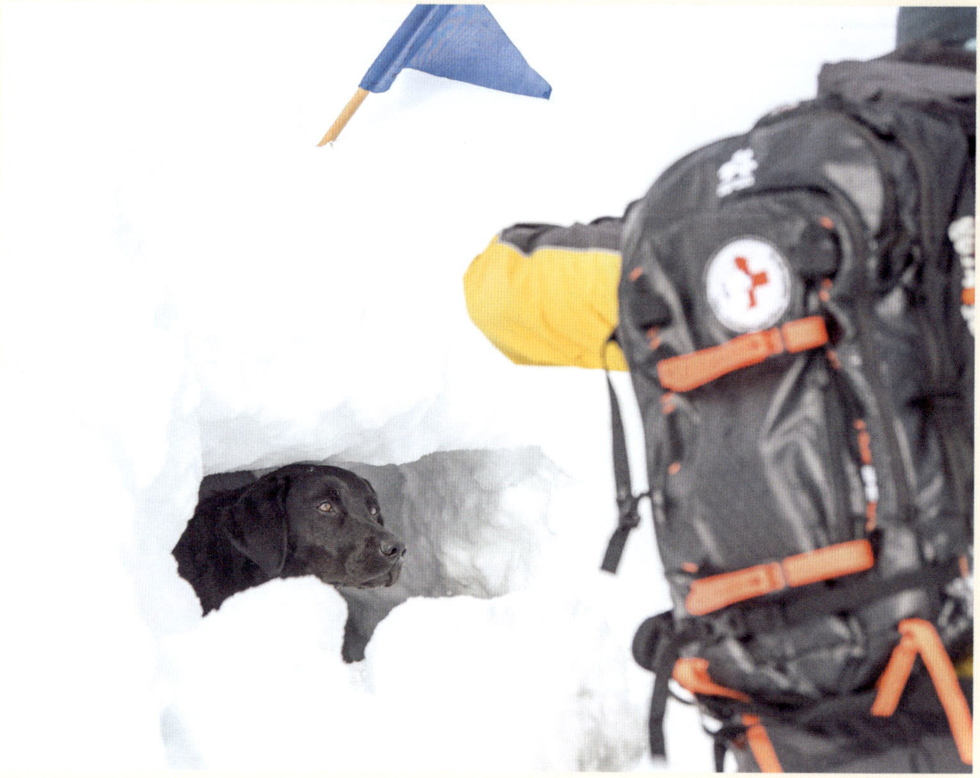

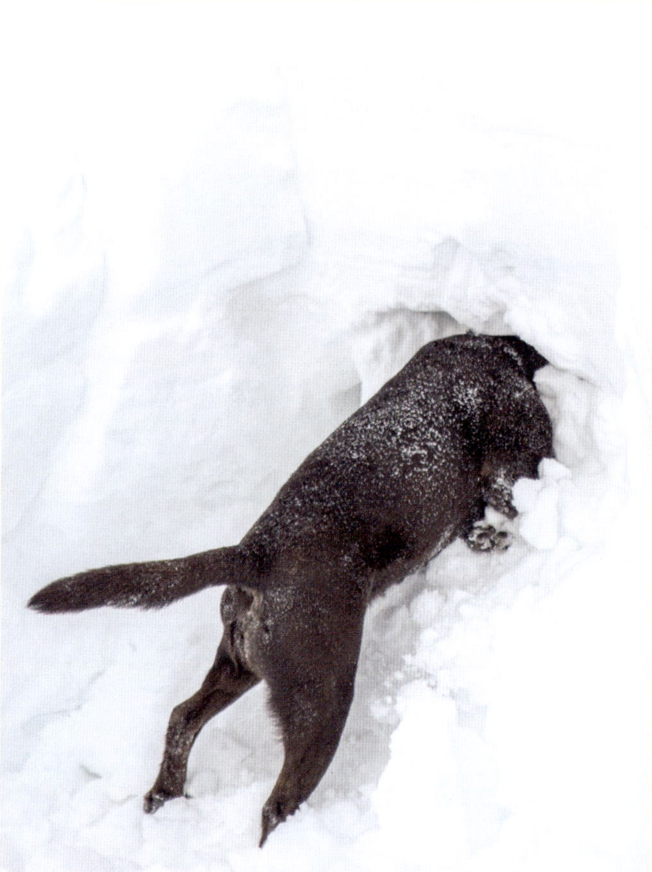

BOTTOM LEFT A digging dog is a great sign, as that means they are on the scent of a person. The handlers do not help the dogs with their digging, as it may influence the dogs to give up or look for help.

TOP LEFT & BELOW The dogs are taught to stay in the hole with the person they found until their handler arrives. The handler will mark the hole and provide details about when the person was found, which is incredibly important to medical teams as they determine how to treat the rescued person.

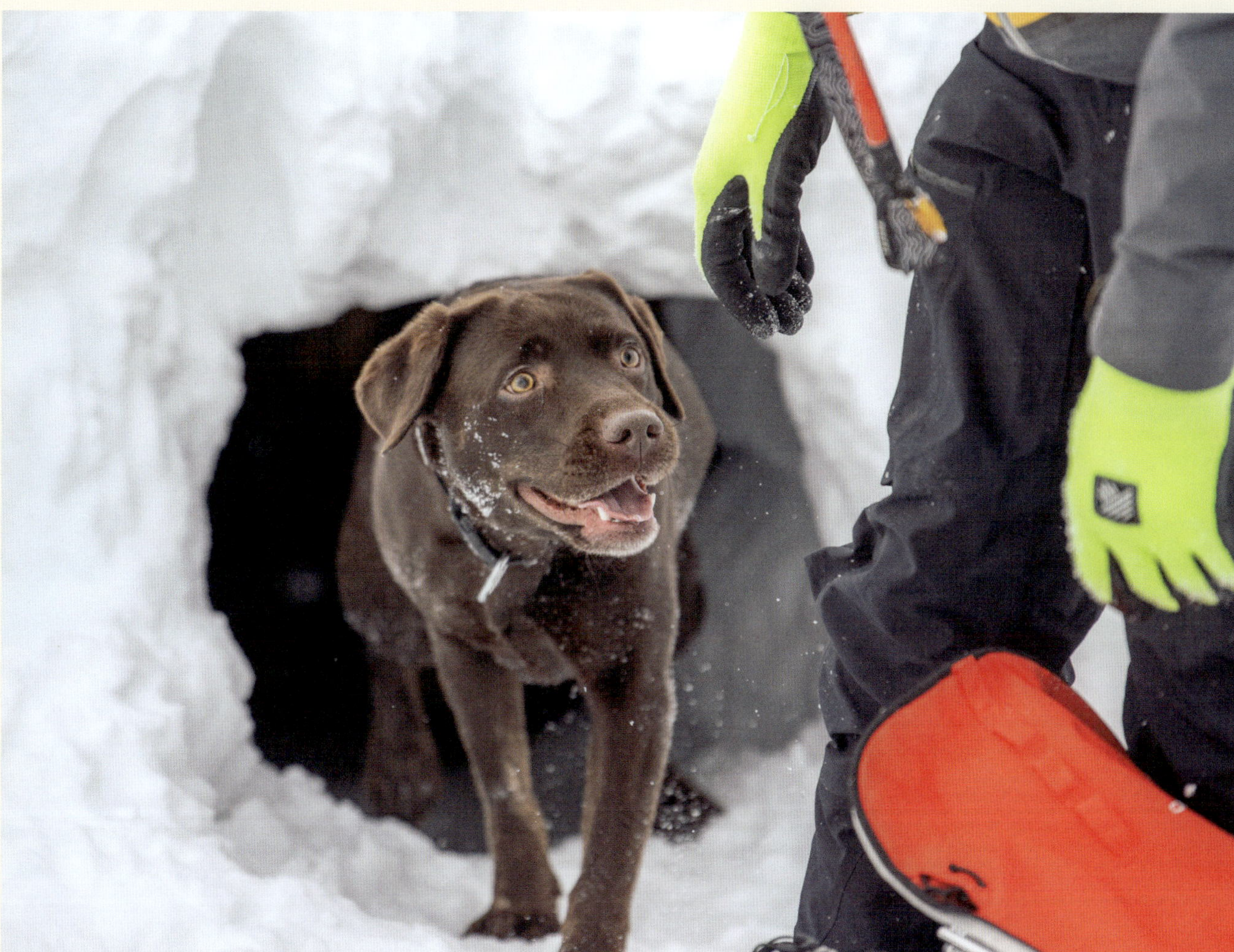

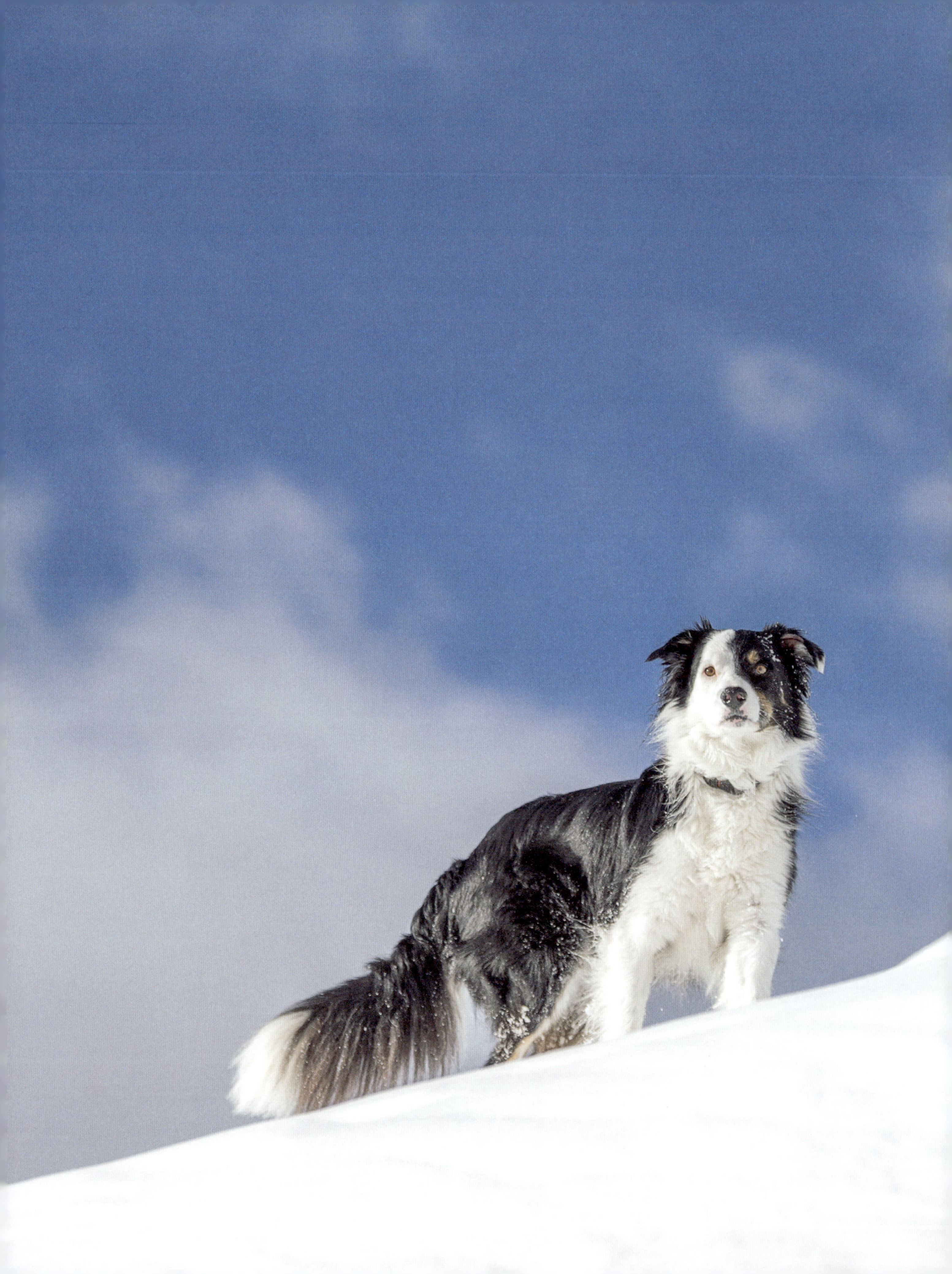

LEFT Dogs will run up and down the mountains, often using peaks to survey the area. Handlers also use high vantage points to watch their dogs scan the area. They want to keep an eye on the dogs, because if they disappear, it means they have found a person.

BELOW I had the opportunity to stay in a hole and wait to be found. After about 20 minutes of silence, I heard a rumbling outside the hole. Paws started digging and then a beautiful, golden head peeked through the snow, ready to save the day.

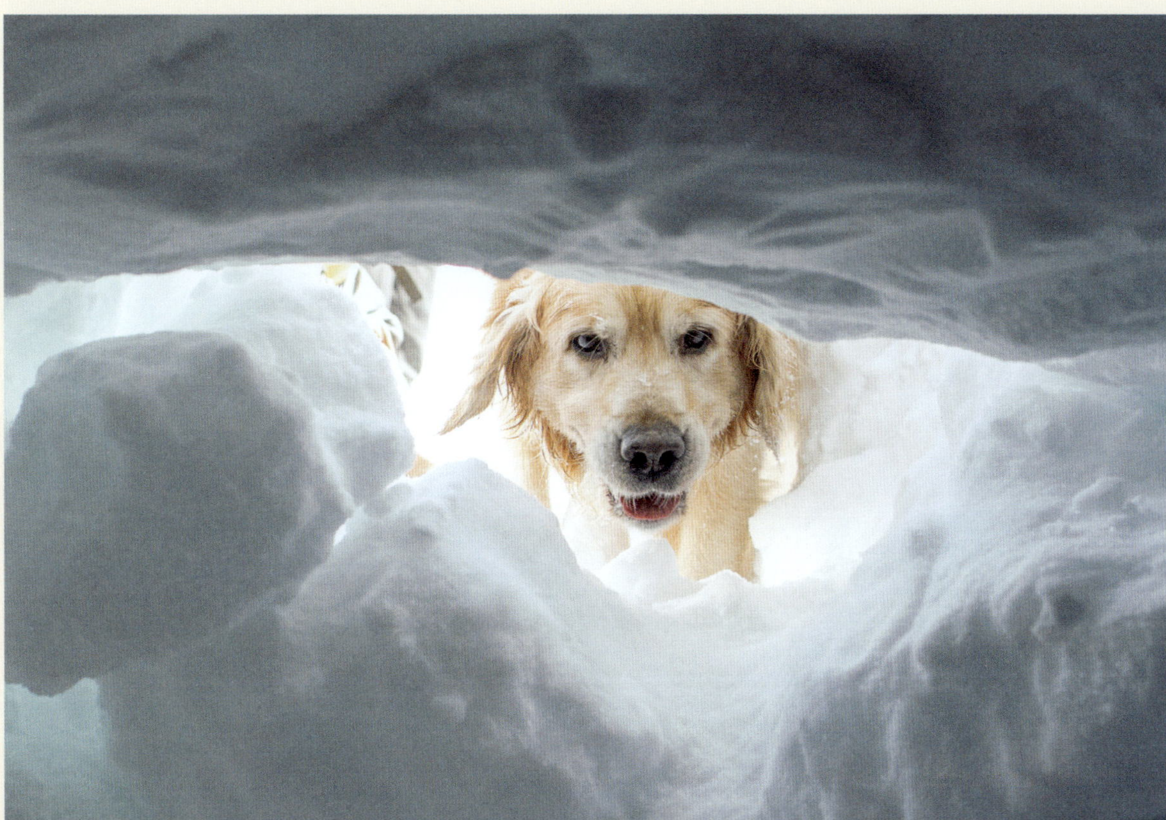

RIGHT After each team successfully finished training, with every dog finding the people buried in the snow, the group got together to recap the sessions.

BELOW In the afternoon, the group had a bit more fun. They performed search activities that were much shorter and easier for the dogs. It is important to make this work fun for the dogs, as it will motivate them to do it when it matters most.

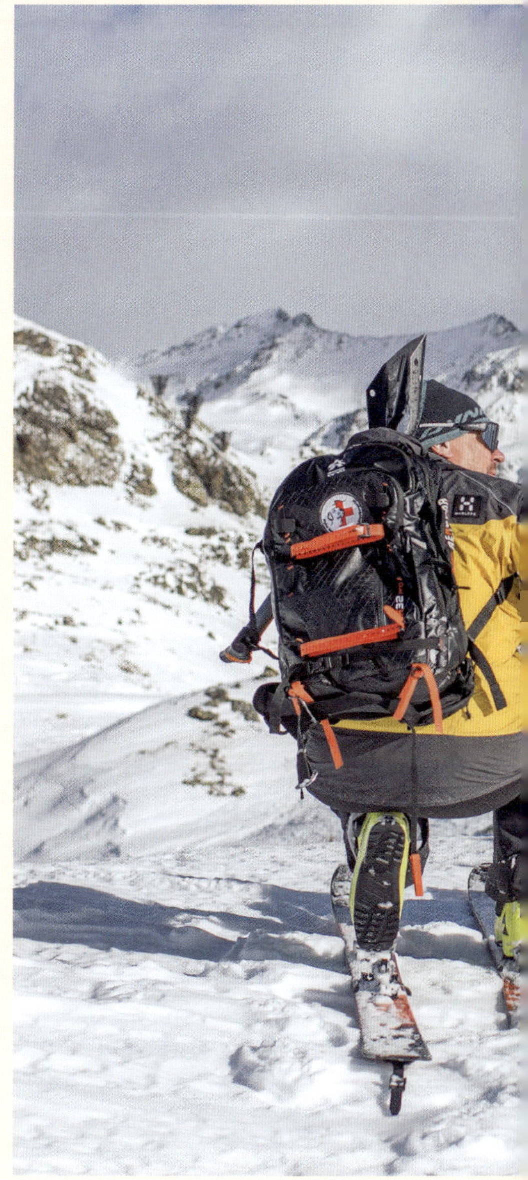

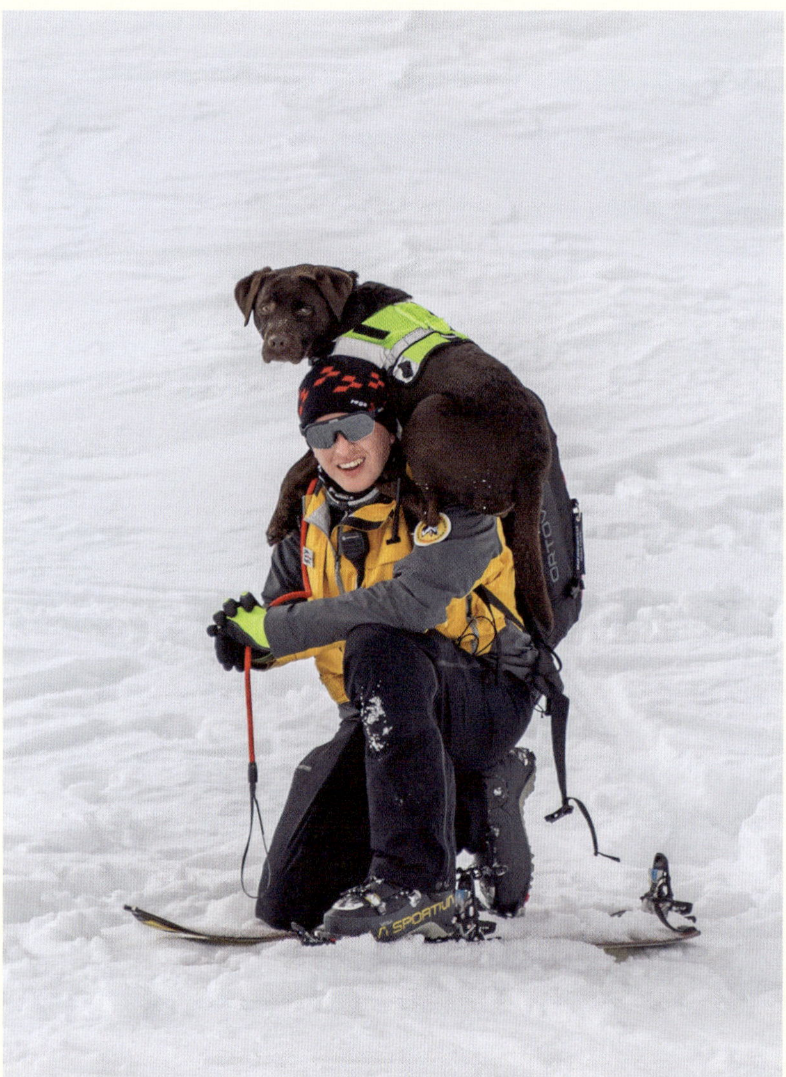

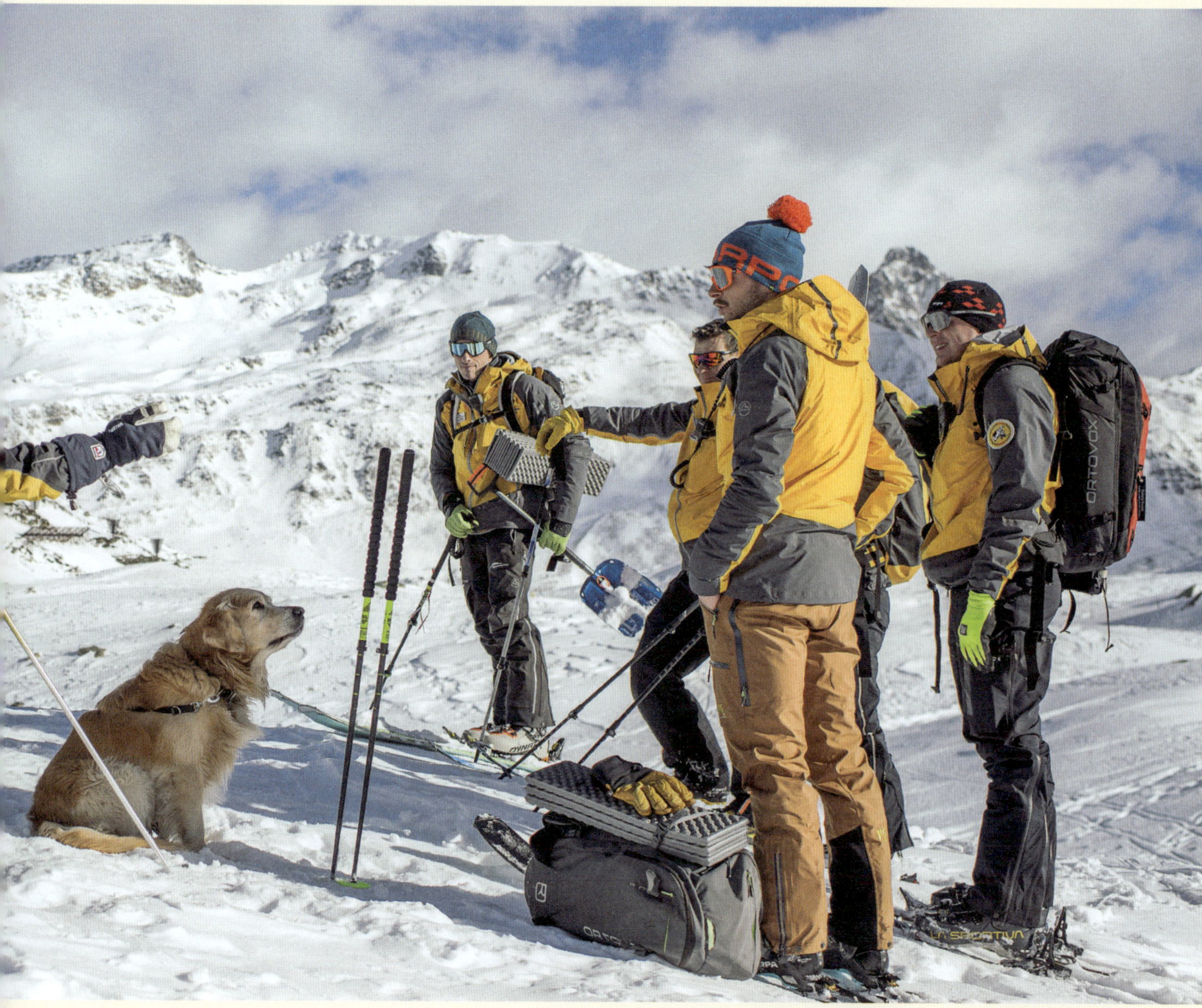

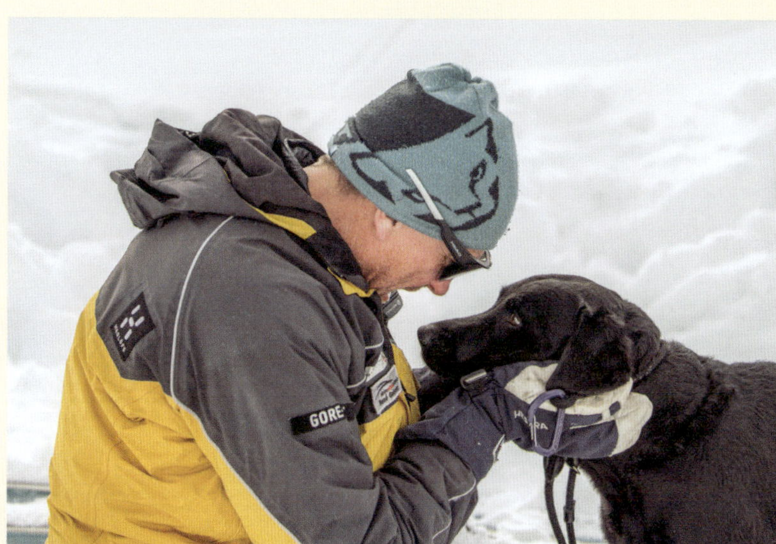

RIGHT With every working dog, it comes down to mutual trust and a strong bond between the handler and dog.

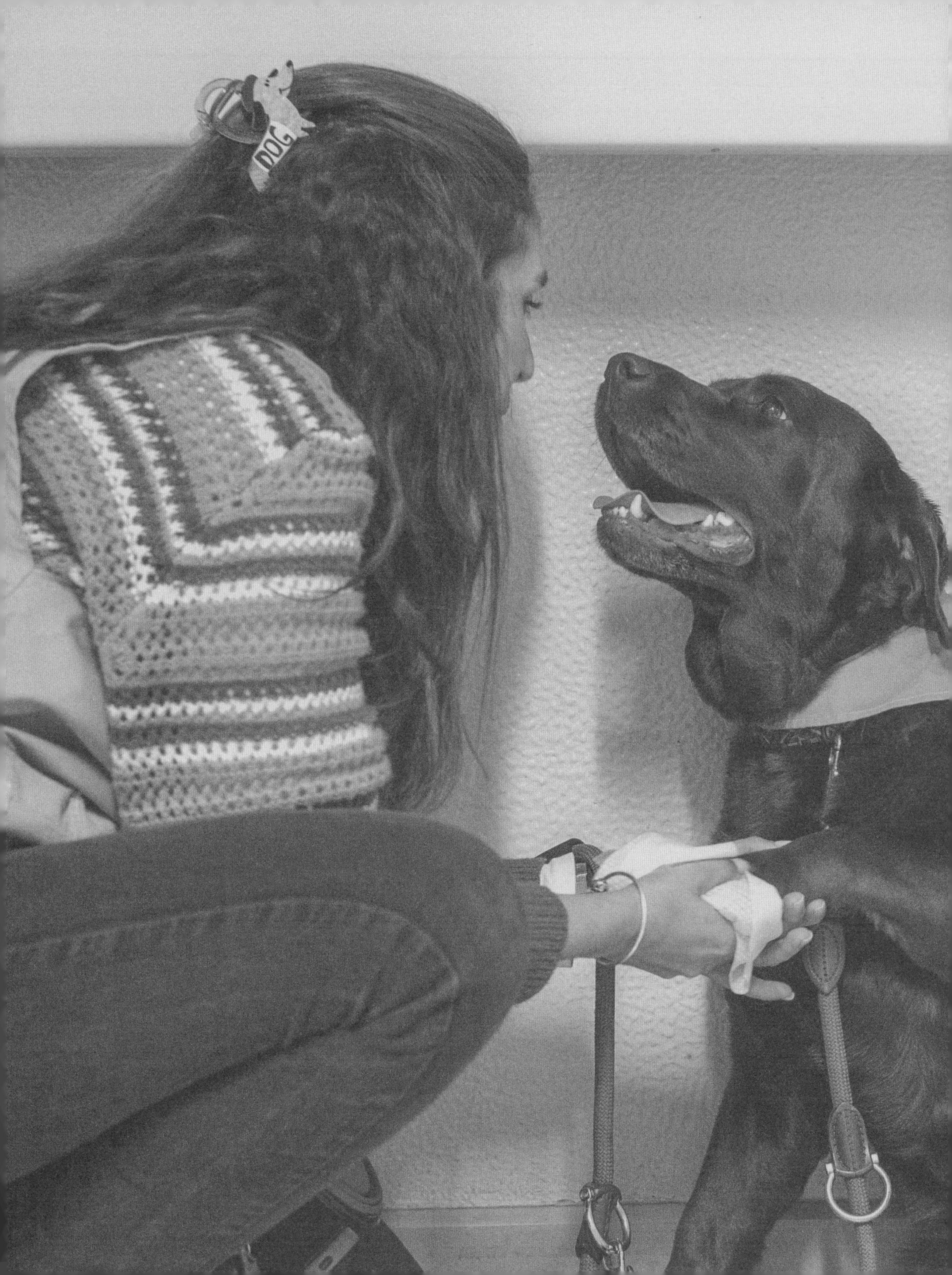
DOG

LOCATION	BREEDS	TASKS	SKILLS
Lisbon, Portugal and Buffalo, USA	Rescue, Labrador, Bernese Mountain Dog, Golden Retriever, Beagle Mix, and Shih Tzu	Comforting, Getting Pet, Lying Down	Calmness, Sociability, Responsiveness

HOSPITAL THERAPY DOGS

THE POWER OF DOGS is clear when they walk into a hospital. Their presence alone can completely shift the mood of everyone in the room, patients and hospital staff alike. In a place where things often get heavy, therapy dogs stroll in with a certain lightness that allows people to forget, even for just a moment, the weight of the world.

I photographed hospital therapy dogs in Portugal and the United States, where I witnessed the monumental impact of the work these dogs do in both countries.

ÂNIMAS has paw prints all across Portugal. They provide therapy dog training and services, including visits to hospitals where the dogs have developed strong relationships with long-term patients. Across the Atlantic Ocean, the Volunteer Services team at Roswell Park organizes visits from local, certified therapy dogs. They work with the dogs' handlers to schedule which areas of the hospital each dog will visit.

During my visits, I found that hospital therapy dogs come in varying breeds and sizes, but they had one overwhelming similarity: a gentle presence. They enjoyed human attention and were content spending long periods of time on the floor, on laps, and in hospital beds, providing calm companionship.

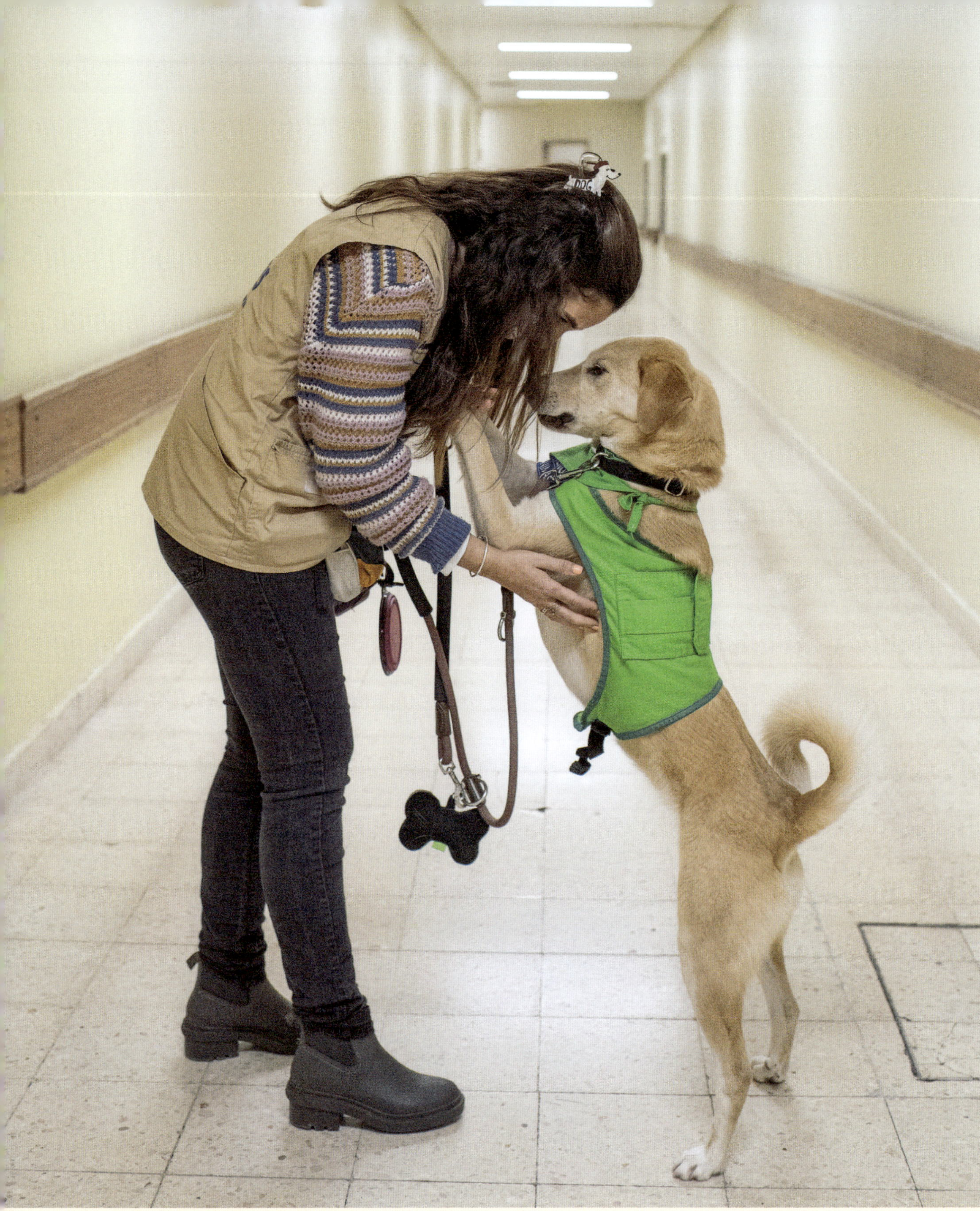

ABOVE Inês Chambel works for ÂNIMAS, helping them to provide therapy dog visits to hospitals in Portugal. During my trip, we visited two hospitals in the Lisbon area: Garcia de Orta and Amadora-Sintra. Inês does therapy work with her two personal dogs, a mixed breed named Jamaica and a Labrador named Nairóbi.

BELOW LEFT The first step before visiting patients is to completely disinfect the dogs with wipes. Jamaica knew the drill and calmly accepted the cloth treatment before going to work.

BELOW RIGHT Before she was a therapy dog, Jamaica was a classic underdog. She was a stray who was rescued by the perfect owner, Inês, who recognized her potential as a working dog. Now, Jamaica brings so much joy during her hospital visits, putting smiles on the faces of both patients and staff.

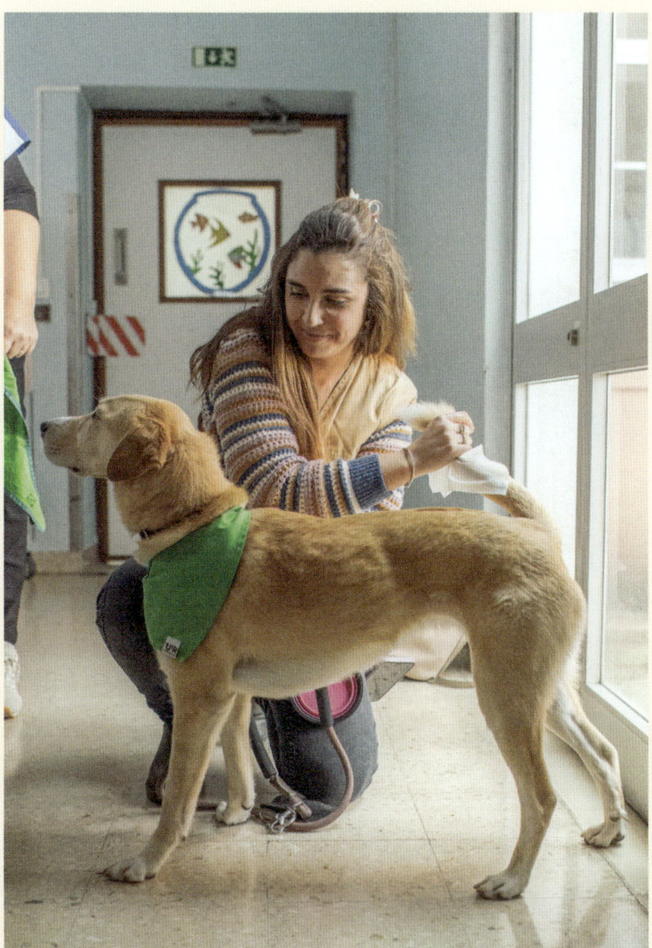

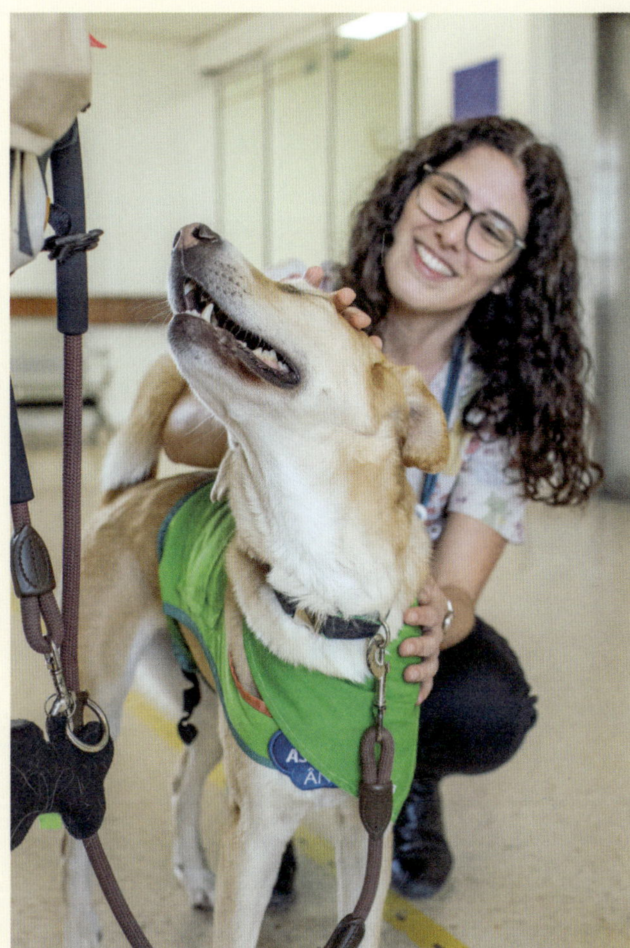

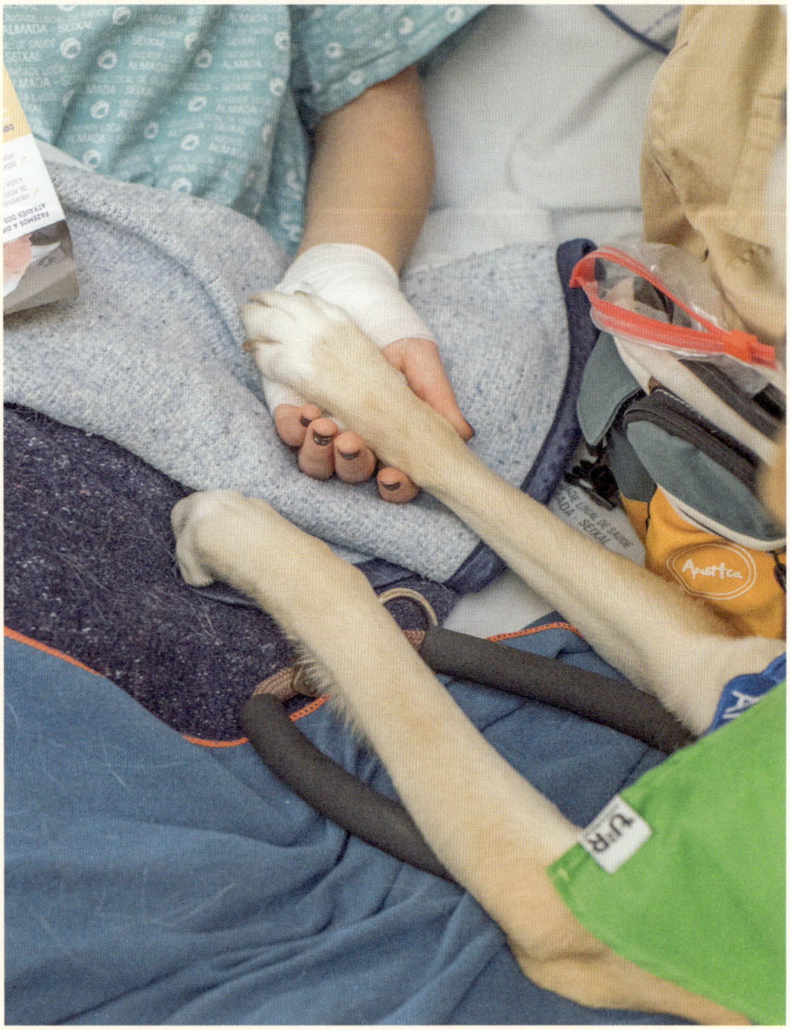

214

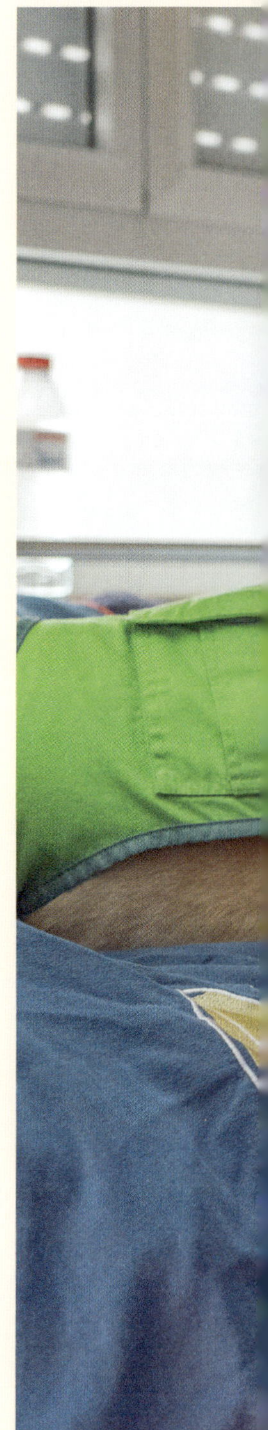

ABOVE & RIGHT The first patient visit was enough for me to recognize the impact of therapy dog work. Jamaica hopped up onto the hospital bed and calmly laid her head down, letting the patient pet her head. The moment became emotional to the point that everyone in the room had tears in their eyes. Days in the hospital can be long and monotonous, and it was very clear that a visit from a dog is a touching experience.

Days in the hospital can be long and monotonous, and it was very clear that a visit from a dog is a touching experience.

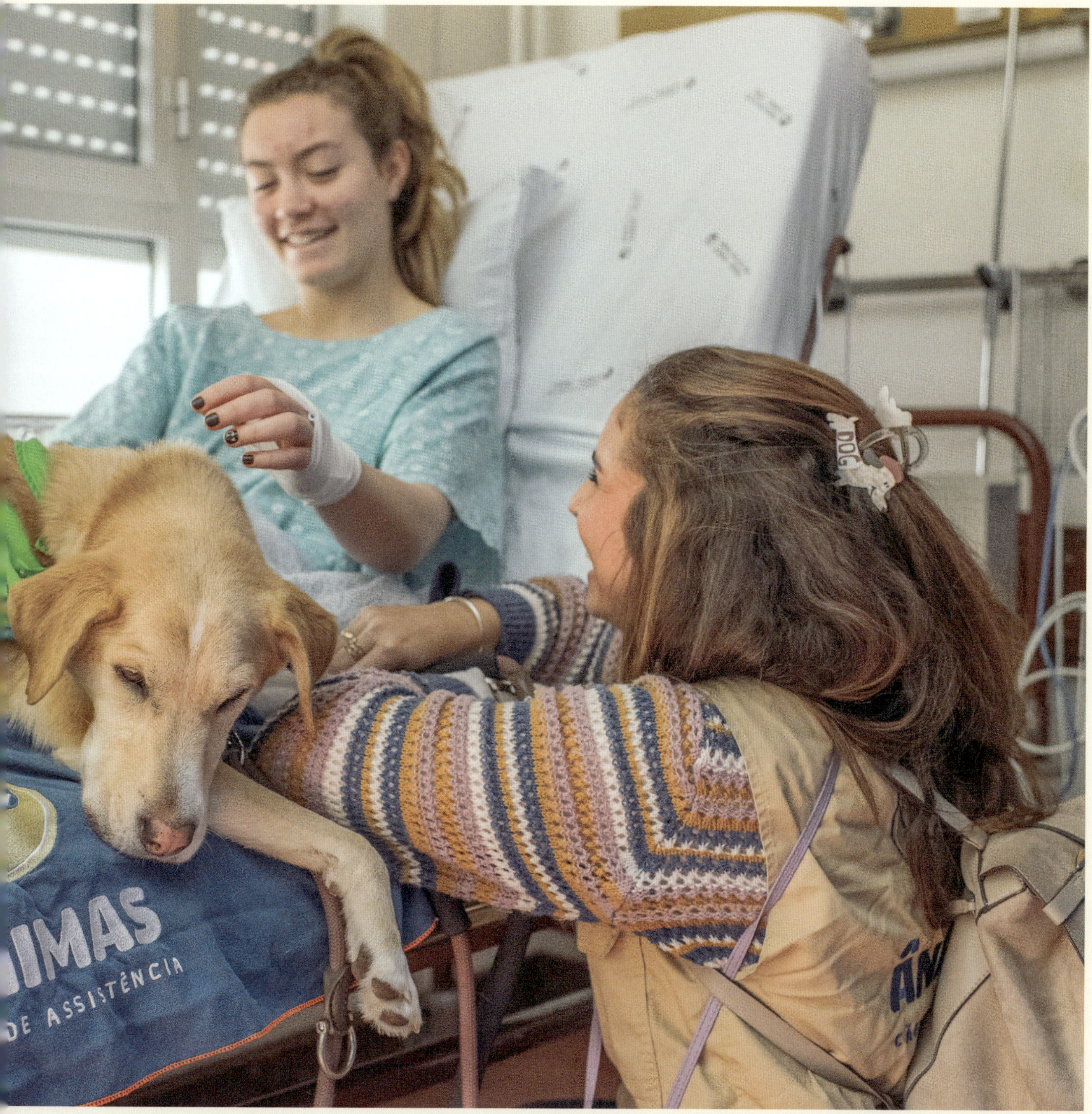

BELOW & RIGHT Some kids who have regular treatments schedule their hospital visits to align with the days that therapy dogs will be there. Kids don't want to go to the hospital for any reason, especially not as a patient. But if they know there is going to be a dog there, it makes the visit a little more inviting.

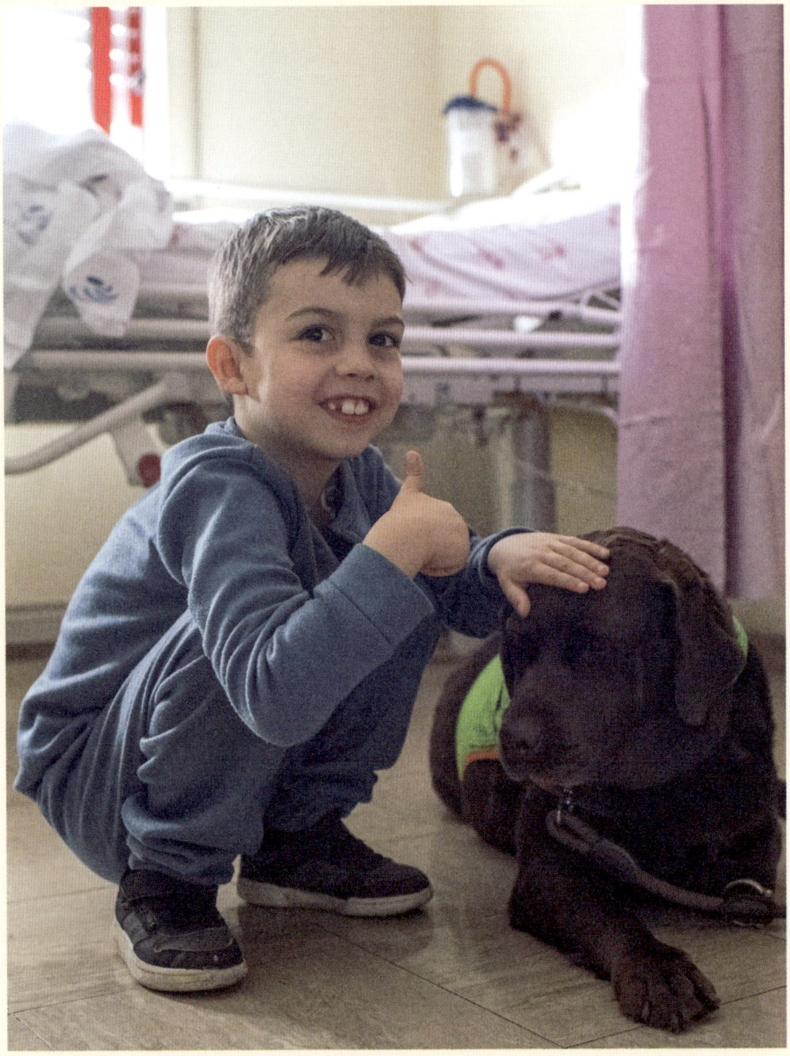

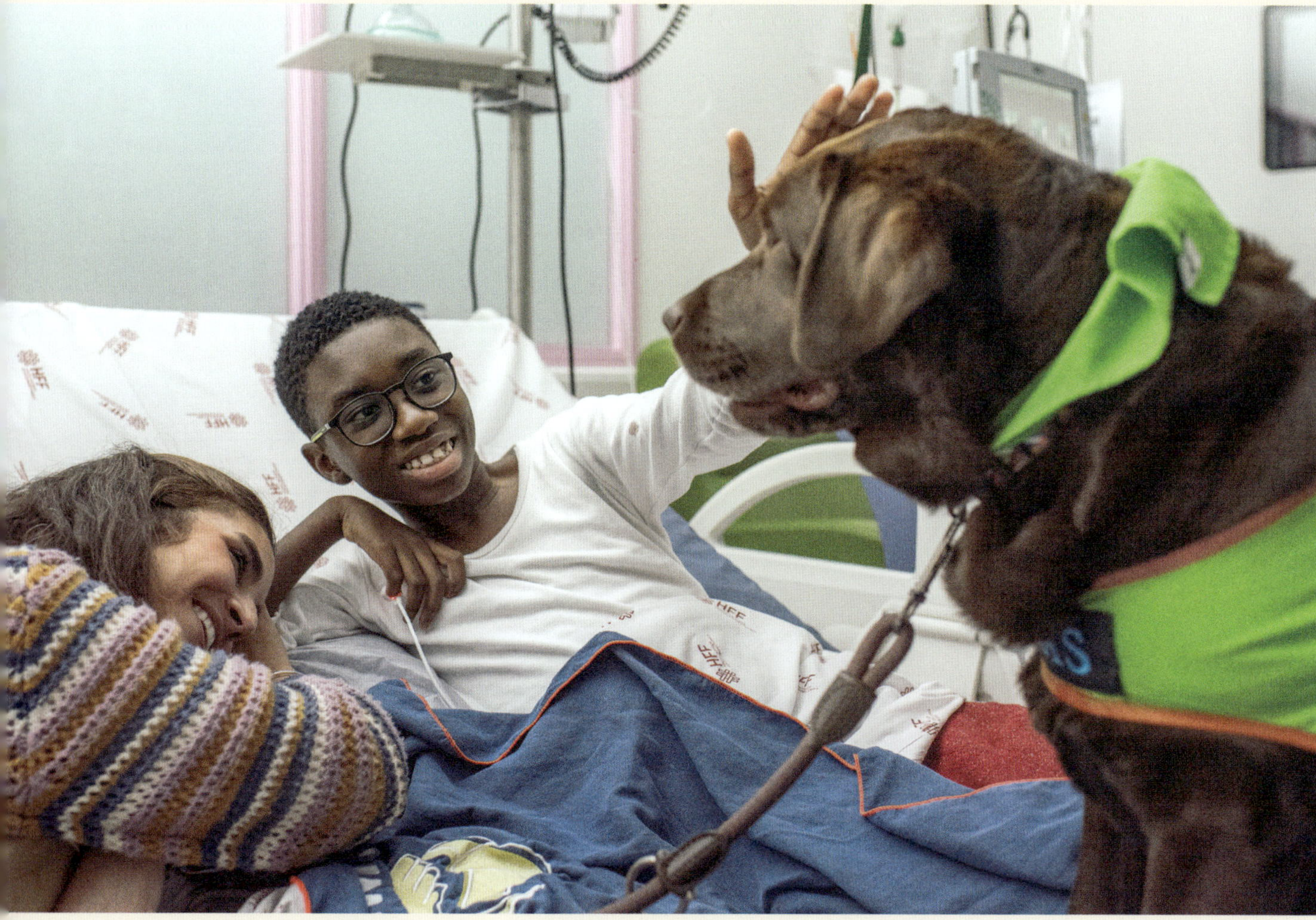

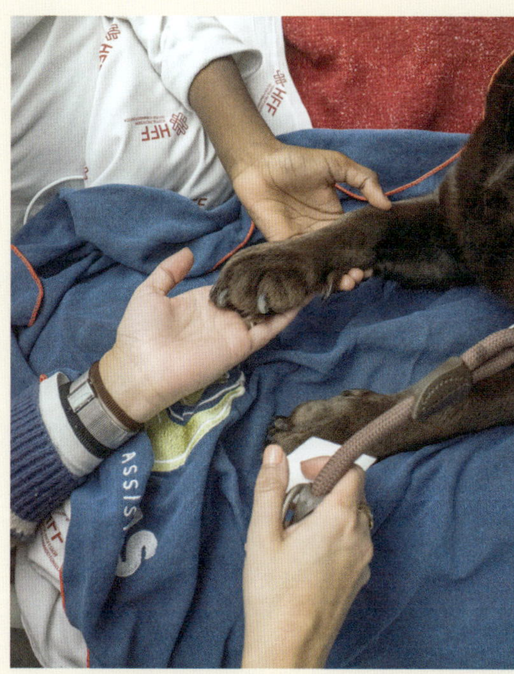

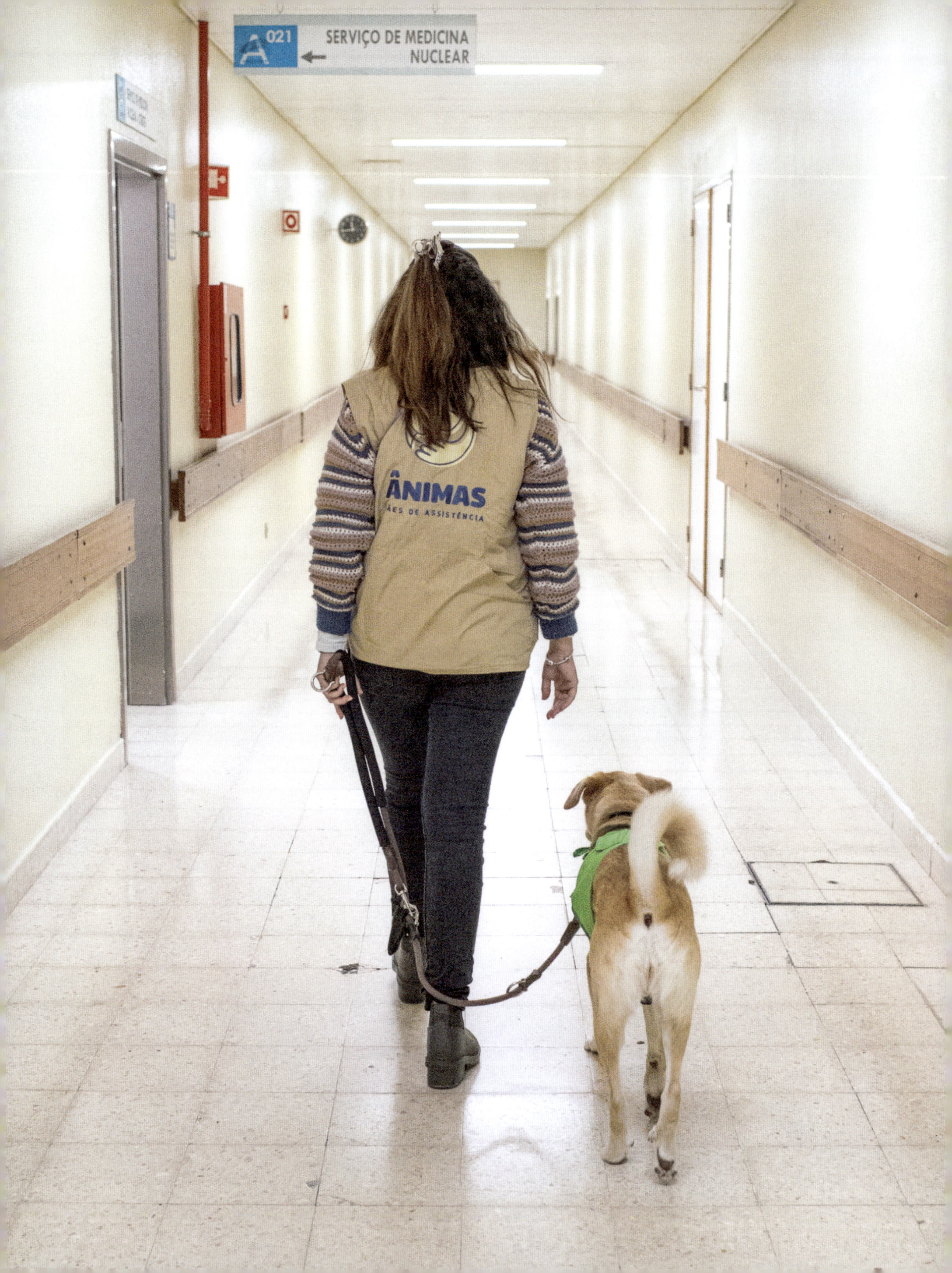
021
SERVIÇO DE MEDICINA
NUCLEAR
ÂNIMAS

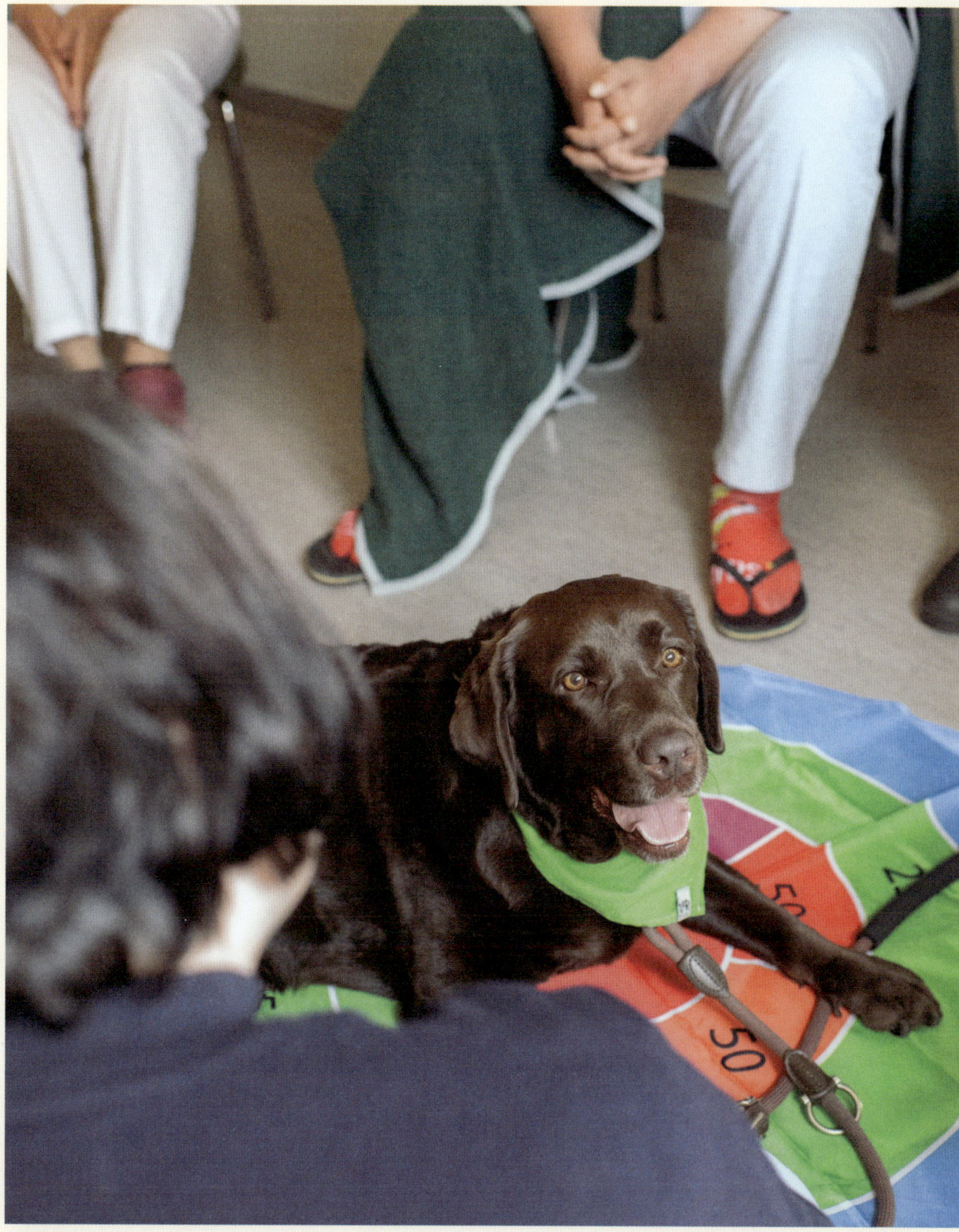

LEFT Inês is so good at her job: Working with dogs clearly comes naturally to her. But she also has an infectious, positive personality that pairs perfectly with the work of her therapy dogs. I don't speak Portuguese, but I was still able to recognize how quickly Inês connects with patients. Her bedside manner is elite, and the joy she and her dogs bring to hospitals is such a gift.

ABOVE The room seems to revolve around the dogs when they enter. People want to talk about the dog and tell stories about their own. The presence of a therapy dog is an immediate connection to something good.

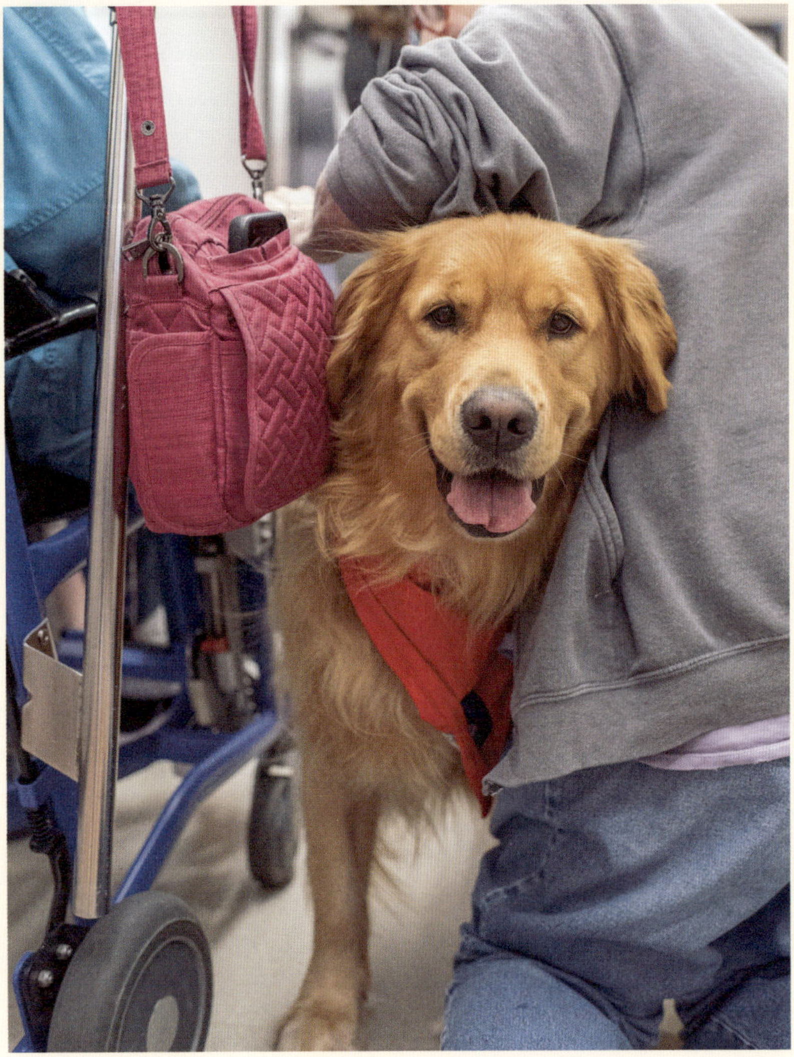

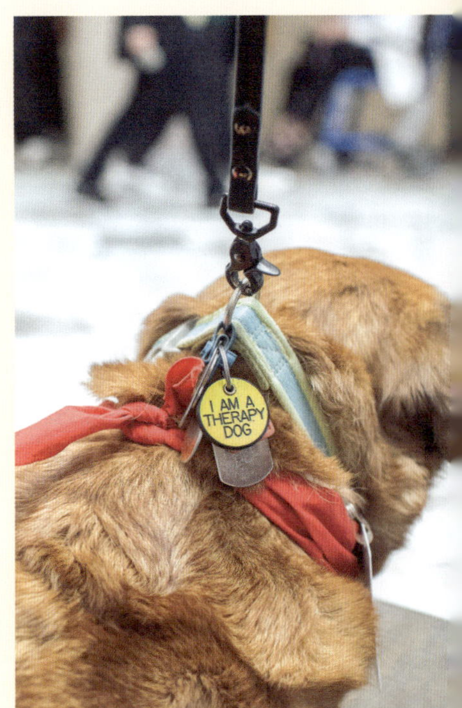

ABOVE & RIGHT Roswell Park is a world-renowned cancer research and treatment center located in Buffalo, New York. At the hospital, therapy dogs are an important part of patient care. They come in all shapes and sizes, from the big Bernese Hudson down to little Louie the Shih Tzu. No matter their size, they all do exceptional work.

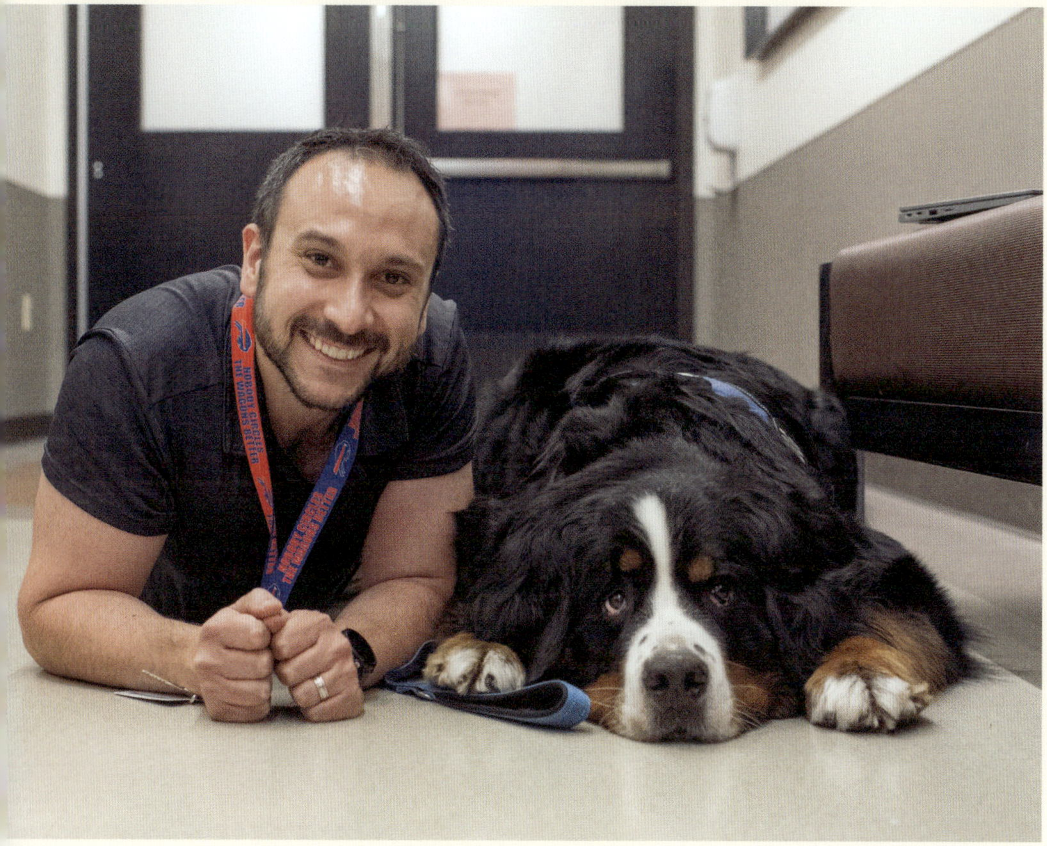

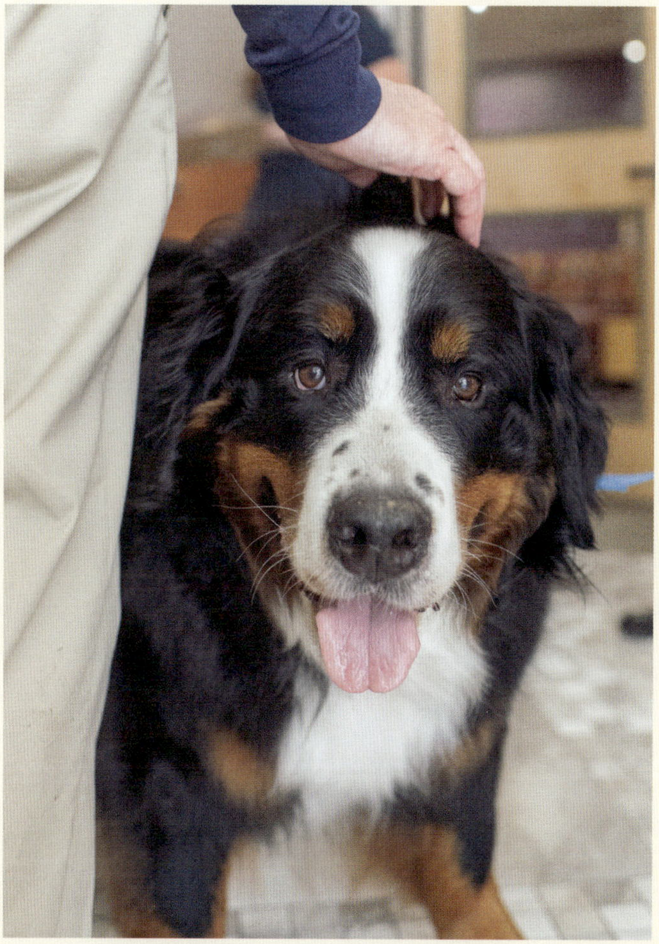

ABOVE & RIGHT Dogs have a funny ability to get people to do things out of the ordinary. Most work days at the hospital don't involve lying belly flat on the floor, but that standard changes when there's a photo op with a dog.

Kids don't want to go to the hospital for any reason, especially not as a patient. But if they know there is going to be a dog there, it makes the visit a little more inviting.

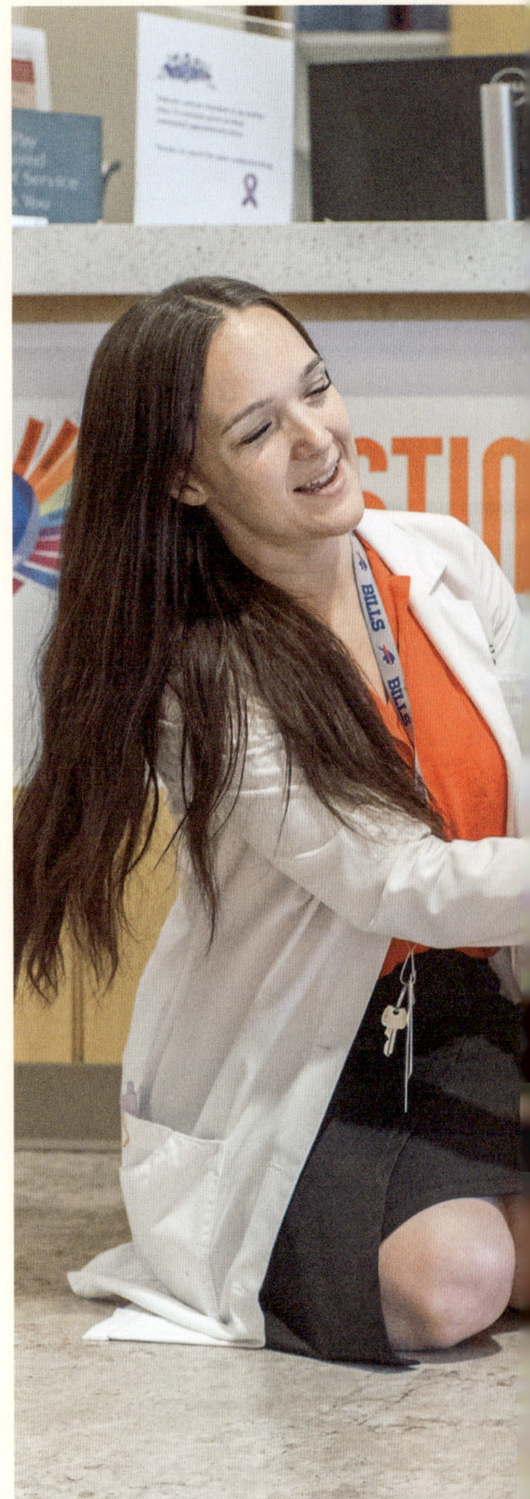

RIGHT Some departments have their favorite dogs, and for the Gynecology Center, Paddington is their star. He receives a hero's welcome whenever he shows up and he knows it's coming. He runs right into the waiting arms of the staff as the highlight of their workday.

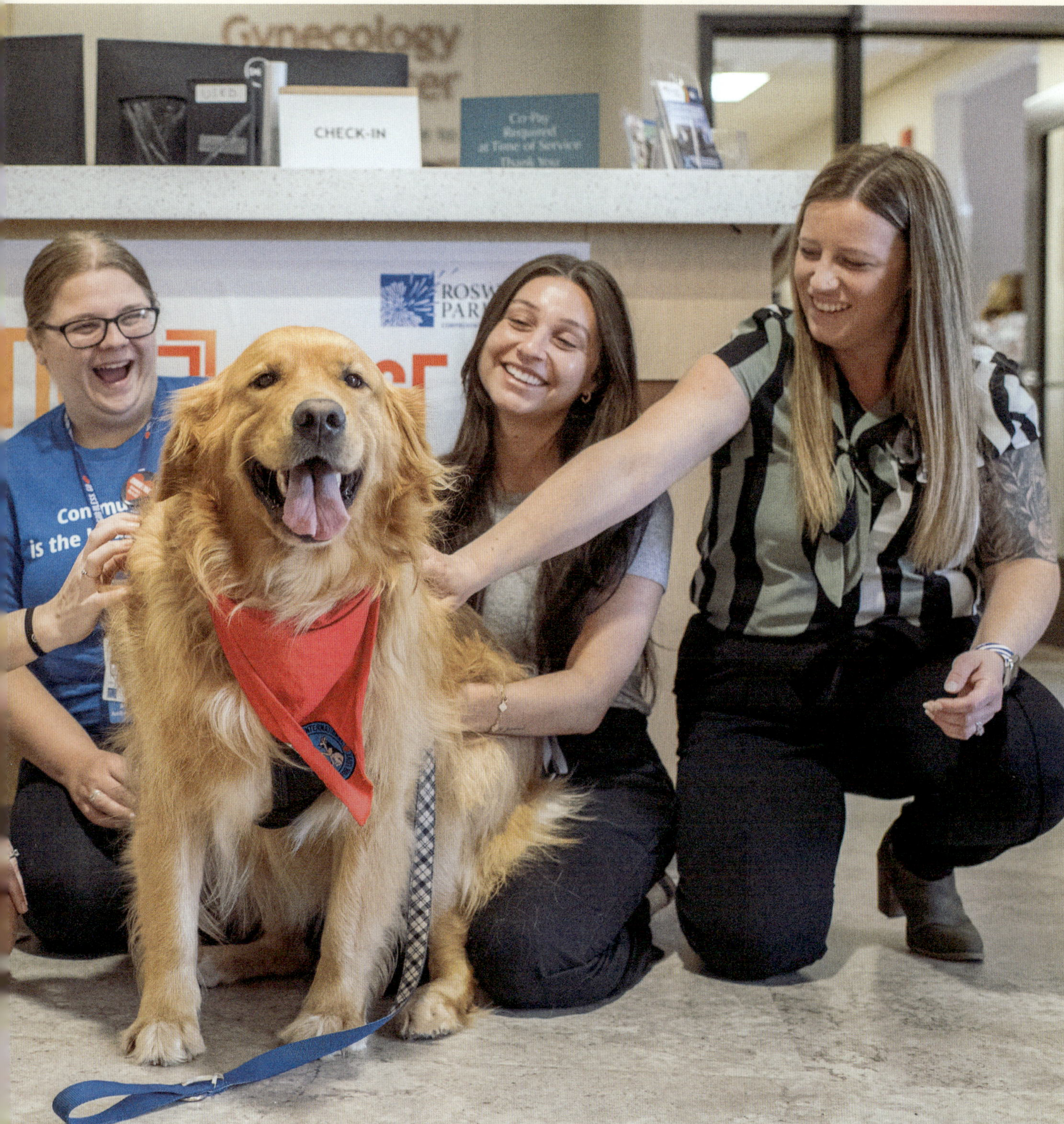
Gynecology
CHECK-IN
Co-Pay
Required
at Time of Service
Thank You

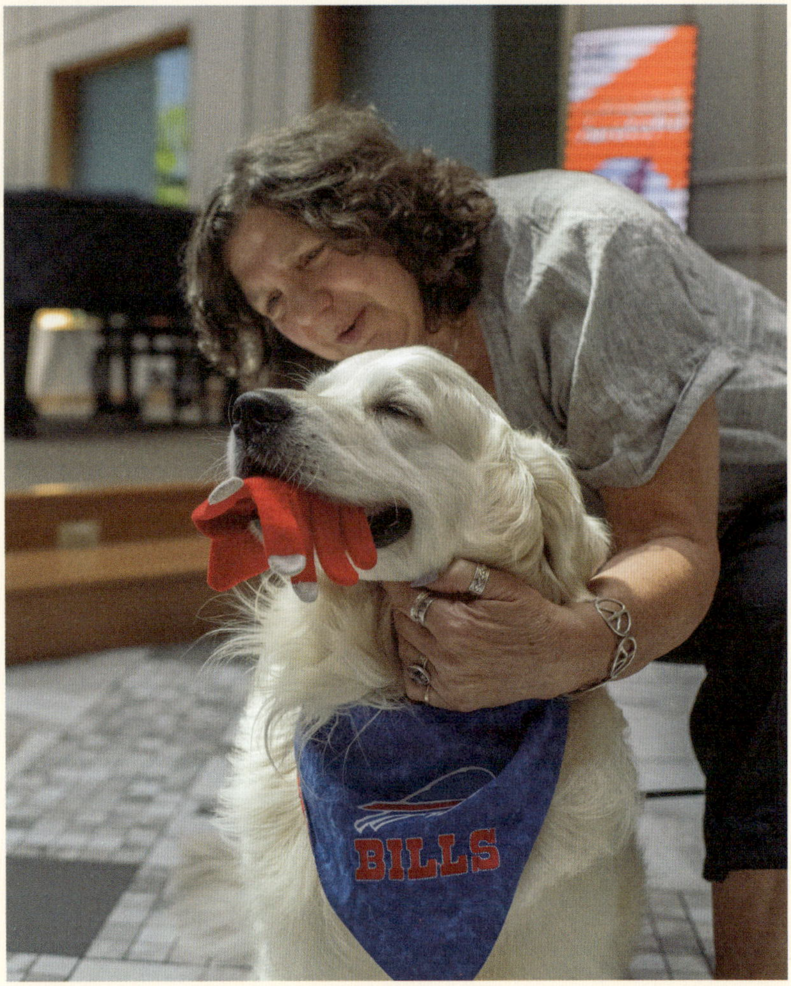

ABOVE The unsuspecting moments are really special. This woman stopped Lumi in the lobby and asked if she could pet him. She spent a few minutes sitting with him while Lumi basked in the attention. When she said goodbye with tears in her eyes, she thanked Lumi's owner for making her day.

BELOW Even when the therapy dogs stay in the lobby, they draw a crowd. Adults and kids alike are drawn to them, for a quick pet or a moment to sit with them – anything to make their days a bit better.

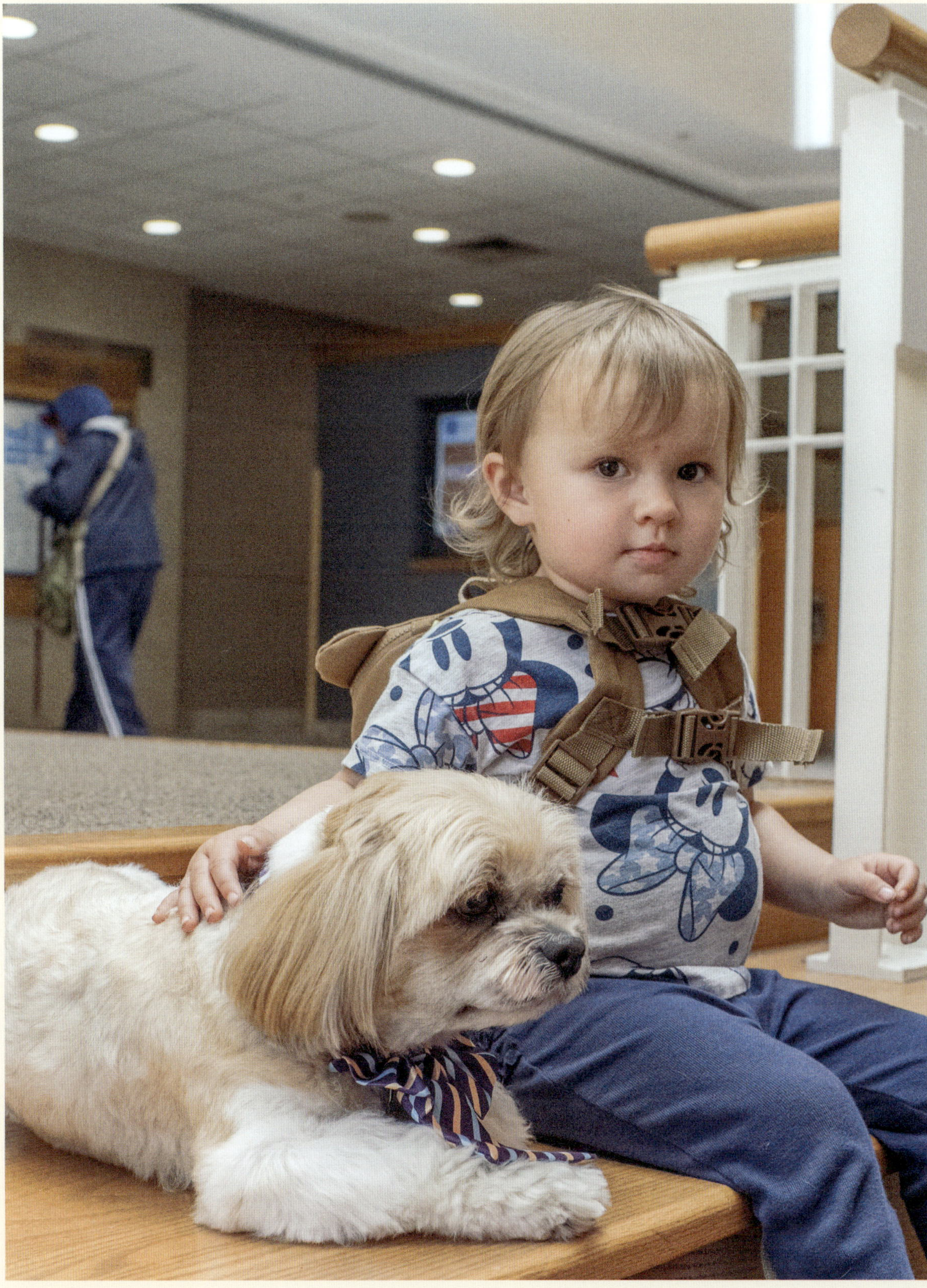

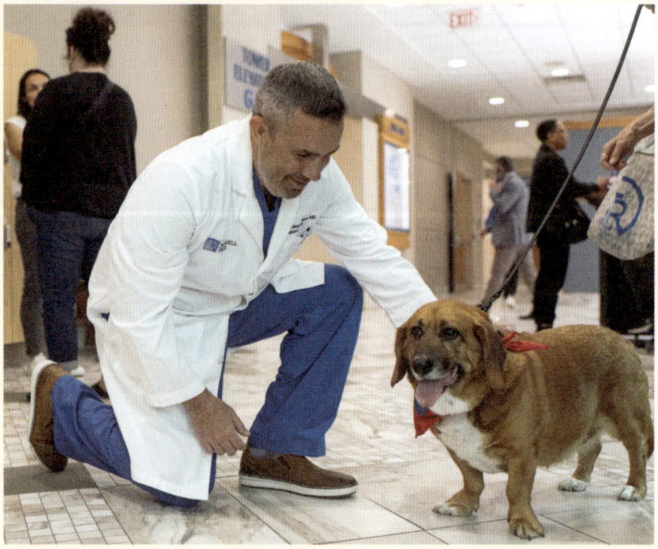

LEFT Two big dogs. One is an actual dog, the other is my brother. They do incredible work at Roswell Park. I love them both.

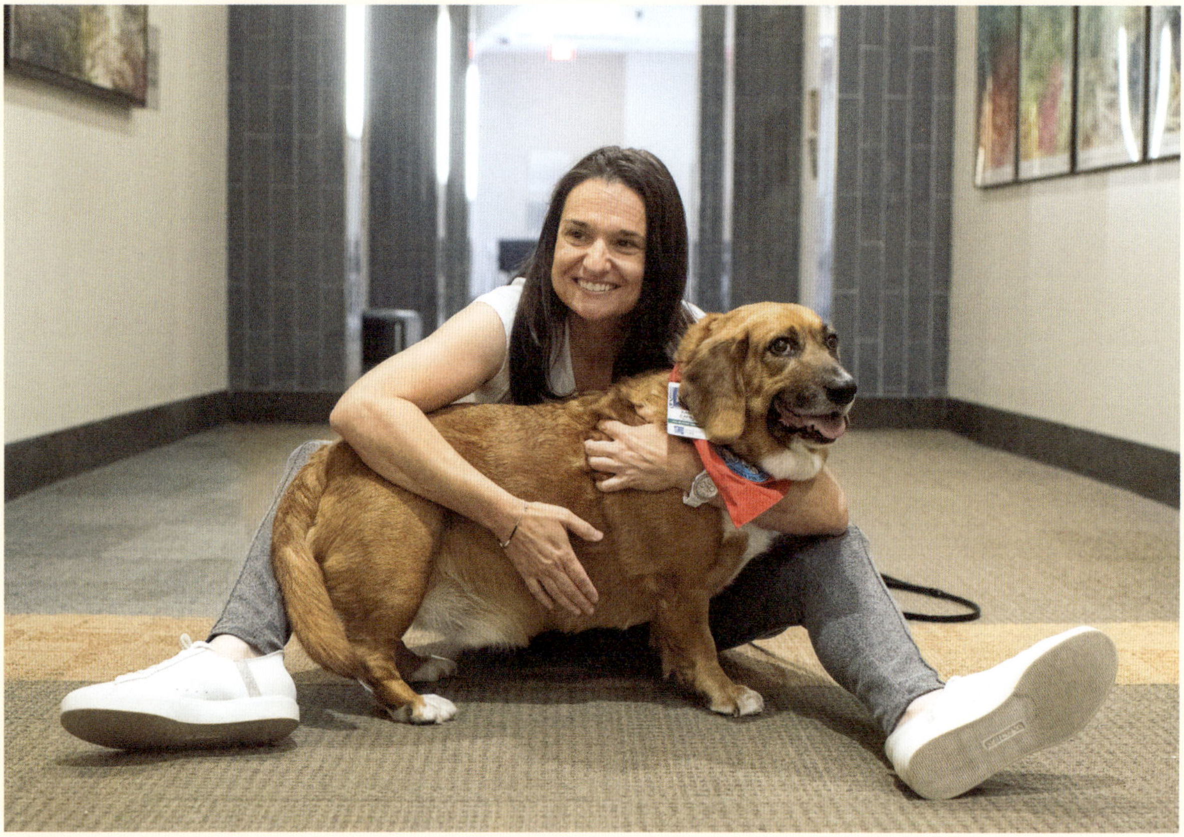

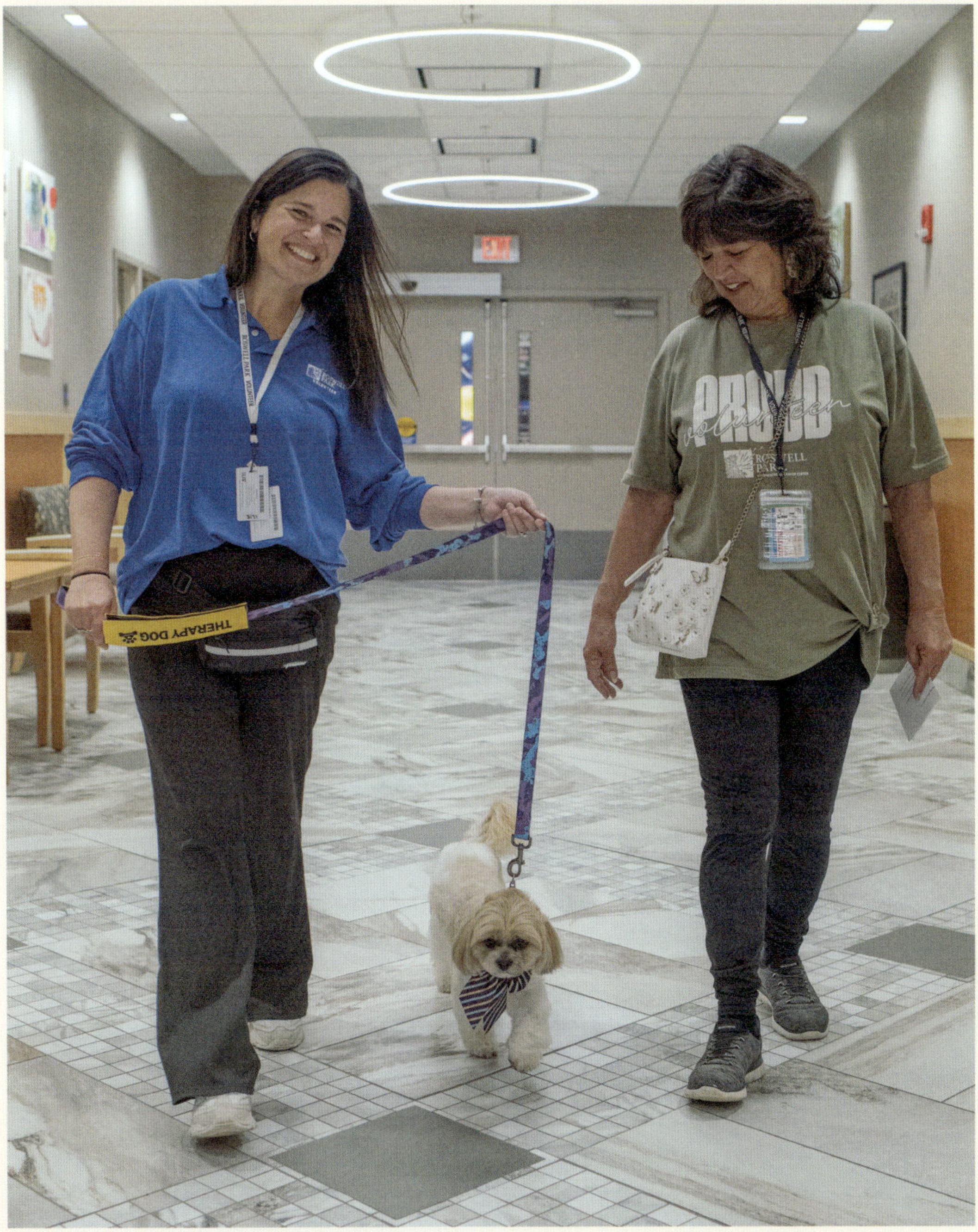

LEFT Deanna works at Roswell Park and helped organize my visit. She said she loves working at a place with people who genuinely care about their community, who show up every day to ease burdens, offer hope, and walk alongside patients and families through their hardest chapters. She plays an instrumental role doing all those things through her work with the therapy dogs.

ABOVE So much credit is due to the volunteers who offer their time to visit the hospital with their therapy dogs. The resounding sentiment is that it is such a rewarding experience to see the positive impact their dogs have at the hospital.

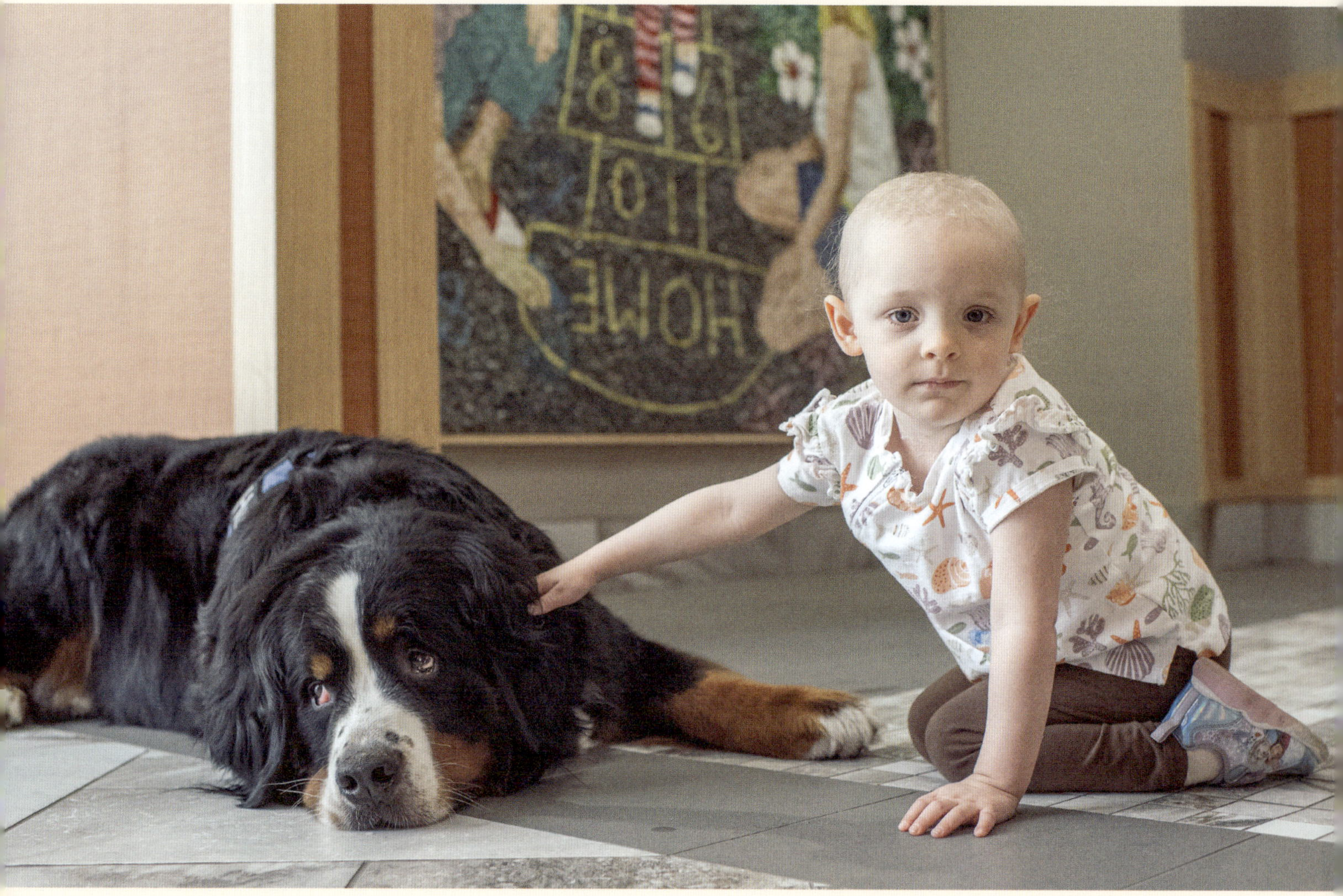

ABOVE When Hudson walks into the pediatric unit, something special happens. The kids get to forget: about the hospital rooms and the appointments and the doctors. For a few minutes, they hug the gentle giant, shake his big paws, lay with him on the ground, and, more than anything, they just get to be kids.

When Hudson walks into the pediatric unit, something special happens. The kids get to forget: about the hospital rooms and the appointments and the doctors.

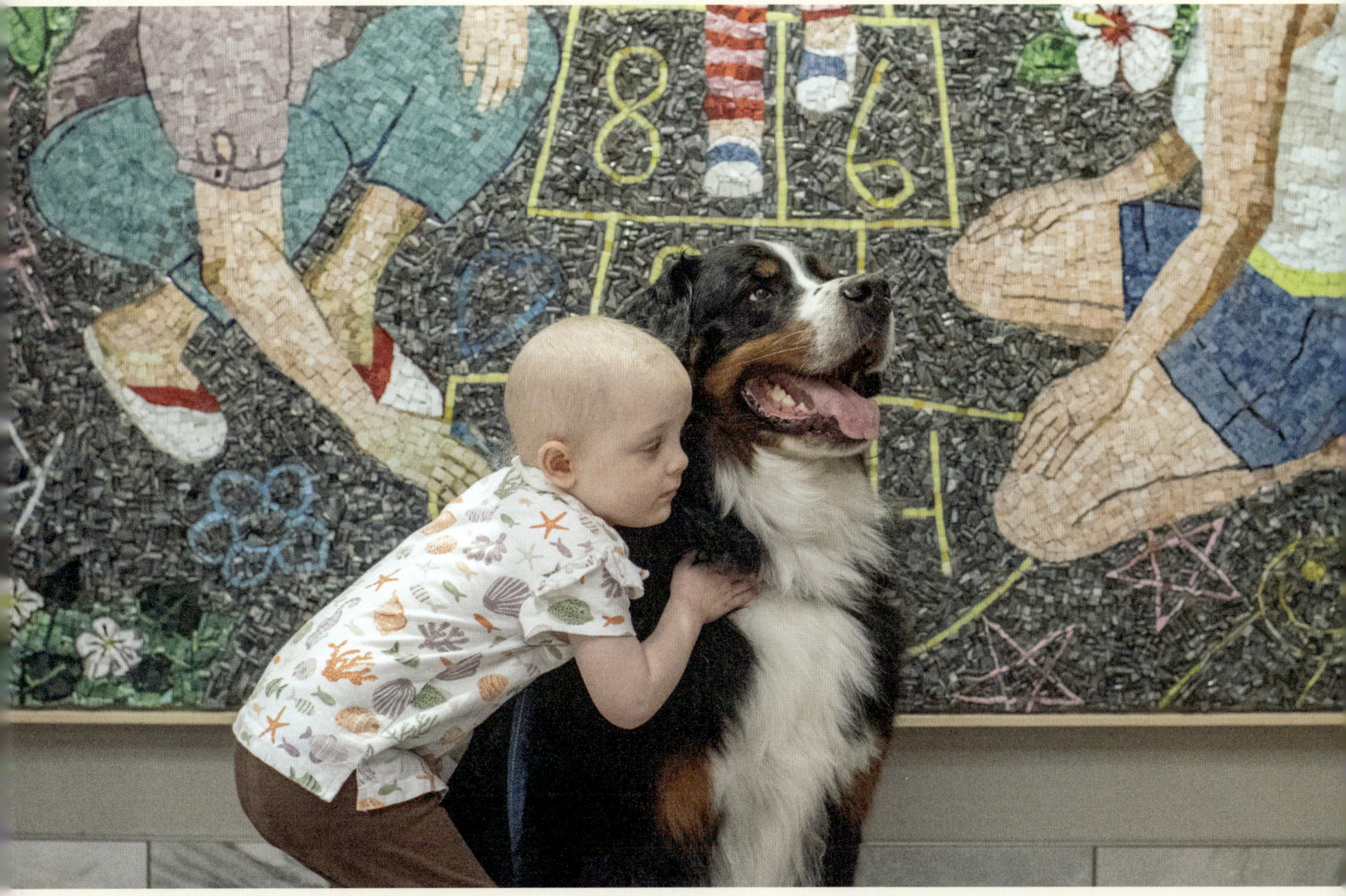

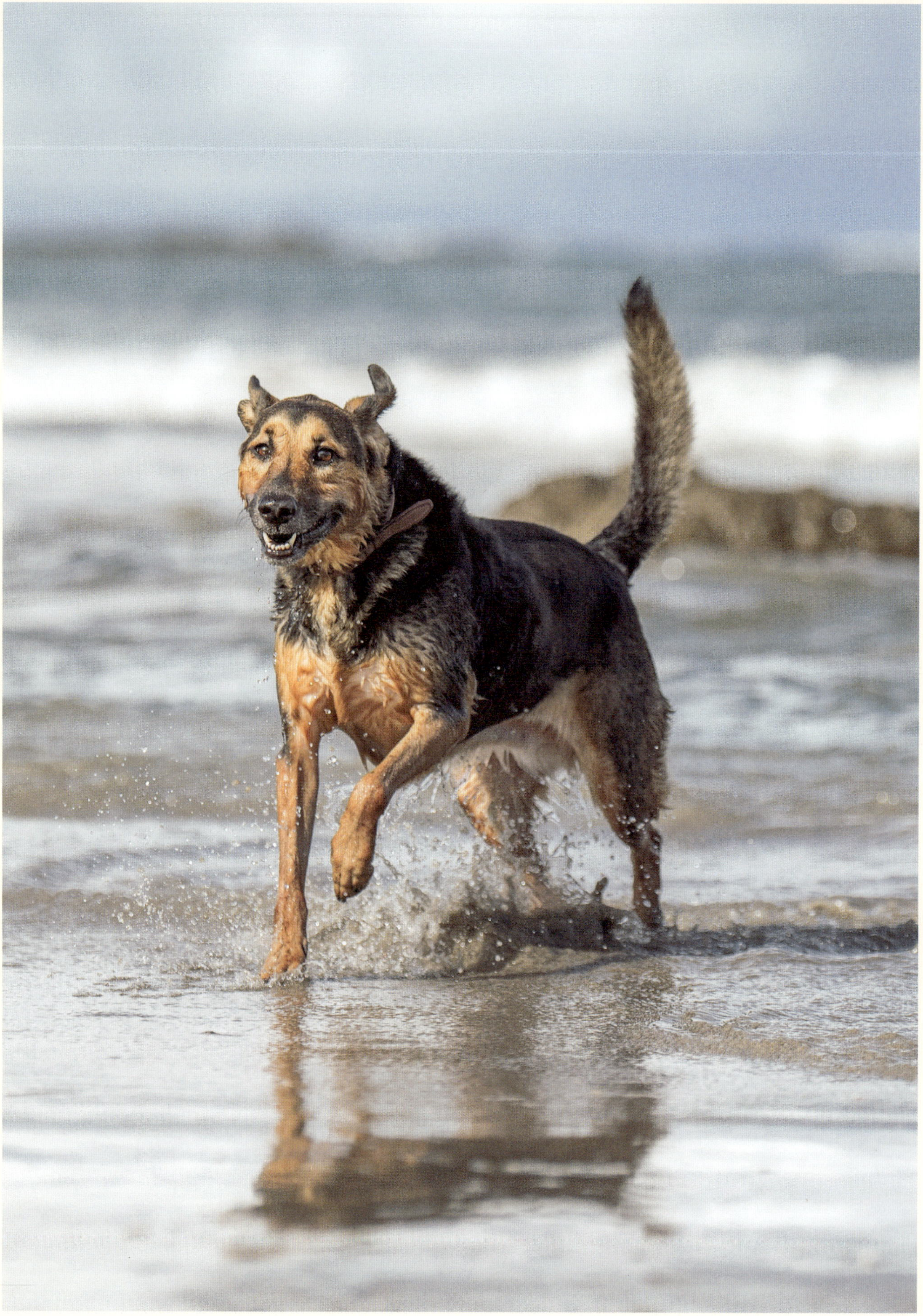

ABOVE *Viola, my favorite model.*

ABOUT THE AUTHOR

John Fabiano is an international dog photographer and the founder of *Wags Around the World*. His work explores the diverse relationships between dogs and humans in different cultures.

John is drawn to capturing authentic moments between dogs and humans. He has been recognized for his work internationally, including being named the 2024 International Documentary Dog Photographer of the Year.

He lives in Amsterdam with his wife, Stephanie, and his dog, Viola. He continues to eye up trips abroad to tell the stories of unique human–dog relationships.

His work and travels can be found on his *Wags Around the World* social media accounts.

ACKNOWLEDGEMENTS

This book exists because of the generosity of strangers around the world who opened their lives to me. To all the people and dogs I photographed throughout my travels – including those not in this book – I am so thankful that you helped me pursue my passion.

Thank you to my parents for their unwavering support, even when I'm sure my life choices didn't make much sense to you. To my five older siblings, thank you for paving the way. Steve, no one helped my dream come to life more than you.

Trae and Nikunj, thank you for your support and encouragement in the early days. Colin Gordon, thank you for teaching me how to use a camera and motivating me to become a better photographer.

I'll forever be grateful to Elle Luna for authoring *The Crossroads of Should and Must*, a book that had a monumental impact on my life.

Thank you to those who helped me coordinate trips – Abílio Leite, Chris Wesley, Shun Adachi, Saki Daorana, Sabine Alder, Sandy Van Zyl, and Roswitha Dannenberg. Thank you especially to Guy Hull, for taking me on an incredible trip to see the dogs of Australia.

Thank you to Megan Cuthbert and Avery Hayes at Smith Street Books. You hatched this idea and provided me with much-needed editing and guidance as we brought it to life.

To the dogs of my life – Duffy, Lola, Dina, Nola, Loki, and Viola – you all shaped my love and appreciation for your species. V, you are my favorite model and my muse.

Finally, and most importantly, Steph. Thank you for going on a first date with an unemployed, wannabe dog photographer. Your support has been constant, and I can't imagine this journey without you. I love you.

Smith Street Books

Published in 2026 by Smith Street Books
Naarm (Melbourne) | Australia
smithstreetbooks.com

Distributed outside of ANZ, North & Latin America by
Thames & Hudson Ltd., 6–24 Britannia Street, London, WC1X 9JD
thamesandhudson.com

EU Authorised Representative: Interart S.A.R.L.
19 rue Charles Auray, 93500 Pantin, Paris, France
productsafety@thameshudson.co.uk; www.interart.fr

ISBN (US & UK edition): 978-1-9235-0317-5
ISBN (Australia edition): 978-1-9235-0349-6

Smith Street Books respectfully acknowledges the Wurundjeri People of the Kulin Nation, who are the Traditional Owners of the land on which we work, and we pay our respects to their Elders past and present.

PUBLISHER: Megan Cuthbert
EDITOR: Avery Hayes
DESIGN CONCEPT & LAYOUT: Susan Le
PROOFREADER: Ariana Klepac
PRODUCTION MANAGER: Aisling Coughlan
PRE-PRESS: Megan Ellis

Printed & bound in China by C&C Offset Printing Co., Ltd.

Book 472
10 9 8 7 6 5 4 3 2 1

FSC MIX Paper | Supporting responsible forestry FSC® C008047 www.fsc.org